Collard's volume analyses the challenges facing the Emmanuel Macron presidency in France. Over and above this, it shows us the opportunities and pitfalls of political leadership in a complex modern democracy.
—**John Gaffney**, *Aston University, United Kingdom*

Dr Collard has compiled an impressive range of scholarship to offer comprehensive and original insights into the presidency of Emmanuel Macron, illuminating the intractable difficulties of effecting political change in France.
—**Helen Drake**, *Loughborough University London, United Kingdom*

REVOLUTION REVISITED: EMMANUEL MACRON AND THE LIMITS OF POLITICAL CHANGE IN FRANCE

This book provides timely assessment of the extent to which Emmanuel Macron's declared presidential goal – to bring in radical transformation of French politics, indeed a revolution, albeit a democratic one – has been achieved.

This analysis of his presidency provides a framework for reflection on 'immobilism' in French politics, and how enduring transformation has remained much more elusive to most of those who promised it. With a wide a range of underlying, seemingly intractable and unresolved structural issues dominating French society, the book asks whether the young 'disrupter' has succeeded in reforming France where others had failed. What can we learn about the processes of political change from analysing Macron's successes and failures in working through his ambitions for France?

This book will be of key interest to scholars, students and followers of French politics/studies and society, gender studies, media studies and more broadly European studies.

Susan Collard is Senior Lecturer in French Politics and Contemporary European Studies at the University of Sussex, UK.

Routledge Advances in European Politics
Rethinking European Social Democracy and Socialism

The History of the Centre-Left in Northern and Southern Europe in the Late 20th Century
Edited by Alan Granadino, Stefan Nygård and Peter Stadius

From Reception to Integration of Asylum Seekers and Refugees in Poland
Karolina Sobczak-Szelc, Marta Pachocka, Konrad Pędziwiatr, Justyna Szałańska and Monika Szulecka

The Integration of Refugees in the Education and Labour Markets
Between Inclusion and Exclusion Practices
Edited By Karolina Sobczak-Szelc, Marta Pachocka and Justyna Szałańska

Politicisation, Democratisation and EU Identity
National EU Discourses in Germany and France
Claudia Wiesnar

Political Behaviour in Contemporary Finland
Studies of Voting and Campaigning in a Candidate-Oriented Political System
Edited by Åsa von Schoultz and Kim Strandberg

How Migrants Choose Their Destinations
Factors Influencing Post-EU Accession Choices and Decisions to Remain
Dominika Pszczółkowska

Civic and Uncivic Values in Hungary
Value Transformation, Politics, and Religion
Edited by Sabrina P. Ramet and László Kürti

The Parliamentary Dimension of the Conference on the Future of Europe
Synergies and Legitimacy Clashes
Edited by Karolina Borońska-Hryniewiecka and Lucy Kinski

Revolution Revisited: Emmanuel Macron and the Limits of Political Change in France
Edited by Susan Collard

For more information about this series, please visit: www.routledge.com/Routledge-Advances-in-European-Politics/book-series/AEP

REVOLUTION REVISITED: EMMANUEL MACRON AND THE LIMITS OF POLITICAL CHANGE IN FRANCE

Edited by Susan Collard

Routledge
Taylor & Francis Group

LONDON AND NEW YORK

Designed cover image: Gerard Julien via Getty Images

First published 2025
by Routledge
4 Park Square, Milton Park, Abingdon, Oxon OX14 4RN

and by Routledge
605 Third Avenue, New York, NY 10158

Routledge is an imprint of the Taylor & Francis Group, an informa business

© 2025 selection and editorial matter, Susan Collard; individual chapters, the contributors

The right of Susan Collard to be identified as the author of the editorial material, and of the authors for their individual chapters, has been asserted in accordance with sections 77 and 78 of the Copyright, Designs and Patents Act 1988.

All rights reserved. No part of this book may be reprinted or reproduced or utilised in any form or by any electronic, mechanical, or other means, now known or hereafter invented, including photocopying and recording, or in any information storage or retrieval system, without permission in writing from the publishers.

Trademark notice: Product or corporate names may be trademarks or registered trademarks, and are used only for identification and explanation without intent to infringe.

British Library Cataloguing-in-Publication Data
A catalogue record for this book is available from the British Library

ISBN: 978-1-032-34664-9 (hbk)
ISBN: 978-1-032-34661-8 (pbk)
ISBN: 978-1-003-32325-9 (ebk)

DOI: 10.4324/9781003323259

Typeset in Sabon
by Deanta Global Publishing Services, Chennai, India

CONTENTS

List of figures	*ix*
Notes on contributors	*x*
Preface	*xii*

1 Introduction: How Disruptive Can a French President Be? 1
   Susan Collard

2 Emmanuel Macron: The Paradoxes of a Disruptive
   Presidency 24
   Sylvie Strudel

3 Democracy in France under Emmanuel Macron: From a
   Crisis of Representation to a Crisis of Regime? 41
   Susan Collard

4 Political corruption in France and the 'Moralisation of
   Public Life' under Emmanuel Macron 65
   Susan Collard and Françoise Dreyfus

5 Political Parties After the 2017 Earthquake 88
   Elodie Fabre

6 Macron, the Media and Political Communication 113
   Raymond Kuhn

7   Towards a 'Sovereign Europe'? Macron's European policy
    between conceptual fireworks and national interests   133
    Jörg Monar

8   Macron and the Economy: A Labour-Market Perspective   155
    Brigitte Granville

9   Emmanuel Macron's Reform of the Higher Civil Service:
    Transforming the State Nobility into 'Can-Do Managers'?   180
    Jean-Michel Eymeri-Douzans

10 Education under Emmanuel Macron: Some Market-
    Inspired Change and Much Continuity   201
    Nicolas Charles and Andy Smith

11 A Paler Shade of Green: Emmanuel Macron's Policies on
    the Environment and Climate Change   220
    Charlotte Halpern

12 Protest and Repression During Emmanuel Macron's
    Presidency   241
    Olivier Fillieule, Fabien Jobard, and Anne Wuilleumier

13 Macron's Africa Policy: Promises, Practices and Path
    Dependencies   263
    Tony Chafer

14 Macron's New Beginning: Coming to Terms with the
    Colonial Past Through Restitution, Recognition and
    Empathy   283
    Martin Evans

15 Recognition and Surveillance: Emmanuel Macron's
    Religious Policy   302
    Philippe Portier

Epilogue: 6 January 2025   323
    Susan Collard

Index   334

FIGURES

5.1	Results of 2017 French presidential elections	91
5.2	Composition of the French National Assembly, 2017	92
5.3	Placement of French parties on the left–right and socially liberal vs conservative (gal–tan) axes, 2019	96
5.4	Results of the 2014 and 2019 elections to the European Parliament	98
5.5	Results of the 2021 regional elections (metropolitan France and Corsica only)	99
5.6	Results of French presidential elections 2022	104
5.7	Composition of the French National Assembly, 2022	107
8.1	Monthly unemployment rate, total, % of labour force, January 1983–December 2021	157
8.2	Labour participation: employment rate total, % of the working-age population	158
8.3	Tax wedge total, % of labour cost, 2000–2021	163
8.4	Financial balance of the unemployment insurance in € billions	172

NOTES ON CONTRIBUTORS

Tony Chafer
Emeritus Professor of African and French Studies, University of Portsmouth

Nicolas Charles
Maître de Conférences, University of Bordeaux
Faculty of Sociology UMR / CNRS Centre Emile Durkheim

Susan Collard
Senior Lecturer in French Politics and European Studies
Department of Politics, University of Sussex

Françoise Dreyfus
Emeritus Professor in Political Science, University Paris I / Centre européen de sociologie et de science politique

Martin Evans
Professor of Modern European History, University of Sussex

Jean-Michel Eymeri-Douzans
Professor of Political Science and Deputy Vice-Rector Sciences Po Toulouse, responsible for International Relations, LaSSP, University Toulouse Capitole

Elodie Fabre
Lecturer in Politics in the School of History, Anthropology, Philosophy and Politics
Queen's University Belfast

Olivier Fillieulle
Professor of Political Sociology, University of Lausanne, UNIL-IEP-CRAPUL, research centre on political action

Brigitte Granville
Professor of International Economics and Economic Policy, Head of the Department of Business Analytics and Applied Economics
School of Business and Management
Queen Mary University of London

Charlotte Halpern
Senior Researcher at Sciences Po Paris, Centre for European studies and comparative politics (CEE), Paris, CNRS, France

Fabien Jobard
Senior researcher at CNRS and Centre de recherche sociologique sur le droit et les institutions pénales (CESDIP) Saclay, director of the Groupe Européen de Recherche sur les Normativités (GERN).

Raymond Kuhn
Emeritus Professor, School of Politics and International Relations
Queen Mary University of London

Jörg Monar
Honorary Professor, European Interdisciplinary Studies Department and former Rector, College of Europe, Bruges

Philippe Portier
Professor of History and sociology of secularisms, Director of Studies at the Ecole Pratique des Hautes Etudes (PSL-Sorbonne), Paris

Andy Smith
Research professor at the Centre Emile Durkheim-Sciences Po Bordeaux

Sylvie Strudel
Professor of Political Science, University of Paris-Panthéon-Assas, CECP / CEVIPOF

Anne Wuilleumier
Researcher at IHEMI (Institut des Hautes Etudes du Ministère de l'Intérieur) and associate researcher at CESDIP (Centre de recherches Sociologique sur le Droit et les Institutois Pénales), Paris

PREFACE

This book has been conceived and written for all those with an interest in French politics, not just students and fellow academics, but general readers as well. My aim was to combine the rigorous academic research of experts in their fields with an accessible style, and the chapters have all been structured to provide some background knowledge and context for those who have no formal knowledge of the French political system. For reasons explained in the introduction, the presidency of Emmanuel Macron is a unique opportunity to explore recent events in contemporary politics through the lens of political change, which poses problems for France that are not experienced in the same way elsewhere. In deciding to explore Macron's proposed 'Revolution', I was faced with the dilemma of selecting which aspects to focus on, and I am aware that there are many areas of politics and policy that are not touched on in this volume. In particular, an important chapter on inequalities regrettably had to be abandoned by the author for personal reasons. But in every other respect, the final choice of topics was mine and however partial the coverage, I hope this volume will make a useful contribution to our understanding of French politics as played out under Emmanuel Macron. Preparing the manuscript has taken considerably longer than anticipated, partly because that is the way in academia, but also because of the ongoing twists and turns in French politics that have made it hard to reach a suitable stopping point. Originally planned as an evaluation of the first presidency, with a possible second edition if Macron won another term of office, the circumstances of his re-election in 2022 were such that this analysis finally stopped in July 2024, with the situation of political chaos created by the president himself in calling a snap election, which most observers saw as an act of incomprehensible self-harm. By the time this book is published, events should have moved on from the current situation of political stalemate, though the direction (and pace) of travel are impossible to predict. However the future unfolds, this volume will hopefully provide a solid foundation for those wishing to gain a better grasp of French politics in all its compelling complexity.

I would like to express thanks to Adam Steinhouse for his valuable help in establishing UK equivalents for French terminology relating to the civil service and to my 'lay readers' Paul Bennell and Marie Lapierre for their helpful feedback on some of the chapters.

Sue Collard, July 2024.

1
INTRODUCTION: HOW DISRUPTIVE CAN A FRENCH PRESIDENT BE?

Susan Collard

Abstract

This chapter explains the rationale of the book, which is to assess the extent to which Emmanuel Macron was able to bring about the 'Revolution' to which he aspired as presidential candidate. The analysis of Macron's presidency is framed within broader questions about the difficulties of implementing political change in France, and the historical problem of political 'immobilism' derived from traditional resistance to change. In recent decades, the pursuit of political change has revolved largely around attempts to introduce structural reforms associated with neoliberal policies that are resisted by a majority of the population, especially on the left, but considered essential by most political elites. Macron's election in 2017 owed much to his capacity to present the need for reform with a positive spin, but his exercise of power failed to deliver the positive transformation he hoped for, as demonstrated in the contributions to this volume. These are summarised in this chapter, before some conclusions are drawn in the final comments.

> We want change, but we don't want it enough. If we want to move forward, to make our country successful and prosperous in the 21st century in line with our History, we must act. Because the solution lies within us. It won't come from making a list of proposals that won't be implemented. It won't emerge from making flawed compromises. It will come as a result of different solutions which require a profound democratic revolution. It will take time. It will depend on just one thing: our unity, our courage, our common will. This is the democratic revolution that I believe in.
> Emmanuel Macron, *Révolution*, XO Editions, 2016, p. 9

DOI: 10.4324/9781003323259-1

Introduction

The election of Emmanuel Macron to the presidency in 2017 was a watershed moment in contemporary French politics: he defied all the established rules for securing this high office, and his ambitions to fundamentally 'transform' France and French politics were intentionally 'disruptive'. But would this young political novice be successful where others before him had failed? The implementation of political change in France has historically been as tumultuous as it has been difficult, producing several revolutions and 17 constitutions. Under the Third (1870–1940) and Fourth (1946–1958) Republics, persistent conservatism and resistance to change that prevented adaptation to rapid socioeconomic change was referred to as *immobilisme*. More recently, under the Fifth Republic, this has presented an ongoing challenge for successive presidents and governments, particularly since the 1970s and 1980s. Paradoxically, whilst presidential elections are frequently won on a mandate for change, attempts at reform are often met with strong resistance, much of it in the streets, forcing governments to withdraw key proposals.

This has led to what is known as *dégagisme*: a tendency to vote out whoever is in power, as if no leader can ever satisfy the electorate. From 1981, with some exceptions, a pattern of *alternance* set in, whereby the presidency regularly alternated between the left and the right. Yet Emmanuel Macron broke this pattern in two ways: first, by winning the election in 2017 from a position which claimed to be 'neither right nor left' and, second, by becoming the first president to be re-elected in 2022 without the benefit of an intervening period of 'cohabitation', as was the case for both François Mitterrand in 1988 and Jacques Chirac in 2002. The circumstances in which Macron came to power, and the nature and scale of his ambitions, set out in his manifesto book *Revolution*, published in 2016 to launch his election campaign, thus created a unique set of parameters that make Macron's presidency particularly conducive to analysing the problem of political change in contemporary France.

The initial aim of this volume was to assess the extent to which Macron was able to pursue his political ambitions during his first presidency, with a view to a second edition if he secured another mandate. Academic experts working in areas of particular significance to Macron's programme were invited to evaluate his record in their subject areas, examining the factors that inhibited or facilitated the passing of reforms in a wider political context where the formal powers of the French president are said to be greater than those of leaders of most other Western democracies. However, as students of French politics will know, what can in fact matter more than formal, constitutional powers are the informal constraints that can undermine a president's position. Macron's presidency has provided a vivid illustration of this struggle between formal powers and informal power which, at the time of finalising this manuscript in July 2024, remains ongoing.

Indeed, the original plan to focus on the first presidency was disrupted by Macron's failure to win an absolute majority in the National Assembly (NA) after his re-election in 2022, since this outcome offered the irresistible prospect of assessing the new limitations on the president's power with only a 'relative' majority to approve legislation. The problem then arose of finding an appropriate point at which to conclude the analysis, pending a further update at the end of the second presidency; the outcome of the European elections in early June 2024 seemed to offer the most suitable moment since Europe has been so central to Macron's agenda. However, the catastrophic results in those elections for his supporters, 'Besoin d'Europe', which only won 13 seats compared to 30 for the far-right National Rally, drove him to take the unexpected and highly controversial decision to dissolve the National Assembly, triggering unscheduled legislative elections in late June and early July. The cutoff point for the book was therefore once more extended.

However, the legislative election results did not produce the 'clarification' that Macron had hoped for, since no party or group of parties won enough seats to constitute a workable majority, an outcome that was totally unprecedented in the Fifth Republic. His own alliance, 'Ensemble', once again made significant losses, down from 250 seats to 166, while the far-right National Rally won an unprecedented 123 seats, more than any other single party; the various parties of the left, who, despite the many tensions between them during the European election campaign, had unexpectedly signed a hasty agreement to form an electoral alliance (the 'New Popular Front' or NFP) in order to limit the gains of the far-right, unexpectedly won the most seats (184). Thus, the new composition of the Assembly was deeply divided into roughly three blocs. Macron, having rejected the candidate proposed by the NFP, Lucie Castets, on the grounds that the other parties would immediately censure her government, decided to postpone the nomination of a new prime minister and government till after the Olympic Games. This decision provided the opportunity to draw a (temporary) line under his record and assess his political legacy up to that point in July 2024. Since the contributions to this volume were finalised at various points during the spring of 2024, a few of them require minor updates, which I provide in the summaries of the chapters that follow. In the concluding paragraphs, I draw on these different studies to offer a general assessment (to date) of this very unique presidency and its attempt to implement major political change.

But before dipping into these summaries, a brief reminder of Macron's overall ambitions is in order, especially since these have not changed during his time in office. His political project was set out in his 2016 campaign book, *Revolution*, in which he explained his conviction that France, still locked into the socioeconomic model established during the post-war era, was now in urgent need of further modernisation through fundamental structural reforms that had been postponed for decades as a result of the 'immobilism' of French politics and the blockages caused mainly by what are referred to as 'intermediary bodies' (*corps intermédiares*). Specifically, Macron pointed the finger at organisations that he accused of focusing on their own interests over those of the country at large, imposing their rules on others – such as political parties, trade unions, the media and, interestingly (since he was himself a top civil servant), the top echelons of the Administration. These were all entities that, for him, were no longer fulfilling their role in structuring French democracy. He was particularly frustrated by 'rent-seekers' – those who enrich themselves through the security of entrenched, privileged positions in society (*la rente de situation*) without giving back to society or the economy, rather than creating wealth through innovation (*la rente d'innovation*). His idea of waging a war against 'rent-seeking' in its many different guises is one which recurs repeatedly in Macron's discourse, reflecting the fact that he is, at heart, an entrepreneur who values risk-taking and believes in work as the only way to emancipation.

For Macron, social justice can best be achieved by ensuring that formal rules and rights are the same for everyone, establishing a level playing field in pursuit of maximising life chances, but also by enabling France to move on from a society regulated by 'statutes' to one of greater mobility, driven by entrepreneurial spirit: equal opportunities rather than equality. Nevertheless, the state retains an important role to play in this process, correcting imbalances and intervening where the market struggles to perform, as well as adapting the institutions to enable necessary cultural and behavioural change. Macron presented himself as a pragmatist, not an ideologue, placing a high value on efficiency. His project, therefore, was, and remains, resolutely economically liberal or, rather, neoliberal; it relies on the theory of 'trickle-down' economics, recast as the theory 'of the lead-climber', which involves supporting employers to innovate to create growth, assisted by greater flexibility in the workplace. This means helping workers to retrain and adapt to changing economic circumstances and, for this reason, the education system requires adaptation, as does the state administration.

None of this was radically new: since the oil crises and economic recession of the 1970s and the failure of the Socialist Experiment to 'break with capitalism' in the early 1980s, political elites on both left and right in France had tacitly accepted the need to adapt to the neoliberal model espoused by Margaret Thacher in the United Kingdom and Ronald Reagan in the United States. But successive governments had struggled to wean France off its generous post-war social model: strong popular resistance and a tradition of effective street protest had repeatedly caused governments of both left and right to withdraw unpopular, liberalising measures. Whilst privatisation was first openly advocated by the Gaullist right under Jacques Chirac as prime minister in 1986, this was ideologically more problematic for the left. The failure of the Socialist Experiment did not trigger a French equivalent of the official conversion of the German socialists to 'liberal socialism' at the Bad Godesberg conference in 1959, which had involved the renunciation of orthodox Marxist policies and the acceptance of free market principles, albeit within a regulated market. Instead, French official socialist discourse after 1984 (when the communists left the government) quietly dropped its critique of capitalism and adopted the language of 'modernisation' without any formal acknowledgement of this significant shift in the party's position. With its internal divisions unresolved, the Socialist Party oscillated between radical ideas in opposition and a more 'responsible' approach to governing once in power: François Hollande won in 2012 by promising radical 'Change Now', but as president, he reneged on important campaign pledges and introduced liberalising reforms (largely influenced by Emmanuel Macron), making him so unpopular by the end of his mandate that even his own party did not want him to stand again. Thus, the social democratic left failed to persuade its electorate that liberal reforms could deliver any benefits, and the language of neoliberalism remained taboo for them.

Where Macron innovated was in managing to present his project not as a programme of neoliberal reforms aimed at the 'marketisation' of society, subjecting France to the forces of globalisation, but as socially progressive, motivated by the goal of social justice and efficiency through the promotion of 'inclusive growth', wider access to previously closed venues for personal advancement, and the encouragement of individuals to maximise their life chances by becoming more autonomous and competitive. Putting this positive spin on neoliberalism enabled him to build a political force in the centre of French politics, claiming to be neither (or both) of the left or the right whilst 'at the same time' attracting support from both camps amongst those who accepted the neoliberal agenda with a human face. His masterstroke was to successfully position himself as the progressive, pro-European bulwark against the rise of the nationalist, Eurosceptic far right, a position crucial to his electoral success. Besides, for Macron, his proposed domestic reforms were closely linked to France's position in the EU, seen by political elites as a multiplier of French influence more than as an inhibitor of national sovereignty: his ambitious proposals for reforming the governance structures of the Eurozone were conditional on the success of structural reforms in France, intended to convince Germany to soften its approach to tight fiscal restraint.

With a score of 66 per cent in the second round of the 2017 presidential election and a solid absolute majority in the National Assembly, Macron could claim a strong mandate for implementing the transformation he promised. However, his victory was, in reality, more nuanced: a high abstention rate on the second round meant that he only polled 43.6 per cent of registered voters and, of the 24 per cent who voted for him in the first round, only 54 per cent said that they did so because of his programme – the rest were voting tactically;[1] this would have important implications for the way in which Macron's presidency subsequently evolved. The following summaries of the chapters in this volume provide a series of snapshots of how Macron's transformation of France developed between 2017 and July 2024 in specific areas, followed by some general conclusions regarding Macron's legacy to date.

Assessing the limits of political change under Emmanuel Macron

In Chapter 2, Sylvie Strudel discusses Macron's presidential style through the articulation of what she defines as three paradoxes: the monarchist–populist, the Jupiterian–participatory and the 'both left and right'. These are worked through by means of what she describes as personalisation, managerial disintermediation and a rightward shift in policies and electoral support. Set within the historical context of the presidentialisation of politics under the Fifth Republic, she shows how Macron developed the idea of 'verticality' in decision-making, played out notably in relation to his prime ministers, who he has treated as servants of the Head of State. Before he was even officially a candidate, he had already said that France needed a 'Jupiterian' leader, in contrast to Hollande's 'normal' presidency which for Macron represented a loss of authority;[2] the reference to Roman mythology enabled him to encapsulate the idea of strong leadership alongside a protective role whilst also remaining above the melee and its partisan quarrels.

Once elected, he insisted that being Jupiterian would not mean he would constantly intervene in government business but that he would restore the original spirit of presidential pre-eminence intended by de Gaulle. In practice, the idea of self-imposed aloofness and parsimonious public comment very soon gave way to the sort of hyper-presidential intervention that was the hallmark of President Sarkozy. Strudel brings interesting detail to the creation of the image that the president chose to convey of himself, illustrating her portrait with lesser-known anecdotal evidence about the president's apparent inability to recognise when he has spoken for long enough. Her analysis concludes with the appointment in January 2024 of Gabriel Attal, widely seen as a clone of Macron himself, the ultimate example, she argues, of a narcissistic pathology. Although Attal was a former socialist, his appointment confirmed the turn to the right of Macron's politics over time, bringing to an end the early claim to be neither left nor right. This is the only dimension of Macron's style of presidency to constitute political change: in all other respects, his approach has remained resolutely vertical and Jupiterian.

The apparent contradiction between the president's Jupiterian exercise of power and the pursuit of greater participation by ordinary citizens is discussed in more detail in Chapter 3 (Susan Collard), which explores how the president hoped to transform French democracy, widely agreed to be in urgent need of 'renovation'. Given the extent of his presidential powers, further strengthened by a comfortable and docile parliamentary majority, it is remarkable how little he was able to achieve in this area. His proposals for institutional reform were potentially far-reaching and included modifying the electoral system for legislative elections to include some degree of proportional representation – which had wide support – while at the same time planning to reduce the number of parliamentarians in both chambers, which was more controversial. Resistance from a politically hostile Senate was predictable but could have been better managed if the various components of the three different laws presented by the government had been more coherently packaged. But the Senate, which managed to assert itself as an effective check on executive power, was not the only obstacle to Macron's programme for democratic renovation: the suspension of parliamentary debate on these reforms was triggered by entirely unconnected events leading to the 'Benalla Affair'. This was the first political scandal of the presidency, concerning allegations of misconduct made against one of the president's closest security advisors.

As for Macron's agenda to revive citizen participation, the initiative was very soon stolen from him by protesters in the Yellow Vests movement, which forced the president to revise his political agenda. Here, we also see a contrast between a harsh and repressive police response and a more conciliatory verbal attempt to recognise failures of policy-making and of personal governing style. This was combined with the promise of a Great National Debate to allow all citizens to express their grievances and make proposals for change, followed up with a Citizens Convention on the Climate (CCC) as an experiment in deliberative democracy. Jupiter thus transformed a vast and unmanageable movement of anger and discontent against himself and his policies into a public relations exercise to restore his reputation, confirming the very monarchical style of his presidency, despite explicitly recognising that it was this that had inspired much of the anger.

Chapter 3 also engages with the underlying problem of democracy with regard to increasing hyper-presidentialism in the Fifth Republic, which reached its zenith in Macron's ultra-solitary exercise of power. This is best illustrated by his high-risk decision to call a snap election in June 2024 – a decision taken, by all accounts, behind closed doors, in collaboration with only a few close advisors: not even his prime minister was consulted. Following the chaotic situation of deadlock produced by this election, he told TV journalists that he assumed full responsibility for it and had no intention of resigning. He refused to appoint a new prime minister until after the Olympic Games, pushing the ball into the court of the newly elected deputies in the NA to find ways of working together in the absence of any clear majority. In so doing, he was avoiding facing the consequences of his decision by adopting the role of 'umpire' above the spectacle of bickering parties that had underpinned de Gaulle's conception of the presidency, enshrined in Article 5 of the Constitution.

In Chapter 4, Susan Collard and Françoise Dreyfus assess a different aspect of Macron's plan to renovate democracy: the drive to 'clean up' French politics and restore morality into public life, which constituted an important act of political communication in the context of the accusations of corruption against the *Républicains*' candidate, François Fillon, during the 2017 election campaign. In terms of legislative output, there was a marked contrast here with the failed institutional reforms discussed in Chapter 3, in that these laws were given high priority after the 2017 elections and were promulgated in September. The perceived need to legislate for the 'moralisation of public life' is explained in the first half of the chapter, which shows how political corruption in France had developed over the Fifth Republic, encouraged by its institutional framework and feeding off embedded beliefs and ideas that have historically permeated French politics. While political scandals were the main trigger for legislation, this was also influenced, from the 1990s onwards, by the global turn towards the need for greater transparency in governance, enabling anti-corruption agencies to become established with government recognition and accreditation. This did not, however, prevent many high-profile politicians, including prime ministers and presidents, from engaging in various types of corruption, the most emblematic examples of which involved former President Sarkozy. Macron has not been the subject of any such allegations, although the second half of the chapter shows that he has sometimes taken questionable stances regarding the behaviour of ministers in his governments. Dreyfus's analysis of 'compliance' by politicians, with all the various rules imposed on them by the increasingly onerous legislative framework, reveals a mixed bag of responses, but perhaps most importantly, it highlights the significant but little-known role of the agency set up to monitor the application of the regulations, the High Authority for Transparency in Public Life (HATVP), whose approval is now needed before any ministerial appointments can be confirmed. It is hard to draw conclusions as to how much real change has been brought about as a result of Macron's law on the moralisation of public life as tensions remain between the rule of law and embedded political behaviours, but the absence of any major political corruption scandal under Macron's watch suggests, at the very least, some evolution in the right direction.

In Chapter 5, Elodie Fabre analyses the changes in the main French political parties and the party system since Macron's disruptive election in 2017, which gave credence to the idea that the old divisions of right and left were no longer pertinent to French politics. Macron's newly created party LaREM (*La République en Marche*, Republic on the Move) was based on the idea of 'transcending' these cleavages and espousing a more pragmatic idea of politics based on 'what works'. Fabre describes Macron's meteoric rise to power and the building of political support via a digital network and explains his victory over the other parties in 2017 before comparing the results with those of sub-national elections during his first presidency, in which Macron's party failed to build local support. By the time of the 2022 elections, developments within LaREM and the other parties had created a different dynamic, especially the rise of Marine Le Pen's party based on her strategy of 'de-demonisation', including a change of name to National Rally (RN) in 2018. These elections confirmed a tri-polar division, in which Macron's alliance was increasingly challenged by the growth of the radical left – now united in the NUPES alliance led by Jean-Luc Mélenchon – and of the radical right, including the controversial candidacy of Eric Zemmour. Despite a hung parliament, Macron's alliance was still able to command a 'relative' majority, but, as discussed in Chapter 3, his governments struggled to pass legislation and increasingly looked to the mainstream right for support, confirming the rightward turn of *macronisme*. In the National Assembly, deputies from Mélenchon's party LFI (*La France Insoumise*) pursued disruptive tactics for which they received a record number of suspensions, while the National Rally, with its unexpected windfall of 89 seats, conducted itself impeccably, determined to show that it was a responsible party fit to govern. Some of Macron's deputies defected over his forcing through the pension reform in 2023, and his majority looked increasingly fragile as the European elections approached in June 2024.

Since Fabre's chapter concluded just before these elections, some updating is required here. The European election campaign had highlighted fundamental disagreements between the different parties in the NUPES alliance, especially over the situation in the Middle East. The various components of NUPES therefore led separate campaigns, and the socialists won more seats than LFI, reversing its previous position of relative weakness. This, no doubt, gave Macron reason to believe that, in calling new legislative elections, he could win back some of the more moderate socialists into his camp. However, to everyone's great surprise, within 48 hours of Macron's announcement, the parties of the left had formed a new alliance called the 'New Popular Front' (NFP) and pledged a series of electoral agreements designed to minimise the gaining of seats by the National Rally. Even more surprisingly, this alliance went on to win more seats than any other group in the new tri-polar composition of the National Assembly, enabling it to claim that it had won the election, despite being about 100 seats short of an absolute majority.

Meanwhile, on the right, the dissolution triggered a dramatic split within the *Républicains*, when its president, Eric Ciotti, unilaterally announced an electoral alliance with the RN. This was however rejected by the majority of the party, causing a split amongst its deputies: a group of 47 deputies formed called *La Droite Républicaine*, whilst Ciotti's group of 16 took the name of *A Droite*. A legal battle for the 'ownership' of the party ensued. The new leader of *La Droite Républicaine,* Laurent Wauquiez, determined to preserve the party's identity, indicated that his group would work on a 'legislative pact' (but not a coalition) with the presidential majority's group, from a position of 'constructive opposition' to avoid a government of the left. However, the numbers would still not deliver a viable majority. This position arguably left the mainstream right in a fragile position, in the shadow of the RN, which increased its presence from 88 seats to 123. Emmanuel Macron had, once again, disrupted the party system but no longer to his advantage: his hope of forming a coalition of parties within 'the republican arc', excluding both extremes (LFI and RN), now looked out of reach, and the president had to face the seemingly intractable problem of how to avoid a drift into 'immobilism'.

In Chapter 6, Raymond Kuhn analyses Macron's relationship with the media and assesses his mixed record of success in managing his political communication. Kuhn begins by contrasting the nature of Macron's presidential election campaign in 2017 – when novelty made him the preferred candidate of many media outlets – with that of 2022, when he became the preferred candidate to criticise. In 2017, despite being, in other ways, a very private person, Macron did not shy away from allowing the spotlight to be shone on his unusual marriage to Brigitte but, by 2022, he presented himself more as an international statesman, focused on seeking a resolution to the Russian invasion of Ukraine. Although the Elysée plays a role as the 'primary definer' of the news media in France, Macron initially planned to keep journalists at arm's length by moving the press office out of the main Elysée building. Nevertheless, as time went on, his personal style of communication changed, and the president was soon omnipresent in all media outlets, often to his detriment. Notable failures of communication were the Benalla Affair (discussed in Chapters 3 and 4) and the 2023 pension reform. Off-the-cuff comments made in public places were also important examples of very poor communication that were highly damaging to his image.

In describing the evolving media landscape in France, Kuhn highlights the importance of the impact on public opinion of news channels and especially, *CNews*, owned by media magnate Vincent Bolloré, whose opponents accuse him of running a Christian crusade against 'wokism' and Islam, holding him responsible for fuelling support for the RN by mainstreaming their views. Bolloré has been working for some time towards increasing the influence of his own views in public debate, including support for the 'union' of all the parties of the right: in the 2024 elections, he openly endorsed the decision by LR President, Eric Ciotti, to form an electoral alliance with the RN. In February 2024, a landmark decision by the Council of State[3] confirmed that *CNews* had, indeed, evolved from a news channel into an opinion channel. Bolloré's activities also came under scrutiny in the public debate over the concentration of media ownership, which had been the subject of a Senate enquiry in March 2022. In this context, Macron had been working since 2020 on a plan, revived in 2023 and due to be taken through Parliament in 2024 by the new Minister of Culture Rachida Dati, to bring together *France Télévisions* (the public TV channels), *Radio France,* the *Institut National de l'Audiovisuel* (INA), *France24* and *Radio France Internationale* (RFI) into one large organisation to be called *France Médias,* supposedly modelled on the BBC. It was strongly criticised by employees fearing for their jobs and by the left, who saw it as an attempt to 'Macronise' public broadcasting. As it had not been debated in parliament before the dissolution of June 2024, its future depends on future political developments.

In Chapter 7, Jörg Monar assesses Macron's European policy, arguably the centrepiece of his political project. Many of his planned domestic reforms were intended to strengthen the French economy and bring it more into line with the German economy in order to persuade Germany to agree to his ambitious plans for reforming the governance of the Eurozone. However, as Monar explains, the change of German leadership pushed the president into looking beyond the Franco–German tandem for support and, especially, towards the Central and Eastern European countries. Monar argues that Macron made a distinctive effort to re-conceptualise the idea of Europe as a sovereign and protective power, set out in an important speech delivered at the Sorbonne in September 2017 in which he also made 'an avalanche' of proposals but which did not yield many concrete results, especially regarding his ambitions for European defence. However, he was more successful in consolidating the agreement for the post-Covid recovery package 'Next Generation EU', a major breakthrough in terms of collective debt management, which Germany had previously refused. Macron was also the driving force behind the 'Conference on the Future of Europe', though here, again, there were few tangible results. Finally, Macron's attempts to negotiate with President Putin over Ukraine were a dismal failure, though they enabled the president to show himself as an international statesman during the 2022 election campaign. The fact that in the European elections of June 2024, Macron's alliance won under half the number of seats as the National Rally was a disastrous indictment of the president's European policy: his failure to convince French citizens of his vision for the EU is attributed by Monar to an overestimation of his own powers of persuasion and a misplaced use of political spin in talking up the threats facing Europe. France's traditionally strong position in the EU has also been severely weakened by the domestic political crisis and by the latest figures showing an alarming level of national debt and budget deficit, triggering formal repercussions from the EU Commission. This could not be further from the outcome to which Macron aspired in 2017.

In Chapter 8 by Brigitte Granville, the subject of Macron and the economy, including its European dimension, is discussed from a labour-market perspective. Since the 1970s, France has grappled with high unemployment of around 10 per cent, and successive presidents have failed to tackle the problem effectively. Taking as her starting point Macron's proclaimed goal of employment reform, Granville first explains the economics of France's historically 'dysfunctional labour market' in language accessible to those without specialist knowledge of economics. She then discusses Macron's labour reforms, which built on the controversial El Khomri Law of 2016, passed with Macron's support as Economics Minister under François Hollande. Although this law had been strongly contested because of the 'liberalising' provisions on working hours and conditions, once president, Macron went further and passed a series of measures that introduced greater flexibility in labour legislation and decentralised collective bargaining down to the company level, which implied weakening the role of the unions. Once again, this triggered street protests – but Macron stood firm, arguing that he had been elected on a mandate for reform. He followed up with a law designed to empower working people to gain better control over their professional development, offering training opportunities and other adaptations to their working lives and prioritising vocational training. Here again, the role of the unions was weakened, and large companies were encouraged to set up their own apprenticeship training centres. Another reform involved changes to the employment-insurance system; interestingly, it extended benefits to the self-employed and facilitated voluntary career changes, especially involving re-skilling. However, there were also reductions and other adverse modifications to entitlements. Disrupted by the pandemic, they were picked up again under the second presidency, leading to structural changes across the various agencies delivering employment policies.

In conclusion, Granville explains the difficulty of assessing the effectiveness and impact of structural reforms, noting that the reduction in unemployment from 9.6 to 7.8 per cent between 2017 and 2020 cannot be imputed to reforms sponsored by Macron. Besides, this period was significantly disrupted by the pandemic, distorting any relevant data. Nevertheless, she notes Macron's determination to address persistent hurdles and classifies some of his reforms as 'pivotal achievements'. She also identifies two significant constraints on the effectiveness of structural reform in bringing about sustained long-term improvements in economic performance: France's deteriorating public finances and the top-down technocratic approach to carrying out reform. Many aspects of Granville's analysis will, no doubt, be disputed by other economists, but she delivers an important reminder that evaluating economic change cannot easily be contained within a politically defined time frame.

A similar conclusion is drawn by Jean-Michel Eymeri-Douzans in Chapter 9, when he points out in his analysis of Macron's reform of the Higher Civil Service that long-term outcomes are hard to assess, given the administration's skill in 'digesting' reforms. The French system of 'Administration' is at the heart of all policy-making in France, but its complexity makes it hard for outsiders to grasp. The French state is a mastodon that employs 25 per cent of the country's workforce and is in a constant process of reform, to which Macron has attempted to add his mark by tackling the apex of this system – the top civil servants or *hauts fonctionnaires*. As Eymeri-Douzans explains, this small elite of technocrats, a sort of 'state nobility', has traditionally emerged from a highly competitive and supposedly 'meritocratic' system of selection, managed through the *grandes écoles*, which delivers – for those who are successful – a highly prestigious career path at a young age, not only providing total job security for life but also allowing its members to move in and out of politics or the private sector at will, in the knowledge that their post will remain open should they wish to return to it. A 'super-elite' is composed of those who perform well enough during the selection process to choose to join the most prestigious *grands corps*. What makes this system so distinctive is the way in which these technocratic elites enter the political system, creating a 'technocratisation' of politics: five out of eight presidents – including Macron – and many prime ministers were *hauts fonctionnaires*, not to mention the legions of ministers and their advisors and other politicians. This system of self-perpetuating elites dominating policy-making has been a significant factor in driving strong anti-elite feelings amongst the French citizenry, illustrated by the Yellow Vests demonstrations.

Although Macron was a product of this system, he chose to forfeit his lifelong tenure as Finance Inspector when he resigned in order to stand as a presidential candidate. Moreover, in *Revolution*, he criticised senior civil servants as constituting a 'caste', running the country's affairs from the shadows and he argued for systemic reform. Eymeri-Douzans explains how, once elected, Macron broke with tradition by taking immediate measures to ensure political control of the administration, then oversaw a law opening up recruitment to applicants from more socially diverse backgrounds, which Eymeri-Douzans argues is a real cultural revolution. He also closed the National School of Administration (ENA), causing shock and horror in government circles: following delays caused by the pandemic, in January 2022, it was replaced by the National Institute for Public Service (INSP), and a new *corps* of general state administrators was created. Eymeri-Douzans argues that this major reform, which represented a major Macronian 'disruption', can be summarised as transforming the 'state nobility' into 'can-do managers'. However, most importantly in his view, Macron's reforms represent the French incarnation of a common trend observed in many post-modern democracies towards a growing 'functional politicisation' of top civil servants, summoned to be more docile towards ever-more 'presidentialised' executives. In this respect, the reform is perfectly aligned with Macron's consolidation of vertical decision-making that has been the hallmark of his presidency.

In Chapter 10, by Nicolas Charles and Andy Smith, the importance of the French state is investigated from a different perspective – that of the education system which, like the administrative system, was highlighted by Macron as central to his ambitions to transform French society. This analysis sets out to identify areas of change in education brought about during Macron's presidency in contrast to those where continuity prevailed. To this end, the authors begin by explaining the historical underpinning of the education system and its republican commitment to the idea of meritocracy, born of the Revolution of 1789: educating all children in a similar way via a body of teachers employed as national civil servants was historically used both to consolidate the republican approach to citizenship and to deepen identifications with France 'the nation' (as opposed to its regions) and the principle of meritocracy itself. However, by 2017, it was widely admitted that the Republican ideal of educational justice for all had simply not been achieved, and Macron's manifesto clearly prioritised the need to address this problem. Charles and Smith argue that he did this by introducing changes which destabilised the established principle of meritocracy within education in the name of individual freedom and competition, targeting the political economy of the education sector from the angle of marketisation to allow more competition and choice, which lay at the heart of his vision of social justice.

Whilst some of Macron's reforms represented institutional continuity, others were explicitly disruptive of existing norms, such as the launch of 50 experimental schools in Marseilles and the introduction of flexibility and choice at the level of the *baccalauréat* which the authors – and most teachers – saw as introducing inequality. In higher education, a new web portal procedure – *Parcoursup* – for regulating access to most Higher Education (HE) establishments, was also seen as challenging equality amongst applicants and initiating more systematic competition between institutions and the marketisation of education. The authors are cautious as to the extent of change brought about by these policies; nevertheless, they argue that their market-based logic contains the potential for deep structural change, driven by a highly liberal, top-down political enterprise whose commitment to social justice has been framed around greater competition.

In Chapter 11, Charlotte Halpern assesses Macron's achievements in the field of environmental and climate policy (ECP). France has often been portrayed in comparative research as a case of 'failed institutionalisation', in that the state has struggled to effectively structure the diverse activities and groups, both within the state and outside it, which have developed since the emergence of environmental issues in the 1970s. Decentralisation, since the 1980s, has further fragmented policy organisation, resulting in high levels of differentiation and territorial diversity, which do not conform to the 'clichéd' view of France as an archetypically strong, centralised and unified state. As Halpern demonstrates, this has strong implications for the presidency's capacity to drive change.

Although environmental issues had not played a very prominent role in Macron's 2017 campaign, his high-profile promise to 'make our planet great again' after President Trump withdrew the United States from the Paris Agreement on Climate Change, raised high expectations, reinforced by his appointment of one of France's most popular environmental activists, the TV journalist, Nicolas Hulot, as Minister for Ecological and Inclusive Transition. The president singled out 'green issues' as a cornerstone of his modernisation agenda, putting the green economy at the heart of his plans to transform French society and agriculture as well as in his efforts to reassert France's leadership in Europe and globally. However, his ambitions were very soon thwarted not only by the resignation of Hulot – on the grounds that he had 'a little influence but no power' to resist powerful lobbies protecting vested interests – but also by the eruption of the Yellow Vests movement, triggered by policy instruments designed to tackle climate change. This led to the adoption of a strategy of conflict avoidance to justify prioritising small steps – and controversial decisions such as the use of pesticides were increasingly transferred to the EU level. There were, however, positive outcomes such as the European Green Deal and the Covid recovery package, Next Generation EU (NGEU), which included incentives for technological innovations furthering the green transition. The invasion of Ukraine highlighted the urgency of rethinking the EU's energy supplies, and Macron called for major new investment in nuclear reactors whilst also pushing aggressively, at EU level, for nuclear energy to be classified as a green investment under the EU taxonomy.

Halpern's overall conclusion is that the fight against climate change under Macron has been impeded by climate delaying and the politics of small steps. Although his use of 'green' rhetoric was instrumental in promoting his programme for the French economy, unforeseen events disrupted his agenda. Although he was partly able to turn this to his advantage, the discrepancy between ambitious 'heroic' discourse and the reality of complex policy processes that encroached on his capacity for policy-making means that it is unlikely that his legacy will match the climate emergency.

Chapter 12, by Olivier Fillieulle, Fabien Jobard and Anne Wuillemier, offers a different discussion of the Yellow Vests protest movement by focusing on the police response to it and, by extension, considers the broader issue of repressing protest during Macron's presidency. The authors' analysis of this question is based largely on a research project that involved extensive interviews which bring fascinating insights to bear on the details of police operations. The French police have established an international reputation for their particularly brutal tactics when dealing with street protests, and this chapter explains why this was the case for the Yellow Vests protests. It begins by setting out the complex institutional organisation of the various police forces in France, all of which are reinforced by state-appointed prefects across all French territory who are responsible to the Interior Minister for law and order in their areas; in Paris, given its turbulent history, there is also a special Police Prefect. Since the 1970s, different policies have been implemented – including 'community policing' under the left and 'governing through crime' under the right – but it was the dramatic terrorist attacks of 2015 and 2016 that put the police at the forefront of the political agenda and which justified the declaration of a state of emergency that was still in force when Macron was elected.

The new president initially took a resolutely progressive position on policing and was critical of police behaviour towards ethic-minority youth in the suburbs or *banlieues*. But when the Yellow Vests protests broke out, the sheer extent of demonstrations was such that he called for massive police mobilisation, including the special riot-police units. However, budget cuts to policing, implemented following the financial crisis of 2008, meant that these forces were depleted, curtailing their operational capacity. Traditional methods of crowd policing had been replaced by 'judicialisation', maximising arrests as indicators of 'results and performance' as protest policing became aligned with crime control. Faced with the Yellow Vests protests, a repressive paradigm therefore took hold, which led to unprofessional management of the demonstrators. The authors question whether this repressive policy was a deliberate manifestation of Macron's neoliberal determination not to give in to street protest or whether he found himself entrapped by the police who had become indispensable to maintaining law and order, including his own personal security. There is evidence to support either interpretation and the truth probably lies somewhere between the two. In any case, police repression continued in response to the pension reform protests, environmental demonstrations and incidents involving suburban youth but not, interestingly, against the farmers' protests of early 2024.

In Chapter 13, Tony Chafer assesses Macron's Africa policy through his attempt to change the dependent pathways of '*La Françafrique*' embedded in the politics of the Fifth Republic and he finds that the president's ambitions to break with the past, like his initially progressive positions on policing, did not resist the pressures of political and institutional realities. France had established a model of neo-colonial relations with its former African colonies following their independence, based on the goal of preserving exclusive rights to developing resources and markets and asserting the right to use military intervention to protect its interests. Economic control was further embedded through the maintenance of a common currency, the CFA franc. All French presidents since 1981 had announced plans to transform this unhealthy relationship, but continuity had prevailed. Chafer shows how Macron's approach was significantly different to that of any predecessors in several ways relating to military, economic and political relations, most notably his attempt to build a new partnership focusing on youth and civil society in Africa and to develop a more multilateral model of military intervention. He also created a new advisory body, the Presidential Council for Africa, by-passing the usual channels in search of more independent advice; however, the rhetoric was not matched by positive results.

In terms of military policy, Macron sought to maintain the ongoing Operation Barkhane, aimed at driving out Islamic militants from the Sahel, by creating the G5 Sahel Joint Force (G5SJF) in the hope that it would, eventually, be able to take over counterterrorism operations from Barkhane, reinforced later by the creation of an international Coalition for the Sahel. However, the worsening of the security situation on the ground and a series of military coups led to the end of that operation and to the forced withdrawal of French troops from Mali, Burkina Faso and Niger. As the traditional *gendarme* of Africa', Macron found himself trapped in a 'logic of intervention' from which he could not escape – and accusations of neo-colonial interventionism persisted. France was criticised for its double standards, and its failure either to deliver improvements in security and governance or to promote development, played into the narrative that France was in the Sahel, above all, to defend its own interests.

With regard to economic ties with Africa, Macron's instincts as an economic liberal were to attempt a 'reset' of the economic and business relationship partly to reverse the declining share of French companies in trade with Francophone Africa but also to free them from the networks and 'closed shops' of *la Françafrique*. However, vested interests were resistant, particularly over continuing arguments about the CFA franc and its future, which have still not been resolved. As for the political relationship, one notable innovation by Macron was the holding of a new-format Africa–France summit in Montpellier in 2021 to which *les acteurs du changement* were invited, but no African heads of state. This venture, however, backfired on the president when France was accused of arrogance and hypocrisy, promoting democracy in Africa whilst mired in issues of racism at home. Likewise, his attempt to promote the French language through *Francophonie* was condemned as condescending and paternalistic. Overall, therefore, despite an attempted change of rhetoric and style, Chafer shows how Macron's Africa policy failed to escape the weight of the past, and his own personal missteps and policy errors were emblematic of the difficulty of breaking with the cultural legacy of French domination.

In Chapter 14, Martin Evans assesses Macron's efforts to address the painful legacies of French colonisation, especially of Algeria, which he described during his presidential campaign as 'a crime against humanity'. Evans focuses on two key processes that Macron initiated: the restitution of African artefacts acquired during colonisation and the search for truth and reconciliation over the Algerian War. On restitution, after announcing (in Ouagadougou) his aim of returning to Africa the objects 'acquired' in various illicit ways during France's colonial past, Macron commissioned the Sarr-Savoy report whose inventory counted 88,000 artefacts, of which about 70,000 were in the Quai Branly Museum in Paris, commissioned by President Chirac. The report recommended that the terms of restitution should depend on the context of the acquisition, and the first, unambiguous, returns were made to Benin in November 2021. However, a further report published in April 2023 by the former president of the Louvre argued for modifying the criteria for restitution; the Council of State subsequently issued a judgement in March 2024 that raised a complex legal issue regarding terms of their 'ownership', after which the process of legislating to allow the release of the remaining restitutions was suspended. Given the current political uncertainty, the future of this initiative is now on hold: having been at the forefront of the movement for cultural restitution, France seems to have lost its vanguard position.

With regard to Algeria, the new president felt that his youth enabled him to re-set the historical dial, both in an effort to improve poor inter-state relations and to address the alleged link between the Algerian War and the alienation of French citizens of Algerian heritage that he considered to be a factor in the growth of homegrown Islamist 'separatism' – and, by extension, terrorism. Of all French colonies, Algeria stood out by the longevity of colonial rule (132 years) and the violent nature of the fight for independence, which had far-reaching consequences for a number of specific communities in France, each with their own different memory narratives. Macron's ambition to initiate a process of reconciliation led to the commissioning of a report by the well-known historian Benjamin Stora, which highlighted the stark contrast between official memorial narratives in both countries. In France, it could be summarised as collective amnesia whilst, in Algeria, it was one of hyper-memory, marked by a proliferation of commemorative events and memorials to the martyrs. Response to the report was predictably very varied but did not trigger any reconciliation, despite Macron's decision to create specific memorial days encapsulating the different memory narratives.

Frustrated by the lack of positive response, in the autumn of 2021, the president changed tack, and when hosting an event at the Elysée, he described the Algerian regime in place as a 'political-military system' whose backbone was ongoing exploitation of memory (*'rente mémorielle'*) and 'hatred of France'; he then cut visas for Algerians (and Moroccans and Tunisians), producing a diplomatic furore. Although, once re-elected, he made an official visit to Algeria, a scheduled return visit by the Algerian President Tebboune has still not materialised and, at the end of July 2024, Algeria withdrew its ambassador from France following Macron's declaration of support for the Moroccan plan for the autonomy of Western Sahara. These recent events occurred after the conclusions drawn by Evans, which highlight the fact that Macron, as president, never repeated the phrase 'crimes against humanity'; nor did he ever go beyond the language of recognition and empathy to embrace the idea of apology. In the current political climate, Franco-Algerian relations seem no closer to any kind of reconciliation and, after the major riots provoked by the unlawful killing by the police of Nahel, a youth of Algerian descent, in June 2023, Macron's ambition of appeasing the tensions in French society seems highly optimistic.

The alienation of descendants of Algerians in France is also discussed in Chapter 15 by Philippe Portier in his analysis of Macron's religious policy, which reflects the president's concerns regarding the turn towards 'separatism' by part of the Muslim population in France. Portier delivers well-evidenced insights into Macron's thinking around the question of religion, which is more central to his diagnosis of the problems facing France than hitherto credited, and he highlights two elements, 'recognition and security', which he argues are driven by a fear of 'anomie' (social instability resulting from a breakdown of values). The wider context for this analysis, the historical origins and significance of French secularism, is explained in Portier's introduction, which sets out the fundamental principles of the religious neutrality of the state, enshrined in the famous 1905 Law of Separation of Church and State, which officially relegates religion to the private sphere, free from interference from the state. However, in the 1980s, demands by young Muslims of immigrant descent for differentiated treatment, such as the wearing of headscarves in the traditionally neutral educational space, ignited tensions later exacerbated by the onset of terrorist attacks attributed to Muslim Islamists. Secularism then underwent what Portier calls a 'substantialist turn' in the early 2000s: the 'values of the Republic' were reasserted as the fundamental framework within which the rights of the individual must be contained, as confirmed in the 2004 law banning conspicuous religious symbols in state schools.

Portier then explores Macron's thoughts about how the transition to modernity has created a risk of alienation and separation that undermines national cohesion and republican values. Macron believes that religion is a stabilising force in society and a factor of identity and has often referred to France's 'Christian roots'. But while Catholicism is often seen as central, he also acknowledges the contribution of Protestantism and Judaism to shaping the nation's character. The president attaches particular importance to discussions with religious authorities, including the Pope – a form of 'recognition' that, for Portier, bears witness to a certain 'corporatisation' of French politics. However, the relationship between the two is asymmetrical, and the government retains the final decision, such as the ban on holding Mass during the Covid pandemic. Regarding Islam, a debate has sprung up in France around a greater observation of ritual obligations, which is often accompanied by a distancing from political law: for advocates of liberal secularism, this is not necessarily in contradiction with the republican concept of 'living together', whilst, for others, it is a worrying development that feeds into 'communitarianism' and terrorism. Macron's position, expressed in many speeches, aligns with the second of these perspectives, as was articulated in the 2021 law 'reinforcing respect for the principles of the Republic', which was much criticised globally as being Islamophobic. Portier argues that this law, extending the scope of state intervention into many other sectors such as associations, health, education and sport, and reducing the scope for religious freedom, constitutes a vast reform of the secular laws of the Third Republic. Moreover, Macron's attempt to establish institutionalised control over the Muslim faith in order to build 'an Islam of the Enlightenment' is a move in the same direction, as is his programme of 'civic rearmament', under the authority of strict secularists. Portier concludes that Macron's policies on religion represent the continuation of the model for the public management of religious affairs first established in the early 2000s, which curtails freedoms, in the name of material and cultural securitisation, rather than preserving them.

Concluding comments

What conclusions can be drawn from these different analyses about the capacity for political change in a country led by a president with extensive formal powers that can be seriously undermined by informal constraints and unexpected events? Based on the cases examined here, it appears that Macron had only limited success in implementing his 'revolutionary' programme, even during the first presidency, when he benefitted from a strong and docile majority in the National Assembly to pass legislation. Institutional factors played a part in this, as did unpredictable events like the pandemic and the invasion of Ukraine, but, above all, it was personal factors, the personality and 'management' style of the president, combined with unpopular policy reform, that encroached most on presidential power, as was the case for his two predecessors. The scale of protest in the Yellow Vests movement forced Macron to seriously reschedule his political agenda, even though it paradoxically enabled him to reassert his personal authority, as did the pandemic. Yet growing hostility towards the president undermined his legitimacy, further weakened by his 'semi-victory' of 2022. This hostility was triggered by a combination of personal style and political misjudgement: his 'Jupiterian' interpretation of the exercise of power inspired not just anger and resentment towards a monarchical leader but also intense personal hatred. The very symbolic abolition of the ISF wealth tax, widely seen as unjust, quickly labelled him as the 'president of the rich' and, only a year after his election, in April 2018, during the demonstrations against one of his early reforms of the 'privileged' status of employees of the state-run railway company SNCF, an effigy of the president was first hanged then set on fire.

During the Yellow Vests protests and other demonstrations, there were countless similar scenes, calling for the president's resignation and making threats to his life. Macron's habit of making tactless and often insulting off-the-cuff remarks has inspired deeply felt indignation and resentment, fuelling the image of an arrogant leader, totally disconnected from, and uninterested in, the lives of ordinary people: the unemployed horticulturalist told to cross the road and get a job in a café, the comment at a meeting of 'startuppers' about how a station is a place where there are some people who succeed and others who 'are nothing' (*qui ne sont rien*) are but two examples. Despite repeated claims to be 'listening', he gave the impression of not hearing, and his openness to dialogue too frequently ended in monologue. During the pandemic, he created an outcry by saying that he wanted to 'annoy the shit out of' (*emmerder*) people who refused to get vaccinated. Thus, personal rejection of the president became a self-inflicted form of constraint on his power, to which he responded by ratcheting up the use of authoritarian methods, creating a pernicious cycle of protest and repression.

Indeed, beyond the allegedly unjust and unpopular policies themselves, it is the 'undemocratic' way in which Macron is accused of imposing them on a largely unwilling population, especially the pension reform of 2023, that aggravated the unrest. Moreover, despite making many concessions – especially in response to the Yellow Vests – and despite repeated promises to 'change his method' or 'govern differently', he has not in any way given up on the overall goal of implementing his programme of reforms. This is not just personal stubbornness on his part: his determination to see through his goal of transforming France is derived from the firm conviction that these structural reforms are essential to restoring economic prosperity and creating a more efficient and just society – and he remains convinced that his diagnosis is the right one.

These strong views are said to owe much to Macron's participation in the work of the Attali Commission, appointed by President Sarkozy in 2007 to make recommendations on how to liberate growth through structural reforms (Godin, 2022). The commission's report, claiming to be non-partisan, argued that, although elites of both left and right had, since the failure of the Socialist Experiment in the early 1980s, reached tacit agreement on the need for neoliberal reforms to bring France into line with other economies, especially Germany, successive governments had shied away from them, preferring political compromises over holding firm in the face of popular protests: the French population was firmly attached to its generous social model and not easily persuaded that Thatcher's Britain was a preferable alternative. The Attali Commission recommended a more radical approach to introducing structural reforms, and Godin (2022, p. 111) argues that this was the genesis of *macronisme*.

Macron remains committed to his neoliberal project to transform France: like Margaret Thatcher (with whom comparisons are frequently made), this president is not for turning. Already, back in September 2017, during early demonstrations against his labour reforms, he made it clear that he would not give in to protest and would see through his programme with absolute determination. The use of forceful (albeit constitutional) tactics to implement the 2023 pension reform with only a relative majority showed that he was prepared to ignore popular opinion in pursuit of this agenda. Given the long history of concessions granted by previous leaders over unpopular reforms, it is not hard to see why the most widely used word in France to describe Macron's hard-nosed approach is 'brutal'. Given, too, the emphasis he placed in *Revolution* (2019, p. 254) and repeated elsewhere, on the need to '*convaincre*', to win support for his policies through the power of persuasion, the strength of opposition against him must be seen as Macron's personal failure to convince the French people that his vision for social justice is the best for France.

At the time of writing, in late July 2024, Macron's political future and legacy hang in the balance and the prospect of his accomplishing France's conversion to neoliberalism seems in doubt; this is almost certainly the end of '*la macronie*', with Jupiter's disillusioned troops abandoned by the wayside, even if his personal capacity for resilience should not be underestimated. Several contributors to this volume point out that the impact of deep policy change (such as education, state reform and the economy) is hard to evaluate within the political time frame of a presidency: it is possible that, in years to come, Macron's reforms will deliver more tangible results, be they positive or negative. It is even plausible that, given the curious tendency in France to rehabilitate once unpopular politicians (François Hollande is the latest example), the legacy of Emmanuel Macron may one day be re-evaluated in a more positive light in the popular imagination. For now, however, France has been politically immobilised by the president's impulses for disruption, which have so far proved to be self-defeating, not just for himself but for the whole political system.

Notes

1 https://www.opinion-way.com/fr/sondage-d-opinion/sondages-publies/politique/presidentielle-2017.html 'Sondage jour du vote au premier tour.'
2 https://www.challenges.fr/politique/macron-ne-croit-pas-au-president-normal-cela-destabilise-les-francais_432886
3 https://www.conseil-etat.fr/actualites/pluralisme-et-independance-de-l-information-l-arcom-devra-se-prononcer-a-nouveau-sur-le-respect-par-cnews-de-ses-obligations#:~:text=Par%20sa%20d%C3%A9cision%20du%2013,homme%20et%20des%20libert%C3%A9s%20fondamentales

References

Godin, R. (2022) *La guerre sociale en France*. Paris: Editions La Découverte.
Macron, E. (2016) *Révolution*. Paris: XO Editions. English edition: Macron, E. (2017) *Revolution*. London: Scribe.

2
EMMANUEL MACRON: THE PARADOXES OF A DISRUPTIVE PRESIDENCY

Sylvie Strudel

Abstract

This chapter explores the ways in which Emmanuel Macron has used the powers granted to the President of the Republic since his election on 7 May 2017. The author's analysis answers the central question: what kind of holder of office has this youngest President of the French Republic made, having never been previously elected and without any real history of party activism – supported by a movement (En Marche!) *that did not even exist a year before the presidential election and promoting a political project claiming to be 'both left and right'? Strudel highlights three paradoxes (monarchical–populist, Jupiterian–participatory and 'both left and right'), which she considers to be particularly illuminating, both in shedding light on Macron's presidential project and his exercise of power and in understanding how each of these paradoxes has been worked through over the past seven years of his mandate: through what she describes as personalisation, managerial disintermediation and a rightward shift in his policies and support.*

Introduction

Since 1958, every President of the Republic has left his mark on the presidency by his governing style: Charles de Gaulle had crafted the Constitution of the Fifth Republic, establishing the image of a majestic president, driving a revitalised sovereign state, guiding the people and embodying a deeply rooted nation. Valéry Giscard d'Estaing transgressed the conservative codes of Gaullism and Pompidoulism, setting in motion a sort of presidential marketing that resonated with societal demands (real or supposed). Then, despite his determined opposition to de Gaulle and his undeniable republicanism,

DOI: 10.4324/9781003323259-2

over the course of his two seven-year terms, François Mitterrand brought back the charismatic image of the president as a true 'constitutional pontiff' (François, 1992). Though Jacques Chirac was able to ensure respect for the solemnity of the function, he came across as empathetic and sympathetic, while Nicolas Sarkozy, described as the 'ultra-president', replaced presidential reserve and the aloofness of the position with unrestrained communication and often-unbecoming responsiveness. Finally, seeking a break with the media hysteria surrounding his predecessor, François Hollande displayed a mix of sobriety and normalisation – as if the institutions of the Fifth Republic could be satisfied with a 'normal president'.

Beyond personal styles, two mutually reinforcing trends have been discernible over the years: a progressive presidentialisation of the regime and an increasing personalisation of the presidential office. These trends are, at the same time, the consequence of constitutional changes, adjustment to circumstances, individual choices and major social and political developments that have also been observable at the international level.

'A Constitution is a spirit, institutions and practice', said Charles de Gaulle in a press conference held on 31 January 1964.[1] The intention of the authors of the Constitution of 4 October 1958 and of the text itself was to restore a stable executive branch by giving precedence to the President of the Republic, considered the 'cornerstone' of government institutions – all this while, according to Michel Debré, labelling the form of government as 'parliamentary' due to the flexible separation of powers. From this point on, the president would be able to appoint the prime minister (Article 8), to submit bills of all kinds to referendum (Article 11) and to dissolve the National Assembly (Article 12).[2] As head of the armed forces, the president alone may resolve to use nuclear force, and diplomacy is their second 'reserved domain'.[3] That said, France is not the United States. The Fifth Republic gave the president significantly greater powers than those of the president under the Third and Fourth Republics, but the form of government, though certainly no longer fully parliamentary, is not fully presidential either. Legal experts and political scientists have been debating how to label the current political system since 1958 but have failed to reach a consensus: for Raymond Aron, it is an 'Imperial Republic', for Maurice Duverger, a 'semi-presidential system' and for Pierre Avril, a 'hybrid system' (Donegani and Sadoun, 1998).

At least two constitutional revisions have been made that contributed to changing government dynamics by placing the presidential election at the heart of the French political system. The election of the President of the Republic by direct universal suffrage, as desired by Charles de Gaulle and adopted by referendum on 28 October 1962, gives the Head of State a political legitimacy derived directly from the people, though not excluding the possibility of plebiscites. The adoption of the five-year term by the constitutional law of 2 October 2000 (subsequent also to a referendum held on 24 September 2000) and the synchronisation of the electoral calendar (as a result of which the legislative elections follow immediately after the presidential election) have, in turn, reinforced the pre-eminence of the President of the Republic. By reducing the possibility of cohabitation, this dual reform helped to remove the risk of weakening the power of the presidency. From a political point of view, these constitutional revisions also impacted on the political parties, transforming them into machines focused on the presidential elections (Cole, 1993; Portelli, 1980). Multiple variations of this reinforcement of executive power have taken place, both in France (Roussellier, 2015) and beyond (Poguntke and Webb, 2005), since it might be said that the process of 'presidentialisation' has now affected all forms of government, even its parliamentary forms (Foley, 2000).

Another large-scale phenomenon, amply documented over a long period of time, now also affects most democracies: that of the personalisation of political competition (Kirchheimer, 1966; Wattenberg, 1991). Media overexposure, combined with the ever-more-pervasive influence of social networks, as well as the role of spokespersons and the emphasis placed on polls have all contributed to a progressive intimisation of politics, a de-ideologisation of political programmes turned 'catch alls' and, ultimately, to the emergence of populist leaders. Some authors have even alluded to the emergence of 'personal parties' (Calise, 2000; McDonnell, 2013).

Emmanuel Macron, like his predecessors, is part of the same succession that began in 1958, but there are certain specific aspects that differentiate his rise to power and his exercise of the office of president. How has he used the powers granted to the President of the Republic since his initial election on 7 May 2017 at just 39 years old? What kind of holder of office has this youngest President of the French Republic made, having never been previously elected and without any real history of party activism – supported by a movement (*En Marche!*) that did not even exist a year before the presidential election and promoting a political project claiming to be 'both left and right'? How have the paradoxes at play – clearly displayed during his rise to power, in keeping with his 'at the same time' (*en même temps*) doctrine – stood the test of the exercise of power and of the trials and crises that have arisen (such as the Yellow Vests, Covid-19 or pension reform)? How can we evaluate them in light of the promises of *Revolution* (Macron, 2016a) that were made before the election? Three paradoxes (monarchical–populist, Jupiterian–participatory and 'both left and right') would appear to be particularly illustrative, both to shed light on Macron's presidential project and his exercise of power and to understand how each of these paradoxes has been worked through over the past seven years of his mandate: through personalisation, managerial disintermediation and a rightward shift in his policies and support.

The monarchical–populist paradox

The election of Emmanuel Macron in 2017 was, in part, an unexpected one – 'disruptive', to use the candidate's management terminology. His candidacy did not respect the usual pre-requisites for winning a presidential mandate, as if it were *precisely* his violation of the two golden rules – to have been prime minister or several times minister and to be supported by an established party, well-organised and powerful – that clinched his access to the nation's highest office (Dolez, Fretel and Lefebvre, 2019; Strudel, 2017). The same disruption of the conditions of access to the presidential mandate which Macron so often theorises about, setting the rules of a 'new world' against those of the 'old world', can also be seen in his ideas about the presidency of the republic. Indeed, looking at his writings, Macron avails himself of two contradictory imperatives in regard to the figure of the president: the view from above – or the distanced perspective – and the perspective of proximity. In an interview held in July 2015 with journalist Éric Fottorino for the weekly *Le 1*,[4] he said:

> Democracy suffers from a sense of incompleteness, because democracy is not sufficient unto itself. There is something missing in the democratic process and the way it functions. In French politics, this absence is the presence of a King; and I think fundamentally that the French people did not want the death of the King. The Terror created an emotional, imaginary, collective void: the King was gone! Then we tried to fill that void, to place other people there, like when we had Napoleon or de Gaulle, for instance. However, the rest of the time, French democracy has failed to fill that empty space.

At the same time, however, in his book *Revolution*, published a year later, candidate Macron (2016a, p. 244) had lucidly analysed the French situation:

> What fuels the anger or rejection of our fellow citizens is the conviction that power is in the hands of leaders who no longer resemble them, no longer understand them and no longer care about them. That's the root of our whole predicament.

Does there not seem to be a certain aporia, an irresolvable contradiction, in the ambitions of Emmanuel Macron, whose fantasies of continuity go hand-in-hand with plans for a break with the past?

A good illustration of this can be seen in an analysis of the tension that Macron creates between contradictory principles and when we look at how those contradictions are resolved. A previous article drew upon iconographic analysis to demonstrate the narcissistic bias created by Macron's public relations choices (Strudel and Vedel, 2021). Indeed, looking carefully at the official portrait of the President of the Republic, certain things can be seen that help to shed light on everything else about his time in office. In fact, the official photograph[5] combines two spectacular though implicit dimensions: the president's public face and his private face, both the institutional dimension and the personal dimension of the head of state, call to mind the *King's Two Bodies* thesis (Kantorowicz, 1957). The photograph can be visually divided into two sub-parts. The upper part very explicitly fits the format of the official photographs of Emmanuel Macron's predecessors: a president shown in a frontal view, posing in his office in the Élysée with a window in the background looking out over the park, flanked by French and European flags. The lower part, on the other hand, which only occupies a third of the photograph, completely disrupts the usual photographic codes; the image is loaded with deliberately placed items, whose meaning can be ascertained only because they were intentionally described by the press officer for the head of state. The president is leaning back against his desk, with both hands resting on its edge; to the left, we see two smartphones placed one on top of the other in front of an open book from the *Bibliothèque de la Pléiade*, towered over by a rooster inkwell; to the right, there is a clock and two other closed books from the *Pléiade* collection. Paradoxically, these objects, which are in fact barely discernible, have attracted a good deal of attention and commentary, thanks to the release of an official video posted online by the Élysée's press officer, Sybeth Ndiaye, which was made at the time of the photo shoot.[6] In the video, she mentions the titles of these works, which otherwise could not be discerned. They are *War Memoirs* by Charles de Gaulle (the open book), *The Red and the Black* by Stendhal and *The Fruits of the Earth* by André Gide (the closed books). The most significant element here, it would seem, is not so much the opposition between tradition and modernity (which dominated the comments) but that between public and private, between the institutional and intimate dimensions. Though the upper part of the photograph is clearly a concession to the 'required elements' to be included in the head of state's official photograph, the lower part displays more of the intimate realm. It gives the general impression of an affirmation of physical presence, as well as a more relaxed (even familiar) posture – the kind that one might more readily adopt amongst loved ones or at an informal meeting rather than in an official situation – and includes multiple items referencing personal history and individual tastes. The photograph as a whole conjures up a juxtaposition of the mystical body and the carnal body, whose respective attributes are suggested by the saturation of signifiers by the items shown (heroic relationship to power, physical commitment, the modernity of the 'start-up nation', the continuity of political time, ambition and initiation, etc.). This calculated saturation was literally staged by Emmanuel Macron to assert his obsessive control of his image and fill out his complex conception of the presidential role.

This tension between distance and proximity is also found in the linguistic registers used by Macron: conceptual,[7] technocratic or managerial,[8] affected[9] and 'at the same time' relaxed,[10] frontal[11] or even insulting.[12] Furthermore, he is not afraid to come into contact with the French public, at times getting 'close enough for a shouting match'[13] – and even close enough for a slap in the face, as occurred on 9 June 2021 in Tain l'Hermitage while mingling with the crowd on the sidelines of a visit to a hotel management school.

His management of major crises has also tended to show the personal predilections that have characterised his time in office. This was the case during the Yellow Vests movement and the Covid-19 crisis and in the pension reform episode. Consider the following two examples. The unstructured Yellow Vests movement, which started to emerge between May and October 2018 – leading to road blockades and street protests from November 2018 – and continued until June 2019, originated from calls to demonstrate (broadcast via social networks) against rising fuel prices as a result of an increase in taxes on fuel and energy products. The demands very quickly grew beyond tax issues, however, to focus on the living conditions of the middle classes, the sense of neglect experienced in certain regions and the distrust felt towards politicians and intermediary organisations such as political parties and trades unions, expressed in particular by demands for direct and participatory democracy. The conflict in this crisis had a dual front. On one side were demonstrators directly targeting Emmanuel Macron, demanding his resignation, burning his official portrait in multiple cities and even decapitating an effigy of him in Angoulême on 22 December 2018. On the other, Macron, in response, willingly placed himself on the front lines.

This is how he was able to co-opt the participatory potential of the Great National Debate activities – which were set up to help find a solution to the crisis – monopolising them for his own benefit while dominating the public and political stage. One significant illustration of this took place on 18 March 2019, when 64 dignitaries chosen from among France's most distinguished intellectuals (Nobel Prize winners, prestigious academics and renowned researchers) were invited to the Elysée Palace to submit their observations and put questions to the President of the Republic, as a contribution to the Great National Debate. Given the very high number of speakers (indeed, too many), they were each instructed to limit their speech to two minutes to allow for questions and answers. These exchanges started shortly after 6 p.m. and continued until 2.45 a.m., turning the occasion into a marathon that lasted 8 hours and 15 minutes.[14] At first, the length of the president's responses – made to each group of four presentations by these intellectuals – varied from 6 minutes and 40 seconds to 16 minutes and 15 seconds each.[15]

However, from 11 p.m. onwards (i.e., after five hours of debate), the tempo changed: the intellectuals' speeches were addressed in groups of six or seven instead, and the president's response times lengthened to 23 or 24 minutes each. After a final speaking time of 20 minutes, granted at 1.30 a.m. to the four government ministers present (Education, Higher Education, Culture, Ecological and Inclusive Transition), the president concluded the debate with a 39-minute speech, delivered to a room that had gradually been emptied of its participants; around 10 of them left before they had a chance to speak due to this unreasonably extended timing. Looking back on their participation in this debate, certain participants, such as the sociologist Dominique Méda, said she felt as though she had been taken hostage[16] in a fake debate – because it was devoid of any opportunity for a real dialogue or exchange of views and invited speakers had simply been used to show the president in a favourable light. In fact, to venture a musical metaphor, it felt as if, over the course of the evening, the orchestral symphony (where each musician can be heard) gradually became a concerto, with a soloist stretching out the duration of his showpieces as much as possible to show off his physical performance and virtuosity.

A few months later, the Covid-19 crisis offered the young president an opportunity to regain a new legitimacy and to continue to express his vision (and his practice) of the task of the presidential office. Omnipresent in the media (12 television appearances between 12 March 2020 and 9 November 2021), Macron took to the stage on all fronts (visiting hospitals, engaging in European negotiations) – even allowing his entourage to declare that 'the president has become an epidemiologist' (*Le Monde*, 30 March 2021) to justify his positions, which sometimes ran contrary to the advice of scientists. What does all this show? That Macron's predilection is both to respect and to break the codes and to combine some traditional components with forms of communication that are at times innovative but struggle to maintain the juxtaposition between presidentiality and incarnation, often resolving the tension between the two in self-ostentation.

The Jupiterian–participatory paradox

This strong personalisation of the presidential role goes hand-in-hand with a strong 'verticalisation' of the presidential exercise of power, resulting in a lonely and top-down decision-making process or 'disintermediation' (Dolez, Douillet, Fretel and Lefebvre, 2022). This 'Jupiterian' dimension of presidential power was suggested and theorised by Macron in his book *Revolution*, which shows the strategic and intellectual configuration underlying this simultaneously conventional and transgressive candidate.[17] By adopting the posture of the providential man, he reactivated the constituent components of the Gaullian imagination: the 'meeting of a man and a people' on the basis of a presidential election; the affirmation of a strong presidency and of the verticality of political power;[18] the condemnation of a republic trapped 'in a web of political structures' and 'in divisions inherited from another era' (Macron, 2016a, p. 43); diagnosing the party system as having outlived its useful life and prescribing the transcendence of parties; passing judgment on the weakening of the left/right divide; and calling for unity and for unity among all 'progressives'. In this way – consistent with convention – he asserted his claim to a presidential monarchy, anchoring him to the fundamentals of presidential practice under the Fifth Republic. Yet, at the same time, he proclaimed his confidence in the resources of citizen expertise, transversal organisation or even direct public speaking, marking something of a convergence with reformist models and ideas from the start-up world (risk enhancement, small teams and bottom-up communication).

The exercise of power would, nevertheless, gradually bend the tension within this vertical–horizontal paradox towards verticality alone, giving rise to an essentially top-down operation. His relationship with the prime minister is the perfect illustration of this. Although the diarchy of the executive branch is considered to be one of the constitutional originalities of the Fifth Republic, because it places a prime minister as head of government[19] opposite the president as head of state, Macron advocated a more Gaullian rhetoric and practice. In other words, he sought to transform the diarchy into a hierarchy and to make the prime minister a servant of the head of state. Others before him had sought to do much the same: de Gaulle, of course, with Maurice Couve de Murville; Georges Pompidou with Pierre Messmer; Valéry Giscard d'Estaing with Raymond Barre; François Mitterrand with Pierre Bérégovoy and, closer to the present day, Nicolas Sarkozy with François Fillon.[20] To protect his presidential pre-eminence, Macron would break with his prime minister, Edouard Philippe, as soon as he perceived him to be a potential competitor,[21] replacing him on 3 July 2021 with Jean Castex, a top civil servant and locally elected official, who was seen as more of a 'technocrat' than a politician of national stature. Macron's decision, made the day after his re-election on 16 May 2022, to appoint as prime minister Elisabeth Borne, a civil engineer and graduate of the highly prestigious *École Polytechnique* and his Minister of Labour, Employment and Social Solidarity in the previous government, falls within the same logic, preferring highly technically focused administrators over those with political magnetism.[22] Under Macron, the prime minister acts more as a coordinator of ministerial action than the leader of a political majority.

A second illustration of this lonely and top-down decision-making process can be seen in certain presidential speeches. Ministers are often pre-empted in their announcements, stripped of responsibility for certain dossiers or have their decisions overturned by a president who has made himself 'minister of everything' (*Le Monde*, 16 May 2023). Macron announced the

'Water Plan' on 30 March 2023, even though Elisabeth Borne had planned to announce it alongside the Minister for Ecological Transition; during his speech on 20 March 2020, Macron announced the closure of all school premises, from nurseries to universities, even though Minister of National Education Jean-Michel Blanquer had declared only a few hours earlier that total closures were 'not the way we do things'. These situations appear quite remarkable in light of a previous highly critical text regarding the office of the president, which had held that 'political decisions can no longer come from a single voice' (Macron, 2011, p. 114).

Members of the government are not the only ones marginalised by the president's independence and distrust towards them; political parties, unions and local elected officials have all found themselves in this position. Here, again, Macron's approach to the management of major crises has been revealing. In the midst of the Yellow Vests protest movement, while Laurent Berger, leader of the *Confédération française démocratique du travail* or CFDT (the biggest union in France), was submitting multiple proposals to end the crisis and give intermediary organisations like the unions a central role, Macron remained deaf to his appeals. For him, economic, social and political transformation cannot come through unions, which he sees as a relic of the 'old world'. The same scenario occurred again during the Covid-19 crisis, as discussed above. Lastly, the long series of protests against pension reform are an illustration of the top-down approach tinged with authoritarianism that has characterised this president. A power struggle immediately arose, starting on the first day of the demonstrations on Thursday 19 January 2023, only nine days after the prime minister first presented the pension reform proposals, which provided, among other things, for a raise of the retirement age from 62 to 64 years. The response was unprecedented: the eight trade-union confederations joined together for the first time in more than 12 years to form a solid coalition, which succeeded in mobilising 1.12 million demonstrators across France, including 80,000 in Paris alone, according to the Ministry of the Interior. The demonstration in Paris was so massive that a second protest route had to be opened to relieve congestion in the crowded Place de la République. The crowds included teachers, firefighters, students, police officers and hospital staff, as well as private-sector employees. They were all there to protest against the pension reforms, which were considered unfair and brutal – but there were other demands too: an increase in wages to keep pace with inflation, a more equitable distribution of wealth, the taxation of excess profits and the overall questioning of Macron's policies were also central to the demonstrations. In the face of the protests, Macron remained focused on his pension reform, condemning the unions' approach to the issues as conservative (archaic, even) and prioritising his own political ambitions over the consensus, which dominated amongst protestors. During an official visit to

Barcelona, Macron stated that the government would press forward with its pension reform 'with respect and in a spirit of dialogue but with determination and responsibility'. Three months after a massive social movement, a chaotic legislative process[23] and with public opinion resolutely against it,[24] the law was approved by the Constitutional Council on 14 April 2023 and enacted into law the same day. The president had remained steadfast and unyielding.

Nevertheless, Macron's exercise of power is not as solitary as one might believe at first glance. 'Disintermediation' (Dolez et al., 2022, p. 16) does not necessarily imply isolation. One interesting analysis has argued that 'this exercise of power is not so much solitary as it is informalised' (Gaïti, 2021). The paradox with this high-flying *énarque* (graduate of the top administration school, the ENA) is in the way he so readily goes over the head of established negotiating partners, in particular the top civil service (and even the entire network of 'intermediary' organisations), preferring instead to bring in consulting firms (*cabinets de conseil*) and create *ad hoc* bodies such as the Covid-19 Scientific Council. This independent advisory board, set up at Macron's request in March 2020 as part of the state of emergency to deal with the pandemic, was made up of 10 experts under the chairmanship of Professor Jean-François Delfraissy, a doctor specialising in internal medicine and immunology. Among the criticisms levelled at the council were that it was an '*ad hoc* expert body with ill-defined boundaries' to the detriment of existing health agencies,[25] that Jean-François Delfraissy's opinions were not always accepted by his political masters (Vautier-Chollet, 2022), and even that it was 'exploited' by politicians, as its chairman himself admitted at a press conference held to mark the end of the Scientific Council's term of office in July 2022.

With regard to the use of consultancy firms, a report from the *Cour des Comptes* (Court of Accounts: the French supreme audit institution), published on 10 July 2023, found that public expenditure on this tripled between 2017 and 2021, amounting in that year to 232 million euros.[26] On 11 July 2023, the newspaper *Libération* ran the story on the front page, with the headline '*addiction salée*', a subtle play on words modifying the popular expression *une addition salée* (a pricy bill at a restaurant) with the word *addiction* (dependence on a drug). The *Cour* condemned this as an easy fix, presented by the executive as a mark of administrative modernity. The Covid pandemic, though it was exceptional, provided a striking example of how private firms (in particular the firm McKinsey[27]) were put in charge of vaccine policy in France, sometimes even in lieu of the minister's office. The increasing trend in outsourcing tasks that could arguably have been entrusted internally to highly qualified civil servants constituted a loss of competence or experience within the administration and took place without proper management or oversight, sometimes proceeding on the basis of criteria based on personal connections. These mechanisms not only raise questions about the new decision-making networks at the executive level (which have become multiple and unstable) but also show who has benefitted from this introduction of competition between decision-making bodies. In fact, it has served to justify the 'verticalisation' of presidential power, which thus emerges as the only way to organise this disorder and is also the main beneficiary of this managerialisation of decision-making circuits.

The 'both left and right' paradox

The election of Emmanuel Macron in 2017 resulted from a combination of unexpected events and methodical preparation, which contributed to creating an expansive central political space for candidate Macron (Strudel, 2017). The two open primaries fought on the right and left attracted those whom American political scientists have described as 'hardcore partisans' (Norrander, 1989): voters who accentuate the ideological polarisation of elections and help to nominate candidates who are more radical than the party line, such as François Fillon – a very conservative candidate within the *Les Républicains* party – and Benoît Hamon, representative of an anti-liberal (in the French sense of the word) utopian socialism within the Socialist Party. Added to this were a number of factors: François Hollande's (reluctant) decision not to seek re-election, announced on 1 December 2016, the *Canard Enchaîné* newspaper's cut-throat serial coverage of what would come to be known as 'Penelopegate' or 'the Fillon affair' starting on 25 January 2017, the endorsement of Macron by the centrist François Bayrou on 22 February 2017 and, finally, the anticipation of Marine Le Pen's presence in the second round. These elements created a very broad central political space and helped to reinforce the 'both left and right' project espoused by Macron. The candidate's methodical preparation was based on the political diagnosis presented in his book *Revolution* (Macron, 2016a). In it, he observed the gradual falling apart of the Socialist Party, revitalised by François Mitterrand at Épinay after 1971 on the model of 'synthesising' its disparate factions, the breakdown of party identity within *Les Républicains*, the threat represented by the presence of Marine Le Pen and the weakening of major divisions, particularly between left and right. 'In my eyes, the real divide in our country (...) is between progressives and conservatives; that's the divide I want to rebuild now', he declared in an interview with the newspaper *Le Monde* on 23 April 2016 (Macron, 2016b). In seeking to do so, Macron claimed inspiration from proposals 'from both the left and the right', assuming a position he considers to be one of 'pragmatism'. Thus was born his catchphrase 'at the same time' (*en même temps*).

With regard to ideology, Nicolas Truong, writing in the newspaper *Le Monde*, highlighted the influence on Macron's thinking of the philosopher

Paul Ricœur (for whom he had briefly worked as a research assistant), in terms of respecting opposing points of view when they are presented in the context of a rational argument: 'Macronism is a kind of syncretism. It is both social bonapartism and liberal progressivism, both oligarchical dissolutionism [*dégagisme*] and transcendental liberalism' (Truong, 2015). Falling politically within the traditions of the 'third-force' coalition established during the Fourth Republic, Macron's approach sought to go beyond the hitherto unsuccessful efforts of Jean Lecanuet in 1965, Alain Poher in 1969 and François Bayrou in 2007, to make it personal, which Michel Rocard or Jacques Delors (seen as 'centrist' socialists) would never have permitted themselves to do. Only Valéry Giscard d'Estaing in 1974 had believed that he could really 'govern from the centre', with the support of 'two out of three French people', before being overtaken by the rightward turn of French centrism and eventually defeated by a united left in 1981.

In fact, the election of Emmanuel Macron on 7 May 2017 was indeed a victory 'for both the left and the right'. This was evident from the first round of voting on 23 April. Although according to a much-cited quotation attributed to François Mitterrand, 'the centre is neither left nor left',[28] the 24 per cent of those who voted for Macron from the start were more centre than centrist although they were, nonetheless, left-leaning. Perceived as a more centre-left candidate, he found his primary support in voters from the left and the centre. Starting even from the first round, he won over 45.7 per cent of those who had voted for Hollande in 2012 and 24.6 per cent of those who had voted for environmentalist candidate Eva Joly in 2012, 11.1 per cent of Jean-Luc Mélenchon's former supporters on the radical left, 39.8 per cent of the centrist François Bayrou's supporters and 16.6 per cent of Sarkozy's – but only 3.5 per cent of Marine Le Pen's. Here, we can clearly observe a fracturing not only of the social-democratic 'synthesis' in the Socialist Party but also of the exit strategies employed by right-wing voters. Macron took advantage of this and of the problems within *Les Républicains,* as well as the pressure of 'tactical voting' that started in the first round in an effort to prevent another 21 April 2002, when Jean-Marie Le Pen had unexpectedly managed to reach the second round of the presidential election, defeating the socialist candidate Lionel Jospin. However, although he was able to make use of the latent weakening of the structural power of the left/right divide and hear the demands of an increasingly defiant public opinion, his electoral success in the first round – confirmed in the second round – was achieved only thanks to the support of a hybrid electorate (Strudel, 2017).

Yet, five years later, on 24 April 2022, Macron was re-elected President of the Republic, having won over 1.1 million more votes in the first round than he won in 2017 (with 27.8 per cent of the votes cast in the first round in 2022). However, this was less of a victory than it appeared to be in two ways. On the one hand, unlike in 2017, Macron did not go on to obtain an absolute majority of deputies in the legislative elections that followed in June. On the other hand – and above all – this election was not a continuation of the previous one: between the two elections, his electorate had profoundly changed. As much as his victory in 2017 was due to his 'both left and right' positioning, his win in 2022 was characterised by a clear rightward shift. Now perceived as a centre-right or even a right-wing candidate (Martigny and Strudel, 2022, p. 172), his voters were themselves primarily from the right. Moreover, the ideological and sociological structures of the Macron vote changed significantly between 2017 and 2022, reflecting the contribution of part of the Fillon vote in 2017 and the rightward shift of Macron's electorate. Although in 2017, the Macron vote contributed to a significant reduction in the votes won by socialist candidate Benoît Hamon, in 2022, this was reversed, mainly to the detriment of right-wing candidate Valérie Pécresse (*Les Républicains*). Whilst the Macron vote in 2017 essentially reflected a 'catch-all electorate' (Strudel, 2017, p. 218) not characterised by marked antagonisms of a generational or class nature, in 2022, it was indicative of a moderate-right electorate, quite traditionally elderly and well off.

Significantly, support for Macron had begun shifting to the right in the summer of 2017, after the 'asymmetric signals' (Strudel, 2019) sent on the one hand to the most privileged classes – transforming the 'Wealth Tax' (ISF) into the 'Property Wealth Tax' (IFI) and introducing the 30 per cent 'flat tax' on capital gains in the 2018 draft budget – and, on the other, to the less-privileged – the gradual reduction of employment benefit starting from 1 September 2017, the insecurity-generating El Khomri law [*loi du travail*], a reduction of five euros per month in the housing-assistance programmes taking effect from 1 October and announcements of tobacco and fuel tax hikes.

Conclusion

In attempting to make an overall assessment of a completed presidential term (and a second term that has been underway for over two years), one must not allow promises in Macron's *Revolution* to obfuscate either the deviations that have taken place under the pressure of events or the lines of continuity, even if due only to the inertia of the multiple social processes and institutional constraints weighing upon government action. Since 7 May 2017, Macron's mandates have been punctuated by several major crises: the Yellow Vests movement, the Covid-19 pandemic, street mobilisation against the pension reform, the urban riots that were triggered by the killing of a teenager by a police officer in July 2023 or the farmers' protests in February 2024. Critics have most often targeted the president's legitimacy and personal aura, in spite of his sometimes unorthodox responses, such as departure from traditional financial wisdom in favour of the 'whatever it takes' approach to costs taken during the Covid pandemic and introducing deliberative concessions in seeking to put an end to the Yellow Vests episode with the Great National Debate. However, setting himself up as a target for criticism is something to which the president has regularly and willingly exposed himself. For example, with the hyperbolic use he makes in his public discourse of the verb *assumer* (to take full responsibility for something), Macron is signalling semantically that he is the sole legitimate authority for decision-making. He has thus given a very presidentialist reading of the Constitution of the Fifth Republic, with increasing emphasis on its personal, 'vertical' and right-wing dimensions. The appointment of Gabriel Attal as prime minister on 9 January 2024 is the latest example of this egotistical pathology and right-wing drift. On the one hand, the mirror effect with the Emmanuel Macron of 2017 is striking: same youth (34 years old for the youngest Prime Minister of the Fifth Republic and 39 years old for the youngest President of the Republic), same audacity, same 'flexible' ideology (coming from the left but with economically liberal tendencies), same pragmatism (action and results count more than doctrine) and same popularity in the polls. Commentators were not mistaken: 'a clone of himself', according to *Le Monde* (de Royer, 2024), *Macron Premier ministre* headlined the front page of *Libération* on 10 January. On the other hand, the turn to the right has been openly acknowledged: not only does Gabriel Attal embody order and rules, appealing to the right-wing electorate seduced by his acts of authority as former Minister of National Education (banning the *abaya* and establishing measures against bullying in schools),[29] but also his government, formed on 11 January, has seen the arrival of two former Sarkozyist ministers (Rachida Dati appointed to Culture and Catherine Vautrin to Labour, Health and Solidarity) and the retention of right-wing 'heavyweights' (Bruno Le Maire and Gérald Darmanin) in the key ministries of Finance and the Interior. In this respect, the appointment of Gabriel Attal conceals a powerful contradiction: it reflects both a reincarnation of the Emmanuel Macron of 2017 *and* the disappearance of the initial 'left and right' Macronism. Although, as a candidate in 2017, Emmanuel Macron embodied promises of modernity and change, as president, he has failed to hold together the dual propositions underpinned by the idea of being 'at the same time' one thing and another, the idea that gave his campaign its originality. Each time, these stimulating paradoxes have shifted in one direction only, generating disappointment, distance and mistrust among a significant proportion of citizens.

Notes

1 Charles de Gaulle, radio and television broadcast of 20 September 1962.
2 Conversely, parliament can overturn the government (Article 49).

3 All the powers specifically granted to the President of the Republic are listed in Articles 5–19 of the Constitution of 1958.
4 Emmanuel Macron, '*Il est urgent de réconcilier les France*', interview with Éric Fottorino, *Le 1*, 121, 13 September 2016.
5 https://www.elysee.fr/emmanuel-macron/2017/06/29/portrait-officiel-du-president-de-la-republique.
6 https://twitter.com/sibethndiaye/status/880381431603658752.
7 Such as in the speech delivered on 9 April 2018 before the Bishops of France at the Collège des Bernardins in Paris: https://www.elysee.fr/emmanuel-macron/2018/04/09/discours-du-president-de-la-republique-emmanuel-macron-a-la-conference-des-eveques-de-france-au-college-des-bernardins.
8 Such as when he refers to the 'start-up nation' or 'bottom-up democracy'.
9 Such as when he uses obsolete or little-used words like '*antienne*' [antiphon], '*galimatias*' [balderdash] or '*logorrhée*' [logorrhea].
10 Such as in the soundbite 'We pour an insane amount of money into social benefits', spoken by the president during an informal interview with his advisors at the Élysée Palace on the evening of 12 June 2018 and posted on the social network Twitter the same day: https://www.youtube.com/watch?v=rKkUkUFbqmE.
11 On 4 January 2022, Emmanuel Macron stated in an interview with the newspaper *Le Parisien* that he wanted to maintain his Covid vaccination guidelines despite opposition from the unvaccinated: 'I really want to annoy the shit out of them and so that's what we'll continue doing to the bitter end': https://www.leparisien.fr/politique/emmanuel-macron-determine-a-emmerder-les-antivax-04-01-2022-EOBO25O4DJHURHCNXVRTGRDKA4.php.
12 On 29 June 2017, the President of the French Republic participated in the inauguration of Station F, the largest start-up campus in Europe, which was built in a former warehouse at Austerlitz railway station in Paris. At the event, he delivered a speech 'without looking at any notes and obviously improvised' to an audience of business owners and caused quite a stir by saying: 'A train station is the kind of place where successful people cross paths with people who are nothing. Because it's a place we're just passing through. Because it's a place we all share'. https://www.youtube.com/watch?v=B-SBJjIjqYY.
13 To use a favourite expression of Gérard Larcher, President of the Senate, who sees this as a virtue in mayors as popularly elected local representatives.
14 https://www.youtube.com/watch?v=WvO_k_NxWEM.
15 Survey and calculations of speaking times prepared by the author.
16 https://www.liberation.fr/debats/2019/03/19/grand-debat-des-intellectuels-pris-en-otage_1716086/.
17 For example, Macron prefers to describe his proposals as 'projects' rather than programmes, such as 'My project for France', presented on 2 March 2017.
18 Referred to in an interview as early as 20 March 2015 (www.dailymotion.com/video/x2k3dd4).
19 During periods of cohabitation (1986–1988, 1993–1995 and 1997–2002), executive power was able to operate more as a real diarchy without being submitted to the hierarchy of presidentialisation.
20 In August 2007, at a lunch with journalists from the regional daily press, Nicolas Sarkozy is quoted as
saying: 'The Prime Minister is a "*collaborateur*"; I'm the boss'.
21 As others before him – Charles De Gaulle did the same with Georges Pompidou in 1968, Georges Pompidou with Jacques Chaban-Delmas in 1972 and François Mitterrand with Michel Rocard in 1991. Jacques Chirac's resignation letter to Valéry Giscard d'Estaing (1976) demonstrates the unusual independence of the prime minister's decision to resign from the president. Chirac wrote: 'I do not

have the means that I consider necessary today to effectively carry out my role as Prime Minister and in these conditions, I have decided to terminate it'.
22 As a former advisor to Lionel Jospin at Matignon, Elisabeth Borne has the double merit of being a recognised representative of the Macronist left but sufficiently reformist to not frighten the right.
23 Around 20,000 amendments were tabled in advance of the review of the pension reform bill by the National Assembly (including 13,000 by *La France Insoumise*) in order to slow down the procedure; however, the government was able to bypass these tactics by using Article 49-3 on 16 March (see Chapter 3). A cross-party motion of no-confidence in the government was proposed by opposition parties on 20 March but was rejected by nine votes (278 votes for the no-confidence motion out of the 289 necessary for its adoption). This very small margin of victory for the government shows how the executive branch had been weakened, in the wake of the demonstrations against the pension reform.
24 An *Ifop* poll taken for *L'Humanité* on 15 January 2023 found that 68 per cent of French people opposed the reform bill. Opposition was particularly strong among those under 35, the working and middle classes and the unemployed – but lower among retirees.
25 Report by the Senate Committee of Enquiry on the lessons of the Covid-19 pandemic, December 2020. https://www.senat.fr/rap/r20-199-1/r20-199-122.html (last accessed 24 February 2024).
26 https://www.ccomptes.fr/system/files/2023-07/20230710-Recours-par-Etat-aux-prestations-intellectuelles-cabinets-conseil_0.pdf.
27 Whose activities during Covid were called into question during the 2022 presidential campaign, resulting in the National Financial Prosecutor's Office opening two separate investigations.
28 http://www.centrisme.free.fr/le%20florilege%20de%20citations%20sur%20le%20centrisme.htm
29 According to an IFOP poll published on 22 January 2024, 73 per cent of those who voted for Pécresse (the *Républicain* candidate) in 2022 were satisfied with Attal compared with a national figure of 49 per cent. https://www.ifop.com/wp-content/uploads/2024/01/120529-Indices-de-popularite-Janvier-2024.pdf (accessed 2 March 2024).

References

Calise, M. (2000) *Il partito personale*. Roma-Bari: Laterza.

Cole, A. (1993) 'The presidential party and the Fifth Republic', *West European Politics*, 16(2), pp. 49–66.

De Royer, S. (2024) 'Avec Gabriel Attal à Matignon, Emmanuel Macron concède qu'il a besoin de sa popularité pour redonner souffle et vie à son mandat', *Le Monde*, 10 January.

Dolez, B., Douillet, A.-C., Fretel, J. and Lefebvre, R. (2022) 'A l'épreuve du pouvoir. L'entreprise Macron entre continuités et singularités', in Dolez, B., Douillet A.-C., Fretel, J. and Lefebvre, R. (eds) *L'entreprise Macron à l'épreuve du pouvoir*. Grenoble: Presses Universitaires de Grenoble, pp. 11–19.

Dolez, B., Fretel, J. and Lefebvre, R. (eds) (2019) *L'entreprise Macron*. Grenoble: Presses Universitaires de Grenoble.

Donegani, J.-M. and Sadoun, M. (1998) *La Vème République: naissance et mort*. Paris: Calmann-Lévy.

Foley, M. (2000) *The British presidency: Tony Blair and the politics of public leadership*. Manchester: Manchester University Press.

François, B. (1992) 'Le Président pontife constitutionnel. Charisme d'institution et construction juridique du politique', in Lagroye, J. and Lacroix, B. (eds) *Le Président de la République: usages et genèses d'une institution*. Paris: Presses de la FNSP, pp. 303–332.

Gaïti, B. (2021) 'La décision dans la crise sanitaire ou la logique du désordre', *The Conversation*, 21 April.

Kantorowicz, E. (1957) *The king's two bodies*. Princeton, NJ: Princeton University Press.

Kirchheimer, O. (1966) 'The transformation of the western European party systems', in La Palombara, J. and Weiner, M. (eds) *Political parties and political development*. Princeton, NJ: Princeton University Press, pp. 177–200.

Macron, E. (2011) 'Les labyrinthes du politique. Que peut-on attendre pour 2012 et après?', *Esprit*, April–May, pp. 106–115.

Macron, E. (2016a) *Révolution*. Paris: Pocket.

Macron, E. (2016b) 'La gauche aujourd'hui ne me satisfait pas', *Le Monde*, 23 April.

Martigny, V. and Strudel, S. (2022) 'Une popularité en trompe-l'œil?', in Dolez, B., Douillet, A.C., Fretel, J. and Lefebvre, R. (eds) *L'entreprise Macron à l'épreuve du pouvoir*. Grenoble: Presses Universitaires de Grenoble, pp. 163–178.

McDonnell, D. (2013) 'Silvio Berlusconi's personal parties: from Forza Italia to the Popolo della Libertà', *Political Studies*, 61(1), pp. 217–233.

Norrander, B. (1989) 'Ideological representativeness of presidential primary voters', *American Journal of Political Science*, 33(3), pp. 570–587.

Poguntke, T. and Webb, P. (eds) (2005) *The presidentialization of politics. A comparative study of modern democracies*. Oxford: Oxford University Press.

Portelli, H. (1980) 'La présidentialisation des partis français', *Pouvoirs*, 14, pp. 97–106.

Rousselier, N. (2015) *La force de gouverner*. Paris: Gallimard.

Strudel, S. (2017) 'Emmanuel Macron: un oxymore politique?', in Perrineau, P. (ed.) *Le vote disruptif*. Paris: Presses de Sciences Po, pp. 205–220.

Strudel, S. (2019) 'Quand le premier de cordée dévisse', in Cautrès, B. and Muxel, A. (eds) *Histoire d'une révolution électorale (2015–2018)*. Paris: Classiques Garnier, pp. 265–276.

Strudel, S. and Vedel, T. (2021) 'Les deux corps du président Macron', in Ignazi, P. and Reynié, D. (eds) *La vie politique*. Paris: Presses de Sciences Po, pp. 87–96.

Truong, N. (2015) 'Petite philosophie du macronisme', *Le Monde*, 15 May.

Vautier-Chollet, M. (2022) 'Fin du Conseil Scientifique : ces huits avis (suivis ou pas) qui ont marqué ses deux ans et demi d'existence', *France-Inter*, 31 July, https://www.radiofrance.fr/franceinter/fin-du-conseil-scientifique-ces-huit-avis-suivis-ou-pas-qui-ont-marque-ses-deux-ans-et-demi-d-existence-4747800 (accessed 2 March, 2024).

Wattenberg, M.P. (1991) *The rise of candidate-centered politics. Presidential elections of the 1980s*. Cambridge: Cambridge University Press.

3
DEMOCRACY IN FRANCE UNDER EMMANUEL MACRON: FROM A CRISIS OF REPRESENTATION TO A CRISIS OF REGIME?

Susan Collard

Abstract

This chapter discusses an important component of Emmanuel Macron's intended 'Revolution': the revival of French democracy, said to be in need of urgent 'renovation'. Whilst for many, the fundamental problem lies in the imbalance between executive and legislative power, this was not the issue for Macron, who openly embraced a monarchical style of presidency. His proposals focused, rather, on the renewal and 'moralisation' of the political class, on new structures to encourage greater citizen participation and on reforms designed to streamline the legislative process, including reducing the number of parliamentarians and introducing a partial form of proportional representation for legislative elections. However, despite extensive presidential powers, he failed to overcome parliamentary resistance to these reforms, and his albeit innovative forays into participatory and deliberative democracy with the Great National Debate and the Citizens Convention on the Climate were essentially motivated by his attempt to quell the protests triggered by the Yellow Vests movement. Further disadvantaged in his second presidency by the loss of an absolute majority in the National Assembly, Macron's momentous decision in June 2024 to call a snap election threw the system into further disarray and uncertainty, leaving French democracy in an unprecedented state of crisis that many argue might best be resolved by his own resignation.

Introduction

The emergence of democracy in France was a long and tumultuous process that continues to cast a long shadow over politics even today. After the Revolution of 1789, France lurched from one regime to another, following what Malcolm Slater (1985, p. 9) described as the 'pendulum of constitutional development' between executive and legislative dominance in a quest to replace the absolute monarchy of the *Ancien Régime*. Following the demise of the short-lived First Republic, swept away by Napoleon Bonaparte's first empire, there followed two types of constitutional monarchy, two more revolutions (1830 and 1848), a second republic and a second empire until, finally in the 1870s, the Republic became firmly established as the nation's political system, though not without a struggle against recalcitrant monarchists. Although this Third Republic did not survive the onset of the Second World War, giving way to a personal dictatorship during the Occupation, there was no question of a return to monarchy when the Fourth Republic was created after the Liberation. However, this parliamentary regime did not withstand the political crisis triggered by the Algerian War for independence, which opened the way for Resistance hero General de Gaulle to negotiate his way back from 'retirement' to impose a new constitution for a Fifth Republic in 1958.

This was radically different from the previous two, where the president's role had been mainly honorific. De Gaulle argued for a much stronger presidency with sufficient powers to tackle political crises, and his new constitution established an institutional framework which put the president at the centre of decision-making. The usurping of parliamentary sovereignty by the new institutions of the Fifth Republic was then – and has continued to be – strongly contested. Yet over time, presidentialism became accepted as the new normal, with presidential elections attracting higher turnout, at around 80 per cent, than other elections. In recent decades, however, growing opposition to the emergence of 'hyper-presidentialisation' has been accompanied by calls, mainly from the radical left, for a new, Sixth Republic, to restore a greater balance between executive and legislative power. Rising rates of abstention in presidential elections, especially in 2022, indicate an underlying rejection of the excesses of a 'monarchical presidency'.

Nevertheless, as demonstrated in Sylvie Strudel's Chapter 2 in this volume, when Emmanuel Macron was elected in 2017, in many ways, he modelled his 'vertical' and 'Jupiterian' presidency on that of de Gaulle, even suggesting that the French people retain a lingering nostalgia for monarchical authority. In what Strudel describes as the 'monarchist–populist paradox', Macron's analysis of the problems undermining French democracy, outlined in his campaign book *Revolution* (2016), lay not in the excesses of presidential power but in the fact that, despite citizens' deep desire for political engagement, 'democratic fatigue' and anger had taken root in response to a sense that the country's destiny was controlled by a small elite who were unrepresentative of the French people and who did not understand or care about them. What was needed, he argued, was not a programme of major constitutional reform but a renewal of the whole political class in order to address the long-standing 'crisis' of political representation; this could be achieved by encouraging 'new blood' into the system, through a transformation of the parties – who he accused, as de Gaulle had done, of abandoning the general interest in the pursuit of their own agendas dominated by self-seeking party officials. Democracy would also be enhanced, he said, by streamlining the parliamentary process to make it more efficient and by encouraging better evaluation and control of public policy, which also implied reform of the administrative system: 'Public policies are more effective when they are developed together with the citizens who will be affected by them' (2016, p. 256). This also meant redefining the status of civil servants (*fonctionnaires*) in favour of a new 'contractualisation' of the Republic to deliver a more democratic and pragmatic distribution of power (*un nouveau partage démocratique*; 2016, p. 259), even if he believed the state should maintain its role in key, 'regalian' sectors. Macron's idea of a healthy modern democracy involved active citizens participating in the transformation of the country, 'for they are our everyday heroes'.

Macron's conception of the democratic renewal necessary to transform France was therefore far-reaching, and would involve disrupting existing practices in many key areas of politics and public policy, set out in his manifesto proposals for 'a renovated democracy'.[1] His proposals for the 'moralisation of political life' are discussed in Chapter 4 of this volume, while the reforms involving the contractualisation of the administration are assessed in Chapter 9. This chapter shows how Macron's other ambitions for democratic revival were very soon thwarted by unforeseen events that he struggled to control: after failing to pass any of his proposed institutional reforms, he found himself the target of angry protest from the Yellow Vests movement. He tried to turn this to his advantage by instigating the 'Great National Debate' (GND) and subsequently setting up the Citizens Convention on the Climate (CCC), promoted as innovations in participatory and deliberative democracy. However, critics dismissed them as simply operations of political communication, pointing to other ways in which democracy under Macron was being curtailed, especially during the Covid pandemic. By the time the president stood for re-election in 2022, the increasing fragility of French democracy was reflected in the generally high rate of electoral abstention and the fact that he subsequently failed to win an absolute majority in the National Assembly (NA). Although this could have potentially triggered a transition towards a better balance between executive and legislative power, in fact, it led to a further tightening of presidential dominance over the parliamentary agenda, best illustrated by the forcing through of a pension reform in 2023 despite massive opposition. This showed the paradoxical weakness of a president with extensive constitutional powers but no reliable political majority to do his bidding: Macron had become a lame-duck president. His 'disruptive' decision to dissolve the NA in June 2024 after the announcement of the results of the European Elections, which saw the far-right win twice as many seats as his own party, was a desperate attempt to seek 'clarification' of a very troubled political situation – but which instead resulted in further confusion. Far from renovating French democracy, Macron had instigated an unprecedented political crisis, just as the Olympic Games were about to open in Paris, putting France at the centre of global media attention.

Early ambitions: political renewal and institutional reform

In 2017, for the legislative election campaign, Macron took the lead by example in trying to achieve better parliamentary representation of the French population by driving the idea of the renewal of the political class in the way that candidates were selected for what became his formal party, *La République En Marche* (LREM). Free from the problems of incumbency known to favour men (Murray, 2008), selection criteria prioritised gender parity, ethnic diversity, a broad geographic representation and political 'novices' from civil society. In the newly elected NA, 42 per cent of deputies held no other mandate, compared to 16 per cent in 2012 and 7 per cent in 2007 (Andolfatto, 2017). Altogether, 415 (72 per cent) were 'primo-deputies' (compared to about one-third normally) – even more than the socialist renewal in 1981 (44 per cent) – and only 48 were elected for a fourth mandate. The average age also dropped from 54 to 49, reversing the previous continuous upward trend. By winning 308 seats out of 577, LREM thus seemed to make a significant contribution to the renewal of the Assembly elected in June 2017.

However, other factors also played a role in this renewal: first, increasing adherence by most parties to the gender-parity laws (partly to avoid financial penalties) meant better representation for women – rising from 27 to 39 per cent after the election – and the significant loss of seats by incumbents from the Socialist Party (PS) and *Les Républicains* (LR) also had an impact. Second, the implementation, for the first time in 2017, of a law passed under the Hollande presidency that imposed new limits on multiple office-holding (when deputies also retain executive roles such as mayors or leaders in subnational levels of governance) meant that some deputies had preferred to keep their local mandate, thus freeing up seats for new blood. Moreover, in terms of occupation, there was a clear professionalisation, with 70 per cent of seats occupied by those in the private sector, *professions libérales et cadres* and fewer lawyers, doctors, teachers and top civil servants, all previously dominant professions in the NA. Andolfatto (2017) argued that this 'renewal' was thus not a real rupture with the past but a transition, while Rouban (2017) highlighted the emergence of a new socio-professional *élite* that mirrored the *fracture sociale* separating *élites* from ordinary people and which did not resolve the crisis of representation that Macron had identified as problematic. Subsequent academic analysis concluded that the increased 'representativity' of LREM deputies was largely illusory since the positive attributes associated with greater diversity were in fact largely concentrated in a small number of individuals, for example, a young female of ethnic origin from civil society elected for the first time (Bresson and Ollion, 2022). Moreover, the novices struggled to play more than a symbolic role in the Assembly and were unable to introduce any new ways of 'doing politics differently' (Ollion, 2021). The failure to fundamentally renew the composition of the NA to make it more representative of French society was further entrenched by the elections of 2022 and 2024, where even gender parity took a downward turn (Goannec, Huet and Poinssot, 2024).

Once elected – and despite previously playing down the importance of introducing major institutional reforms – Macron first confirmed his intention of doing that very thing in July 2017 in his inaugural speech to both chambers of parliament sitting as the 'Congress' in the special chamber reserved for this purpose in the palace of Versailles.[2] Setting out his vision for a progressive project for change and deep transformation, he spoke of the need to make the legislative process more efficient, confirming his proposal to reduce the number of parliamentarians by a third, enabling them to be better resourced. He also reiterated his intention to introduce a degree of proportionality into the electoral system, to limit in time the number of mandates held by parliamentarians and to reform the Economic, Social and Environmental Council (CESE), making it the 'forum of our Republic' representing civil society.

Newly elected French presidents frequently announce plans for constitutional reform and usually appoint a political heavyweight to lead a commission of experts to make recommendations. However, Macron broke with this tradition by asking the presidents of the NA and the Senate to submit their own proposals to feed into the government's plans, enabling him to establish what their 'red lines' would be in terms of proposed changes. Unsurprisingly, whilst the NA's report[3] delivered ideas in line with the president's plans, the report[4] from the Senate (where Macron's party and allies did not have a majority) contained proposals that were mainly at odds with his ambitions. After long deliberations, the government eventually unveiled its final plans for reforms in April 2018, to be dealt with in three separate laws:[5] a Constitutional law, an 'Organic' and an 'Ordinary' law, all of which would, however, be closely linked under the heading of 'Laws for a more representative, responsible and efficient democracy'. The decision to separate a complex set of proposals in this way, given the strong opposition to some of the key reforms from the Senate, was puzzling since, if one part of it should fail, the overall 'package' would be compromised (Savonitto, 2020). Moreover, the difficulty of achieving constitutional revision was well known since it requires approval not only by majority votes in both chambers of parliament but also by either a referendum or by a three-fifths majority vote by parliamentarians meeting together in Congress. Several attempts at constitutional amendment have failed at this hurdle, with the most recent constitutional reform, under Nicolas Sarkozy in 2008, passing by only one vote. Some of the major changes now proposed by Macron, such as the reduction of the number of parliamentarians and modification of the electoral system, did not require a constitutional amendment, so could have been passed separately, yet this was not what was proposed.

The Constitutional law[6] was the first bill sent to the NA for deliberation in May 2018 and included a rather mixed bag of 18 articles (Sergues, 2018), many of which involved parliamentary procedure (in particular, restricting the right of amendment), the reform and renaming of the CESE as the Chamber of Civil Society and the granting of the right to differentiation for territorial 'collectivities' in certain conditions, including Corsica. The Organic Law[7] included the proposal for the reduction by 30 per cent of the number of parliamentarians – from 577 to 404 – and 244 senators, down from 348, which would require controversial boundary changes. It also proposed that elected mandates be limited in time to three identical terms of office for deputies, senators and Members of the European Parliament (MEPs) and elected executive positions at sub-national levels, to encourage renewal. The Ordinary Law[8] proposed that 15 per cent of deputies (61) would be elected by PR using a national list system applying the same rules as for other list systems at sub-national level. Voters would be able to cast two votes, one in their constituency and one for PR (to include the deputies for overseas citizens, reduced from 11 to 8). These two laws were scheduled for parliamentary debate in the Autumn, after the anticipated approval of the Constitutional law in late July, since they were known to be strongly opposed by the Senate, whose approval was also required for the Organic Law.[9]

The details of these laws are too complex for detailed discussion here (see Claret and Savonitto, 2020), but, from the outset, opposition parties strongly resisted the procedural reforms underpinning the government's attempt to strengthen its already dominant position over parliament and which were especially detrimental to the Senate – the traditional bastion of the right. The government, on the other hand, justified its proposals in the name of greater efficiency in the legislative process, reputedly far too slow. One notable example of the struggle between executive and legislative powers can be seen in the government's attempt to restrict the right to propose amendments, enshrined in Article 44 of the Constitution as the 'principle means of expression' for parliamentarians. Notwithstanding certain limits (notably, amendments must not lead to an increase or reduction in public resources), the right of amendment is considered sacrosanct. However, it can also be seen as a means of obstructing parliamentary business since it is commonplace for thousands of amendments to be put forward on a single text: the most extreme example is that of an energy bill in 2006 to which the opposition lodged a record 137,537 amendments. Nor is there any obligation for an amendment to be different from an amendment proposed by another member (identical amendments) or even to have a direct link with the text in question (*cavaliers législatifs*), and the same amendments can be discussed both at the committee stage and in plenary sessions. It is therefore not hard to see why a government with an ambitious agenda would seek to restrict this practice and to make frequent use of other devices such as the 'accelerated procedure' to speed up the passing of legislation. Equally, parliament understandably wants to cling on to the powers it retains in the face of executive hegemony. In the case of the Constitutional Bill in question, 1,400 amendments were examined in the committee proceedings in June – of which 52 were adopted, significantly transforming the original government bill – before more amendments were added in the plenary sessions in July, reaching well over 2,000 (Savonitto, 2020).

The government was therefore already being seriously challenged over its constitutional reform when Macron made his second speech to the Congress in Versailles in July 2018,[10] acknowledging the delay in progress but reaffirming his belief in this 'reform for trust and strengthening of representation'. However, only days later, parliamentary proceedings were suddenly interrupted by revelations in *Le Monde*[11] of what became 'the Benalla Affair' (Garrigues, 2019), in which one of Macron's close security aides was shown to have assaulted demonstrators on May Day in 2018 whilst officially just an observer. There followed an outcry in parliament as deputies and senators demanded explanations from the Elysée; LREM deputies were thrown into confusion by the resounding silence from the president and his government. The opposition parties denounced a 'state scandal' and set up committees of inquiry in both chambers to establish the facts. Parliamentary debate was paralysed, and the government suspended proceedings. In his speech to mark the 60th anniversary of the constitution in October,[12] Macron said that the reform would be brought back in January. However, the eruption of the Yellow Vests protests in November meant a radical change of priorities, which led to the complete withdrawal of the legislation: the executive was forced to accept a major defeat, and the Senate had successfully asserted itself as a check on executive power. The contrast with the rapid passing of the laws on the 'moralisation of public life' in 2017 (discussed in Chapter 4) was striking.

The Yellow Vests protests and the Great National Debate

Just as the events of May 1968 that paralysed France for weeks were totally unexpected, the Yellow Vests movement, which seriously disrupted

Macron's political agenda, seemed to come from nowhere. Moreover, it represented an entirely new form of protest in France, well-known for its tradition of contentious politics (Tilly, 1986). This episode forced the president to refocus his top-down, institutional approach to democratic engagement around demands expressed by angry citizens demonstrating against him and his 'unjust' policies. The first Yellow Vests protest took place on Saturday 17 November 2018 in response to Facebook posts calling for mobilisation against the government's announcement of a rise in fuel tax to finance climate transition, and asking people who supported the cause to display their high-viz jackets (a legal requirement for all drivers); (Tran, 2020). For the first 'Act' of the protest, people gathered at provincial roundabouts in over 2,000 locations across France to block roads and fuel depots, and this was followed by weekly 'Acts' of defiance every Saturday, bringing together a disparate group of mainly working people with widely different profiles who, whilst rejecting any form of central leadership or *'désintermédiation'* (Lefebvre, 2019), nevertheless shared similar concerns for what they saw as the economic injustice inflicted on them by elites who had no understanding of their predicaments, just as Macron (2016) had accurately noted in *Revolution*. Significantly, they came mainly from rural and peri-urban areas, relied on cars to get to their poorly paid jobs and felt that they were being unfairly and disproportionally burdened with the cost of ecological transition. At the end of November, a list of 42 wide-ranging demands[13] was posted on social media, largely relating to the cost of living and calling for greater fiscal justice (especially the abolition of the wealth tax, the ISF) but also demanding greater government accountability and transparency, with better opportunities for participation in decision-making, especially through calls for the introduction of 'Citizens' Initiative Referendums' (RIC). These demands showed not only how protesters saw themselves broadly as the losers of the globalisation and economic liberalisation advocated by Macron, but they also revealed a bigger agenda, including issues of democratic representation.

In a televised interview on 14 November, just before the first protest, Macron had recognised his failure to reconcile French people with their leaders[14] and, at an Elysée event on ecological transition on 27 November,[15] when the protests were already underway, he acknowledged that many people felt excluded from decisions on these policies and called for a 'new working method' to include those who felt ignored. He therefore announced he would organise a national debate on transition issues with specific reference to including the Yellow Vests in the hope that solutions would be found to the concrete problems expressed by the protesters. After the third 'Act' of protests, he announced the withdrawal of the planned fuel tax; five days later, he delivered a much-watched speech on television,[16] in which he promised a series of economic measures worth 10 billion euros. He also promised to broaden the scope of the proposed debate, which he himself would coordinate, to involve all national and local institutions, social partners and civil society, with a special appeal to the mayors (of whom there were over 36,000) to play a role in facilitating the dialogue. Although some were reticent,[17] others responded, especially in rural areas, by providing 'registers' in which anyone could express their grievances, just as they had done in the *cahiers de doléance* before the 1789 Revolution. This idea came, in fact, not from Macron himself but from some of the protesters in the Gironde area who had initiated it in the early demonstrations. These registers would be open until the official launch of the debate in January 2019 when they would be passed up to the *prefectures* for analysis. In December 2018, the National Commission for Public Debate (CNDP)[18] was asked to organise the Great National Debate (GND), originally planned to last from 15 January to 15 March 2019.[19] However, disagreements soon emerged with its president when it became clear that the government intended to retain a monopoly over the analysis of the results and the conclusions to be drawn from them.[20] The task was therefore given, instead, to two of the prime minister's newly appointed ministers, with a very *ad hoc* organisational structure with no legal basis. A 'college' of five independent 'guarantors' was hastily appointed to oversee the operation and guarantee its integrity, including the renowned political scientist Pascal Perrineau; the National Library (BNF) would digitise all the contributions.[21]

Concerned about the drift of these events, an association called *Democratie Ouverte* (DO),[22] including Yellow Vests, experts, ecologists and participation specialists, published an Open Letter to the president in *Le Parisien* asking for guarantees that the GND would be not just a whitewash but a genuine attempt at democratic renewal. They called for a citizens' assembly on three subjects – climate change, democracy and tax – and worked closely with another association, the *Gilets citoyens* (Citizens Vests).[23] In parallel, an 'Observatory of Debates'[24] was set up in collaboration with academics from the CEVIPOF research centre in Paris to monitor the GND and set up mechanisms to prolong it as an ongoing contribution to the revival of democracy in France. The Yellow Vests were also sceptical of the GND and established an alternative called 'The Real Debate',[25] with the participation of *Cap Collectif*, a start-up that had provided the platform for the government's site. This site was more interactive than the official GND site, inviting citizens to express their demands and grievances on any subject of their choice and enabling voting for proposals[26] (Courant, 2019).

The GND was finally launched on 13 January 2019 when the president published a five-page 'Letter to the French People',[27] in which he responded to the Yellow Vests but reminded them of the project he was elected to deliver and which he was determined to see through. The population was asked to engage with four specific themes chosen by Macron while ignoring some of the key demands from protesters such as fiscal justice, the privileges enjoyed by politicians and the RIC. Macron's themes were tax and public spending, the organisation of state and public services, the ecological transition and democracy and citizenship. On this last theme, he sought proposals relating to his institutional reforms – specifically, on the preferred proportion of PR to be introduced, on the reduction of the number of parliamentarians, on reform of the Senate and the CESE, on the use of referendums and on how to increase participation in decision-making. He committed to 'drawing conclusions' from the debate, which would help to build 'a new contract for the Nation' – transforming people's anger into solutions – but made no solid commitments. Grievances could be expressed through questionnaires on a dedicated website, which also provided resources to support the organisation of meetings or citizens' conferences. Critics complained, however, that the site did not allow interaction or debate and merely produced a series of monologues (Courant, 2019). For the first face-to-face debate in a small town in Normandy, Macron spent seven hours, shirt sleeves rolled up, talking to local people – and this performance would be repeated in numerous debates across France as the president tried to engage with ordinary citizens, though dialogue often became more of a monologue. According to the official website, he participated personally in 16 public meetings, met 2,310 elected representatives and 1,000 young people, taking up 85 hours of his time.

During the three months of the GND, nearly two million contributions were recorded on the site, 10,134 local meetings were held, 16,337 town halls opened grievance registers and 27,374 emails were received. This volume of activity made the results hard to process, but, at the end of the exercise, the website published summaries of contributions on the four themes specified by Macron.[28] On the theme of democracy and citizenship, 62 per cent of respondents agreed with the introduction of some PR for legislative elections, while 86 per cent agreed with reducing the number of parliamentarians, thus endorsing the presidential proposals. More local referendums were wanted by 80 per cent of respondents but only 53 per cent at the national level. Academic research[29] showed, however, that the profiles of the participants, who were obviously self-selecting, were far from being representative of the population as a whole (predominantly retirees and from higher socio-professional groups) and certainly did not resemble those of the Yellow Vests. With regard to democracy, three main demands emerged from this research: greater participation but within the framework of representative democracy, better explanation of public policy and a strengthening of links between citizens at the national level (Rouban, 2019). The final report of the College of Guarantors[30] concluded that, despite certain limitations, especially of time, the GND had fulfilled its mission of allowing citizens to express themselves and that it had delivered a multitude of interesting initiatives; however, it also recognised that the framing of the themes by the president had been problematic. Experts in deliberative democracy found that the GND lacked legitimacy, representativeness and inclusiveness (Dobler, 2020; Fleury and Morel, 2019) and regretted that a good opportunity for serious deliberation had been missed by not following the basic standards of deliberative design (Ehs and Mokre, 2020). Nevertheless, it was also welcomed by some as a valuable experiment in participatory democracy, and overall, it was certainly an original response to an immediate crisis (Buge and Morio, 2019). Its likely longer-term significance and impact were, however, unclear: whilst the government spokesperson, Sibeth Ndiaye, said that 'nothing would be the same again',[31] public opinion was more sceptical. An opinion poll at the end of the GND showed that 79 per cent of respondents thought that it would not offer a way out of the social unrest that was still ongoing and that 76 per cent did not believe that there would be any change of style or method in the remaining years of Macron's presidency.

As for the handwritten 'registers of grievance', they were nearly all transcribed and archived digitally either in the BNF or at the departmental level; however, access has so far been restricted to a few researchers. A report in *Le Monde* said there were 19,899 registers containing over 200,000 handwritten contributions from about 16,500 town halls, mainly rural.[32] The Association of Mayors in the Paris Region published a 48-page synthesis of the (anonymised) 2,865 contributions made in that area, concluding: 'At the heart of the democratic crisis that we are experiencing, we must rebuild a link between the people and their representatives ... establish trust through a new pact between local collectivities and central power'.[33] An association, *Rendez les doléances!* has been campaigning for the archives to be made available to all citizens under open access and argues that anonymisation would not be as onerous as the government claims. Meanwhile, this treasure trove of documents remains largely out of reach for those citizens who contributed to it.

Macron Act II

To mark the end of the GND, Macron held his first press conference at the Elysée on 25 April 2019.[34] He began by drawing lessons from the Yellow Vests protests, recognising the profound sense of injustice and abandonment experienced by many and a lack of trust in all élites, especially himself. He acknowledged having made mistakes and promised a new, 'more human', mandate and 'a very deep change of method' for the '2nd Act' of his presidency. But whilst accepting the need for a change of style, he remained convinced that his project for transforming France remained the right one and he would not change direction from the programme on which he was elected, which he claimed was already starting to deliver positive results. He spelt out numerous measures to be taken, including a significant package of economic measures to benefit the most disadvantaged. On citizenship and democracy, he returned to his manifesto proposal to introduce some PR, now set at 20 per cent, a compromise reached after negotiations with the president of the Senate and MoDEM leader, François Bayrou. The reduction of parliamentarians would be set somewhere between 25 and 30 per cent, and the time limit of three identical mandates was maintained. Local petitions would be facilitated, and the requirements for holding a 'Shared Initiative Referendum' (Référendum d'Initiative Partagé or RIP) would be relaxed; however, he rejected the demand for a Citizens' Initiative Referendum (RIC) on the grounds that this would undermine representative democracy and the role of parliament. The suspended institutional reforms were sent back to parliament in August 2019, but, after the failure to reach an agreement with the president of the Senate over the summer, this important legislation was quietly and curiously allowed to slip into the long grass, from where it never returned.

The Citizens Convention on the Climate

Following on from the GND, the president announced another experiment in democratic engagement in the form of a Citizens Convention on the Climate (CCC), to be composed of 150 citizens chosen (not quite[35]) at random as a sample of the French population, using a methodology originally put forward by the CNDP for the GND. The CCC is considered in some detail in Chapter 11 in this volume, but a brief discussion is required here since it represented a new attempt at deliberative democracy to emerge from the Yellow Vests protests. The idea of citizens' assemblies had originally been proposed in January by the associations DO and *Gilets citoyens*[36] mentioned earlier, and in building on this idea, Macron changed the name from Assembly to Convention and restricted its focus to climate change. It was organised under the authority of the Council for Economic, Social and Environmental Council (CESE; which Macron had planned to reform) and was conducted in a more professionally controlled environment than the hastily structured GND: a governance committee of 15 was established to assist the participants, including Thierry Pech of the 'progressive' think-tank Terra Nova, originally close to the socialists before embracing the ideas of Macron. They took part in six weekend workshops in the chamber of the CESE in Paris from early October to late January 2020 and they were asked to make proposals for achieving, 'in a spirit of social justice', a reduction in greenhouse emissions of at least 40 per cent (compared to 1990) by 2030.

Macron committed, at the outset, to allowing the CCC's proposals to be put either to referendum or to parliament, but, when the 149 proposals[37] were delivered to the government in June, he immediately rejected three of them[38] (or six, according to the participants)[39] and a highly mediatised debate ensued over how the remaining proposals should be taken forward. In practical terms, since the nature of the different measures proposed meant implementation using different types of legal process in line with the complex mesh of existing international (especially EU), national and sub-national legislative frameworks, the complexity of turning well-intentioned ideas into law became immediately evident.[40] Indeed, a fundamental problem emerged concerning the legitimacy of the CCC with regard to its relationship with existing political institutions, as did the ambiguity of Macron's promise to submit the CCC's proposals to them 'without filter', as pointed out by the distinguished sociologist Dominique Schnapper:[41] many Convention members had taken it as a pledge to apply their proposals, yet, the CCC had no legal basis as a legislative body. Ultimately, in a representative democracy, parliament trumps citizen participation: the Minister for Relations with Parliament and Citizens Participation, Marc Fesneau, reminded CCC participants that those who take the final decisions are the government and parliament when it votes laws (Gourgues and Mazeaud, 2022). This brought into question the feasibility of citizens' conventions as a way forward for democratic renewal, but which Thierry Pech sidestepped by proposing to allow a role for 'pre-legislative' deliberation on laws before the vote in parliament since such processes could be facilitated within the existing institutional framework.[42] Nevertheless, in the case of the CCC, 'participationism' seemed to be less about reforming and improving democracy than about strengthening the government's hand (Gourgues and Mazeaud, 2022), and it was argued that, far from representing a break with the presidentialisation of the institutions, these innovations in citizen participation, in fact, simply emphasised their monarchical nature (Gossement, 2020).

As Halpern points out in Chapter 11, the fate of most of the CCC's 149 proposals became the subject of many claims and counter-claims, but the 'monarch' did agree in July 2020 to transmit to parliament the CCC's proposals for referendums; in December (delayed by the pandemic), he confirmed that a referendum would be held on amending Article 1 of the Constitution to include a guarantee by the Republic to preserve biodiversity, the environment and the fight against climate change. A Constitutional law to this effect was presented to parliament in January 2021, but, after six months of debate, agreement could not be reached on the wording of the text – notably the use of the word 'guarantee', which the Senate majority refused to accept – and, in July 2021, the prime minister announced its withdrawal. Although the long-term significance of the CCC has been widely downplayed, there are those – like American political scientist Hélène Landemore – who see it as a real advance, offering a basic model that should be permanently institutionalised (Wakim, 2024).

54 Revolution Revisited

The reform of the CESE

One of the CCC's proposals which was taken forward quite readily because it concurred with the presidential agenda, was the reform of the Economic, Social and Environmental Council (CESE), previously abandoned as part of the constitutional reform. The CESE was an advisory body, located in the impressive Palais d'Iena, which formally acted as a sort of 'third chamber' but which played an inconsequential role in French politics. Macron wanted to make it 'a Chamber of the future to bring together all the living forces of the nation', connecting civil society with the political institutions in social dialogue, as originally intended – but downplaying the role of established *corps intermédiares* such as trade unions ('rent-seekers' delegitimised in his eyes by their self-interested agendas), in favour of more-direct citizen engagement with long-term policymaking discussions, to be called the 'Council of Citizen Participation'. This reform was now separated from the other more contentious proposals in the constitutional reform and was presented to parliament in September 2020 using the 'accelerated procedure'. Agreement was reached by December, and the law was promulgated in January 2021. Some significant changes were introduced without changing the name – which was resisted by the Senate: membership was reduced, the signing of petitions was facilitated and members were allowed to take more initiatives on public consultations. However, this reform was far from the flagship transformation that Macron had hoped for and, despite ambitions by its former President Patrick Bernasconi to restore confidence in French democracy,[43] the CESE remains essentially a consultative body, said to be the guardian of a palace rather than a real driver for a renewed form of citizenship and participatory democracy (Padovani, 2022). It was, nevertheless, the chosen forum for a consultative assembly on 'the end of life,' in 2023,[44] which Macron heralded as contributing to the 'democratic reinvention' to which he aspired.[45]

With the prospect of the 2022 elections drawing closer, MoDEM leader François Bayrou made a last-ditch attempt to persuade the president to introduce some form of PR for the forthcoming legislative elections;[46] although it was widely supported by other parties, time was too short, and once again, it fell by the wayside. As the end of Macron's first presidency approached, there was little evidence of the promised democratic transformation. The president had failed to overcome Senate resistance to his institutional reforms and, although the GND and the CCC were clearly innovations, they remained, nevertheless, reactions to a political crisis and were widely seen as public relations exercises by a president who was happy to debate with citizens in front of TV cameras but who, ultimately, did not want citizen participation to infringe upon his Jupiterean style of decision-making, despite repeated promises to change his 'method'. Furthermore, when the Senate published its report in March 2022 into the government's controversial use of consultancy agencies, it revealed that the delivery of 'citizen's participation' had been largely sub-contracted at huge cost to private consultants, justified on the grounds of their expertise (Vaudano, Romain, Martinon and Sénécat, 2022). Besides, these two experiments had highlighted the fundamental problems of how to combine the output of citizens' participatory activities with the legal realities of law-making by elected representatives. Nor was there any attempt to explore the institutionalisation of citizen participation within the state apparatus other than through the managerial principle of 'participative governability' under the authority of executive power (Gourgues and Mazeaud, 2022). The Covid pandemic from March 2020 had also reinforced the 'verticality' of political power over citizens when all decisions relating to the *crise sanitaire* were taken behind closed doors in a *Conseil de défense* (François, 2022): record numbers of citizens lodged complaints with the Council of State in its role as top administrative court, relating to various kinds of constraints on their basic rights and freedoms during the pandemic's 'state of emergency' and, although normally a docile servant of the executive, it made some notable judgements against the government. Its annual report in September 2021 cited a fear of exacerbating the weakness of representative democracy to justify recommending stronger limits on the executive's powers to prolong a state of emergency, involving parliamentary approval and inclusion in the constitution.[47]

Macron's second presidency: from crisis to crisis

In his (brief) presidential campaign for re-election in 2022 under the slogan *Avec Vous (With You)*, overshadowed by the Russian invasion of Ukraine, Macron once again promised a renovation of the institutions, blaming the opposition for blocking his proposals but also acknowledging that some reforms had been carried out in a rather cavalier manner (*à la cavalcade, à la hussarde*). He repeatedly promised a 'less vertical' style of presidency and pledged a 'change of method' by the creation of a 'transpartisan commission' to consider constitutional reform and a 'permanent great debate' with the French people to share the responsibility for reforms needed. In his election-night speech on the Champ de Mars, he said that the next presidency would not mean continuity with the first but would trigger the 'collective invention of a *méthode refondée*' for a new era.[48] Although he was comfortably re-elected with 58.55 per cent of the vote, this was down from 66.1 per cent in 2017, with 3 million (6.2 per cent) blank or spoiled votes[49] and 13.6 million (28 per cent) abstentionists on the second-round run-off against Marine le Pen. Macron was thus elected by only 38.5 per cent of registered voters (compared to 43.6 per cent in 2017). In the following legislative elections, turnout was low in both rounds, with more abstentionists than voters,[50] confirming the sense that French democracy was still 'fatigued'.

The fact that Macron's party, now renamed *Renaissance*, failed to obtain an absolute majority in these elections with its electoral allies the MoDEM and *Horizons* (under the collective name *Ensemble*), raised the question of whether he would be able to pursue his programme of reforms. It is a fundamental paradox of the Fifth Republic that, despite very significant constitutional powers, a president cannot effectively pursue their political programme without a majority in the NA to pass laws (even if certain measures can be implemented by decree). Since *Ensemble* formed the biggest alliance, with 250 seats (42 per cent), this did, however, represent a 'relative majority', with significantly more seats than any other group, enabling the president to appoint a prime minister from his own camp, unlike 'cohabitation' where an opposition party wins a majority of seats.

A relative majority is an infrequent outcome in a political system that has seen the gradual emergence of stable majorities following the introduction of a majoritarian electoral system (in two rounds) and the presidentialisation of party politics. Nevertheless, from 1988 to 1991, following the re-election of François Mitterrand, Prime Minister Michel Rocard managed such a situation quite successfully by 'opening out' his government to figures from civil society, by espousing a more consensual style of politics and by reaching out for support to pass legislation on a case-by-case basis. He also made frequent use of the powerful set of constitutional devices that allow a government to force through laws against a reluctant parliament if necessary – the most notorious of which is Article 49.3, which allows the prime minister to push through a law without a vote (Rocard used it 28 times). Although its use is always controversial and is strongly criticised by opponents as anti-democratic, all governments have used it. However, to limit abuse, in a rare concession to parliament, the constitutional revision of 2008 restricted its use to only once per parliamentary session (except during the budget legislation). The only way for the opposition to fight back when Article 49.3 is used is to table a censure motion (a vote of no confidence) against the government, which, because it requires a majority of votes, is very hard to achieve. A government with only a relative majority regularly relies on the fact that the political differences between the various components of the opposition usually prevent them from joining forces to vote together against it.

This was especially pertinent to the fragmented NA elected in 2022 since there was now a significant presence of more radical parties on both the left and the right: the radical left alliance, NUPES, held 151 seats and the National Rally (former National Front) had unexpectedly won 89 seats. Nevertheless, the smaller the government's majority, the more fragile its position: while Rocard's government held 275 seats – not far off an absolute majority of 289 – Macron's new government was in a weaker position with 250. In theory, this situation could have been seen as an opportunity for the opposition to try and clip the wings of the presidential majority and for the

NA to reassert itself against the executive. It could also have represented an opening for Macron to pursue his ambition of reaching beyond the traditional cleavages to build a broader coalition. However, the politics of his second presidency took a different turn, and the heavy-handed approach taken by the government simply reinforced the widespread sense that French democracy still needed a major overhaul.

After his 'semi-victory' in the elections, Macron initially proceeded with announcements in line with his campaign promises to reinvigorate democracy: government spokesperson Olivier Véran also became the Minister for 'Democratic Renewal', to include citizen participation and supervision of a new body, the *Conseil National de la Refondation* (CNR), intended to give substance to Macron's idea of introducing a 'new method' of governing 'in the spirit of dialogue and shared responsibilities'– to foster unity instead of division.[51] In practical terms, the goal was to bring together people from different fields of activity to discuss themes such as housing, education and health – mainly at the local level – and to work together to find solutions to problems. However, many organisations and opposition parties and some of the trade unions and other *corps intermédiares* refused to participate because it was seen as potentially undermining parliamentary authority; thus, this venture never really got off the ground. Indeed, all presidential attempts to organise experiments in participatory and deliberative democracy continued to be overshadowed by the actions and style of his presidency and new government, led by a 'technocrat' and former socialist, Elisabeth Borne, under close 'supervision' from the Elysée. She initially declared her intention to 'govern differently', based on the idea of building majorities around specific pieces of legislation (*'majorités de projet'*) as Rocard had done. However, having failed to reach an agreement with other groups, determined to remain autonomous, she resorted to pushing through government reforms using the constitutional devices at its disposal: during the passing of the budget in the autumn of 2022, she invoked Article 49.3 ten times.[52]

The most emblematic illustration of this resort to the hard-line approach came with the pension reform, debated in parliament in early 2023, which was widely described as a 'brutalisation of democracy' imposed by the president himself. First, the government controversially chose to present it as a finance bill amending the 2023 budget,[53] which enabled it to trigger Article 47.1 of the Constitution, never used before in this way, to significantly limit the duration of debate. Consequently, only 2 out of 20 articles were discussed in the NA. Other constitutonal devices were also used, such as the 'blocked vote' (Article 44), which allows only government amendments to be retained. In the NA, members of the radical-left party *La France Insoumise* (LFI) used 'obstructionist' tactics, presenting thousands of amendments, causing major disruption in the chamber and triggering a record number of sanctions for misconduct. In the streets, massive popular protests were supported by the unprecedented formation of a united coalition of resistance from all the trade unions – the *intersyndicale*. The intensity of hatred towards Macron personally was visible in the many effigies, and portraits of him paraded in the massive street protests alongside reminders of the 'decapitation' of Louis XVI: this was not the Revolution that Macron had intended. Nevertheless, the government refused to back down and responded instead, with harsh police repression, as during the Yellow Vests protests. Finally, the prime minister (reluctantly) decided on 16 March to invoke Article 49.3 in order to pass the bill without a vote, triggering a rare 'transpartisan' censure motion sponsored by a small independent group of deputies and which failed by only nine votes. In April, the law was promulgated after approval by the Constitutional Council.[54] Many constitutional experts nevertheless considered the legislative process adopted by the government as anti-parliamentarian and undemocratic: Macron may have won his battle for pension reform, but the strength of opposition to it simply reinforced the wide gulf between citizens and their leaders that he himself had previously deplored – and, increasingly, his position was seen as illegitimate.

After the promulgation of the law, Macron addressed the French people[55] and spoke of the need for a 100-day period of 'appeasement', to last till the national holiday on 14 July commemorating the 1789 Revolution. However, when he travelled around the country to meet ordinary people to try and win them over, he and his ministers were met with angry crowds banging saucepans, *les casserolades*, and when he attended the final match of the Coupe de France at the Stade de France in April, he had to present the cup to the winners from the safety of the tribune rather than out on the field to avoid a hostile onslaught from the crowd, which had become a regular occurrence on such occasions. By the end of the 100 days, France was in the throes of more violent street riots after the unlawful killing by a policeman of an adolescent of part-Algerian descent, riots which once again highlighted the controversial role of the police in maintaining law and order, endorsed by the government.

Mindful of the difficulties that his government would face in pushing on with his political agenda, Macron then adopted a strategy in late Summer of inviting all the party leaders and the presidents of the NA and Senate to try and identify areas of agreement on key subjects due for debate in the autumn like the forthcoming immigration bill and institutional reforms. However, these *Rencontres de Saint Denis* failed to deliver any concrete results, and three of the parties – LFI, the PS and LR – withdrew from the talks in November, accusing Macron of stoking the crisis of democracy by multiplying initiatives outside the existing institutions.

Once again, the prime minister had to use Article 49.3 to pass her budget in autumn 2023, and in December, a controversial Immigration Bill, criticised on the left for being too tough and on the right for being too soft, was blocked in the NA by a *motion de rejet préalable*,[56] unusually supported by almost all the opposition deputies on both the left and the right. Accused of being 'in denial of democracy' (*déni de démocratie*) over what many saw as a political crisis, the Elysée minimised it as a simple parliamentary incident and rejected the idea of a dissolution called for by the RN. This kind of blocking motion, lesser known than the 49.3, is easier to pass than a censure motion, but it cannot bring down a government – it simply rejects a text. Determined to push through this flagship bill, Macron urged Borne and the Interior Minister, Gerald Darmanin, to seek a compromise with the parties of the right in a *Commission Mixte Paritaire* (CMP), a parliamentary committee designed to thrash out a settlement in cases of disagreement. Agreement was finally reached at the cost of numerous concessions to parties of the right, most of which, as the government anticipated, were subsequently rejected by the Constitutional Council.[57]

The resolution of this parliamentary crisis over the Immigration Bill confirmed that Macron's government had clearly veered to the right and that the presidential mantra of balancing left and right *en même temps* was no longer tenable. It also triggered deep divisions within the presidential camp, with 20 deputies voting against the final text and 17 abstaining, representing 20 per cent of *Renaissance* deputies – a significant loss for a relative majority. With the scope for further reform seriously limited by his increasingly fragile majority, the president promised a 'new direction' in January 2024. As is traditional in French politics under the Fifth Republic, this meant changing the prime minister – the 'fuse' to be replaced when a president is in difficulties. In view of the European elections in June, Macron chose the young and popular Education Minister, Gabriel Attal, the 'mini-Macron', whose new government included several ministers close to Nicolas Sarkozy – still an influential visitor to the Elysée. Attal approached the problem of legislating in a hostile parliament by saying that he would make astute use of executive decrees on high-profile issues, like his popular ban on the wearing of the Muslim *abaya* in schools when he was Education Minister. However, there are limits to ruling by decree, and in the six months of his government, he was unable to make real progress on any of his priorities: education, health and housing. Media reports evaluating his first 100 days in office concurred that, despite his good intentions, the political stalemate he inherited made him a lame-duck prime minister to a lame-duck president. Most importantly, he failed to revive the fortunes of the presidential camp in the face of strong competition from the young RN leader, Jordan Bardella, whose victory in the EP elections of June 2024 sealed the fate of Attal's short-lived government when Macron announced his momentous decision to dissolve the NA and hold new elections, a decision taken without even consulting his prime minister.

Initiated by the president to seek 'clarification' of a seemingly intractable political situation in which he retained little room for manoeuvre, these elections simply created even greater deadlock, producing a split of the 577 seats into roughly three main blocs, none of which had enough deputies to command a viable majority: Macron's supporters, 'Ensemble', dropped from 250 to 166 seats; the hastily agreed left-wing alliance, the New Popular Front (NFP), surprisingly won 184 seats (compared to 142 for the NUPES alliance in 2022); the National Rally (RN) increased its presence from 88 to 123, making it the biggest single party, and with support from the 17 members of the breakaway group from *Les Republicains* under the leadership of Eric Ciotti, this far-right block together won 143 seats. This was an atypical election outcome, not previously produced by the majoritarian system of the Fifth Republic, which usually delivers a majority (either absolute or relative). It was partly distorted by the impact of the 'republican front' agreed between the NFP and Macron's alliance 'Ensemble', whereby candidates agreed to stand down in the second round in favour of the leading 'republican' candidate to limit gains by the 'unrepublican' far-right National Rally (RN) and its allies (though the NFP was more consistent in sticking to this agreement than 'Ensemble'). This meant that many voters were voting 'against' rather than 'for' the candidates in their constituencies, and were thus deprived of a real choice. The increased recourse to this kind of tactical voting suggests a need for electoral reform.

If Macron's proposal to introduce some form of PR had been implemented, it would no doubt have delivered similar or possibly greater fragmentation. Paradoxically, and notwithstanding any distortions of tactical voting, this three-way split could be seen as a positive indicator for democracy, in that it probably delivers a fairly accurate political representation of the electorate, which is also 'fractured' into three main camps, since Macron's unpopular record of governing from the centre has led to the growing polarisation of opposition on both right and left against him. Moreover, another positive for democracy was that this election outcome was delivered by a significant increase in voter turnout to nearly 67 per cent on both rounds, the highest in a legislative election since the last 'unscheduled' election in 1997.[58]

Tension is thus discernible between the aims of representivity and governability: if the political preferences of the French electorate are to be more faithfully represented within a more fragmented composition of the NA (all the more so if PR were to be introduced), its members must surely move away from the current adversarial political culture to find ways of working together. Yet the idea of compromise is often negatively associated in French political culture with *compromission* or 'selling out'. Coalitions were accepted practices under the Third and Fourth Republics, but as mentioned in the introduction, they tended to create instability and 'immobilism' because of the strength of resistance to change, and the Fourth Republic in particular has a poor reputation. Under the Fifth Republic, the presidential system has increased governability but has reduced representivity, and the growing electoral success of the far-right has compounded this problem. It is hard to see a way out of this conundrum, which raises the question of whether this is an institutional or a political crisis: can it be resolved by future elections and a change of leadership or does it require institutional and/or electoral reform? Although the introduction of some degree of PR might seem an attractive proposition to many, previous debates show that consensus on a specific model is likely to be elusive, and French political culture will struggle to adjust. Can the regime of the Fifth Republic adapt to changing circumstances or has it reached the end of its shelf life? Is it time to usher in a Sixth Republic, as advocated by the radical left under Jean-Luc Mélenchon?

There is no shortage of suggestions from experts with regard to possible ways forward, but the problem remains of how any institutional or electoral change might be implemented in the current political configuration, especially since it is unclear how much capacity any future government will have to address these fundamental questions: the risk of being censured by opposition forces will remain ever present, at least until further elections, which cannot take place before July 2025. Meanwhile, can Jupiter survive his disruptive decision by securing some kind of 'grand coalition' of the 'republican arc', excluding both extremes (LFI and the RN) or might he succumb to calls for his resignation? At the time of writing in late July 2024, the future of democracy looks very uncertain in this land of eternally contentious politics.

Notes

1. https://www.aefinfo.fr/assets/img/modules/comparateur/docs/6/Programme-Emmanuel-Macron.pdf
2. https://www.elysee.fr/emmanuel-macron/2017/07/03/discours-du-president-de-la-republique-devant-le-parlement-reuni-en-congres
3. https://www2.assemblee-nationale.fr/static/reforme-an/Rapport-1-GT.pdf
4. https://www.senat.fr/fileadmin/import/files/fileadmin/Fichiers/Images/presidence_senat/40_propositions_du_groupe_de_travail_du_Senat_sur_la_revision_constitutionnelle.pdf
5. A Constitutional law amends the Constitution, an Organic Law relates to the Constitution and must be approved by the Constitutional Council and an Ordinary Law only concerns matters specifically ceded to Parliament in Article 34 of the Constitution.
6. https://www.assemblee-nationale.fr/dyn/15/textes/l15b0911_projet-loi
7. https://www.assemblee-nationale.fr/dyn/15/textes/l15b0977_projet-loi
8. https://www.assemblee-nationale.fr/dyn/15/textes/l15b0976_projet-loi
9. Ordinary laws can be passed as a last resort without approval of the Senate but not Organic Laws.
10. https://www.elysee.fr/emmanuel-macron/2018/07/12/discours-du-president-de-la-republique-devant-le-parlement-reuni-en-congres-a-versailles

11 https://www.lemonde.fr/politique/article/2018/07/18/le-monde-identifie-sur-une-video-un-collaborateur-de-m-macron-frappant-un-manifestant-le-1er-mai-a-paris_5333330_823448.html
12 https://www.elysee.fr/emmanuel-macron/2018/10/05/transcription-du-discours-du-president-emmanuel-macron-au-conseil-constitutionnel
13 https://blogs.mediapart.fr/jeremiechayet/blog/021218/liste-des-42-revendications-des-gilets-jaunes
14 https://www.rtl.fr/actu/politique/emmanuel-macron-je-n-ai-pas-reussi-a-reconcilier-le-peuple-francais-avec-ses-dirigeants-7795578839
15 https://www.vie-publique.fr/discours/207388-emmanuel-macron-27112018-strategie-et-methode-transition-ecologique
16 https://www.lemonde.fr/politique/article/2018/12/10/le-verbatim-de-l-allocution-televisee-du-president-de-la-republique_5395523_823448.html
17 Only weeks before the first protests, Macron had downgraded the annual presidential meeting with France's mayors.
18 The CNDP was created in 1995 as a form of 'institutionalised citizen participation' to take responsibility for organising public debates on subjects with a significant impact on the environment, and in 2002, it became an independent administrative authority.
19 https://www.debatpublic.fr/en
20 https://www.archives.debatpublic.fr/sites/cndp.portail/files/documents/01-rapport-missiongd_ok-1.pdf
21 https://granddebat.fr/
22 https://www.democratieouverte.org/nos-actions-plaidoyer-campagnes
23 https://giletscitoyensorg.wordpress.com/
24 https://www.participation-et-democratie.fr/observatoire-des-debats-0
25 https://levraidebat.org/
26 https://aoc.media/analyse/2019/04/09/petit-bilan-grand-debat-national/
27 https://www.elysee.fr/emmanuel-macron/2019/01/13/lettre-aux-francais
28 https://granddebat.fr/
29 https://www.sciencespo.fr/cevipof/fr/content/lobservatoire-des-debat-0.html
30 https://granddebat.fr/pages/le-college-des-garants
31 https://www.bfmtv.com/politique/gouvernement/apres-le-debat-sibeth-ndiaye-promet-que-rien-ne-sera-comme-avant_AN-201904070009.html
32 https://www.lemonde.fr/societe/article/2024/01/18/les-milliers-de-cahiers-de-doleances-une-mine-pour-les-chercheurs-cinq-ans-apres-les-gilets-jaunes_6211449_3224.html
33 https://amif.asso.fr/vie-de-l-association/nos-publications-vie-de-l-association/etudes-et-rapports/rapport-d-analyse-des-cahiers-de-doleances-d-ile-de-france/
34 https://www.elysee.fr/emmanuel-macron/2019/04/25/conference-de-presse-grand-debat-national
35 https://blogs.mediapart.fr/association-sciences-citoyennes/blog/161219/convention-citoyenne-pour-la-democratie-continue-contre-la-manipulation-du-pouv
36 https://giletscitoyensorg.wordpress.com/la-convention-citoyenne/
37 https://www.conventioncitoyennepourleclimat.fr/
38 https://www.vie-publique.fr/en-bref/274866-convention-citoyenne-climat-les-reponses-du-president-de-la-republique
39 https://giletscitoyens.org/2020/07/10/les-150-face-au-president-quel-bilan/
40 https://laviedesidees.fr/Decider-ensemble.html
41 https://www.telos-eu.com/fr/politique-francaise-et-internationale/un-parlement-qui-nen-est-pas-un.html
42 https://www.lagrandeconversation.com/debat/politique/la-convention-citoyenne-une-innovation-democratique/

43 https://www.info.gouv.fr/communique/12705-communique-de-presse-du-premier-ministre-jean-castex-remise-du-rapport-de-m-patrick-bernasconi
44 https://www.lecese.fr/convention-citoyenne-sur-la-fin-de-vie
45 https://www.vie-publique.fr/discours/288866-emmanuel-macron-03042023-fin-de-vie
46 https://www.leparisien.fr/politique/francois-bayrou-la-proportionnelle-est-une-obligation-democratique-et-morale-06-02-2021-8423594.php. Bayrou's party had won 19 per cent of votes in the first round 2007 but only three seats.
47 https://www.conseil-etat.fr/publications-colloques/etudes/les-etats-d-urgence-la-democratie-sous-contraintes
48 https://www.vie-publique.fr/discours/284950-emmanuel-macron-24042022-presidence-de-la-republique
49 Blank votes (*votes blancs*) are empty envelopes, whereas spoiled votes (*votes nuls*) contain ballot papers that have been written on, torn or contain several ballot papers.
50 https://www.archives-resultats-elections.interieur.gouv.fr/
51 https://conseil-refondation.fr/
52 There is no limit to the usage of this article during budget debates.
53 Technically, this is known as a *projet de loi de financement rectificative de la sécurité sociale* or PLFRSS.
54 The CC did not validate some of the elements in the bill (*les cavaliers sociaux*) considered inappropriate for a finance bill.
55 https://www.elysee.fr/emmanuel-macron/2023/04/17/adresse-aux-francais-2
56 https://www.vie-publique.fr/fiches/292343-quest-ce-quune-motion-de-rejet-prealable
57 https://www.conseil-constitutionnel.fr/decision/2024/2023863DC.htm#:~:text=LE%20CONSEIL%20CONSTITUTIONNEL%20A%20%C3%89T%C3%89,le%20Pr%C3%A9sident%20de%20la%20R%C3%A9publique
58 https://fr.statista.com/statistiques/716531/participation-legislatives-france/

References

Andolfatto, D. (2017) *Revue politique et parlementaire*. No. 1083–1084. https://www.revuepolitique.fr/la-nouvelle-sociologie-de-lassemblee-nationale-renouvellement-ou-cercle-ferme/

Bresson, J. and Ollion, E. (2022) 'Que sont les deputes novices devenus?', in Dolez, B., Douillet, A.-C., Fretel, J. and Lefebvre, R. (eds) *L'entreprise Macron à l'épreuve du pouvoir*. Grenoble: Presses Universitaires de Grenoble, pp. 115–130.

Buge, E. and Morio, C. (2019) 'Le Grand débat national, apports et limites pour la participation citoyenne', *Revue du Droit Public et de la Science Politique en France et a l'Etranger*, 5, pp. 1205. https://hal.science/hal-04418338

Claret, P. and Savonitto, F. (2020) *La réforme institutionnelle sous le quinquennat d'Emmanuel Macron*. Paris: L'Harmattan.

Courant, D. (2019) *Petit bilan du Grand Débat National*. AOC. https://aoc.media/analyse/2019/04/09/petit-bilan-grand-debat-national/

Dobler, C. (2020) 'The 2019 Grand Débat National in France: A participatory experiment with limited legitimacy', *Democracy International*, Research Note. https://www.democracy-international.org/sites/default/files/PDF/Publications/gdn_france_research_note_0.pdf

Ehs, T. and Mokre, M. (2020) 'Deliberation against participation? Yellow Vests and Grand Débat: a perspective from deliberative theory', *Political Studies Review*, 19(2), pp. 186–192.

Fleury, M. and Morel, B. (2019) 'Le Grand Debat, vrai symptôme et fausse solution au malaise démocratique'. https://blog.juspoliticum.com/2019/04/03/le-grand-debat-vrai-symptome-et-fausse-solution-au-malaise-democratique-par-marine-fleury-et-benjamin-morel/#:~:text=3%20avril%202019-,Le%20Grand%20d%C3%A9bat%2C%20vrai%20sympt%C3%B4me%20et%20fausse%20solution%20au%20malaise,les%20citoyens%20et%20l'ex%C3%A9cutif

François, B. (2022) 'Macron et les institutions: rien de nouveau sous le soleil?', in Dolez, B., Douillet, A.-C., Fretel, J. and Lefebvre, R. (eds) *L'entreprise Macron à l'épreuve du pouvoir*. Grenoble: Presses Universitaires de Grenoble, pp. 41–52.

Garrigues, J. (2019) *Les scandales de la République de Panama à l'affaire Benalla*. Paris: Nouveau Monde.

Gossement, A. (2020) 'La convention citoyenne pour le climat est profondément monarchique', *Reporterre*, 5 February. https://reporterre.net/La-convention-citoyenne-pour-le-climat-est-profondement-monarchique

Gourgues, G. and Mazeaud, A. (2022) 'La démocratie participative selon Emmanuel Macron: la participation citoyenne au service de la monarchie républicaine', in Dolez, B., Douillet, A.-C., Fretel, J. and Lefebvre, R. (eds), *L'entreprise Macron à l'épreuve du pouvoir pouvoir*. Grenoble: Presses Universitaires de Grenoble, pp. 53–66.

Lefebvre, R. (2019) 'Les gilets jaunes et les exigences de la représentation politique', *La Vie des idées*, 10 September.

Macron, E. (2016) Révolution. Paris: XO Editions. English edition: Macron, E. (2017) Revolution. London: Scribe.

Murray, R. (2008) 'The power of sex and incumbency: a longitudinal study of electoral performance in France', *Party Politics*, 14(5), pp. 539–554.

Ollion, E. (2021) *Les candidats. Novices et professionnels de la politique* Paris: PUF.

Padovani, J. (2022) 'La réforme du Conseil économique, social et environnemental: une citoyenneté en question', *Revue des Droits de l'Homme*, 22.

Rouban, L. (2017) *L'assemblée élue en 2017 et la crise de la représentation*. Paris: Sciences Po, Research Report. https://sciencespo.hal.science/hal-03458680

Rouban, L. (2019) 'Le Grand Débat National et la Démocratie: première synthèse', Cevipof https://www.sciencespo.fr/cevipof/sites/sciencespo.fr.cevipof/files/Version%202_Grand%20de%cc%81bat_de%cc%81mocratie_premie%cc%80re%20synthe%cc%80se_LR_2019.pdf

Savonitto, F. (2020) 'Itinéraire d'un abandon', in Claret, P. and Savonitto, F. (eds) *La réforme institutionnelle sous le quinquennat d'Emmanuel Macron*. Paris: l'Harmattan, pp. 19–52.

Sergues, B. (2018) 'Le projet de loi constitutionnelle de 2018: entre sydrôme aigu de réformisme constitutionnel et necessaire mutabilité du corpus juridique suprême', *Politeia*, 34.

Slater, M. (1985) *Contemporary French politics*. Basingstoke: Macmillan.

Tilly, C. (1986) *The contentious French*. Cambridge, MA: Harvard University Press.

Tran, E. (2020) 'The Yellow Vests movement: causes, consequences and significance', in Drake, H., Cole, A., Meunier, S. and Tiberj, V. (eds) *Developments in French politics 6*. London: Bloomsbury, pp. 179–196.

Vaudano, M., Romain, M., Martinon, L. and Sénécat, A. (2022) 'Comment l'exécutif a confié l'organisation des concertations citoyennes à des cabinets de consultants privés', *Le Monde*, 26 March.

Wakim, N. (2024) 'Interview with Helene Landmore', *Le Monde*, 22 July. https://www.lemonde.fr/chaleur-humaine/article/2024/07/22/climat-si-on-leur-donnait-les-moyens-de-participer-a-la-transition-beaucoup-de-citoyens-seraient-partants_6255161_6125299.html

4
POLITICAL CORRUPTION IN FRANCE AND THE 'MORALISATION OF PUBLIC LIFE' UNDER EMMANUEL MACRON

Susan Collard and Françoise Dreyfus

Abstract

This chapter discusses the problem of political corruption in France through the discussion of a law 'on the moralisation of public life' passed by President Macron to tackle it. This legislation was precipitated by the eruption during the election campaign of the 'Penelopegate' affair, incriminating the 'Republicains' candidate François Fillon and his wife Penelope, but the law also sought to address a more deep-seated set of problems relating to political corruption said to be undermining public trust in politics. The chapter provides some historical background explaining the development of political corruption during the Fifth Republic and its negative impact on trust in politicians, summarising the laws passed over several decades to stop corrupt political practices, particularly with regard to party finance. The second part of the chapter uses official data to assess the extent to which politicians comply with the legislation. It shows that not only was there limited enthusiasm amongst parliamentarians for accepting the demands imposed on them but also, at the level of government ministers and their advisers, a number of cases of misconduct in office led to resignations and sanctions that tarnished Macron's presidency, which has not delivered the 'exemplary republic' to which he aspired.

Introduction

This chapter evaluates President Macron's attempt to 'moralise public life' within the wider context of political corruption as an ongoing public problem in France. Although his prioritisation of these problems was precipitated ostensibly by the eruption during the 2017 election campaign of the 'Penelopegate' affair, incriminating the *Republicains* candidate François Fillon and his wife Penelope, the concerns addressed under Macron were, in fact, more deeply embedded, and the legislation he introduced – rather than innovating – built on a series of laws introduced over several decades. The chapter therefore begins by explaining why political corruption had emerged as a salient public problem in the late 1980s and how it was tackled by successive governments up to 2017. It then sets out the measures introduced by Macron in his attempt to 'clean up' French politics, before assessing – through an analysis of the responses of political elites to the many laws and regulations imposed on them – the extent to which they have brought about any real change. We conclude that, whilst significant efforts have been made to change practices through legislation, reinforced by the growing influence of international norms of transparency, the attitudes and behaviours of the French political class, imbued with an 'inherited' sense of privilege, have still not fully made the transition from the 'old world' to the 'new world' that Macron said was central to his vision of political transformation in France.

Political corruption in France

Historically, France has been no stranger to corruption, however it is defined; before the Revolution of 1789, favouritism and privilege were the norm, but the upheaval of values that accompanied the overthrow of the monarchy and the abolition of feudal privileges meant that denouncing abuses of power became a civic duty espoused by the revolutionaries and the notion of corruption was redefined in the Penal Code of 1810 under Napoleon I (Mattina and Monier, 2018). After the Revolution, defence of the definition of 'the general interest' against individual interests by the people's representatives was an important (at least theoretical) ongoing concern (Lascoumes, 2022). However, the 'virtuous' republic failed to live up to its founding ideals: in 1889, the offence of 'trading favours' was added to the code following a major scandal involving the selling of honours by the son-in-law of the president of the Third Republic (1870–1940) which, along with the Panama Scandal and the Stavisky Affair, gave it the reputation of being corrupt (Girling, 1997). Yet, most of the scandals during this period involved financial speculation or fraud rather than political misconduct (Garraud, 1999), which only became a major public problem well into the Fifth Republic.

To outsiders, the most striking observation about French attitudes with regards to political corruption is the traditional absence of any concept of conflict of interest, seen as an 'anglo-saxon' idea and only given legal definition in 2013. This, as Yves Mény has argued, enabled the development of a range of practices that became systemic:

Corruption in France is derived from mechanisms, values and rules that are totally integrated and legitimised by the political system. Corruption does not occur in the margins of the system but lives in symbiosis with it.
(Mény, 1992, p. 23)

He cites, in particular, the example of porous boundaries between the public and private spheres, allowing top civil servants in the *grands corps* to build their careers using a system of *pantouflage* or revolving doors (discussed in Chapter 9), and the tradition of multiple office-holding that developed under the Third Republic, perpetuating 'networks of connivance' between local and national politics and facilitating the growth of fiefdoms under powerful *notables*. At the same time, Mény adds, the 'tentacular' nature of the administrative state, creaking under the pressure of its own excessive rules and regulations, means that the system can only function by producing *arrangements* or workarounds that can easily slip into corruption. This is accentuated by the fact that social and political pluralism in France is historically weak:

We have a weak stomach for pluralism ... diverse points of view, behaviour and opinions have always been viewed with suspicion ... they must always bow to the superior interests of the state. ... As a result, conflicts of interest make little sense, because the only valid interest is the superior interest of the state.
(Mény, 2013, p. 5)

A second observation that helps to contextualise political corruption in France is the '*de facto* politicisation' of the judiciary (Evans, 2002). Its long history of subjugation to political power is reinforced by the institutions of the Fifth Republic, allowing 'affairs' involving politicians to be swept under the carpet by tacit collusion between political power and the law (Garraud, 1999). Although the judiciary is formally independent, as enshrined in the Constitution, the 'public prosecutor's office' (*le parquet*) is under direct control of the Ministry of Justice, and it is widely believed to have been 'instrumentalised'. However, in the late 1980s, there was a backlash of 'judicial activism', led by rebellious 'red' lawyers like Renaud Van Ruymbeke, who were determined to break free from the political hold on them and who brought to justice certain high-profile politicians from the 1990s onwards. A 'new professional culture' transformed the relationship between politics and the judiciary, described by Garraud as 'the judicialization of politics' (1999, p. 134).

Closely connected is the role of the media, historically entwined with the worlds of business and politics (Jeanneney, 1984). Alongside the emancipation of judges and magistrates, a similar awakening took place among certain French journalists who worked with the judiciary in the 1990s to bring cases of political corruption into the public domain in a wave of editorial denunciations of the political class (Marchetti, 2002). Journalism, like the judiciary, was traditionally deferential to political power, and at the beginning of the Fifth Republic, the context of the Algerian War enabled de Gaulle to establish direct executive control through a Ministry of Information that literally dictated what news was for public dissemination through the state-controlled media monopoly, *Radio-Télévision Française*. The press was less tightly controlled, enabling the satirical weekly paper *Le Canard Enchaîné* to uncover various scandals during the Gaullist era – but their revelations reached only a limited audience because they were not relayed by other media sources: most mainstream journalists did not see themselves as 'guard dogs' (Marchetti, 2002) and feared that committing *lèse-majesté* could jeopardise their careers. This changed in the 1980s and 1990s with the appearance of investigative journalists like Edwy Plenel and others who worked closely with the judiciary to reveal multiple cases of political corruption, establishing a symbiotic relationship of 'connivance' (Dupin, 2001) to their mutual benefit in furthering their shared objective of resisting political pressure.

These deeply embedded features of the French political system are reinforced by the institutions of the Fifth Republic, where executive power is highly concentrated around the president, who is above the law and cannot be charged with any offence except treason while in office. To understand how all these elements moulded the situation that Emmanuel Macron inherited, the following section explains how political corruption developed between 1958 and 2017, from a focus on systemic corruption of party finance in the late 1980s–1990s to the (reluctant) internalisation of international norms in the early twenty-first century.

The changing nature of political corruption in the Fifth Republic 1958–2017

Unchecked corruption 1958–1988

The type of political regime is a significant factor in determining how corruption is articulated in any particular context (Johnston, 2005), and Mény (1992) was the first to show how this relates to France. In 1958, de Gaulle used the political crisis triggered by the Algerian War to impose a new constitution strengthening the presidency. Political opponents claimed that executive dominance of the new institutions, including the judiciary and the police, enabled those in power to pursue self-interested illicit activities. Corrupt and illegal practices were indeed widespread, even systematised, under de Gaulle's watch (Denoël and Meltz, 2023; Garrigues, 2019); 'the

Gaullist party and its candidates were favoured by privileged relationships with industrial and business lobbies and therefore ... were the "natural" party of corrupt governance' (Pujas and Rhodes, 1999, p. 695). Much corruption was associated with property deals, facilitated by massive post-war construction, yet these practices were not widely reported, and even when they were, they had limited national impact (Maisetti, 2018).

Another widespread form of corruption during this era, involving *all* parties, was a system of 'municipal racketeering' in which companies wanting to build offices or, notably, supermarkets and hypermarkets, had to pay the local authority a 'fee' (Denoël and Garrigues, 2014), through building or utility contracts negotiated using bogus 'consultancy' firms (*bureaux d'études*) organised by the parties. Creating fictitious jobs on local government payrolls to fund party activists was also commonplace (Knapp, 2002). Given the rising costs of 'political communication' from the 1960s, such practices became the 'systemic method of financing political activity' (Mény, 1996, p. 163). Illegal party financing developed because parties were unable to raise sufficient funds legally: de Gaulle's scornful attitude towards parties meant that they had no legal status in the constitution and had to form as 'associations', which limited their capacity to charge membership fees and accept donations. State funding only covered minimal campaign expenses. This problem was often discussed in parliament, but 29 proposals for regulation were unsuccessful (Doublet, 1997). It was not until the unprecedented experience of conflictual political cohabitation from 1986 to 1988 between the Socialist President François Mitterrand and Gaullist Prime Minister Jacques Chirac, that intensified party competition led to the legalisation of party funding.

The regulation of party finance 1988–1995

The trigger for calling time on this systematised illicit party funding was the revelation of two scandals, the *Carrefour du Developpement* and the Luchaire Affair (Garrigues, 2019), which involved allegations of illegal practices linked to party funding that implicated the socialists. Following an 'arrangement' between the president and the prime minister, two laws were hastily passed on 11 March 1988 (just before the legislative elections that ended cohabitation) to regulate 'financial transparency in public life'[1] and were followed by other laws passed in 1990, 1993 and 1995, as successive governments of left and right refined and updated the terms and conditions of party finance in a process designed to stop – or at least be seen to address – illicit practices (Clift and Fisher, 2005). The 1988 laws gave legal status to political parties and established a complex system of public funding to cover running costs and campaigns for presidential and legislative elections, based on the number of seats won.[2] Personal enrichment would be monitored by requiring declarations of assets at the beginning and end of electoral mandates, while parties had to start submitting annual accounts to a newly created Commission for the Financial Transparency of Public Life (CTFVP); sanctions for non-compliance involved up to a year of ineligibility for candidates and the loss of state funding for parties (Drysch, 1993) though these were rarely applied.

In 1990, following more scandals revealing massive illegal party financing by the socialists, new laws 'limiting electoral spending and clarifying the financing of political activities'[3] extended the 1988 rules to all elections and introduced various other changes, notably the legalisation of donations to parties (Clift & Fisher, 2005; Fay, 1995; Lascoumes, 2001) and a requirement for more detailed party accounts to be scrutinised by a new National Commission on Campaign Accounts and Political Finance (CNCCFP). Controversially, the legislation also included an amnesty for offences committed before 15 June 1989 relating to the financing of parties and campaigns, except personal enrichment. The governing socialists, who had always presented themselves as occupying the moral high ground (Mény, 1996), were much criticised for what was seen as a 'self-amnesty', even though it did not include parliamentarians.

A new prime minister, Pierre Bérégovoy, promised to 'urgently burst the abscess' of corruption, now acknowledged as extending beyond politics into economic affairs,[4] and in 1993, the Sapin law (after Michel Sapin, Minister of Economy and Finance) on 'the prevention of corruption and transparency in economic life'[5] introduced further regulation, extending beyond party finance into economic and financial affairs (Fay, 1995; Lascoumes, 2001). It created the Central Service for the Prevention of Corruption (SCPC), tasked from within the Ministry of Economics and Finance with three roles: to centralise information helping to prevent corruption, to answer requests for advice from political, administrative and judicial authorities and to train (mainly private) companies in corruption prevention. After much debate (Phélippeau, 2018), the legality of business donations was maintained but was conditional on the publication of donors' details. However, the publication for the first time in 1994 by the CNCCFP of candidates' accounts in the 1993 elections showed the extent of party funding by big business; this influenced the controversial decision to ban them in new laws passed in 1995,[6] which increased public funding and amended the regulation of wealth of politicians and dealings with public procurement (Fay, 1995; Lascoumes, 2001).

Despite all this legislation on party finance (or perhaps because of it), the number of corruption scandals involving politicians reached a crescendo in the 1990s, and the Mitterrand presidency ended in 1995 in a wave of sleaze (Collard, 1996). The regulation of campaign expenditure, especially for the presidential election where the political stakes were highest, did not deter candidates from seeking 'alternative' funding sources, and Edouard Balladur and Nicolas Sarkozy were both charged with various types of corruption in this context.[7] President Chirac was convicted after the end of his mandate for offences committed while he was mayor of Paris, as was his prime minister, Alain Juppé. Political corruption was therefore rife in high places, but many local politicians were also still disregarding the rules: embedded practices and attitudes still frequently trumped respect for the new legislative framework.

The emergence and recognition of anti-corruption

This eruption of political corruption as a public problem galvanised a new generation of journalists like Edwy Plénel and judges like Thierry Jean-Pierre and Renaud Van Ruymbeke into working together, as discussed earlier, to try to change the practices and mindsets that they saw as derived from archaic notions of privilege amongst political elites, who consider themselves to be above the law. Their mission was assisted by the 'global turn' in problematising corruption in the 1990s when concerns for 'good governance' developed (Dreyfus, 2022). International norms established by organisations like the World Bank, the OECD (Anti-bribery Convention, 1997), the Council of Europe (GRECO, 1999) and the UN (Convention Against Corruption, UNCAC 2004) were gradually accepted in France, and their regular reports started to impact on debates around corruption. Several Non-Governmental Organisations(NGOs) also emerged, driven by the search for 'transparency': Transparency International (TI), created in 1993 by a group of retired World Bank officials, opened a 'chapter' in France in 1995,[8] followed by two French associations – Sherpa in 2001[9] and Anticor in 2002.[10] These developments contributed to a gradual emancipation of the judiciary from political control (Dreyfus, 2022; Garraud, 1999; Roussel, 2002). Since 2007, presidential candidates have been pressed to take positions on corruption, and successive presidents have declared their commitment to 'an exemplary Republic' – yet the many charges of corruption brought against Sarkozy since the end of his mandate show that he, for one, did not apply this principle to himself.

'Transparency in Public Life' and the recognition of conflicts of interest

When François Hollande became president in 2012, he espoused a more ethical approach to politics, but in March 2013, the investigative news website *Médiapart* (created by Edwy Plénel) revealed that the socialist Budget Minister Jérôme Cahuzac had a secret bank account in Switzerland (Denoël and Garrigues, 2014). After repeated denials in the National Assembly (NA) and to the president's face, Cahuzac eventually admitted guilt and was charged with tax fraud and money laundering. He was sentenced on appeal in 2018 to four years in prison (two of them suspended) and banned from eligibility for public office for five years.[11] In response to this scandal, laws were passed in October 2013 relating to 'Transparency in Public Life',[12] extending the remit of earlier laws and establishing stronger institutions to monitor their application: the newly created High Authority for Transparency in Public Life (HATVP)[13] replaced the CTFVP established in 1988 and widely considered to be more of a 'political gesture' than an effective authority (Lascoumes, 2001). Significantly, these laws included a definition of conflict of interest as 'any situation of interference between a public interest and public or private interests that may influence, or appear to influence, the independent, impartial and objective exercise of a role'. A further law passed in December 2013 on 'the fight against tax fraud and serious financial crime'[14] created a public prosecutor for financial affairs and reorganised the legal framework for the prevention of tax fraud. It also, with a view to strengthening the role of civil society in the fight against corruption, enabled anti-corruption organisations such as TI-France and Anticor to seek accreditation (*agrément*), under certain conditions, enabling them to request investigations into suspected cases of corruption.[15] This would prove to be a significant tool for anti-corruption campaigners: TI-France received its first accreditation in 2014, Sherpa and Anticor in 2015.

In response to reports by the EU in 2014[16] and the HATVP in 2015,[17] another law was passed in December 2016 'relating to transparency, the prevention of corruption and the modernisation of economic life', known as Sapin II[18], because it built on the 1993 Sapin I anti-corruption law. Aiming to increase transparency in public decision-making processes and tackle economic fraud, it created the French Anti-Corruption Agency (AFA)[19] (replacing the SCPC created by Sapin I), under the joint authority of the ministries of Justice and the Budget, to monitor the implementation of internal anti-corruption programmes. It also increased protection for whistle-blowers and tackled more explicitly the thorny issue of lobbying, seen in France as contradicting its universalist commitment to the 'general interest' over private interests. However, attitudes were evolving: following a parliamentary report in 2008[20] arguing that expert opinion could make a valuable contribution to policymaking as long as lobbyists were ethically regulated, both chambers had created internal registers of lobbyists (*les représentants d'intérêts*) in 2009.[21] Sapin II now required all lobbyists to register their parliamentary activities, creating an online directory managed by the HATVP (Courty and Millet, 2018). Thus, by 2017, when Emmanuel Macron was elected, France arguably already boasted a robust legislative framework to tackle both political and economic corruption. Yet, the ongoing evidence of corruption and misconduct in high places and the use of (deliberate?) legal loopholes to find workarounds such as micro-parties for campaign funding (François and

Phélippeau, 2018) indicated the resilience of deep-seated attitudes. To what extent would President Macron, committed to throwing out the 'old world' to usher in the new, succeed in imposing his project for 'revolution' with regard to moralising public life?

Emmanuel Macron and the 'moralisation of public life'

Given the increasing political prominence of the issue of corruption, Macron could not fail, as candidate, to take a position. In his manifesto[22] (p. 12), he said that he wanted to put an end to privileges, 'arrangements', fraud and corruption and made several proposals for a major law 'moralising public life' (p. 27). During the campaign, allegations of corruption against the *Republicains* candidate Francois Fillon[23] – former prime minister under Nicolas Sarkozy and strong favourite to win the election – made the issue even more salient. Fillon was accused of having employed his wife, Penelope, 'fictitiously', as his parliamentary assistant; although it was commonplace and legal for parliamentarians and ministers to employ their relatives in such roles, it was claimed that Fillon's wife had not actually been doing the work she was paid for. In response to these allegations, Macron issued a decree soon after taking office, banning ministers and executive-level advisors from employing members of their immediate family as *collaborateurs*. He then oversaw the immediate (and somewhat hasty) preparation of two laws[24] to implement his manifesto pledges. These laws were initially promoted by the new Minister of Justice, François Bayrou, a long-standing centrist politician who withdrew his presidential candidacy to support Macron; a central plank of this agreement was a commitment to legislating on what Bayrou initially called 'the moralisation of public life'– intended as a *choc de confiance*, a 'boost of trust' in political life to strengthen the links between elected representatives and ordinary citizens. However, within just weeks, allegations surfaced that his party, the MoDEM, had used parliamentary assistants to MEPs, paid for by Brussels, to work for the party in France, and this precipitated his resignation, along with two other MoDEM ministers.

There was clearly some conceptual and practical confusion as to what exactly was meant by the 'moralisation of public life'; the terms 'moralisation' and 'probity' were not clearly defined, and the name of the laws changed several times during the parliamentary process before finally arriving at 'laws for trust in political life' (Lascoumes, 2017). These laws largely involved a tightening up or extension of existing regulations: they introduced modifications regarding the declaration of the president's assets (*patrimoine*) and added stricter verification of parliamentarians (including MEPs) with regard to tax declarations, tighter controls over consultancy activities and greater transparency regarding their business connections. Penalties were increased for non-compliance, and there was stricter regulation of conflicts between the public and private interests of parliamentarians. Rules designed to ensure greater transparency and control over party financing were modified, especially with reference to election campaigns, when party accounts would have to be controlled by the Court of Accounts (Blachèr, 2018).

But there were also innovations: first, following 'Penelopegate', the ban (by decree) on hiring close family members as *collaborateurs* was extended from ministers to parliamentarians and those in local leadership positions, with harsher penalties for failure to comply. Second, the 'parliamentary reserve' was abolished: this had been a sum of money made available, by informal convention and with no legal basis (Lemaire, 2017), to each deputy and senator to apply to spend as they chose, usually by contributing funds towards local projects or subsidising activities of local associations. This practice had been increasingly criticised for facilitating clientelism and was identified as problematic in the 2016 GRECO report evaluating the prevention of corruption in France;[25] parliamentarians who were also mayors could spend their whole allocation on their own municipality, and until 2014, no details of how this money was spent were publicly accessible.[26] Third, *une obligation de déport* required parliamentarians to refrain from voting on laws when they had declared an interest in that subject on the parliamentary registers of interests. Fourth, following many reports of abuse of the system, parliamentary expenses (at that time a monthly fixed payment) would only be refunded on the provision of receipts. Finally, the financing of election campaigns would be facilitated by creating a 'Bank for Democracy'.[27] Macron chose to highlight the importance of these laws by inviting the press to witness him signing them in his office – a very unusual practice. Whilst they were presented as a major step forward in strengthening ethics in political life, critics emphasised the weaknesses and limitations of these laws and doubted their capacity to create a real 'boost of trust' (Lascoumes, 2017; Untermaier-Kerléo, 2018).

In 2019, a law on the transformation of the civil service gave the HATVP the additional functions of the previous Commission of the Civil Service's Code of Conduct (created in 1990). The HATVP's opinion must now be sought by ministers, senior civil servants and ministerial advisors – but not by parliamentarians due to the separation of powers – wishing to work in the private sector, regarding any potential conflict of interest between their previous and new roles before accepting. The same process applies for those in the private sector wanting to work in the public sector.

How were these laws received? A 2020 GRECO report (para. 18, p. 8) recommended that the mechanisms in place concerning top executive roles should be extended to the president's office.[28] It made explicit reference to the case of Macron's chief security aide, Alexandre Benalla, who was filmed assaulting demonstrators on May Day in 2018 whilst officially just an observer. The unravelling by the media of what rapidly became the

'Benalla Affair' – and the president's curiously indulgent response to it – led ultimately to a political crisis in parliament, resulting in the abandoning of the government's important constitutional reform programme then under discussion. When Macron finally broke his long silence, it was to say that he 'refused to sacrifice top civil servants, ministers or advisors on the altar of populism', adding provocatively that, if anyone was responsible, it was him (Garrigues, 2019). The affair triggered enquiries by the National Assembly and the Senate; the latter's report[29] identified serious misconduct in the Elysée's handling of the affair and, controversially, referred to the public prosecutor's office certain very senior presidential advisers accused of trying to bury evidence; although their cases were not taken forward, Benalla was found guilty in September 2023 of 'voluntary violence'– a conviction confirmed on appeal in June 2024 – and he was also convicted of three other offences in cases that are still ongoing. This was the first political scandal of Macron's presidency, and it marked the end of the 'honeymoon' period that followed his election.

In 2021, the National Assembly conducted a *mission d'évaluation* of the 2017 laws on trust in political life. During the enquiry, deputies were asked to complete a questionnaire, and 50 individuals gave evidence, including leading representatives of the HATVP, AFA, Anticor and TI-France. The general thrust of responses was that, while the 2017 laws delivered some progress, there was still much room for improvement. Anticor's president, Elise Van Beneden, pointed to various loopholes in the new regulations, such as the use of *emplois croisés* – when parliamentarians, banned from hiring close members of their own families as assistants, simply made arrangements with colleagues to hire one another's family members.[30] TI-France's assessment also minimised progress and pointed to the negative impact of the 'affairs' involving the probity of ministers (discussed below) who were allowed to remain in office despite being formally under investigation.[31] The final report made 50 proposals for improvements in four key areas: the prevention of conflicts of interest, exemplarity and probity, transparency and political finance.[32] There were, however, no more relevant laws passed during the second presidency.

How seriously do politicians take these rules and codes of conduct?

Annual reports by the parliamentary commissioners for ethical standards clearly illustrate the reluctance of some parliamentarians to follow the rules, even those they have themselves approved (Wickberg and Phélippeau, 2022). The NA ethics commissioner has a mainly advisory role, with no powers to investigate or deliver sanctions, which in any case are more or less limited in practice to a public exposure of the breach – or 'name and shame'. Since its creation in 2014, the HATVP has assumed responsibility for monitoring declarations of assets and income at the beginning and end of mandates, required since 1988 for parliamentarians (and certain public officials). Since the 2013 laws, parliamentarians and ministers must also submit a separate declaration setting out their interests and activities. Both declarations are sent to the HATVP, which verifies the content and makes the declarations of assets, interests and activities publicly available: the interests and activities declaration is accessible online, while the assets and income declaration is only accessed physically in the relevant prefect's office. Citizens, journalists and anti-corruption associations can therefore act as a further control by signalling potential omissions or false declarations. Alerts from such sources increased from 2 in 2015 to 53 in 2020 (Wickberg and Phélippeau, 2022).

Parliamentarians

The HATVP sent, in 2017, information to newly elected deputies explaining what 'declarations of assets' are and how to organise them and offered further assistance by phone. Despite this, only 494 of the 577 members of the National Assembly made their declaration on time (within two months of their election), with others taking over a month longer. When control of the declarations of assets reveals missing information or the possibility of offences being committed, the HATVP informs the public prosecutor: in 2014, there were around 30 cases, 9 in 2017, 31 in 2018 (15 of which concerned a misappropriation of the allowance representing their expenses) and 10 in 2020. In 2020, a year that saw the election of 178 senators and of councillors in municipalities with over 20,000 inhabitants – plus a change of government – altogether, the HATVP received 17,113 declarations of assets and interests.[33] However, among the 2,457 verified declarations, only 52.9 per cent complied with the requests for full details, accuracy and honesty; for 21.9 per cent of the cases, supplementary declarations were requested and, in 24.6 per cent of the cases (concerning mainly those elected locally), reminders had to be sent. By contrast, in 2022, the year of the presidential and legislative elections and the appointment of a new government, almost all the members of the National Assembly[34] sent in their declarations on time (HATVP, 2022). However, only 33.2 per cent of 4,170 declarations were deemed accurate: the HATVP asked for modifications in 60.6 per cent of the cases, and 51 files were sent to the public prosecutor, 10 of which were due to a lack of probity. The HATVP's annual reports show that declarations concerning activities and interests are the most problematic. When the HATVP considers that a parliamentarian's activity or interests are incompatible with their parliamentary mandate, it can only take this information to the relevant chamber (because of the principle of the separation of powers).

The codes of conduct of the two chambers of parliament state that parliamentarians must abstain from taking part in legislative debates and/or voting on any subject that might bear any relation to personal or family interests. Since the 2017 laws, parliamentarians in both chambers must indicate on a public register of abstentions (*registres de déport*) every time they abstain from participating and their reasons for doing so. The registers posted online[35] show that few parliamentarians believe that they have a conflict of interest worthy of abstention, although women in the National Assembly declare a concern more frequently than men. However, abstentions are increasing over time, reaching 38 in 2023, suggesting a slow 'appropriation' of the rules. In the Senate, only five abstentions were registered between November 2020 and March 2023.

Ministers

Once appointed, ministers are no longer permitted to intervene in any way in fields related to their former activities or interests: decrees give the prime minister jurisdiction over these subjects. Some ministers fail to comply with the rules – such as Jean-Paul Delevoye, a politician with a long career in various elected and ministerial positions, who supported Macron in 2017. He was appointed in September 2017 as High Commissioner for the reform of the retirement system and, in September 2019, entered the government attached to the Ministry of Health. His declaration of interests was presented to the HATVP 10 days after the deadline and subsequently posted online, with both the HATVP and journalists finding a number of activities and interests missing. It transpired that he had 'forgotten' about 10 activities, two of which led to a conflict of interest. Faced with a media campaign and despite presenting a revised declaration, he resigned in December. Nevertheless, the HATVP, applying the law of October 2013, referred the case to the public prosecutor and, in October 2021, he was condemned to a four-month deferred sentence and a fine of €15,000.

Other problems arising may be solved by the president or the prime minister if they consider it necessary. In December 2023, the interim Minister for Health, Agnès Firmin Le Bodo, was put under formal investigation (*mise en examen*). Before being appointed to replace the minister who resigned, she was already his junior minister in charge of the territorial organisation of the medical professions so her declarations were already controlled by the HATVP. It turned out that, before entering the government, she had owned a pharmacy and had accepted gifts from a pharmaceutical firm to favour their products, even though such exchanges have been forbidden by law since 1993; she had also omitted to declare the gifts in her tax return. She was not appointed to Attal's new government in January 2024 but remained a deputy and was re-elected in the June 2024 elections.

Conflicts of interest

A striking case of 'lack of awareness' of potential conflicts of interest is that of the controversial Minister of Justice, Eric Dupond-Moretti, formerly a renowned criminal barrister. After his appointment in July 2020, he initiated disciplinary proceedings against certain *magistrats*[36] with whom he had serious disagreements while he was conducting the defence of Nicolas Sarkozy, on trial for various types of corruption. The anti-corruption organisation Anticor lodged a complaint against him in autumn 2020 for 'illegal taking of interest' (*prise illégale d'intérêts*), following which he was put under formal investigation in July 2021 and ordered to appear before the Court of Justice of the Republic (CJR) in October 2022, with a trial in November 2023. This was the first time that a minister in office had been tried in the CJR since its creation and the fact that he was Minister of Justice made it even more controversial. The public prosecutor called for a one-year deferred sentence; however, this was not upheld by the CJR, which decided that, even if the minister's decisions *did* constitute an illegal conflict of interests, he was not aware of this and was thus not guilty! This decision may be seen as purely political – which is generally the case for most sentences issued by the CJR – and very poorly grounded from a legal perspective.

Indeed, the CJR has been politically controversial since 1993 when it replaced, for ministers, the role of the High Court of Justice, which is empowered to judge the President of the Republic. Historically, France had rejected the idea that politicians should be tried by the justice system – seen as being either too autonomous or too easily manipulated – and the constitutions of the Fourth and Fifth Republics both endorsed the principle of allowing the judgement of ministers and parliamentarians by a political institution composed only of parliamentarians (Lascoumes, 2022). But given the strength of popular indignation over the contaminated blood scandal, demand for a more independent court grew, and the CJR was a compromise, including 12 parliamentarians (six from each chamber) and 3 members of the judiciary. It has been much criticised for three reasons: first, it reinforces the sense that political elites are given special treatment 'above the law'; second, its field of jurisdiction lacks clarity with regard to other courts and third, because of the clemency of sanctions imposed compared to criminal courts. Lascoumes (2022, pp. 27–28) has described this as 'a justice "between friends" (*de l'entre-soi*) transgressing democratic principles of equal treatment between citizens and the exemplarity of their leaders'. Despite many recommendations to reform or abolish the CJR, none has yet been taken forward; Macron's proposals for constitutional reform (discussed in Chapter 3) included its suppression, but this legislation was abandoned in the wake of the Benalla Affair. The CJR's lack of impartiality and the failure to introduce reform was also criticised in the compliance report by GRECO in April 2024, which recommended 'that, with regard to acts of corruption relating to the performance of their duties, government members be brought before a court that ensures total independence and impartiality, both real and perceived'.[37]

The case of Dupond-Moretti also reopened debates over whether ministers should be allowed to remain in office if they are formally placed under investigation or charged with an offence. An informal convention often referred to as the 'jurisprudence Balladur' had, in the 1990s, established the principle that ministers placed under formal investigation should resign. Macron endorsed this in relation to the case of François Fillon during the presidential campaign. However, when Dupond-Moretti was formally placed under investigation in July 2021, the president refused to ask him to resign, arguing that all ministers benefited from the 'presumption of innocence' unless found guilty.[38] He reportedly said in the *Conseil de Ministres*: 'The judiciary is an authority, not a power. I will not allow the justice system to become a power' (quoted in Trippenbach, 2022). He had appointed Dupond-Moretti because he admired his 'disruptive' profile, but the unions of *magistrats* saw his appointment as a declaration of war against them, symptomatic of a deeper ongoing struggle. After his re-election in 2022, Macron reappointed Dupond-Moretti and raised his government ranking (*rang protocolaire*) from tenth to fourth, despite strong negative messaging from the *magistrats*. Their unions even asked the President of the EU Commission for support in maintaining the independence of the judiciary (Deléan, 2022), but Macron resented what he saw as an attempt to control ministerial appointments and challenge his authority. Thus, old debates over the independence of the judiciary were revived. When Dupond-Moretti was cleared of misconduct by the CJR, Macron could claim that his position was vindicated, even if it was political – indeed, it was an assertion of presidential power. Moreover, when Gabriel Atal became prime minister in January 2024, his appointment of Rachida Dati as Minister of Culture disregarded the fact that she was under investigation for 'passive corruption' and 'concealment of abuse of power' (*recel d'abus de pouvoir*) in the Carlos Ghosh affair. Besides, four other ministers had also been maintained in post despite charges against them.

Advisors

Since October 2013, ministerial and presidential advisors must also submit declarations – of assets and of interests and activities – controlled by the HATVP (Kerléo, 2020). However, the General Secretary of the Presidency of the Republic, Alexis Kohler, the closest person to Macron within the presidential staff, was put under formal investigation in September 2022 for 'illegal taking of interest' (*prise illégale d'intérêts*) following a complaint by Anticor. These allegations were linked to his relatives' interests, his position as a senior civil servant and advisor to Macron at the Ministry of Finance between 2009 and 2016 and to his position in his relatives' private shipping company before the presidential election. As in the ministerial cases described above, the president defended the presumption of innocence unless proven guilty and reportedly even intervened on his behalf to prevent an investigation into his activities in 2019 (Orange, 2020). In March 2023, two further top civil servants were included in the investigation, which is still ongoing.

If, when they leave their posts, ministers and advisors want to create or work for a private company, they must seek the advice of the HATVP. Their recommendations, published online, provide a picture of the applicants' understanding of conflicts of interest: almost 90 per cent of the proposed projects are only authorised with strong reservations, and around 6 per cent are declared incompatible, demonstrating that the concept is not yet well understood. The fact that several former ministerial advisors wish to create consulting agencies illustrates their difficulty in separating public and private interests and past and future activities, the former activity enabling the next job (France and Vauchez, 2017).

Consultancy

This frontier between public and private interests is also blurred by a tendency for ministers to turn to international and national consultants for advice that would traditionally have been provided by civil servants. This trend started on a major scale during the Sarkozy presidency when the 'General Revision of Public Policies (GPPR)' was conducted by private consultants who often had social links with politicians in power (Gervais, 2012). Less used under Hollande, external consultancy became widespread after 2017, especially during the Covid pandemic. The very high costs charged by consultants, the conditions of the procurements and the questionable usefulness of their work led the Senate, in 2021, to launch an enquiry into the 'growing influence of private consultants on public policies'. The final report, issued in March 2022,[39] criticised the system, and the Senate initiated a bill that should have been sent to the National Assembly in 2024. Amongst other recommendations, senators proposed that a declaration of interests submitted by applicants to public procurement contracts should be controlled by the HATVP. The US consultancy firm McKinsey came under particular scrutiny due to its close connections with Macron, with leaked emails revealing that at least 10 McKinsey employees had worked on the *En Marche!* manifesto in 2017; since their contribution was not recorded in the campaign accounts, allegations of corruption were made in the media, but the CNCCFP, which validated them, said there had been no irregularities.

Lobbies

Efforts to develop codes of conduct have also been made in a bid to control the influence of the various lobbies; however, being documented on a public register is not necessarily an effective way to control lobbyists' activities. Preparing amendments to laws debated in parliament is common practice and has increased over the last decade. In December 2019, the president of the HATVP, Jean-Louis Nadal, advocated stronger control over the lobbies' interventions in parliament. For him, citizens have the right to know how a law is drawn up; and therefore, all meetings between parliamentarians and lobbyists should be made public, as in the United Kingdom. Up to now, this has not been the rule, and it is uncertain whether it would be effective, since the lobbies have more than one trick up their sleeve (Horel, 2018).

Nevertheless, the Senate Ethics Committee recently ordered a company, which had given fabricated arguments to justify its proposed amendments (which were adopted), to comply with the code of conduct set out in the Sapin 2 law – mainly those concerning probity. Of course, such a warning remains symbolic, as there is no sanction imposed by the law, but it shows that parliamentarians should be cautious and aware of influence based on lies. It also means, however, that information was forthcoming, attesting to the lobby's dishonest behaviour as a result of four NGOs contacting the Senate committee, which could then investigate and conclude as it did.

In this case, as in many others, the role played by civil society – NGOs, the media and whistle-blowers – was especially useful in exposing the lobbyists' well-hidden cases of misconduct. In this respect, it should be noted that the status and protection of whistle-blowers have improved since the Sapin 2 law, when their existence was first taken into consideration. However, the compulsory transposition of the European Directive of 2019 providing better protection for whistle-blowers, triggered opposition to the protection of various kinds of secrets (business, privacy), before its final adoption in 2022. At the end of 2023, the government's decision not to renew Anticor's accreditation to take civil action before the courts, as discussed earlier, could be seen as revenge on the part of the Minister for Justice, since his indictment emanated from Anticor. However, in response to a ruling by the Paris Administrative Tribunal on 4 September 2024, the outgoing prime minister, Gabriel Attal, finally renewed the accreditation for a further three years.

Parliamentary expenses

The 2017 laws replaced the tax-free fixed payment, the *Indemnité représentative de frais de mandat* (IRFM) – considered as a 'top-up' salary – by the *Avance sur frais de mandat* (AFM), which requires the submission of receipts to justify expenses and sets a maximum monthly amount.[40] Each chamber sets its own rules for managing this in consultation with its ethics advisors. The National Assembly put in place a system, in February 2018, with which the independent *déontologue*, Agnès Roblot-Troizier, had previously identified many issues of concern.[41] Moreover, only 120 out of 577 deputies' claims, chosen at random, are checked in any given year. There was considerable resistance from certain deputies, and the initial process was said to have been 'chaotic', with 82 per cent of the cases examined failing to comply with the new regulations. However, by 2019, things had improved (Lascoumes, 2022), and in April 2023, the National Assembly *déontologue's* annual report said that deputies were increasingly assimilating the rules, and only a few cases had required intervention.[42] Allowances not used are returned to the National Assembly, and in 2022, this amounted to over 10 million euros, suggesting that having to provide receipts for expenses was indeed an effective way of increasing integrity. The Senate chose to use a system of direct payment for expenses such as travel, controlled internally by the *Comité de déontologie* but seemingly more generous than its predecessor (Blachèr, 2018). Despite the two chambers' efforts to guard the monitoring of these expenses, several deputies such as Marion Lenne[43] post their expense claims online in the interests of transparency.

Conclusion

To what extent has President Macron brought about the 'moralisation of public life' that he promoted in 2017? There has clearly been no revolution, but there has been discernible evolution, in both practices and attitudes associated with political corruption. The 2017 laws have contributed to the ongoing process of incremental change initiated several decades ago, subjecting this 'public problem' to increasing scrutiny. The process has been driven both internally – largely prompted by scandals – and externally, in response to tightening international standards. The 1990s represented a turning point, in that excessive political corruption triggered a backlash at a time of global awakening to the need for greater transparency. Scandals of illicit party financing, now more tightly regulated, are no longer making media headlines. Yet, certain embedded attitudes remain resistant to legal or institutional regulation, such as the lingering notion of privilege and difficulty in grasping the concept of conflict of interest. Despite a legal framework reputed to be one of the most developed, parliament remains adept at exploiting 'loopholes' or finding workarounds.

High-profile cases of corruption, such as those involving former President Sarkozy (still an influential visitor to the Elysée), may lead to assumptions – both at home and abroad – that French politicians are all corrupt. But public opinion with regard to political corruption is complex (Lascoumes and Tomescu-Hatto, 2008): although opinion polls repeatedly testify that around 70 per cent of the French population perceive politicians to be corrupt, this does not stand out in comparison with other EU countries.[44] Besides, it is hard to establish any evidential basis for these opinions: research shows that there is greater trust in local politicians, even though they are not necessarily less corrupt, because they can deliver more tangible local benefits than national politicians (Lascoumes, 2010). Indeed, the word 'corruption' may be used as an umbrella term to convey discontent with – and disconnection from – political elites, without necessarily associating them with any specific allegations (Dreyfus, 2020): a disconnect that reached a crescendo during the Yellow Vests episode, discussed elsewhere in this volume. The lack of trust in the state's political institutions and administration, identified by successive governments as the major driver behind anti-corruption legislation, may therefore have less to do with perceived political corruption than with the system's inability to address popular expectations – and the repeated failure by political leaders to demonstrate the 'exemplarity' aspired to simply reinforce the gulf between them and ordinary citizens. It is striking that, despite all the laws and institutions established to prevent misconduct by political and administrative elites, most of them, like the very substantial work of the HATVP,[45] remain unknown by the great majority of citizens (Kerléo and Monnery, 2022). Instead of more political gestures, there is a case for raising popular awareness of the existing legal and institutional framework for preventing corruption: the moralisation of public life should be the concern of all citizens, not just the elite.

Notes

1 The Organic Law made changes to the electoral code: https://www.legifrance.gouv.fr/loda/id/LEGITEXT000006069060/, while the Ordinary Law introduced changes to political finance: https://www.legifrance.gouv.fr/jorf/id/JORFTEXT000000321646.
2 The principle of 'free candidacy', which allows for candidates to stand for election independently of a political party means that a distinction is made between general party finance and election campaign funding. Whilst in practice, there is usually a close connection between candidates and their parties, this principle underpins a system of financing, which refunds candidates rather than parties but allows parties to make donations to candidates for their campaigns. Candidates can seek non-party funding for their campaigns and commonly create *comités de soutien* for this purpose (Farouz-Chopin, 2003). This has also given rise to the creation of 'micro-parties' as a way of getting around funding caps (François & Phélippeau, 2018).
3 https://www.legifrance.gouv.fr/loda/id/JORFTEXT000000341734
4 https://www.vie-publique.fr/discours/196642-declaration-de-politique-generale-de-m-pierre-beregovoy-premier-minist
5 https://www.legifrance.gouv.fr/loda/id/JORFTEXT000000711604
6 https://www.legifrance.gouv.fr/loda/id/LEGITEXT000005617565 and https://www.legifrance.gouv.fr/jorf/id/JORFTEXT000000165391
7 Complex legal proceedings against Sarkozy are still ongoing.
8 https://transparency-france.org/
9 https://www.asso-sherpa-20-ans.org/

10 https://www.anticor.org/
11 Few politicians given prison sentences actually go to prison but serve their sentence wearing an electronic bracelet, as was the case for Cahuzac, who stood as a candidate in the legislative elections of 2024 and came fourth with 14.56 per cent of the vote.
12 https://www.legifrance.gouv.fr/loda/id/JORFTEXT000028056315
13 https://www.hatvp.fr/en
14 https://www.legifrance.gouv.fr/jorf/id/JORFTEXT000028278976
15 https://www.justice.gouv.fr/sites/default/files/migrations/textes/art_pix/JUSD1402112C.pdf
16 https://eur-lex.europa.eu/legal-content/EN/TXT/HTML/?amp;from=IT&uri=CELEX%3A52014DC0038
17 https://www.hatvp.fr/wordpress/wp-content/uploads/2020/12/Rapport-activite-2015-HATVP.pdf
18 https://www.legifrance.gouv.fr/jorf/id/JORFTEXT000033558528
19 https://www.agence-francaise-anticorruption.gouv.fr/en
20 https://www.assemblee-nationale.fr/13/rap-info/i0613.asp
21 Around the same time, in both chambers of parliament, codes of conduct ('deontological codes') were adopted, and Commissioners for Ethical Standards were appointed to monitor compliance: since 2011, there is an external advisor (*déontologue*) for the National Assembly (NA) and for the Senate, since 2009, an internal team of senators forms an ethics committee called the *Comité de déontologie*. The constitutional principle of the separation of executive and legislative powers means that each chamber retains control over its own rules and working practices.
22 https://promesses.fr/programme-emmanuel-macron-election-presidentielle-2017/web-story/
23 The case against Fillon opened in February 2020; both he and his wife were convicted, but Fillon later successfully secured an appeal on grounds of procedural irregularity, which has not yet taken place.
24 Organic Laws require submission to the Constitutional Council, but Ordinary Laws do not; hence, the need for two laws. Organic Law: https://www.legifrance.gouv.fr/jorf/id/JORFTEXT000035567936; Ordinary Law: https://www.legifrance.gouv.fr/jorf/id/JORFTEXT000035567974. Decrees can be issued when relating to the domain of executive power (i.e. here, government ministers and advisors), but a separate law is required for parliamentary matters.
25 https://rm.coe.int/CoERMPublicCommonSearchServices/DisplayDCTMContent?documentId=09000016806c5dfc
26 When a successful campaign by a determined citizen-activist, Hervé Lebreton, president of the association 'For a Direct Democracy', had resulted in agreement – written into the October 2013 laws on transparency in public life – to publish the details as from January 2014, it showed that, for 2016, the amount available to the National Assembly was 81.86 million euros (roughly 130,000 per deputy) and 56 million for the Senate (roughly 153,000 per senator). National Assembly records: https://www.assemblee-nationale.fr/budget/reserve_parlementaire.asp. Senate records: https://data.senat.fr/dotation-daction-parlementaire/.
27 Although this measure was included in the final law, it was abandoned in 2018.
28 https://rm.coe.int/cinquieme-cycle-d-evaluation-prevention-de-la-corruption-et-promotion-/16809969fd
29 https://www.senat.fr/rap/r18-324-1/r18-324-1_mono.html
30 https://www.capital.fr/economie-politique/sur-la-moralisation-de-la-vie-politique-le-bilan-du-quinquennat-macron-est-tres-decevant-1419943

31 https://transparency-france.org/2022/02/17/transparence-de-la-vie-publique-lutte-contre-la-corruption-quel-bilan-du-quinquennat-2017-2022-2/
32 https://www2.assemblee-nationale.fr/15/commissions-permanentes/commission-des-lois/missions-d-information/mission-d-evaluation-des-lois-du-15-septembre-2017-pour-la-confiance-dans-la-vie-politique/(block)/81468
33 https://www.hatvp.fr/rapports_activite/rapport_2020/pdf/HATVP_RA2020.pdf. Annual Reports by the HATVP can be consulted at https://www.hatvp.fr/.
34 Some 99.8 per cent sent their declarations of assets on time, and 98.3 per cent their declaration of interests and activities.
35 For the National Assembly: Assemblée-nationale.fr>dyn>deports; for the Senate: https://data.senat.fr/registre-des-deports/
36 Unlike English magistrates, who are lay volunteers, French *magistrats* are paid members of the professional judiciary.
37 GRECO, *Fifth Evaluation Round, Second Compliance Report, France*, 10 April 2024, pp. 13–14.
38 This position was consistent with that taken in his first speech to the Congress in July 2017 when he called for an end to incessant attempts to create scandals by ignoring this principle.
39 https://www.senat.fr/rap/r21-578-1/r21-578-1.html
40 https://www.leclubdesjuristes.com/politique/tout-comprendre-sur-laugmentation-des-frais-de-mandat-des-deputes-et-senateurs-4788/
41 A confidential report for the parliament news channel LCP (*La Chaîne Parlementaire*) in December 2017, including these remarks, was widely reported in the press, for example in *Le Monde*: https://www.lemonde.fr/politique/article/2017/12/06/la-deontologue-de-l-assemblee-critique-la-reforme-des-frais-de-mandat-des-deputes_5225417_823448.html
42 https://www2.assemblee-nationale.fr/static/deontologue/Rapport_deontologue-2022.pdf
43 https://www.marionlenne.fr/category/afm/
44 Eurobarometer2023 https://europa.eu/eurobarometer/surveys/detail/2968
45 The president of the HATVP, Didier Migaud, was appointed Minister of Justice in the government of Michel Barnier on 21 September 2024, significantly ranked in second place behind the prime minister. Migaud, a former socialist deputy, was the only representative of the left in that government (though he left the socialist party in 2010 when he became president of the Cour des Comptes).

References

Blachèr, P. (2018) 'Moraliser la politique par la loi ? Observations sur les lois "confiance dans la vie politique"', *Revue du droit public*, 2, p. 339.
Clift, B. and Fisher, J. (2005) 'Party finance reform as constitutional engineering? The effectiveness and unintended consequences of Party Finance Reform in France and Britain', *French Politics*, 3, pp. 234–257.
Collard, S. (1996) *Confrères et ennemis sous la fin de l'empire Mitterrand: A bibliographical survey of the end of the Mitterrand presidency*. Birmingham: Aston University, Institute for the Study of Language and Society, Working paper in European politics and society No. 10.
Courty, G. and Millet, M. (2018) 'Moraliser au nom de la transparence. Genèse et usages de l'encadrement institutionnel du lobbying en France (2004–2017)', *Revue Française d'Administration Publique*, 165, pp. 17–31.
Deléan, M. (2022) 'Affaire Dupond-Moretti: les syndicats de magistrats en appellent à la Commission européenne', *Médiapart*, 29 April.

Denoël, Y. and Garrigues, J. (2014) *Histoire secrète de la corruption*. Paris: Nouveau Monde.
Denoël, Y. and Meltz, R. (2023) *Mensonges d'état: une autre histoire de la Republique*. Paris: Nouveau Monde.
Doublet, Y.-M. (1997) *Le financement de la vie politique*. Paris: PUF.
Dreyfus, F. (2020) 'Les citoyens face à la corruption: acteurs moraux ou tolérants ?', *Revue Française d'Administration Publique*, 175, pp. 707–720.
Dreyfus, F. (2022) *Sociologie de la corruption*. Paris: La Découverte (Repères).
Drysch, T. (1993) 'The new French system of political finance', in Gunlicks, A. (ed.) *Campaign and party finance in North America and Western Europe*. New York: Routledge, pp. 155–177.
Dupin, E. (2001) 'La Corruption politique: un mal français', *French Politics, Culture and Society*, 19(1), pp. 42–48.
Evans, J. (2002) 'Political corruption in France', in Bull, J.P. and Newell, J. (eds) *Corruption in contemporary politics*. London: Palgrave Macmillan, pp. 79–92.
Farouz-Chopin, F. (2003) *La lutte contre la corruption*. Perpignan: Presses universitaires de Perpignan.
Fay, C. (1995) 'Political sleaze in France: forms and issues', *Parliamentary Affairs*, 48(4), pp. 663–676.
France, P. and Vauchez, A. (2017) *Sphère publique, intérêts privés. Enquête sur un grand brouillage*. Paris: Les Presses de Sciences Po.
François, A. and Phélippeau, E. (2018) 'Party funding in France', in Mendilow, J. and Phélippeau, E. (eds) *Handbook of political party funding*. Cheltenham: Edward Elgar, pp. 271–290.
Garraud, P. (1999) 'Les nouveaux juges du politique en France', *Critique Internationale*, 3, pp. 125–139.
Garrigues, J. (2019) *Les scandales de la République de Panama à l'affaire Benalla*. Paris: Nouveau Monde.
Gervais, J. (2012) 'Les sommets très privés de l'État. Le "Club des acteurs de la modernisation" et l'hybridation des élites', *Actes de la Recherche en Sciences Sociales*, 194(4), pp. 4–21.
Girling, J. (1997) *Corruption, capitalism and democracy*. London: Routledge.
HATVP (Haute autorité pour la transparence de la vie publique) (2022) *Rapport d'activité*. Paris: La Documentation française.
Horel, S. (2018) *Lobbytomie. Comment les lobbies empoisonnent nos vies et la démocratie*. Paris: La Découverte.
Jeanneney, J.-N. (1984) *L'argent caché. Milieux d'affaires et pouvoirs politiques dans la France du XXe siècle*. Paris: Le Seuil.
Johnston, M. (2005) *Syndromes of corruption: wealth, power and democracy*. Cambridge: Cambridge University Press.
Kerléo, J.-F. (2020) 'L'émergence d'un statut déontologique des conseillers ministériels', *Gestion et Finances Publiques*, 1(1), pp. 63–69.
Kerléo, J.-F. and Monnery, B. (2022) 'Probité et transparence au Parlement: bilan et leçons d'une décennie de changements autour de la HATVP', *Revue Française d'Administration Publique*, 184(4), pp. 1097–1114.
Knapp, A. (2002) 'France: never a golden age', in Webb, P., Farrell, D. and Holliday, I. (eds) *Political parties in advanced industrial democracies*. Oxford: Oxford University Press, pp. 107–150.
Lascoumes, P. (2001) 'Change and resistance in the fight against corruption in France', *French Politics, Culture and Society*, 19(1), pp. 49–60.
Lascoumes, P. (2010) 'Prologue', in Lascoumes, P. (ed.) *Favoritisme et corruption à la française. Petits arrangements avec la probité*. Paris: Presses de Sciences Po, pp. 21–65.

Lascoumes. P. (2017) 'La probité à petits pas', laviedesidees.fr, 12 December. https://laviedesidees.fr/La-probite-a-petits-pas

Lascoumes, P. (2022) *L'économie morale des élites dirigeantes*. Paris: Presses de Sciences Po.

Lascoumes, P. and Tomescu-Hatto, O. (2008) 'French ambiguities in understandings of corruption: Concurrent definitions', *Perspectives on European Politics and Society*, 9(1), pp. 24–38.

Lemaire, W. (2017) 'La réserve parlementaire sous l'angle du droit constitutionnel', *Jus Politicum*, 17. https://juspoliticum.com/article/La-reserve-parlementaire-sous-l-angle-du-droit-constitutionnel-1143.html

Maisetti, N. (2018) 'Dénoncer l'économie politique de la production urbaine durant les Trente Glorieuses', in Mattina, C., Monier, F., Dard, O. and Engels, J. (eds) *Dénoncer la corruption: chevaliers blancs, pamphlétaires et promoteurs de la transparence à l'époque contemporaine*. Paris: Demopolis, pp. 128–135.

Marchetti, D. (2002) 'Le journalisme d'investigation', in Garraud, P. and Briquet, J.-L. (eds) *Juger la politique: entreprises et entrepreneurs critiques de la politique*. Rennes: Presses universitaires de Rennes, pp. 167–191.

Mattina, C. and Monier, F. (2018) 'Introduction', in Mattina, C., Monier, F., Dard, O. and Engels, J. (eds) *Dénoncer la corruption: chevaliers blancs, pamphlétaires et promoteurs de la transparence à l'époque contemporaine*. Paris: Demopolis, pp. 13–31.

Mény, Y. (1992) *La corruption de la République*. Paris: Fayard.

Mény, Y. (1996) 'Corruption French style', in Little, W. and Posada-Carbó, E. (eds) *Political Corruption in Europe and Latin America*. London: Palgrave Macmillan, pp. 159–172.

Mény, Y. (2013) 'From confusion of interests to conflicts of interests', *Pouvoirs*, 147(4), pp. 5–15. Available at: https://www.cairn-int.info/article-E_POUV_147_0005--from-confusion-of-interests-to.htm

Orange, M. (2020) 'How Macron's chief of staff was cleared over probe after president intervened', *Médiapart*, 25 June.

Phélippeau, A. (2018) *L'Argent de la politique*. Paris: Presses de Sciences Po.

Pujas, V. and Rhodes, M. (1999) 'A clash of cultures? Corruption and the ethics of administration in Western Europe', *Parliamentary Affairs*, 52(4), pp. 688–702.

Roussel, V. (2002) *Affaires de juges. Les magistrats dans les scandales politiques en France*. Paris: La Découverte.

Trippenbach, I. (2022) 'Avec l'affaire Dupond-Moretti, l'Elysée a changé de doctrine', *Le Monde*, 3 October.

Untermaier-Kerléo, E. (2018) 'Les lois pour la confiance dans la vie politique: toujours plus de déontologie mais pas de "choc de confiance"' *Droit administratif*, 1, p. 17.

Wickberg, S. and Phélippeau, E., (2022) 'From prohibition to regulation: towards the institutionalisation of parliamentary ethics in France', *Public Integrity*, 1–12. https://doi.org/10.1080/10999922.2022.2079296

5
POLITICAL PARTIES AFTER THE 2017 EARTHQUAKE

Elodie Fabre

Abstract

This chapter examines the recent evolution of the French party system, from the formation of En Marche! to the 2022 elections. It assesses the extent to which the 2017 elections changed the party system and how the other parties, from the radical right Rassemblement National (RN) to the old parties of the left and right, responded to the emergence of a centrist pole. The Macron presidency presented several challenges to the old mainstream parties: Macron's increasingly centre-right positioning weakened the right as he had weakened the left in 2017. Meanwhile, the RN continued its normalisation strategy, and the radical left confirmed its dominance on the left. The 2022 elections strengthened the tripolar and polarised nature of the party system, but the centrist pole came out weaker than in 2017, which leads to questions about Macron's legacy and the strength of the centre after he is forced into retirement at the end of his second term.

Introduction

The 2017 elections marked a remarkable moment in the history of the Fifth Republic: for the first time since 1962, neither of the two main traditional parties of the centre right and centre left received enough votes to qualify for the second round of the presidential election. The victories of Emmanuel Macron and his party LaREM (*La République en Marche*, Republic on the Move) in presidential and parliamentary elections seemed to confirm Macron's assessment that the old left–right cleavage had become irrelevant and that citizens were ready for new politics that cared more about managerial performance.[1] The 2022 election was a test of this diagnosis of the French electorate.

The party system has been evolving for several decades, and as in other European countries, the left–right cleavage has been undermined by the emergence of a new values cleavage and issues relating to globalisation. These long-term trends have transformed party competition: the rise of the *Front National* (National Front, FN) combined concerns with identity and immigration with the disengagement of part of the working class from the parties that traditionally represented it. At the same time, the rhetoric of the Socialist Party (PS, *Parti Socialiste*) on taxing the wealthy and strengthening the state often seemed at odds with its actions once in government, which included privatisations under Jospin's government (1997–2002) and liberal labour-market reforms under Hollande's presidency (2012–2017). On the right, the Gaullist party's embrace of the themes of national identity and immigration pushed the party closer to the FN on identity issues without presenting a strong contrast to the PS in economic terms (Gougou and Persico, 2017).

In this context, this chapter focuses on the period 2017–2022. It asks how Macron won the presidency in 2017 without an established party, how he ended the established pattern of alternation between left and right, how the party system evolved after 2017, how other parties responded to the rise of the centre, and how these trends affected the 2022 elections.

Macron's road to power

To explain the rise of Macron and LaREM in 2016–2017, we must understand the development of his personal ambitions and the formation of the party to support his candidacy. The traditional view of party formation is that parties are created to represent interests and respond to the mobilisation of a social cleavage. Here, we are faced with a much more personal project – initiated by a young technocrat – which developed into a 'proper' party after the 2017 legislative elections.

From personal ambitions to a movement

Macron's personal ambitions crystallised whilst an advisor to President Hollande (Pedder, 2018). In his mid-30s, he grew increasingly frustrated by what he saw as the President's and his left-wing majority's inability to reform France. As Economy Minister (2014–2016), he worked towards reforming the labour market and breaking what he saw as unhelpful monopolies (such as regulated professions). He built a profile as a reformist minister not tied by party allegiances and willing to reach across the aisle to achieve policy outcomes. As he faced obstacles, including the reluctance of many PS deputies to support these reforms, he became an increasingly outspoken advocate for supply-side economic reforms and an opponent of those who view France as 'unreformable'. The idea that generations of politicians have failed to reform France because of entrenched partisan interests and corporatism became a central pillar of Macron's campaign in 2017.

Although not embedded in any of the established parties, Macron was not without resources. As a senior civil servant and government minister, he had built a network of like-minded civil servants who also wanted political and social change. When a senior civil servant in the Ministry of Finance, he was hand-picked to sit as *rapporteur* on the Attali Commission on 'releasing French growth' in 2007, which helped him develop networks in the business and political communities. Having prematurely left the civil service, he spent four years as an investment banker for Rothschild & Co, further strengthening these networks (Offerlé, 2019).

En Marche! (EM) was created in April 2016 – while Macron was still a minister – and was able to grow quickly due to the astute use of social media and Twitter (now X) to secure support and donations. EM was a strange object: organised more like a non-profit than a political party, it was promoted as a new, flexible type of organisation in which members (*marcheurs*, which roughly translates as hikers) would have leeway to organise locally. *Marcheurs* could join simply by registering on the website. Tens of thousands of *marcheurs* joined rapidly. They and *Les Jeunes avec Macron* (JAM), which had close links with Stéphane Séjourné, Macron's political adviser (Tronchet, 2018),[2] were critical to the success of *La Grande Marche* (the Big Walk), a campaign to 'diagnose the country', which saw thousands of *marcheurs* knock on doors and talk with people to discuss what they thought did and did not work in France. This 'consultation' was used to build a 'progressivist programme' (Schwalisz, 2018), which helped to launch Macron's candidacy in November 2016, contributing to the image of a bottom-up, popular movement. However, behind this image was a very centralised organisation that controlled messaging, policy development and campaign strategy. The job of ordinary *marcheurs* was to relay this message locally and mobilise the electorate.

Macron was initially reluctant to present a full manifesto (Cos, 2019), but over the campaign, several elements emerged. His programme mixed typical centre-right liberal economic policies (labour-market flexibility, supply-side policies to encourage investment and tight fiscal rules), welfare reforms designed to add obligations to rights but also to extend some welfare rights, pro-EU rhetoric, socially liberal ideas on personal liberties and gender relations, and security proposals that included more police and prison places (*En Marche!*, 2017). This made Macron and EM centre-right on the economy and security with a moderate social-liberal slant (Gougou and Persico, 2017).

An additional pillar of his campaign message was that the left–right cleavage was obsolete and that political parties were still defending what he described as 'tribal' policies linked to outdated ideological frames. This argument resonated with mainstream voters thanks to what Perottino and Guasti (2020) called Macron's 'technocratic populist appeal'. On the one hand, he used populist tropes: the PS and LR were outdated and no longer worked in the best interest of the people but only in their party's interest and had failed France by not reforming it. On the other hand, Macron argued that he would 'get things done' thanks to his experience as a senior civil servant and his knowledge of the private sector. His rejection of left and right labels was at the service of a supposedly anti-ideological openness to 'what works'. This technocratic argument helped to attract professional and centrist voters who would otherwise reject an outright populist project (Perottino and Guasti, 2020). Meanwhile, Macron's rejection of the FN, which he presented as a party whose values were outside the Republican canon, contributed to his image as an anti-populist politician (Hamdaoui, 2021).

The campaign, which combined traditional meetings and social media, helped Macron to present himself as a new face in French politics; active supporters, enthused by a new political project, promoted the candidate locally. After Macron came first in the initial round (Figure 5.1), it became clear that he would be the next president: although Marine Le Pen (FN) had started her strategy of 'normalisation', she did not seem capable of winning. Macron easily won in the second round with 66 per cent of the vote.

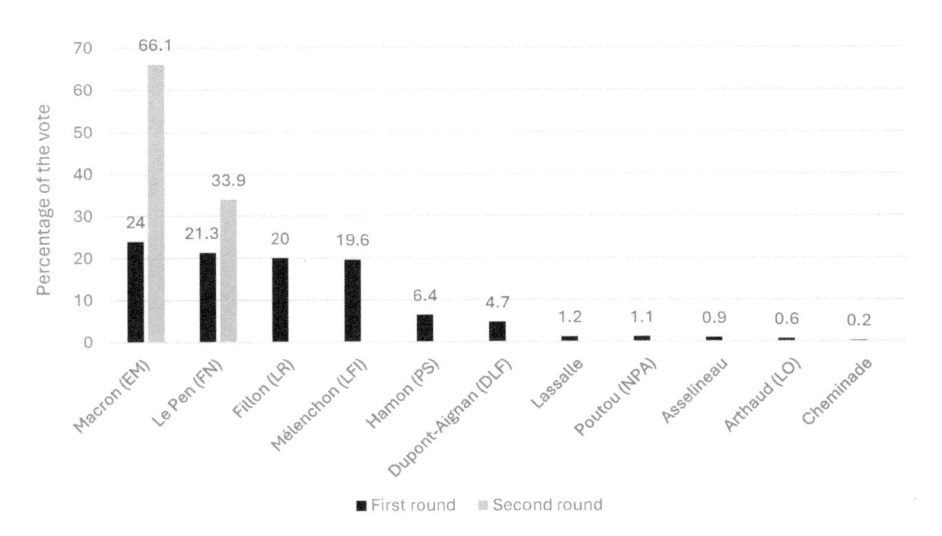

FIGURE 5.1   Results of 2017 French presidential elections

Source: Ministère de l'Intérieur (2017).

Building a parliamentary majority

Since Macron's ability to enact his programme depended on winning a majority in the elections to the National Assembly following the presidential election, he and his team started to organise *En Marche!* for these elections at the start of 2017, turning the movement into a fully fledged party after the presidential election. In early January 2017, EM set up a central candidate selection committee and called for interested individuals to send in their CVs. The party was keen to attract a wide variety of candidates and meet France's strict 50/50 parliamentary gender quota. They received 19,000 applications and fielded 529 candidates (Rouban, 2017a). Some 55 per cent of them had never held elective office, and just over 50 per cent were women (Rouban, 2017b).

Since 2002, legislative elections have followed the presidential election by about a month. The party of the newly elected president has always won a majority since this change to the electoral calendar (Dupoirier and Sauger, 2010). This 'bandwagon' effect also worked for Macron's new party (Figure 5.2). The strategy of including right-of-centre politicians in the first government announced in May 2017 under Prime Minister Edouard Philippe (LR) also allowed LaREM to attract Fillon voters (Evans and Ivaldi, 2017).

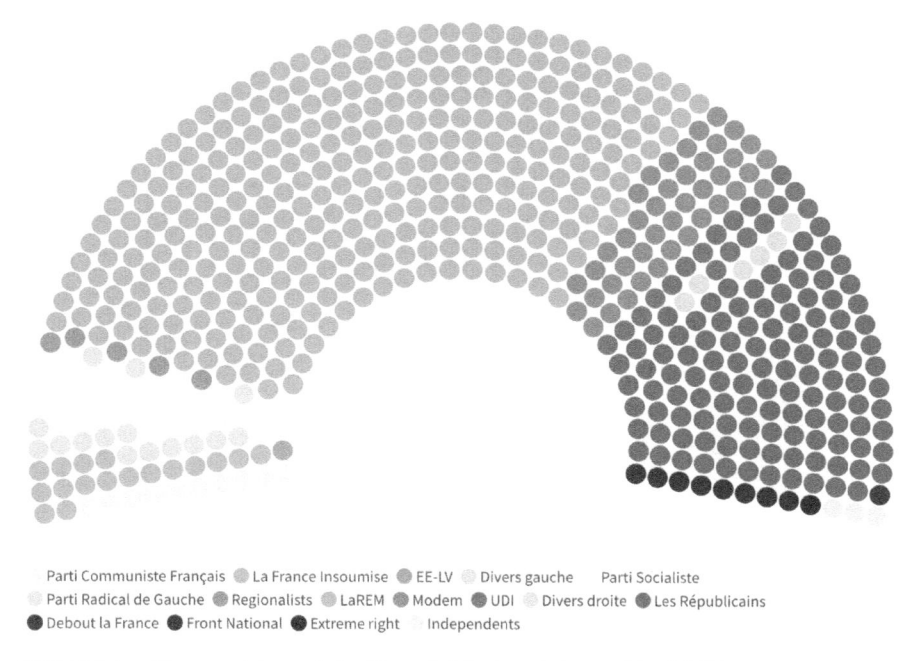

Parti Communiste Français ● La France Insoumise ● EE-LV ● Divers gauche ● Parti Socialiste
Parti Radical de Gauche ● Regionalists ● LaREM ● Modem ● UDI ● Divers droite ● Les Républicains
● Debout la France ● Front National ● Extreme right ● Independents

FIGURE 5.2 Composition of the French National Assembly, 2017

Note: After the June 2017 elections, Macron's parliamentary majority included LaREM and the MoDem (308 out of 577 seats).

The FN failed to confirm their presidential success, winning only eight seats. The previously dominant parties of the centre right (LR, *Les Républicains*) and centre left (PS) saw the size of their parliamentary groups shrink.

Elgie (2018) argues that the composition of the new government, which included a prime minister and two ministers from LR, two ministers from the PS, six from LaREM, one from the *Mouvement Démocrate* (MoDem), two from the centre-left Radical Left Party and 10 'unaffiliated' ministers, combined with the variety of origins of LaREM MPs and the parliamentary support for the Philippe government in its investiture vote show that LaREM is a real centrist *marais* party, a combination of moderate left and moderate right. Within a year, Macron won the presidential election and a parliamentary majority, weakening the traditional parties. He then needed to strengthen this new party to prepare for the next elections (European, local and regional elections) and secure his re-election in 2022.

A new political party in the making

A key to Macron's success was the agility and skills of his core team of former civil servants and people working in tech, who provided the technical and political skills necessary to run a good campaign, harnessing social media and professional and business networks to seek donations. The rapid expansion of the membership of EM was key to his strategy to project an image of political renewal. Once EM was created, the number of *marcheurs* quickly rose to reach 400,000 at the time of the 2017 elections. Joining was easy: it only required providing one's email address on the website. EM did not define itself as a political party, and uniquely, members did not have to pay a fee but instead had the option of making a donation.

After Macron's election victory, *En Marche!* was renamed *La République en Marche*, signalling a change from a campaign movement to a party prepared for government. In September 2017, the party adopted statutes to regulate party life and prepare for future election cycles. The form of organisation chosen by the leadership was somewhat unusual and limited membership participation. The party leader, called a 'general delegate', was elected by the party's Council, of which members represented only 25 per cent. Party members could declare their interest in sitting on the Council and were chosen by sortition (randomly selected by lot), which prevented any form of direct representation of or delegation from the membership (Delaurens, 2018). For many EM founders, the PS, with its internal elections using proportional representation and its local barons, was the example not to follow. Consequently, a very centralised party was created, in which members could promote the party locally but have very little influence centrally. In contrast, the party leadership and the executive had the freedom to set strategic priorities and select candidates for elections.

This lack of membership influence led to disappointment among many members who had hoped for a more participatory party (Fretel, 2019). The high level of membership engagement in the campaign and the party's reliance on the campaign activities of relatively autonomous local committees had led members to expect more influence in the party. The party reached over 200,000 members in 2017 (LaREM later claimed 400,000 members), but only 70,000 voted in the new statutes, which suggests a high level of disengagement of online members (Fabre, 2024).

The centralisation of the party also manifested itself in the expectations placed on its new deputies. The massive influx of LaREM MPs resulted in the youngest Assembly since 1981 – the average age of LaREM deputies was 46 – and the most feminised ever: 46.8 per cent of LaREM deputies were women, more than any other parliamentary group (Rouban, 2017b). However, not all LaREM MPs were novices; 68 had previous association with the PS, 20 with the UDI and 10 with LR (Elgie, 2018). The party and the government expected absolute loyalty, and any rebellion was punished by exclusion from the majority's parliamentary group. Compliance was made easier, at least at the start, by the inexperience of many LaREM deputies, who got engaged in politics to support Macron's agenda and were therefore keen to support the government (Rouban, 2017b).

LaREM went from a weakly structured movement to a centralised political party within a year. During that time, Macron was elected president, and his party won a parliamentary majority. These are exceptional results, unseen in France since 1974. However, LaREM's victory cannot simply be attributed to its popularity and programme. They also benefited from a combination of structural and contextual circumstances that lowered what would otherwise have been high entry barriers for an 'outsider' candidate.

Breaking the PS–LR duopoly

The institutional structure of French politics is not typically beneficial to small or new parties. In 2017, the political context was, however, more favourable to candidates from outside the main parties. Macron benefited from the deep unpopularity of the outgoing president, the scandals that plagued Fillon's (LR) campaign, and the fragmentation and polarisation of the party system that left a large space at the centre.

The two-round majoritarian system used for presidential elections tends to disadvantage small parties without a viable candidate, turning them into 'satellite parties' of larger parties (Elgie, 1997). New candidates and parties may also struggle to raise campaign funds. Established parties with parliamentary representation benefit from significant amounts of public funding, calculated on the basis of past election results and their number of deputies. In 2017, public funding represented half the budgets of the PS and UMP

(Union for a Popular Movement – *Union pour un Mouvement Populaire*) and over a third of that of the RN (Fabre, 2024, p. 71). New parties need to find resources elsewhere, and political donations are restricted: individual donors can only give up to €7,500 per year to parties and up to €4,600 to candidates in a single election, so a new party or candidate requires many small donations. In this context, Macron's connections with business helped his fundraising efforts.

Macron, however, also benefited from a favourable political environment, with a president whose extreme unpopularity prevented him from standing for re-election. Hollande started his presidency with a fairly left-wing economic programme and the goal of being a 'normal' president, but his tumultuous personal life, his fondness for jokes that made him lack gravitas and the divisions in the governing majority, along with his failure to deliver on his promise to increase tax on the wealthy, turned him into a particularly unpopular president (Cole, 2019). Despite his left-wing platform, he chose two prime ministers from the centrist end of the party: neither Jean-Marc Ayrault nor his successor, Manuel Valls, had internal majority support. His promotion of the social liberal Macron as Economy Minister was also perceived as a betrayal by the left of the party. This resulted in a series of crises, with left-wing deputies (*frondeurs* or rebels) voting against several government bills and amplifying party divisions (Sawicki, 2017). Hollande ended his term with very low ratings (10–15 per cent voting intentions in November 2016) and decided, late in the day, not to run again (Martigny, 2017). The 2017 election would not, therefore, have an incumbent candidate, although incumbency had not helped incumbent President Nicolas Sarkozy in 2012.

Both the PS and LR had adopted open primaries to select their candidates, and the process led to them choosing individuals who were more radical than their electorates and struggled to reach beyond the group that selected them. On the left, the 'citizens' primary' pitted former Prime Minister Manuel Valls against former Ministers Arnaud Montebourg and Benoit Hamon. Valls, a centrist, was the continuity candidate, and Montebourg was seen as a leader of the *frondeurs*, while Hamon, also close to the *frondeurs*, appeared as a 'new man' against these two well-established figures. Hamon won with proposals such as a universal basic income, humanitarian visas for refugees and a focus on the country's ecological transition. While on the left of the party, he distinguished himself from Jean-Luc Mélenchon and his radical-left party LFI (*La France Insoumise*, France Unbowed) by rejecting their Euroscepticism. The issue for Hamon was that he would face stiff competition from Mélenchon, a much more experienced campaigner not afraid to court controversies and use populist tropes (Marlière, 2019).

On the right, seven people vied for the candidacy. The three main contenders were former President Sarkozy and former Prime Ministers François Fillon (Sarkozy's only PM) and Alain Juppé (PM under Chirac in the mid-1990s). Sarkozy proposed to continue what he had been doing between 2007 and 2012, with a programme that was economically liberal and right-wing on issues such as security and immigration. Fillon's economic programme was more Thatcherite, while his social positions were typically conservative (Teinturier, 2017). Finally, Juppé was the most centrist candidate – notably on social issues – and appealed more to non-LR voters than Fillon. After Sarkozy's surprise defeat in the first round, Fillon won the second round against Juppé, reflecting the conservative position of party members. However, Fillon's campaign was soon marred with allegations of financial impropriety and corruption in the *Penelopegate* affair, after which he went from frontrunner to loser, having reneged on his promise to resign when he was placed under formal investigation for fraud and influence-peddling in March 2017 (Piar, 2017).

The selection of Hamon and Fillon created more space at the centre (see Figure 5.3). Fillon's political–financial scandals weakened a candidate who could have thwarted Macron's victory. Even with these controversies, Fillon was only 1.3 percentage points behind Marine Le Pen in the first round (Figure 5.1). For Macron, a second round against Fillon would have been more difficult than against Le Pen.

The 2017 election also showed that the party system had changed in the sense that the main competition happened between a strong centre

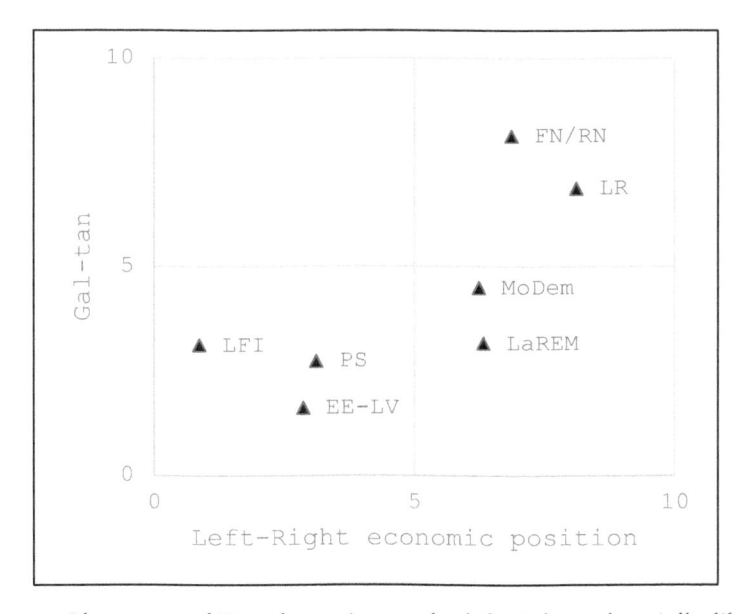

FIGURE 5.3 Placement of French parties on the left–right and socially liberal vs conservative (gal–tan) axes, 2019

Source: Data from Chapel Hill Expert Survey 2019 (Jolly et al., 2022).

and parties at the extremes (Murray, 2021). A weakened PS left room for Mélenchon and LFI to take the leadership of the left; the divisions of the right allowed the FN to present itself as the main opposition to Macron and *En Marche!*.

French parties between 2017 and 2022

Elections between 2017 and 2022 showed a marked contrast between, on the one hand, statewide (presidential, legislative and European Parliament) elections dominated by LaREM and the RN[3] and, on the other, sub-state elections (municipal, departmental and regional), where LR and the PS, older parties with incumbents, were able to maintain their positions. The party system remained fragmented and, despite good intermediary results for the PS and LR, the overall impression was that the 2022 presidential election was going to be a replay of the 2017 contest.

Intermediary elections between 2017 and 2022

Intermediary elections started with those to the European Parliament (EP) in 2019, followed by municipal elections in 2020 and concluding with regional and departmental elections in 2021. Local and regional elections were affected by Covid. Turnout in municipal elections dropped 20 points between 2014 and 2020 (Haute, Kelbel, Briatte and Sandri, 2021). The 2021 regional and departmental elections were postponed from March to June; however, parties were not able to campaign as they normally would (with public meetings, for instance), and turnout also declined (−24 points in the second round) compared to the previous election (Gougou, 2023).

Like the 2017 elections, the 2019 EP elections benefited the RN and LaREM (Figure 5.4). Unlike in 2017, the RN came first – one point ahead of LaREM – and they each won 23 seats. On the left, the Greens of *Europe Ecologie-Les Verts* (EE-LV), who have often done well in EP elections, came third, well ahead of the PS and LFI. On the right, the list of LR and its centre-right allies only received 8.5 per cent of the vote.

In contrast, LaREM and the RN did quite poorly in the sub-state elections. LaREM did badly in the first round of the 2020 municipal elections, even in large cities where its electorate is typically concentrated. Instead, a 'green wave' swept large cities. In the second round, lists merged to help achieve majorities, and LaREM chose to merge with LR lists against the coalition of EE–LV and the left. In the end, LaREM failed to win any city or town council that it did not already hold thanks to defections from the old mainstream parties. Meanwhile, the RN maintained itself in the towns it already governed but made no significant gains. It won two small towns and

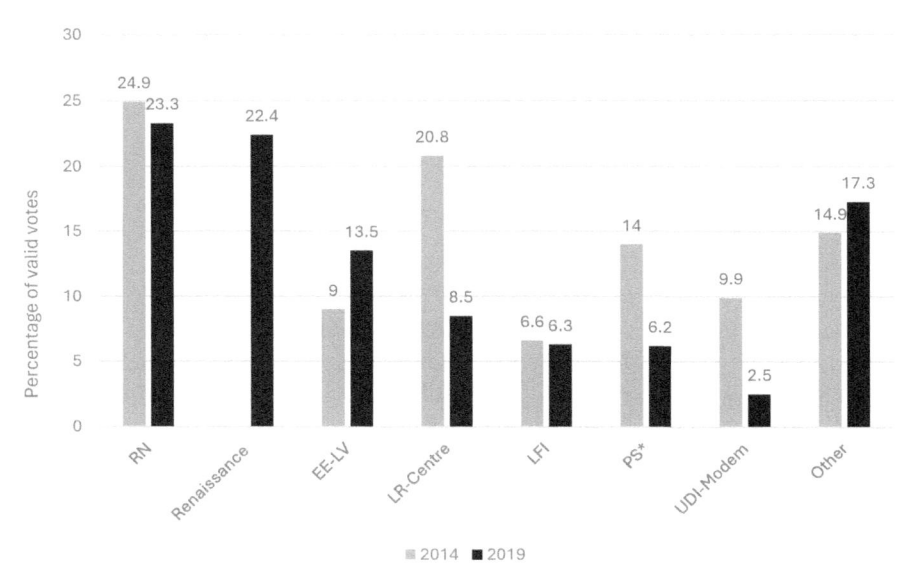

FIGURE 5.4 Results of the 2014 and 2019 elections to the European Parliament

Note: * Union de la Gauche in 2014.
Source: Ministère de l'Intérieur (2019).

one city with a population exceeding 100,000 – Perpignan – where it already had a deputy (see Evans and Ivaldi, 2020 for an analysis of the RN vote).

Following their good score in EP elections, the Greens performed well in the municipal elections. They retained Grenoble and gained several large cities, including Lyon, Bordeaux and Strasbourg, thanks to wide left-wing coalitions. LFI, on the other hand, wounded by the EP elections, did not take a prominent role in these elections and only presented lists under its own name in a few towns and cities, including Paris. LFI candidates mainly joined 'citizens' lists as well as some lists led by other left-wing parties.

Meanwhile, the PS retained its urban strongholds, such as Paris, Clermont-Ferrand, Montpellier, Lille and Rennes, thanks to electoral pacts with other left-wing and green parties. LR incumbents supported by LaREM won in Toulouse, Nice and Calais, among others. LR lost Bordeaux and Marseille but extended its dominance in medium-sized cities and towns. These were good results for the old parties, who thus maintained their presence at the local level.

The last elections before the 2022 presidential election were the regional and departmental ones. Regional elections did not change any governing majority, and departmental elections changed little. Out of 95 departmental councils, the right won two councils and holds 65, the left lost two and holds 27 and the centre lost one, holding three councils (LaREM won in 2 councils). LR held its majority in six regional councils, the centre-right UDI in one and the PS in five, with nationalists retaining Corsica (Figure 5.5).

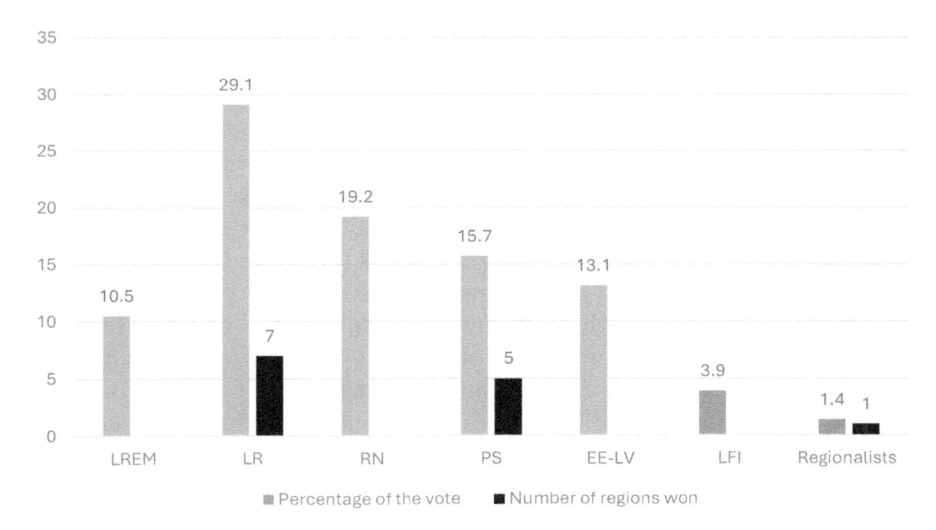

FIGURE 5.5 Results of the 2021 regional elections (metropolitan France and Corsica only)

Source: Gougou (2023).

Overall, French regional elections tend to follow the pattern of second-order elections (Reif and Schmitt, 1980): the main opposition does better than the governing party, with smaller parties performing better than in the previous parliamentary elections. However, Gougou (2023) notes that these good results for LR and the PS are more the result of incumbency and personalised campaigns than of nationwide momentum for these two parties.

Overall, the old parties managed to maintain their positions in sub-state elections, where incumbency and links between citizens and local elites seem to matter more than in national elections. This importance of incumbency on election results was not a good omen for the PS and LR, who could not rely on similar levels of incumbency at the statewide level, where LaREM and the RN dominated.

The centre: LaREM and its allies

Macron and his party had five years to consolidate, develop the party, implement their programme and prepare for the 2022 presidential election. Macron had argued that he could liberalise France's economy and 'at the same time' create a protective state. This 'at the same time' had become a key symbol of his approach and of his rejection of the left–right cleavage.

Over time, his economic reforms (reduction of the wealth tax, flat tax of 30 per cent on income from capital, reduction of housing benefits, cap on compensation for unfair dismissal) and his often-dismissive attitude towards people who struggle economically, all cemented his image of the 'President of the rich' (Knapp, 2022, pp. 502–503; Raymond, 2022). Working-class people and those living in rural or peri-urban areas felt abandoned. Their resentment culminated in the Yellow Vests movement, triggered by the introduction of a new carbon tax in November 2018. The movement turned into a broader protest against elites and against Macron himself and continued well into 2019, with roadblocks, roundabout pickets and violent clashes between demonstrators and the police (Dolez, Douillet, Fretel and Lefebvre, 2022; Schön-Quinlivan, 2019). The president and the government responded with a nationwide consultation (The Great Debate) that failed to meet demands for more participative forms of democracy (Gourgues and Mazeaud, 2022). Time to focus on their political agenda was once again interrupted by the Covid-19 pandemic. This, however, provided Macron with an opportunity to demonstrate his ability to use the strength of the state to protect citizens.

LaREM had adopted new statutes that turned it into a 'proper' political party, with defined roles for the different faces of the party (membership, executive, general delegate, etc.) and formal processes to take decisions and select candidates. The leaders elected in 2017 (Christophe Castaner) and 2018 (Stanislas Guérini) remained overshadowed by Macron's informal leadership, and the party was poorly institutionalised (Houard-Vial and Sauger, 2020). This weakness – and the party's lack of local roots – were particularly visible during the local and regional elections.

The parliamentary majority went beyond LaREM to include the MoDem as its main ally. With its leader, François Bayrou, they took a key supporting role during Macron's first term (Elgie, 2018). The majority also included the group *Agir*, formed by former LR deputies who rejected their party's outright opposition to Macron and favoured a more 'constructive' approach. When LR rejected their strategy, these deputies joined the majority and their president, Frank Riester, was appointed government minister in 2018. These partners became particularly useful when LaREM lost its majority as a single party after a series of defections, mostly on the left of the majority, in 2020. Finally, Edouard Philippe created his own party, *Horizons*, after he left the government in 2021, adding another centre-right party to the centrist pole. After attracting PS members and politicians early on, LaREM in power attracted more on the right, especially centre-right politicians unhappy with LR's move to the right discussed below.

As the 2022 elections loomed, Macron and LaREM could argue that protests and Covid prevented them from implementing parts of the programme that they had been elected to implement and that they needed a second term to fulfil their promises. However, the poor results in local and regional elections led some to wonder whether the party would be able to win a parliamentary majority (Bendjaballah and Sauger, 2022).

The right

Fillon's defeat in the presidential election led to a period of instability for *Les Républicains*, which nonetheless became the main opposition group in the National Assembly with 112 seats. LR was the successor of the UMP – created in 2002 after Jean-Marie Le Pen got into the second round of the presidential election – and was designed to form a single party uniting different traditions of the right (centre-right liberals, Gaullists, Thatcherite liberals, conservatives; Haegel, 2013). However, the success of LaREM tested this coalition to its limits. Disagreements quickly emerged over how to deal with a government including several leading LR members. The leadership quickly decided to exclude them from the party, while those LR deputies who wanted a 'constructive' approach towards Macron and his PM left and joined the parliamentary majority in 2018. As LR looked inward and focused on internal divisions, the RN and Unbowed France were increasingly seen as the main opposition to LaREM, even though they had fewer deputies (Schön-Quinlivan, 2019).

After the 2017 elections, Laurent Wauquiez, president of the Auvergne-Rhône-Alpes region, became party leader. This election confirmed the party's conservative and nationalist turn, combining harsh law-and-order policies, low tax, criticism of the social welfare model, and a defence of 'traditional' France and the peripheries against diverse cities (Bernard, 2018). This same shift under Sarkozy's presidency had alienated the party's moderate electorate (Haegel, 2013), and Wauquiez's election led to the defection of several centrists, including the presidents of the regional councils of Ile-de-France (Valérie Pécresse) and Hauts-de-France (Xavier Bertrand), two politicians with presidential ambitions. Faced with the prospect of some of its remaining voters turning towards the RN, the post-Gaullist right increasingly hardened its position on identity and immigration. After disastrous EP elections in 2019, Wauquiez resigned, and party members chose the leader of the parliamentary party, Christian Jacob, to replace him. Jacob steered the party in a more centrist direction, much to the chagrin of the party's right, who found him too soft. It was in this context of tensions between a consensus-seeking leader and an identitarian and conservative wing that the party selected its presidential candidate via an internal primary, ending its experiment with open primaries. Party members were very divided, with Ciotti receiving 25.6 per cent of the votes, Pécresse 25 per cent, Barnier 23.9 per cent and Bertrand 22.6 per cent in the first round.[4] All the eliminated candidates called for members to vote for Pécresse, the more centrist candidate, against Ciotti, who had refused to ask voters to support Macron against Le Pen in 2017. Pécresse won with 61 per cent of the vote, with a campaign that increasingly appealed to the party's right on social issues, although tensions over the party's direction remained.

The 2017–2022 period demonstrated the failure of the UMP/LR project of a hegemonic party from the centre-right to the conservative right. Macron was able to entice some of its more moderate members and allies, leaving the rump LR divided between anti-Macron centrists and a right wing trying to attract RN voters.

The left

The five years of Macron's presidency were a particularly difficult time for the Socialist Party, previously the dominant party of the left. During this period, the radical-left party LFI and the Greens of EE–LV were on the ascendancy. After Hamon was selected as the PS candidate in 2017, the PS started to splinter. Some of the most prominent centrists defected to Macron, including former PM Manuel Valls and Gérard Collomb, the mayor of Lyon. In 2018, Olivier Faure was elected First Secretary of the PS. He represented some continuity with the Hollande era but, as someone who had opposed Hollande and Valls on key reforms that had divided the majority, he was also compatible with the left of the party. Ahead of the EP elections, the PS formed a common list with *Place Publique* (PP, Public Square), a new pro-EU centre-left movement, with PP writer and filmmaker Raphaël Glucksmann leading the list. The list came sixth, with only 6.2 per cent. Despite this new electoral setback, the PS had good results in municipal, local and regional elections, providing the party with important financial and symbolic resources.

During this period, LFI and its controversial leader, Jean-Luc Mélenchon, had a complicated time. With only 18 deputies, it was a weak force in the National Assembly, though the vocal and sometimes hostile style of its deputies made them highly visible. LFI adopted a 'gaseous' form of organisation, with online networks of sympathisers and self-organised local groups (Alexandre, Bristielle and Chazel, 2021); however, the lack of formal local organisation or strong articulation between the local and national levels made it difficult to mobilise voters on the ground during sub-national elections. This form of organisation also led to accusations of centralisation and lack of internal democracy (Houard-Vial and Sauger, 2020). As a result of a lack of local roots and unstable alliances, LFI failed to win any significant city or region, although it still saw itself as a leader of the left and wanted to unite the left behind Mélenchon's candidacy in 2022.

In contrast, the Greens, who had withdrawn their candidate in favour of Hamon in 2017, had a series of good election results between 2017 and 2022: they came third behind the RN and LaREM in the European elections and did well in municipal elections, with new EE–LV mayors in a number of large cities. As a result, the party warmed to the idea of having their own presidential candidate.

In this context, a primary among all the parties of the left was becoming increasingly difficult, despite pressures from the 'People's Primary' movement (Bendjaballah and Sauger, 2022). As in 2016–2017, Mélenchon refused the principle of a primary and saw himself as the natural leader of the left. However, Mélenchon's divisive personality and some of the party's more extreme positions, notably on foreign policy, made it difficult for other parties to rally behind his candidacy. The Greens decided to present their own candidate, Yannick Jadot; the PS's internal primary selected Paris Mayor Anne Hidalgo; and the Communist Party chose to stand for the first time since 2007 with a charismatic candidate, Fabien Roussel. The left therefore went into the presidential election highly divided.

The Rassemblement National

The aftermath of the 2017 elections was somewhat complicated for the FN. On the one hand, Marine Le Pen had reached the second round of the presidential election and increased the FN vote compared to 2002. On the other, the party only won six seats in the National Assembly, too few to form a parliamentary group. As a result, the party lacked opportunities to shape how the Assembly worked, and its MPs had limited speaking opportunities.

Le Pen's image and the RN's policies seemed to become more mainstream for two main reasons. Firstly, Le Pen and the party's cadres continued their efforts of normalisation (or 'de-demonisation') and were careful to avoid inflammatory and discriminatory language without, however, changing the policies themselves (Mondon, 2015). Le Pen renamed the *Front National* the *Rassemblement National* in 2018 to signal change and to consolidate the normalisation process that she had led since she took over the party in 2011 (Mondon, 2015; Paxton and Peace, 2021). Changing the party's name was designed to suggest that a page was turned in the history of the party. In terms of image, the word *rassemblement* (rally) is softer and less aggressive than the word *front*. It also brings images of togetherness and unity and evoked older names of the Gaullist party, which used this term. Meanwhile, the party kept its nativist and populist message while moving further to the left on socio-economic issues, arguing notably for a more protective state for French citizens (Ivaldi, 2015).

Secondly, other parties increasingly adopted the party's language on issues such as immigration, national identity and security (Marlière, 2022). Even LaREM, which started with Macron's claim that it wanted to fight the RN and oppose populism, was not exempt: its education ministers led debates on 'wokism' in universities and, in a televised debate, Interior Minister Gérard Darmanin criticised Marine Le Pen for being 'too soft on Islam'.

Despite disappointing results in intermediary elections, the RN felt confident that, in presidential elections, they could rely on an electorate that had voted for Le Pen in previous elections and possibly on new voters, as the party's issues were dominating political debates. All predictions suggested that the 2022 elections would be a re-run of the 2017 election.

The 2022 elections: Macron's strange victory

The 2022 election showed signs of both continuity and change: predictions of a re-run of the 2017 election were accurate, suggesting a consolidation of the new party system. However, the failure of *Renaissance* (LaREM's new name) to win a majority opened a period of parliamentary instability and questioned the strength of the changes at the centre. In this context, Macron became the first president to win re-election since 2002 and the first president with a minority government since François Mitterrand (between 1988 and 1993 and after his re-election).

The 2022 presidential and legislative elections

Over 70 per cent of the first-round vote was concentrated on three candidates who were in the top four in 2017, which suggests continuity with 2017 (see Figure 5.6). With 27 per cent in the first round, Macron increased his vote share by three points. Le Pen's score increased by one percentage point and Mélenchon's by two. The second round showed a progression of the radical right, with Le Pen receiving over 40 per cent of the vote (compared

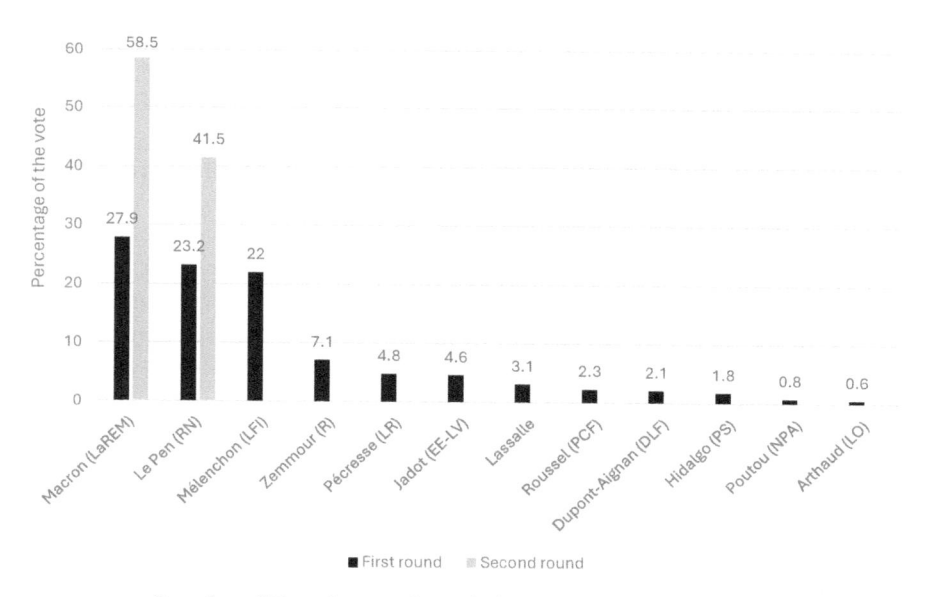

FIGURE 5.6 Results of French presidential elections 2022
Source: Ministère de l'Intérieur.

to 34 per cent in 2017 and her father's 18 per cent in 2002). This election also confirmed the decline of the traditional parties and the tripolar and polarised nature of the party system.

The presidential elections confirmed the strength of the centre/centre-right pole in French politics. Macron entered the campaign late because of a busy international agenda (Durovic, 2023). Cultivating his image of a president 'above the fray' – but also fuelling his elitist image – he refused to participate in debates with other candidates before the first round. His campaign focused on full employment, with compulsory work programmes for the long-term unemployed, and an increase in the retirement age to 65, a measure unlikely to appeal to working-class voters, who usually start to work at a younger age than voters with a professional background. His vote grew in more traditionally conservative parts of the electorate that used to vote LR, a shift probably helped by Sarkozy's support for Macron, while it declined among socialist supporters (Knapp, 2022).

This led to the collapse of the mainstream right, much as the rise of EM had contributed to the collapse of the PS in 2017. Valérie Pécresse's campaign found it difficult to find a space between Macron on the centre-right and Le Pen and Zemmour on her right, and she accused Macron of stealing her party's policies. At the same time, some in her party, most notably Ciotti, pushed her to adopt positions closer to the radical right in the hope of attracting RN voters. She was particularly criticised for using the term 'great replacement', an expression used by far-right conspiracy theorists, in a campaign meeting. Ultimately, the defection of centrist and older voters led to the collapse of the LR vote (Knapp, 2022), and Pécresse had to ask her supporters for financial support because, with less than 5 per cent of the vote, her campaign expenses were not refunded by the state.

The RN campaign focused on presenting Le Pen as a potential president, concentrating less on immigration and more on the economy, including protectionist measures to support French businesses and measures to support lower earners, a key pillar of her electorate (Lorimer and Herman, 2023). Le Pen's normalisation strategy opened some space to the right of the RN and Eric Zemmour, a controversial columnist for *Le Figaro*, occupied that space with his new party *Reconquête* (Lorimer and Herman, 2023). Whereas there were significant similarities between the two candidates in terms of nativism and populism, Zemmour's programme was more economically liberal and reactionary, and he did not shy away from courting controversy, much like Le Pen's father in his time. Le Pen criticised Zemmour's 'endearing yet futile nostalgia for the 1960s' and extreme positions (de Boissieu, 2022), but Zemmour's extremism contributed to making her look moderate. This election emphasised the strength of the radical right as well as its diverse constituencies: whereas Le Pen's electorate is traditionally working- and lower-middle class, Zemmour's is more bourgeois – an electorate that had previously refrained from voting for the RN (Knapp, 2022).

The presidential election also confirmed Mélenchon's leadership on the left. For his third presidential election, Mélenchon came very close to qualifying for the second round with 22 per cent of the vote. His electorate is relatively young and cross-class, perhaps surprisingly so, given Mélenchon's understanding of politics in class terms (Fourquet, 2022). As Mélenchon opposed the Islamophobia of other parties and supported immigrants, he also scored well among Muslims and other minorities (Knapp, 2022). In this context, both Jadot (Greens) and Hildalgo (PS) failed to reach the 5 per cent threshold that would get their election expenses refunded.

The parliamentary elections that followed failed to reproduce the pattern observed since 2002: LaREM – in an alliance called *Ensemble!* (Together!) with the MoDem and former Prime Minister Edouard Philippe's new party, Horizons – failed to win a majority in the National Assembly (Figure 5.7) though they won a 'relative' majority, with more seats combined than any other party. The RN won a record 89 seats and the left, which learned from its past mistakes and adopted a pre-election coalition strategy, won a combined 131 seats as the Nupes (New Popular Green and Social Union, *Nouvelle Union Populaire Ecologique et Sociale*). The new Assembly is therefore a reflection of the presidential election, with three main poles, dominated by *Renaissance* at the centre, the RN on the right and LFI on the left. This polarisation makes it harder for the government to find allies in the National Assembly.

French politics after the 2022 elections: parliamentary instability and planning for the post-Macron era

Although Macron won a second mandate, the task of governing with only a relative majority is difficult, as the government needs to find deputies outside its coalition to support its legislation. The appointment of Elisabeth Borne as Prime Minister in May 2022 was designed to signal a social turn in the presidency, but the new PM was not charismatic, and the government continued with Macron's programme of reforms, reaching out to *Les Républicains* rather than to the left for compromise. Borne regularly used the controversial Article 49.3 of the constitution to pass bills, including the pensions reform that raised the retirement age to 64 after weeks of demonstrations.[5]

Constrained by a two-term limit, Macron is concerned with his legacy. He changed the Prime Minister in January 2024, promoting 34-year-old Gabriel Attal, the popular education minister and an early member of *En Marche!*. Attal was closer to the president – and a more charismatic and political prime minister than his predecessor – and his policy orientations made him more compatible with the right, which he needed to pass

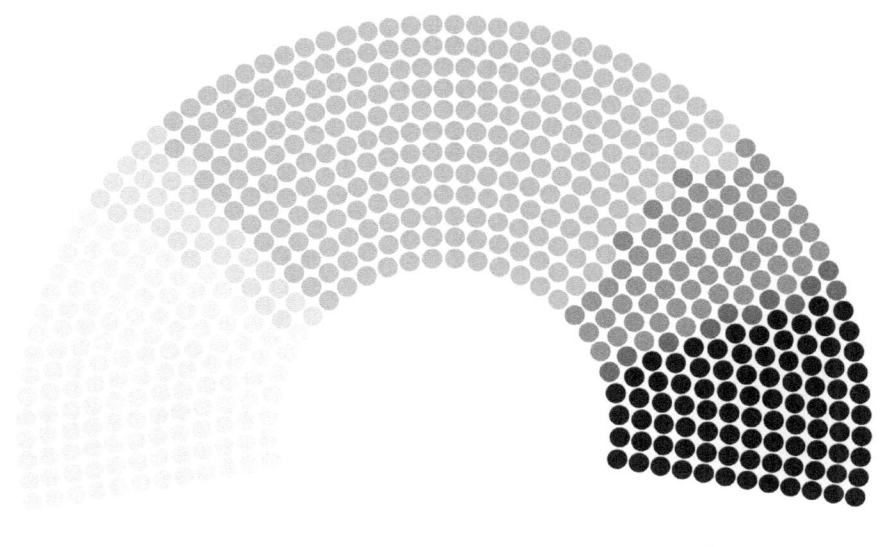

Composition of the French National Assembly

Party	2022	Seat change
Nupes	131	0
Divers gauche	23	0
Regionalist	10	0
Ensemble	245	0
UDI	3	0
Divers centre	4	0
Les Républicains	61	0
Divers droite	11	0
Rassemblement National	89	0

FIGURE 5.7 Composition of the French National Assembly, 2022

legislation. At the same time, Macron was also focusing on less partisan social issues (abortion and euthanasia) to cement his more socially liberal legacy. The two-term limit also means that the centre/centre-right will need a new candidate in 2027. If Attal may see himself as a natural candidate, the exercise of power may have tarnished his aura by then. Meanwhile, former Prime Minister Edouard Philippe is biding his time, as are long-term ex-LR Ministers Gérald Darmanin and Bruno Le Maire. LR will try to regain the ground lost in 2022, but its frequent, if critical, support for government legislation means that its margin for manoeuvre is limited.

Macron's forced retirement may also be an opportunity for other parties. Marine Le Pen left the presidency of the RN to 28-year-old member of the European Parliament Jordan Bardella, whose list was well ahead of that of *Renaissance* in polls before the 2024 EP elections (around 30 vs 17 per cent for *Renaissance*). She focuses on leading the RN's large parliamentary party and presenting herself and her party as respectable president and government in waiting. Zemmour's party, *Reconquête*, chose Le Pen's niece Marion Maréchal as its leading candidate in EP elections but trailed far behind in opinion polls (around 5 per cent), suggesting that the competition from this side might be limited.

However successful the left's union strategy may have been in 2022, its solidity is often tested. LFI deputies often flout parliamentary rules of speech and decorum – to the exasperation of fellow Nupes deputies – and some of their positions have been at odds with Nupes' common positions. Support for European integration was a dividing line between Eurosceptic LFI on the one hand and pro-EU PS and Greens on the other – and the Nupes could not reach an agreement on a joint list for the EP elections. The PS joined forces with *Place Publique* again and LFI and the Greens are presenting their own lists. Unlike in previous elections, the PS–PP list was ahead of the LFI and Green lists in opinion polls. The issue of candidacies for the 2027 presidential election renewed tensions within this bloc. Mélenchon will be 76 in 2027, and it is unclear whether he will stand again – although there is no clear successor. Since October 2023, events in the Middle East have deepened the fractures between members of the Nupes; Mélenchon's strong and outspoken support for the Palestinian cause has also alienated many.

Overall, the 2022 elections strengthened the tripartite division of the party system, leading to the return of a minority government after a long period without either a minority government or cohabitation. Macron is the first French president affected by the two-term limit and the issue of his succession will become increasingly important for *Renaissance* and for the other parties, who may hope that the party's structural weaknesses mean that it was just a one-man operation that will not survive its founder's terms in office.

Conclusion

The 2017 election started a reconfiguration of the party system and the 2022 election confirmed the central position of LaREM/*Renaissance*, which has caused significant problems for the socialists and LR. Macron had presented his programme as an anti-populist project, arguing that governing 'beyond left and right' and delivering on electoral promises would address the rise of populism and weaken the RN. The 2022 elections showed that he failed in this endeavour. He managed to side-line the traditional left–right cleavage parties, which, he had argued, were well past their sell-by date; however, the party system is now highly polarised, with *Renaissance* at the centre-right and its main competitors at the extremes on the left and right. French parties have traditionally been rather weak and unloved (Sauger, 2017). LaREM/*Renaissance* has struggled to retain its early members and build local roots that would help to embed the party locally. In this sense, Macron also failed in his attempt to rebuild trust between citizens and their parties. Macron's second term started with a long wave of protests against his pension reform and his party is trailing behind the RN in opinion polls ahead of the 2024 EP elections. In the context of party system polarisation and uncertainty about the leadership of *Renaissance* after Macron's forced retirement from the presidency in 2027, it is unclear whether the 2017 realignment at the centre will last.

Notes

1 The party was created as *En Marche!* in 2016, but this chapter uses the name *La République en Marche* to refer to Macron's party during the period 2017–2022 because it is the name formally adopted for the legislative elections in 2017. LaREM was renamed *Renaissance* in 2022. The abbreviation LaREM was used by the party, though LREM was also used.
2 Séjourné, an MEP, became leader of *Renaissance* in 2022 and joined the government as Minister for Europe and Foreign Affairs in 2024.
3 The *Front National* was renamed *Rassemblement National* (National Rally or RN) in 2018.
4 Pécresse and Bertrand had re-joined the party to participate in the primary.
5 Article 49.3 of the constitution allows the government to pass legislation without a vote, unless the National Assembly votes a motion of no confidence.

References

Alexandre, C., Bristielle, A. and Chazel, L. (2021) 'From the Front de Gauche to La France Insoumise: Causes and consequences of the conversion of the French radical left to populism', *Participazione e Conflitto*, 14(2), pp. 933–953.
Bendjaballah, S. and Sauger, N. (2022) 'France: political developments and data for 2021', *European Journal of Political Research Political Data Yearbook*, 61, pp. 160–170.
Bernard, M. (2018) 'La reconstruction de la droite sous Laurent Wauquiez ou les risques de l'affiliation identitaire', *Cités*, 74(2), pp. 189–197.
Cole, A. (2019) *Emmanuel Macron and the two years that changed France*. Manchester: Manchester University Press.
Cos, R. (2019) 'De la dénégation du programme à la baisse de la fiscalité du capital. Aspects de la mobilisation programmatique d'*En Marche!*', in Dolez, B., Fretel, J. and Lefebvre, R. (eds) *L'Entreprise Macron*. Grenoble: Presses Universitaires de Grenoble, pp. 39–51.
De Boissieu, L. (2022) 'Présidentielle 2022: Marine Le Pen se démarque d'Éric Zemmour', *Les Echos*, 26 January. https://www.la-croix.com/France/Presidentielle-2022-Marine-Le-Pen-demarque-dEric-Zemmour-2022-01-26-1201196952
Delaurens, D. (2018) 'En marche, la politique moderne?', *Esprit*, 4, pp. 11–17.
Dolez, B., Douillet, A.-C., Fretel, J. and Lefebvre, R. (2022) 'A l'épreuve du pouvoir. L'entreprise Macron entre continuités et singularités', in Dolez, B., Douillet,

A.-C., Fretel, J. and Lefebvre, R. (eds) *L'Entreprise Macron à l'épreuve du pouvoir*. Grenoble: Presses Universitaires de Grenoble, pp. 11–25.
Dupoirier, E. and Sauger, N. (2010) 'Four rounds in a row: the impact of presidential election outcomes on legislative elections in France', *French Politics*, 8(1), pp. 21–41.
Durovic, A. (2023) 'Rising electoral fragmentation and abstention: the French elections of 2022', *West European Politics*, 46(3), pp. 614–629.
Elgie, R. (1997) 'Two-ballot majority electoral systems', *Representation*, 34(2), pp. 89–94.
Elgie, R. (2018) 'The election of Emmanuel Macron and the new French party system: A return to the *éternel marais?*', *Modern and Contemporary France*, 26(1), pp. 15–29.
En Marche! (2017) 'Programme' https://www.aefinfo.fr/assets/img/modules/comparateur/docs/6/Programme-Emmanuel-Macron.pdf
Evans, J. and Ivaldi, G. (2017) 'An atypical "honeymoon" election? Contextual and strategic opportunities in the 2017 French legislative elections', *French Politics*, 15, pp. 322–329.
Evans, J. and Ivaldi, G. (2020) 'Building a local powerbase? The *Rassemblement National* in the 2020 municipal elections in France'. halshs-02977509
Fabre, E. (2024) 'French political parties and democracy', in Poguntke, T. and Hofmeister, W. (eds) *Political parties and the crisis of democracy. Organization, resilience, and reform*. Oxford: Oxford University Press, pp. 58–81.
Fourquet, J. (2022) 'L'archipel électoral mélenchoniste', Fondation Jean Jaurès. https://www.jean-jaures.org/publication/larchipel-electoral-melenchoniste/
Fretel, J. (2019) 'Comment ça marche? La forme partisane de macronisme', in Dolez, B., Fretel, J. and Lefebvre, R. (eds) *L'Entreprise Macron*. Grenoble: Presses Universitaires de Grenoble, pp. 189–200.
Gougou, F. (2023) 'The 2021 French regional elections: Beyond second-order effects', *Regional & Federal Studies*, 33(4), pp. 525–540.
Gougou, F. and Persico, S. (2017) 'A new party system in the making? The 2017 French presidential election', *French Politics*, 15, pp. 303–321.
Gourgues, G. and Mazeaud, A. (2022) 'La démocratie participative selon Emmanuel Macron: La participation citoyenne au service de la monarchie républicaine', in Dolez, B., Douillet, A.-C., Fretel, J. and Lefebvre, R. (eds) *L'Entreprise Macron à l'épreuve du pouvoir*. Grenoble: Presses Universitaires de Grenoble, pp. 53–79.
Haegel, F. (2013) 'Political parties: the UMP and the right', in Cole, A., Meunier, S. and Tiberj, V. (eds) *Developments in French politics 5*. Basingstoke: Macmillan, pp. 128–150.
Hamdaoui, S. (2021) 'Anti-populism during the Yellow Vests protests: from combatting the *Rassemblement National* to dealing with street populists', *British Journal of Politics and International Relations*, 24(3), pp. 493–510.
Haute, T., Kelbel, C., Briatte, F. and Sandri, G. (2021) 'Down with Covid: patterns of electoral turnout in the 2020 French local elections', *Journal of Elections, Public Opinion and Parties*, 31(sup. 1), pp. 69–81.
Houard-Vial, E. and Sauger, N. (2020) 'France: political development and data for 2019', *European Journal of Political Research Political Data Yearbook*, 59, pp. 142–150.
Ivaldi, G. (2015) 'Towards the median economic crisis voter? The new leftist economic agenda of the *Front National* in France', *French Politics*, 13(4), pp. 346–369.
Jolly, S., Bakker, R., Hooghe, L., Marks, G., Polk, J., Rovny, J., Steenbergen, M. and Vachudova, M.A. (2022) 'Chapel Hill expert survey trend file, 1999–2019', *Electoral Studies*, 75, 102420.

Knapp, A. (2022) 'France's party system in 2022', *Modern and Contemporary France*, 30(4), pp. 494–515.
Lorimer, M. and Herman, L.E. (2023) 'The French elections of 2022: Macron's half victory in a changing political landscape', *Journal of Common Market Studies*, 61(1), pp. 80–89.
Marlière, P. (2019) 'Jean-Luc Mélenchon and *France Insoumise*. The manufacturing of populism', in Katsambekis, G. and Kioupkiolis, A. (eds) *The populist radical left in Europe*. London: Routledge, pp. 93–112.
Marlière, P. (2022) 'The French presidential election is in a far-right quagmire', *Open Democracy*, 17 February. https://www.opendemocracy.net/en/france-presidential-election-far-right-great-replacement-eric-zemmour-valerie-pecresse/
Martigny, V. (2017) 'A gauche, la fin de la synthèse social-démocrate', in Perrineau, P. (ed.) *Le vote disruptif. Les elections présidentielles et législatives de 2017*. Paris: Presses de SciencesPo, pp. 44–57.
Ministère de l'Intérieur (2017) 'Résultats des élections présidentielles 2017 – France entière' https://www.archives-resultats-elections.interieur.gouv.fr/resultats/presidentielle-2017/FE.php.
Ministère de l'Intérieur (2019) 'Résultats des élections européennes 2019 – France entière'. https://www.interieur.gouv.fr/fr/Elections/Les-resultats/Europeennes/elecresult__europeennes-2019/(path)/europeennes-2019//FE.html
Mondon, A. (2015) 'The irresistible rise of the *Front National*? Populism and the mainstreaming of the extreme right', in Charalambous, G. (ed.) *The European far right: historical and contemporary perspectives*. London: Friedrich-Ebert-Stiftung and PRIO Cyprus Centre, Report 2/2015, pp. 35–42.
Murray, R. (2021) 'All change? Partisan realignment and parliamentary reform under Emmanuel Macron', in Drake, H., Cole, A., Meunier, S. and Tiberji, V. (eds) *Developments on French politics 6*. London: Red Globe, pp. 57–75.
Offerlé, M. (2019) '"Les patrons" ou "des patrons" avec Emmanuel Macron. Capitaux entrepreneuriaux et capital politique', in Dolez, B., Fretel, J. and Lefebvre, R. (eds) *L'Entreprise Macron*. Grenoble: Presses Universitaires de Grenoble, pp. 79–92.
Paxton, F. and Peace, T. (2021) 'Window dressing? The mainstreaming strategy of the *Rassemblement National* in power in French local government', *Government and Opposition*, 56(3), pp. 545–562.
Pedder, S. (2018) *Revolution Française. Emmanuel Macron and the quest to reinvent a nation*. London: Bloomsbury.
Perottino, M. and Guasti, P. (2020) 'Technocratic populism à la française ? The roots and mechanisms of Emmanuel Macron's success', *Politics and Governance*, 8(4), pp. 545–555.
Piar, C. (2017) 'La présidentielle vue par les JT', in Perrineau, P. (ed.) *Le vote disruptif. Les elections présidentielles et législatives de 2017*. Paris: Presses de SciencesPo, pp. 73–99.
Raymond, G.G. (2022) 'Bottom-up democracy, blame and a republican monarch', *Modern and Contemporary France*, 30(4), pp. 411–425.
Reif, K. and Schmitt, H. (1980) 'Nine second-order national elections. A conceptual framework for the analysis of European election results', *European Journal of Political Research*, 8, pp. 3–44.
Rouban, L. (2017a) *Le profil des candidats investis par La République en Marche: un renouveau limité [Rapport de recherche] CEVIPOF hal-03471789*. Paris: Presses des SciencesPo. https://sciencespo.hal.science/hal-03471789

Rouban, L. (2017b) *L'Assemblée élue en 2017 et la crise de la représentation [Rapport de recherche] CEVIPOF hal-03458680*. Paris: Presses des SciencesPo. https://sciencespo.hal.science/hal-03458680

Sauger, N. (2017) 'Raisons et évolution du rejet des partis', *Pouvoirs*, 163, pp. 16–26.

Sawicki, F. (2017) 'L'épreuve du pouvoir est-elle vouée à être fatale au Parti socialiste? Retour sur le quinquennat de François Hollande', *Pouvoirs*, 163, pp. 27–41.

Schön-Quinlivan, E. (2019) 'France: political development and data in 2018', *European Journal of Political Research Political Data Yearbook*, 58(1), pp. 98–104.

Schwalisz, C. (2018) '*En Marche*: from a movement to a government', *Carnegie Europe*. https://carnegieeurope.eu/2018/04/06/en-marche-from-movement-to-government-pub-75985

Teinturier, B. (2017) 'L'inédite (et dernière?) primaire de la droite et du centre', in Perrineau, P. (ed.) *Le vote disruptif. Les elections présidentielles et législatives de 2017*. Paris: Presses de SciencesPo, pp. 25–41.

Tronchet, S. (2018) 'Jeunes avec Macron: Histoire d'un hold-up politique', *France Inter*, 15 September. https://www.radiofrance.fr/franceinter/podcasts/secrets-d-info/jeunes-avec-macron-histoire-d-un-hold-up-politique-8012266

6
MACRON, THE MEDIA AND POLITICAL COMMUNICATION

Raymond Kuhn

Abstract

This chapter analyses selected aspects of the interdependent relationship between Emmanuel Macron and the French news media, with reference to relevant features of both the political sphere and the media landscape. The first section focuses on Macron's successful attempts to win and subsequently retain the presidency in the 2017 and 2022 elections: Macron as presidential candidate. The second part examines Macron's news management and leadership projection during his period in office: Macron as president. The chapter illustrates the challenges Macron faced in both campaign and presidential communication and assesses his mixed record of success in resolving them.

Winning the competitive struggle for the people's vote: Macron as presidential candidate

To win the French presidency in the two-ballot system of direct election, a candidate has, first, to establish (or confirm) their leadership credentials and presidential status with their party, the media and the electorate; second, to mobilise core voter support in sufficient numbers in the first round so as to be one of the two candidates to proceed to the decisive second-round runoff and, finally, to broaden their electoral appeal between the two rounds in order to attract over half the total vote and ensure victory. Securing party support was not necessary for Macron since he already controlled his party, but he achieved these other objectives, albeit with varying degrees of success, in both the 2017 and 2022 presidential campaigns. It is hugely to his credit

DOI: 10.4324/9781003323259-6

that, in these very different contests, Macron emerged victorious in both, becoming the only presidential candidate in the Fifth Republic to secure two successive direct-election successes without an intervening period of 'cohabitation' between president and prime minister from opposing political camps.

In the light of Macron's markedly contrasting status in the run-up to the two elections, his campaigns were unsurprisingly dissimilar in several key respects. In 2017, he presented himself as the disruptive and transformative newcomer, while, in 2022, he was the incumbent with a five-year presidential record to defend, a legacy that the exercise of power inevitably imposes on the occupant of the Elysée. For several months before the 2017 election, Macron craved the media coverage he required to project his image and differentiate himself from his rivals, whereas, in 2022, he was reluctant formally to enter the electoral arena by officially declaring his candidacy, preferring to use his presidential status for as long as possible to keep himself above the electoral fray. In both cases, however, whether as the projected embodiment of radical reform or as the president-candidate, Macron wanted to maximise control of the news media's campaign agenda and their framing of his candidacy in terms of the content and form of message and imagery alike.

Getting elected: the 2017 presidential campaign

One of the many interesting features of Macron as a candidate in the 2017 presidential election was that he had never previously stood for, far less won, elected office. Unlike previous front-rank candidates, he had never fought an election campaign at any level – local, regional, national or European. Instead, his political background was confined to that of leading adviser to President Hollande from 2012 to 2014, then as Economics Minister under Prime Minister Manuel Valls from 2014 to 2016. During the year before this contest, preparations for Macron's campaign included the establishment of a popular movement, *En Marche!* (taking his initials EM), in the spring of 2016; his highly mediatised resignation from the socialist government in August that year, whereby he publicly distanced himself from both Hollande and Valls; his refusal to participate in the primary contest held by the Socialist Party; the raising of funds from a variety of interested backers to support his presidential candidacy; the publication in November 2016 of his book, *Révolution*, in which he recounted his life story and outlined his ideas for transforming France (Macron, 2016) and, finally, increased use of and presence on the mainstream news and social media networks, particularly after the public announcement of his candidacy in November 2016.

A symbiotic relationship developed between Macron and the media during the long 2017 campaign. Macron systematically marketed himself, his couple and his candidacy, controlling – as much as possible – the images and photos used by the media, just as Nicolas Sarkozy had done in 2007. Moreover, as 'the new kid on the block' – young, fresh-faced, brimming with self-confidence – he was the candidate who benefited the most from the operationalisation of the media's news values, including a focus on the politician as a celebrity and the presentation of news as entertainment – so-called 'infotainment'. Macron helped to create and then surfed on an electoral desire for change, which he articulated in his campaign communication. His discourse was highly person-focused, concentrating more on his dynamic and transformative leadership skills (style and positioning) than on a substantive programme of reform (content) (Mayaffre, 2017). He was also adept at integrating social media into his campaign, targeting specific electoral groups like young voters and seeking to emulate the successful techniques employed by Barack Obama in the 2008 and 2012 US presidential campaigns (Strudel, 2017). Many mainstream media outlets – such as the news magazine *L'Obs* and the weekly photo magazine *Paris Match* – were more than happy to be used by the candidate, covering his campaign in a largely uncritical and supportive fashion. When interviewed about this on French television, Macron argued that he had played no part in the editorial decisions made by these media outlets to publish material sympathetic to his campaign. Although technically accurate, this was also somewhat disingenuous since Macron had provided *Paris Match* with flattering photos via Mimi Marchand, the controversial head of a photographic agency, who advised Macron and his wife, Brigitte, on their image projection.

While the marketing of the private sphere for electoral purposes goes back to Valéry Giscard d'Estaing in 1974 and was particularly used by Sarkozy in 2007, in 2017, Macron stood out as the candidate the most willing to exhibit his private life as an integral part of his electoral communication strategy (Fulda, 2017). He provided the media with a coherent, if selective, career narrative and furnished voter-catching images that frequently focused on the so-called 'fusional relationship' with his wife, including her role as an informal political advisor, spouse and companion. The unusual details of their romance, notably their meeting while he was a pupil at the school in Amiens where she taught and the significant age difference between them (she was 64 by the time of his election victory while he was 39), were a gift for the storytelling celebrity press. Macron even gave the video of his wedding reception to the TV channel *France 3* so that it could be used as part of a favourable documentary, *La Stratégie du météore* (21 November 2016). In short, while newsweeklies such as *Le Point* and *L'Obs* spent months giving significant coverage to Macron's status as a serious presidential candidate, other 'people' magazines like *Paris Match* and *VSD* focused on the Macron couple, with several flattering front-page covers. All of these initiatives effectively formed a bespoke public relations package for editors that required minimal journalistic input before public dissemination (Magnaudeix, 2017, pp. 137–144). The result was a win–win deal for both Macron and the news media (Neumann, 2017, p. 161). He raised his profile in an uncritical context with a targeted section of the electorate, gaining a secondary media 'buzz' when the original story was covered by other media. In return, the media outlet that broke the story benefited directly from a rise in circulation figures and indirectly from free advertising for its content from other media. When allied to the sense that the leader of *En Marche*! and much of the mainstream media shared similar values – pro-Europe, culturally liberal and in favour of economic reform – it was hardly surprising that, in the 2017 campaign, Macron was widely seen as the chosen candidate of the media (Bénilde 2017; Kaci 2017; Lemaire and Roques 2016; Ortiz 2017).

While he skilfully used the news media as a platform for his campaign, they also provided an arena where the candidate pitted himself against his rivals and responded to questions from journalists. He willingly participated in television debates before the first round, neither committing any notable gaffe nor shining in any particular capacity; however, the television debate in which Macron emerged as the clear victor was the second-round live confrontation between him and Marine Le Pen, which attracted a television audience of 16.5 million – a high figure in an era of fragmented media supply but lower in both absolute terms and as a proportion of the total available audience compared with previous second-round debates. While, in 2002, Jacques Chirac had refused to debate with the National Front candidate, Jean-Marie Le Pen, in 2017, there was no way that Macron could repeat Chirac's gambit: during the campaign, he had already participated in television debates including Le Pen, her presence in the second round was not the surprise of 2002, and there was no popular mobilisation against her qualification as there had been for her father. Macron also probably rightly considered that he could deal with any of Le Pen's arguments: not only did the debate demonstrate her weakness on the issues of Europe, the euro and the economy, but it also showed her reliance on notes, whilst Macron appeared in total command. He was not just more knowledgeable, he also was more poised and, while he refused to be ruffled, dealing confidently with his opponent's verbal attacks, Le Pen's discomfiture was obvious at various points. Historically, presidential debates were sometimes heated but were usually characterised by a formal courtesy between the protagonists. The 2017 debate, however, was more of a bruising clash because of Le Pen's aggressive *ad hominem* posture, in stark contrast to the poster slogan of *La France apaisée* that she had used in 2016. The debate was a reminder that, while candidates may benefit from a media appearance, they may also damage their electoral prospects. In short, in 2017, Macron seduced as well as persuaded many French voters; he turned on the charm as well as showcasing his intelligence. As a young, skilful, personable newcomer, he mediatised his marriage to soften his technocratic image and broaden his electoral appeal, presenting himself as socially progressive, economically neoliberal and pro-EU, 'selling' the concept of France as a start-up nation under a transformative president.

Getting re-elected: the 2022 presidential campaign

In the 2022 presidential election, Macron held off officially declaring his candidacy until only days before the formal closing date, choosing to do so in a letter to the French people published in the regional press. Macron's absence from the electoral stage meant that the long campaign period resembled Hamlet without the Prince. Even after he entered the fray, the intense political and media focus on the war in Ukraine diverted attention away from the election. Arnaud Mercier, a leading scholar of political communication, refers to a *drôle de campagne* ('a phoney campaign'), with a statistically evidenced reduction in media coverage compared with 2017 (Mercier, 2022). This, Mercier argues, was caused by the mutually reinforcing interplay of three factors: first, on the demand side, less interest in the campaign from voters than five years previously; second, the non-campaign of Macron even after declaring his candidacy – for example, whereas, in 2017, Macron had organised 12 public meetings (albeit of differing importance) prior to the first round, in 2022, he held only one (Mercier, 2022, p. 106) and, finally, a reduction in the newsworthiness of the campaign, which had to compete for journalistic attention with other events, notably the conflict in Ukraine. In short, voters, the president-candidate and the news media all showed less interest in the 2022 campaign than in 2017: the 2022 presidential campaign began to dominate media coverage only three to four weeks before the first round. The sense of shadow boxing was reinforced by Macron's refusal to debate on television with the other candidates before the first round. He argued, correctly, that no previous incumbent had ever participated in such televised debates. This was yet another reminder that, in 2022, Macron was a president-candidate with a record rather than a new hopeful, and he not unreasonably feared being the object of a combined attack by the other 11 candidates: *Tout sauf Macron* ('Anyone but Macron'). A pre-first-round television debate might have been engrossing for voters but was certainly not in Macron's electoral interest. Moreover, under the long-standing rules that govern the equality of coverage of candidates by broadcasters, there was no obligation on him to appear.

In the first-round campaign, the president-candidate focused on his role as a key player in the Ukraine conflict. Media coverage reinforced Macron's image as an international statesman, and he initially benefited from an upward bounce in his opinion-poll ratings (Holeindre, 2022, p. 115). However, the impact on the partisan preferences of voters in the first round was negligible. The main electoral issue for voters was the cost of living (*pouvoir d'achat*), a theme long championed by Le Pen. Moreover, the downside of Macron's Gaullian approach to a presidential campaign (de Gaulle only very belatedly realised the need to campaign actively in the 1965 election) was that the incumbent came to be regarded as an absent figure: 'Too much president, not enough candidate' (Braun and de la Baume, 2022). His contact with voters was limited, with only one major public meeting, while some policy announcements – for example, on raising the retirement age to 65 and linking employment benefits to work placement schemes – were not universally popular. The second-round campaign in 2022 was more gripping than the first. Macron campaigned much more actively, seeking to win over first-round voters from Jean-Luc Mélenchon, with visits to *quartiers populaires*, toning down some of his reform measures and highlighting his environmental agenda as he sought to broaden his support against Le Pen (Bréchon, 2022). The theatrical highlight was the head-to-head televised debate in the middle of the second week. Having performed disastrously in 2017, Le Pen was desperate to do better. While she achieved this minimal standard, Macron was nonetheless perceived by more voters to have 'won' the debate: one poll put the result at 59 per cent for Macron and 39 per cent for Le Pen. Not surprisingly, 97 per cent of Macron first-round voters declared that their candidate had won the debate; however, even 15 per cent of Le Pen first-round voters came out for Macron, while first-round Mélenchon voters split roughly two to one in his favour (Perry, 2022).

News management and leadership projection: Macron as president

For any president of the Fifth Republic, news management and the symbolic, highly mediatised projection of leadership are determined by a complex interplay of structural and behavioural variables from the realms of both politics and media. These interact to enhance or constrain the president's freedom of manoeuvre as a political communication actor at any given moment of his/her tenure. With specific regard to the Macron presidency, three variables are emphasised in this section: France's hybrid media landscape; the Élysée as a primary definer for the news media and, finally, President Macron's public communicative style.

France's hybrid media landscape

Presidential communication is influenced by the nature of France's media landscape, including its organisational framework, the behaviour of key media actors (owners, news editors and journalists) and audience attitudes and usage. At the start of Macron's first presidential term, the French media landscape was radically different from that of the early Fifth Republic, with only one state-owned television channel, no internet and no social media.

During de Gaulle's presidency, close top-down control over television's news output was managed through the Ministry of Information and the *Office de Radio-Télévision Française* (ORTF). Some liberalisation of state control was introduced by President Valéry Giscard d'Estaing in the 1970s, and this was extended by President Mitterrand through the introduction of a regulatory 'High Authority' at the start of the 1980s. Privatisation of the main channel – TF1 – and the creation of commercial networks further attenuated the traditionally close links between the state and broadcasting from the late 1980s onwards (Kuhn, 1995). In short, by the turn of the millennium, the media landscape had undergone significant economic and political liberalisation. During the Macron presidency, this landscape included a vast range of media outlets, platforms and content (print, broadcasting and online), hypercompetition between infrastructural and content providers, increased supply-side segmentation catering for niche audiences, continuing fragmentation of the mass audience and new patterns of ownership concentration.

The print media of newspapers and news magazines had declined significantly in terms of audience reach, even if newspapers such as *Le Monde* and *Le Figaro* retained their status as elite opinion-formers. By contrast, there had been significant expansion in the broadcasting sector, notably through the arrival of many digital terrestrial television (DTT) channels – free to viewers – and a range of video-on-demand streaming platforms like Netflix. Social media, including YouTube and X (formerly Twitter), became an integral part of this transformed media landscape, whose evolution over the past 25 years has been largely driven by technological change – most notably, the transition from analogue to digital and online. The result was a 'hybrid media system' that blurred the boundaries between print, radio, television and online media sources for content providers and users alike.

What do these structural changes in the French media landscape mean for political communication in general – and presidential communication in particular – during the Macron era? Perhaps less than one might imagine, despite some notable innovations, including a more challenging context for news management. While, on the supply side, there is certainly a plethora of political information available, both online and via rolling news channels, on the demand side, patterns of audience usage have been slower to adapt. Television, particularly news output, remains an important source of political information, particularly for older voters, who constitute a significant tranche of the electorate: they are the most inclined to vote and therefore form a key demographic target for politicians. Television also remains the go-to mass medium for politicians who want to get their message across to a nationwide mass audience; it is therefore unsurprising that Macron has made numerous television appearances during his presidencies to announce important measures, frequently in response to a political crisis. Clips from these television appearances then feature on a whole host of online platforms (the Élysée's official website, mainstream media websites and social media) and are commented on by journalists as the message ripples out from its original source to reach different audiences. Conversely, Macron has also often used social media as his first line of distribution, notably targeting the young; the message is then picked up, reported and commented on by mainstream media outlets – such as when he was interviewed on YouTube by the young video journalist, Hugo Travers, in September 2023 (YouTube, 2023).

During Macron's presidency, three features of this hybrid media landscape that have political ramifications are especially noteworthy. First is the impact of rolling news channels and, in particular, *CNews*. In what has become a crowded market, France currently has four free-to-air rolling news channels: *BFM TV* (the market leader), *LCI* (part of the *TF1* group), *Franceinfo* (run by the public service companies *France Télévisions* and *Radio France*) and *CNews* (part of the Canal+ group and formerly known as *iTélé*). In late 2019, in a bid to differentiate itself from its rivals and improve its audience ratings, *CNews* embraced a highly opinionated form of journalism, including the employment of the far-right polemicist, Éric Zemmour, on its evening programme *Face à l'info*. Zemmour was renowned for his extreme views on immigration and Islam, having published a series of controversial books on what he regarded as threats to French identity posed by allegedly uncontrolled immigration. His comments on the programme led to his being found guilty by the broadcasting regulator of various offences, including incitement to racial hatred. In 2021, Zemmour profited from his controversial status as a journalistic commentator on *CNews* to launch his bid for the presidency. While, in terms of voter support, he failed to outrival Le Pen in the 2022 election, his campaign and television appearances contributed to (though certainly did not cause) a rightist drift in both electoral competition and the political agenda, with his emphasis on alleged links between immigration, insecurity and terrorism (Alduy, 2022). More generally, *CNews* has acquired a reputation for covering topics such as the alleged breakdown of law and order in French society within a right-wing populist framing, encouraging highly opinionated and committed journalism and introducing a US Fox-style combative approach to its political coverage (Cassini 2020). Yet, the public notoriety and political impact of *CNews* have far exceeded its audience ratings.

A second notable feature has been the significant economic concentration of media ownership across the newspaper, magazine, book publishing, radio and television sectors, particularly associated with the activities of the media mogul, Vincent Bolloré. From a purely economic perspective, Bolloré's growing cross-media holdings raise issues of market competition and consumer choice; however, more importantly, they also have a political resonance because of his right-wing views and strong Catholic beliefs as well as his highly interventionist style of ownership. Bolloré has, in recent years, acquired various media outlets, including *Canal+*, *iTélé*, *Europe 1* and *Le Journal du Dimanche*. Following these acquisitions, there were significant protest movements from staff, notably journalists, who opposed a shift in the political line towards the right and, indeed, the radical right. For instance, Bolloré's take-over of *Canal+* was marked by the disappearance of the short daily political satire programme, *Les Guignols de l'Info* and a long-running strike at the news channel *iTélé* (Garrigos and Roberts, 2016). Additionally, in 2023, the appointment as editor-in-chief of *Le Journal du Dimanche* of Geoffroy Lejeune, formerly the editorial head of the far-right magazine *Valeurs Actuelles* and personally renowned for his extremist views, resulted in many journalists leaving the newspaper. The outspoken hard-right populist content of the debate programme *Touche pas à mon poste*, presented by Cyril Hanouna on the *C8 TV* channel (in which Bolloré is a stakeholder), has been criticised as an integral part of Bolloré's 'reactionary ideological project' (Sécail, 2024, p. 76).

Finally, France has very high levels of public distrust in its mainstream media, notably higher than in many other European democracies (Reuters Institute, 2023, p. 24). Only 30 per cent of French citizens trust 'most news most of the time', with 'regional or local papers being the most trusted, followed by public service brands and *Le Monde*, the leading quality newspaper. Commercial TV brands tend to have lower trust levels' (Reuters Institute, 2023, p. 75). Voter trust in politicians is not particularly high either. This combination has made it particularly difficult for President Macron to get his message across. In addition, over half of French citizens suffer from a sense of news overload – what Gault and Medioni term *fatigue informationelle* (2023, p. 15). High levels of political polarisation, a widespread belief that the mainstream media are unduly influenced by economic and political interests, increased support for populist parties and a perception that journalists and politicians engage in too close a cooperative relationship have all contributed to a challenging environment for effective presidential communication.

This was particularly evident in the Yellow Vests crisis during Macron's first presidency when neither he nor the mainstream media were trusted by a significant and highly vocal section of the public. The president was the target of vicious, highly personalised online attacks, while journalists (from *BFM TV*, for example) were regularly insulted and even assaulted by demonstrators. Protestors against government policies on lockdown measures and vaccination during the Covid-19 crisis remained unconvinced by Macron and the mainstream media, not just attacking him for the state's alleged mismanagement of the response to the pandemic, but in some cases preferring conspiracy theories, amplified by social media, asserting that these were far more credible than the presidential message and the alleged mainstream media consensus.

The Élysée as a primary definer for the news media

The French presidency is a very powerful office – whatever the policy-making expertise, leadership qualities, communication skills or political attributes of the incumbent – and it has tended to dominate national news media coverage throughout the Fifth Republic (Kaciaf, 2013); in this respect, Macron's tenure of office is no exception, and he has been determined to use its institutional primacy to the full. Even before his 2017 victory, he had stated his desire to embrace a 'vertical' interpretation of the exercise of power (Leroux and Riutort, 2022), asserting that the French people missed the presence of a monarch as a focal point in the political system. In particular, Macron was at pains to differentiate his view of the presidential office from that of his immediate predecessor, Hollande, who had embraced a vision of a so-called 'normal presidency', thereby downplaying the status of the presidential office. In contrast, Macron sought to build on the myth of Gaullian leadership, which had contributed to French prestige in the 1960s. This top-down model of leadership was described as 'Jupiterean' by Macron (*BFMTV*, 2017).

The central, dominant position of the presidency within the political system ensures that the Élysée is a privileged official source (primary definer) in the process of news management. It seeks to influence, even if it cannot control, the content of the media agenda (agenda-building) and the way in which stories that make it on to the news agenda are covered by journalists (issue-framing). In conjunction with the wider governmental apparatus, the Élysée enjoys the benefit of three key assets that guarantee it privileged access on a routine basis as an official source for the French media: an unrivalled degree of formal political authority enjoyed by the directly elected president; extensive insider knowledge and policy expertise across a range of topics; and structurally embedded organisational resources – finance and personnel – including political advisers, policy technocrats, polling experts and communication specialists. This combination of legitimacy, knowledge and resources gives the Élysée in particular (and the political executive more generally) a favourable inside-track position compared to other sources in the task of news management.

Consequently, the Élysée's perspective on domestic, European and foreign issues is easily articulated across mainstream media outlets. A presidential press conference, television interview or statement at an international summit guarantees substantial media coverage because of the nature of the source, irrespective of the content of the message. Moreover, the Élysée does not just contribute to the professional process of news production in its capacity as an official source; the president is already news simply by fulfilling his leadership role as the chief political actor. Macron and his advisors, therefore, not only help to create the news story and try to spin it to their advantage; Macron frequently *is* the news story in terms of what he says, what he does, where he visits and who he talks to. In short, the president is both the messenger and the message. In performing its news-management function, the Élysée would prefer to be in constant proactive mode, controlling as much as possible the media agenda and issue-framing to serve the president's best interests. However, it also has to be prepared to go into reactive mode, responding to events that come on to the political and media agendas from outside the political executive's initial control. Macron's first presidential term was dominated by the Yellow Vests protests, the Covid-19 global pandemic and, in the final weeks, the war in Ukraine. The two main news stories of the early months of his second term were the pensions reform legislation and a wave of street violence after the killing by police of a teenager of Algerian origin at a traffic stop outside Paris in June 2023. Only the introduction of the pensions reform was a top-down initiative originating from the executive and, even in this case, the Élysée struggled to get its preferred message across. The other four sets of events – all unforeseen in their different ways – emanated either from within French society (Yellow Vests protests, 2023 street violence) or from outside the national political sphere (Covid-19, the war in Ukraine).

Reactive firefighting, therefore, may be more the order of the day than proactive spinning. For instance, the 'Benalla affair', in which one of the president's right-hand men was filmed posing as a policeman and attacking members of the public, erupted out of nowhere in the summer of 2018 following revelations of the incident in *Le Monde* (2023). Damping down the media and political firestorm that resulted from both the newspaper's coverage of the incident and the initial ineffective response by the Élysée in failing to sanction Benalla appropriately meant that Macron was put on the back foot and compelled to try to regain control of a narrative not of his making, with at best very mixed results. The Benalla affair represented an early notable failure in presidential news management during Macron's first term; the Élysée was not just blindsided by the revelations of the incident but also failed to implement an effective communication response, which fed into more general dissatisfaction with the president's performance (Lévrier, 2021, pp. 291–311).

While the presidency is faced with relatively few structural checks and balances within the political system of the Fifth Republic (providing the president has a parliamentary majority), this is less true of news management. The Élysée's attempts to act as a primary definer may be undermined by deliberate counter-briefing or unintentional contradictory statements from other sources, such as leading government ministers. There exists a significant degree of pluralism and competition among official sources within the executive branch, and this often gives rise to confused and conflicting messages that severely undermine any top-down 'command and control' news-management strategy piloted from the Élysée. Pensions reform in Macron's second term was an example of where the Élysée failed to get its explanatory narrative clear from the start, while Prime Minister Borne frequently seemed to be backtracking on previously announced government commitments. The overall picture was that of an executive struggling to construct and then communicate a coherent narrative (Duhamel, 2023, p. 132).

The problem for Macron in this respect has not been a consequence of the structural executive dyarchy between president and prime minister which has, at times, led to competing media briefings. During Macron's first term, his prime minister, Edouard Philippe, sometimes went public over his disagreement with the president – notably during the Covid-19 crisis – but he never sought to challenge him head on, accepting his own secondary status. Neither of Philippe's prime-ministerial successors, Jean Castex and Élisabeth Borne, fell out with Macron in public to any significant degree. In short, in acting as a primary definer, the Élysée has not been systematically undermined by Matignon (the prime minister's office), despite differences of opinion between the head of state and the head of government occasionally aired in the public sphere. Rather, Macron has sometimes been unable to impose a coherent message across the executive branch as a whole. At worst, this has sometimes been due to the president's own lack of clarity or (in the eyes of his critics) coherence in his communication, for instance, in the Élysée's response to the unfolding crisis in Gaza in the autumn of 2023 (Gatinois and Segaunes, 2023). Moreover, since constitutionally Macron cannot stand for a third presidential term in the 2027 election, in the months leading up to this contest, leading ministerial figures, such as Gérard Darmanin and Bruno Le Maire, will undoubtedly cut loose from their supportive stance of Macron to further their own presidential ambitions: such career rivalry will challenge the Élysée's efforts to manage the media on behalf of the president, who may be widely regarded as a 'lame duck' incumbent well before his second term approaches its end.

More broadly, in the process of news management, there is competition among a range of sources to gain publicity, impose issues and influence coverage; however, none have the legitimacy of the Élysée, and few can compare with its knowledge and resources. Some, such as minor political parties and fringe pressure groups, may lack what it takes to make a sustained impact as a primary defining source: they do not have the necessary media capital. Others can, however, hope to benefit from one or more favourable factors – the socio-political context, their celebrity status, their formal leadership role and their media know-how – to shape the media agenda to their partisan advantage in a manner not just different from but also in opposition to that proffered by the Élysée. These counter-sources include leaders of opposition parties – such as Mélenchon and Le Pen – and leading trade-union representatives such as Laurent Berger, a high-profile spokesperson for those opposed to Macron's pension and retirement reforms at the start of the latter's second presidential term, helping to shape media coverage critical of the proposed reform.

In addition, heads of regional councils and mayors of large towns are not just important political actors at the sub-national level but also act as official sources on a range of socio-economic and political issues for regional and local media outlets, which are particularly important in the French media landscape. Some regional and city political bosses are also major figures on the national political stage, further amplifying their authority as a news media source in their locality. Since Macron's supporters are very poorly implanted in elected posts at the sub-national level, the president has lacked embedded spokespersons to advocate the Élysée's policy reforms or simply to defend the president from political attack. Other actors regularly used by the news media as official sources include independent specialists; medical and scientific experts frequently countered the Élysée's preferred version of events during the Covid-19 crisis. It may even happen that a group without any formal organisation or clear leader, such as the Yellow Vests in 2018–2019, may capture media attention and help to set the terms of journalistic coverage through their direct-action protest, their use of violence and their capacity to engage in activities that conform to the media's news values of impact, conflict and human interest (Tran, 2021).

Moreover, the mainstream media themselves are not simply passive recipients of information from sources – journalists exercise a degree of autonomy in challenging the Élyseé's version of events and subjecting it to critical scrutiny. While there may have previously been a strong tradition of journalistic deference shown to the president throughout the Fifth Republic, especially in the broadcasting media, this is now less the case, in part because of the changes in the media landscape described above. The attitudes and behaviour of journalists may constitute, therefore, another barrier to the Élysée's attempts to manage the news. Finally, social-media platforms may spread messages opposed to the official line, over which the Élysée has virtually no control, unless laws (such as those on hate speech) can be used. Fake news and the propensity for some voters to believe conspiracy theories undermine the agenda-building and issue-framing activities of the political executive. In short, while the Élysée under Macron may have hoped to dominate the news field as an official source (with some success, especially in the early part of his first term), it could not expect to exercise anything approaching overarching control.

President Macron's public communicative style

There is a distinctively personal element to presidential communication in the Fifth Republic – what may be called the president's public communicative style – which is partly influenced by the personality of the incumbent and partly fabricated for his/media appearances, often with the aid of communication advisers. This communicative style includes the nature of the president's interrelationship with media personnel, both owners and journalists, as well as the way in which, in performing their leadership role, the president engages in image projection via the media. A president's public communicative style is unique to each incumbent. Yet, even for the same incumbent, the public communicative style must be multi-faceted and capable of adaptation; it varies depending, *inter alia*, on the message, the media outlet and genre, the political context, the intended audience(s) and the desired effect(s).

Both of Macron's immediate predecessors at the Élysée enjoyed close ties with the media, albeit at different levels. Sarkozy was a friend of the owners of several leading private media companies and was prepared to intercede at this level of the chain of command to shape coverage to his advantage. Hollande liked nothing better than talking at length to political journalists, frequently acting as a commentator on his own presidential actions. The publication in late 2016 of a series of on-the-record conversations between Hollande and two journalists from *Le Monde* epitomised this relationship but also demonstrated its dangers (Davet and Lhomme, 2016); the book's embarrassing revelations finally killed off any last hope for a second Hollande candidacy in 2017. Macron was particularly critical of Hollande's intimacy with journalists, believing that this indulgence in self-harm had devalued the currency of the presidential office.

Macron's relationship with media owners and journalists has been more nuanced than that of either Sarkozy or Hollande. While he has enjoyed a close relationship with Xavier Niel (owner of the tech company Free and also a major shareholder in *Le Monde*) and was supported by other media moguls such as Bernard Arnault, his relations with Vincent Bolloré could at best be described as cool, not to say conflictual. Bolloré's hard right-wing views, the populist approach of *CNews* with its anti-elite agenda and the media tycoon's support for Zemmour did not endear Bolloré to the president and his supporters. Nor has Macron sought to construct privileged relations with political journalists, believing that too much coverage of contemporary politics was concerned with process rather than substance, with form rather than content (Davet and Lhomme, 2021, p. 9) and that daily contact with journalists undermined the solemnity of the presidential role (Lévrier, 2021, pp. 41–2). Indeed, in the early period of his first term, he expressed a scornful attitude towards political journalists, giving the impression that they needed him more than he did them; he is reported to have said during the 2017 campaign: 'Journalists have to be kept at a distance … it is important to keep a direct connection with the people, without intermediaries' (Besson, 2017, p.105). His press advisor, Sibeth Ndiaye, even remarked at the start of Macron's first term that she was prepared to lie to protect the president, a public statement that revealed the extent of the gap between the Élysée and the presidential press corps at the time (see Chapter 2). Instead, Macron was more comfortable talking to specialist correspondents in the fields of economics, business, foreign affairs and defence.

This distancing from journalists, which even included an aborted scheme to move the press office out of the main Élysée building (*L'Express avec l'AFP*, 2018), was part of a plan to control the political communication agenda – rather than simply to respond to it – and to create an aura of a president above the hurly-burly of the daily political fray. Macron appeared to be following the advice put forward in the late-twentieth century by Jacques Pilhan, communication adviser to Mitterrand and then Chirac, who believed that rationing contact with the media and appearing relatively infrequently on television amplified the impact of the presidential message when they did speak (Bazin, 2009). However, the idea of minimising contact with the media to support a concept of Jupiterean leadership quickly ran into problems. The presidency was quite understandably regarded by the public as the main source of policy-making – 'the buck stops here' – with a concomitant desire for accountability demanded by voters; the media agenda in the age of rolling news channels and social media platforms was constantly on the move, with an appetite for information that required constant replenishment, and while voters expected their president to incarnate the nation as head of state, they also wanted Macron to understand and deal with their daily problems, such as the cost of living and the provision of public services.

As his presidency ran into difficulties, notably from the Yellow Vests protests, Macron moved away from a highly controlled Jupiterean phase – during which he sought to impose and even to dictate the terms of engagement between political journalists and himself – to more of a transactional relationship in which the president was prepared to engage more readily with reporters and commentators, either on or off the record, as he sought to persuade them of the efficacy of his proposals through his well-oiled mix of explanation and seduction. Any modern-day president interacts with the media on diverse platforms, in various settings and with their appearances subject to different norms and rules of behaviour. At one end of the spectrum, there is top-down presidential communication, such as formal speeches, televised addresses to the nation, articles in print media, the official Élysée website and the president's usage of his 'personal' social-media platforms. Notable examples of this form of communication include Macron's letter to the French people in January 2019 announcing a 'great debate' in response to the Yellow Vests crisis and his letter published in *Le Parisien* in November 2023 condemning anti-semitism. In these settings, the president and his advisers are in total control of the message (though not, of course, of its reception by and impact on audiences). Then, there is interactive communication between the president and journalists/other media actors/members of the public, including print, radio, television and online interviews, press conferences and debate programmes with audience participation. Here, the president has to relinquish control of communication to some extent, as both participants engage in a bilateral exchange relationship, not just answering questions but also responding to criticism. Macron usually performs well in these verbal jousts; for instance, in April 2018, he gave a good performance on *BFMTV* in responding to a particularly hostile line of questioning from the journalists Jean-Jacques Bourdin and Edwy Plenel. In October 2019, in a controversial initiative, he agreed to be interviewed at length by the extreme-right-wing weekly magazine, *Valeurs actuelles*.

Towards the other end of the spectrum, there is professional journalistic reportage and commentary about the president available via a range of traditional outlets in the press and on radio and television as well as on the online sites of these established mainstream media. The president may hope to influence and shape such coverage, but it is not in his control. This is even more true of a range of alternative, participatory and social-media content on the internet, including political blogs, citizen journalism, user-generated content and independent news websites such as *Mediapart*, which, with its strong emphasis on investigative journalism, became established as a powerful critic of Macron (as had been the case with his immediate predecessors), accusing him of a pronounced right-wing drift during his presidencies (*Mediapart*, 2023).

Macron has proved himself to be a particularly able communicator in top-down presidential communication, frequently showing himself to be intelligent, articulate and familiar with policy dossiers across a wide range of topics. He has also ably personified the presidential office, showing the gravitas that French voters expect from their head of state; he generally presents himself as a professional performer in face-to-camera television addresses, though critics say that he speaks for too long (see Chapter 2). The Covid-19 pandemic gave him the opportunity to dominate communication through a series of televised addresses to the nation. In the first such address, in the spring of 2020, Macron declared no fewer than six times that France was 'at war'. He thus sought to present himself as a unifying figure at the time of national crisis, a latter day de Gaulle rallying the people and leading the nation in their fight against an enemy invasion in the form of the virus. Likewise, the Russian attack on Ukraine in February 2022 allowed Macron to emphasise his position as a national protector in the mediated public sphere: only the president could represent the nation in diplomatic talks and international fora – well above party politics and voters' everyday problems. In the first year of his second term, during a visit to New Caledonia, he responded to the unbridled violence that erupted across France after the shooting of a teenager in a Parisian suburb in a long television interview (but effectively a presidential monologue), in which he emphasised the need for 'Order, order, order' and a 'return of authority' (Brunet, 2023).

In exchange-type communication, Macron maintains a very didactic style, responding at length to journalists' questions in what frequently resembles a well-crafted presidential monologue. When the Élysée's technocratic team of presidential advisers was seen as out of touch with popular feeling when the Yellow Vest protests erupted in late 2018, Macron eventually responded not only with substantive concessions but also with a 'great debate'. In communication terms, he committed himself to a series of debates across France in which he sought to present himself in listening mode while, at the same time, engaging in what had become his default communication approach of lengthy authoritative responses. In contrast to this professional approach, however, he has also been prone to off-the-cuff communication errors when speaking to members of the public, often showing his frustration – as when he told an unemployed gardener that he only had to cross the street to find employment in a café or when, very soon after his election, speaking in a former station building, he commented that a station was a place where you could meet both people who were successful and those who were 'worthless' (*les gens qui ne sont rien*) (Public Sénat, 2017).

Conclusion

Sustained and professional public communication is not an option for elite politicians in contemporary advanced democracies; it is a necessity. Operating in highly complex media environments that include traditional print and broadcasting outlets as well as rapidly evolving social-media platforms, they need to engage proactively and responsively to get their message across to voters, maintain their profile and promote their image. Macron well understands the constraints and opportunities of the mediated politics of political leadership: in contrast to his immediate predecessors, he is as comfortable performing in digital and online media as he is in established sectors such as television. He is skilled in question-and-answer sessions with journalists and proficient in formal set-piece addresses to the nation. He is, in many respects, a good communicator: articulate, analytic and, in his best moments, very persuasive, even highly charismatic to his supporters. Yet, overall, his record in public communication has been mixed.

As a presidential candidate, Macron's public communication differed significantly between the 2017 and 2022 contests. In 2017, he sought to co-opt the media to support his candidacy, whereas, in 2022, he tried to keep them at a distance to minimise opportunities for criticism. In addition, in 2022, he made some serious campaign communication errors, particularly between the presidential and parliamentary elections a few weeks later, in failing to outline in sufficient detail the main contours of a second presidential term. This contributed to the significant setback of the result, even if other factors also played a major part – including the weakening of the so-called 'republican front' in voting behaviour (Hewlett and Kuhn, 2022). As president, Macron adapted his relationship with the media during his first term, moving away from keeping journalists at a distance to a recognition of the need to engage with them on a regular basis. The Yellow Vests crisis represented a wake-up call, showing the downside of an aloofness that was widely interpreted as that of a president who was out of touch and uncaring. Both the Covid pandemic and the war in Ukraine provided Macron with the opportunity to use the media to project himself in a 'father of the nation' role, even if the content of his media interventions did not meet with universal approval. During his second term, so far, the failure to win an absolute majority – creating problems with passing legislation – and the constitutional impediment to his standing for a third term have all contributed to the sense of a president on the back foot. This new context has made effective political communication both more urgent and more challenging.

The overall lesson to be learnt from Macron's interdependent relationship with the media is that personal communicative skills have been, in themselves, insufficient to deliver effective public communication, for several reasons. Firstly, the message itself is sometimes unpopular, as with pensions reform; secondly, the messenger was frequently not trusted by voters, as was made clear during the Yellow Vests crisis; thirdly, significant swathes of the public were mistrustful of the media as conduits of reliable information and, finally, other sources contested and undermined the narratives put forward by the Élysée. As a result, for all the prestige and power of the presidential office, public communication has represented a constant and often unrewarding challenge for Macron.

References

Alduy, C. (2022) *La langue de Zemmour*. Paris: Seuil.
Bazin, F. (2009) *Le sorcier de l'Élysée*. Paris: Plon.
Bénilde, M. (2017) 'Le candidat des médias', *Le Monde Diplomatique*, May.
Besson, P. (2017) *Un personnage de roman*. Paris: Julliard.
BFMTV (2017) 'Ce que signifie le président "jupitérien" que souhaite incarner macron'. Available at: https://www.bfmtv.com/politique/elysee/ce-que-signifie-le-president-jupiterien-que-souhaite-incarner-macron_AN-201705180028.html
Braun, E. and de la Baume, M. (2022) 'Macron's campaign problem: too much president, not enough candidat', *Politico*, 9 April.
Bréchon, P. (2022) 'Du premier au second tour présidentiel', in Perrineau, P. (ed.) *Le vote clivé: les élections présidentielle et législatives d'avril et juin 2022*. Grenoble: Presses Universitaires de Grenoble, pp. 225–237.
Brunet, R. (2023) 'Au terme des 100 jours, Emmanuel Macron se pose en président de "l'ordre, l'ordre, l'ordre"'. *France 24*, 24 July. Available at: https://www.france24.com/fr/france/20230724-au-terme-des-100-jours-emmanuel-macron-s-adresse-aux-fran%C3%A7ais-depuis-la-nouvelle-cal%C3%A9donie

Cassini, S. (2020) 'Face à la concurrence, *CNews* fait le pari d'une parole décomplexée', *Le Monde*, 12 September.
Davet, G. and Lhomme, F. (2016) *Un président ne devrait pas dire ça* .... Paris: Stock.
Davet, G. and Lhomme, F. (2021) *Le traître et le néant*. Paris: Fayard.
Duhamel, A. (2023) *Le Prince balafré*. Paris: Éditions de l'Observatoire.
Fulda, A. (2017) *Emmanuel Macron, un jeune homme si parfait*. Paris: Plon.
Garrigos, R. and Roberts, I. (2016) *L'empire*. Paris: Seuil.
Gatinois, C. and Segaunes, N. (2023) 'Emmanuel Macron deroutent son camp par ses tâtonnements, de la scène diplomatique à l'arène politique', *Le Monde*, 14 November.
Gault, G. and Medioni, D. (2023) *Quand l'info épuise*. Paris: Éditions de l'Aube.
Hewlett, N. and Kuhn, R. (2022) 'Reflections on the 2022 elections in France', *Modern and Contemporary France*, 30(4), pp. 393–409.
Holeindre, J.-V. (2022) 'La guerre fait-elle l'élection? Le role du conflit en Ukraine dans l'élection présidentielle 2022', in Perrineau, P. (ed.) *Le vote clivé: les élections présidentielle et législatives d'avril et juin 2022*. Grenoble: Presses Universitaires de Grenoble, pp. 113–120.
Kaci, S. A. (2017) 'Retour sur le traitement médiatique de l'élection présidentielle de 2017'. *Acrimed*, 11 September. Available at: http://www.acrimed.org/Retour-sur-le-traitement-mediatique-de-l-election.
Kaciaf, N. (2013) *Les pages 'politique'*. Rennes: Presses Universitaires de Rennes.
Kuhn, R. (1995) *The Media in France*. London: Routledge.
L'Express avec l'AFP (2018). 'L'Elysée décide de déménager la salle de presse en dehors du Palais'. 14 February.
Lemaire, F. and Roques, T. (2016) 'Emmanuel Macron superstar médiatique', *ACRIMED*, 2 September.
Le Monde (2023) 'Affaire Benalla: cinq ans après "les violences du 1 mai", Alexandra Benalla rejugé en appel', 10 June.
Leroux, P. and Ruitort, P. (2022) 'Emmanuel Macron, la communication et les médias', in Dolez, B., Douillet, A.-C., Fretel, J. and Lefebvre, R. (eds) *L'entreprise Macron à l'épreuve du pouvoir*. Grenoble: Presses Universitaires de Grenoble, pp. 27–40.
Lévrier, A. (2021) *Jupiter et Mercure: le pouvoir présidentiel face à la presse*. Paris: Les Petits Matins.
Macron, E. (2016) *Révolution*. Paris: XO Éditions.
Magnaudeix, M. (2017) *Macron & Cie*. Paris: Don Quichotte.
Mayaffre, D. (2017) 'Les mots des candidats, de "allons" à "vertu"', in Perrineau, P. (ed.) *Le vote disruptif*. Paris: Les Presses de Sciences Po, pp. 129–152.
Mediapart (2023) 'Macron: à droite toute!' Available at: https://www.mediapart.fr/journal/france/dossier/macron-droite-toute
Mercier, A. (2022) 'La "drôle de campagne": l'atonie médiatique de la campagne présidentielle de 2022', in Perrineau, P. (ed.) *Le vote clivé: les élections présidentielle et législatives d'avril et juin 2022*. Grenoble: Presses Universitaires de Grenoble, pp. 99–111.
Neumann, L. (2017) *Les dessous de la campagne 2017*. Paris: Calmann Lévy.
Ortiz, V. (2017) 'Comment les médias ont fabriqué le candidat Macron'. Available at: http://lvsl.fr/medias-ont-fabrique-candidat-macron
Perry, S. (2022) '*Le grand débat*: the return of the return engagement', *Modern & Contemporary France*, 30(4), pp. 479–493.
Public Sénat (2017) 'Macron critiqué pour avoir évoqué "les gens qui ne sont rien"'. Available at: https://www.publicsenat.fr/actualites/politique/macron-critique-pour-avoir-evoque-les-gens-qui-ne-sont-rien-75440

Reuters Institute (2023) *Digital News Report 2023*. Oxford: University of Oxford, Reuters Institute for the Study of Journalism.
Sécail, C. (2024) *Touche pas à mon peuple*. Paris: Seuil.
Strudel, S. (2017) 'Emmanuel Macron: un oxymore politique?', in Perrineau, P. (ed.) *Le vote disruptif*. Paris: Les Presses de Sciences Po, pp. 205–219.
Tran, E. (2021) 'The Yellow Vests movement: Causes, consequences and significance', in Drake, H., Cole, A., Meuiner, S. and Tiberj, V. (eds) *Developments in French politics 6*. London: Red Globe Press, pp. 179–196.
YouTube (2023) 'L'interview d'Emmanuel Macron par HugoDécrypte'. Available at: https://www.youtube.com/watch?v=3Z6HnUJ3hcw

7
TOWARDS A 'SOVEREIGN EUROPE'? MACRON'S EUROPEAN POLICY BETWEEN CONCEPTUAL FIREWORKS AND NATIONAL INTERESTS

Jörg Monar

Abstract

This chapter analyses President Macron's European policy. His forceful reconceptualisation of the EU as a 'sovereign' and 'protective' Europe and the substantial EU reform agenda both helped Macron to get elected and provided him with considerable initial political capital at a European level. After his intended strategic partnership with Germany proved elusive, he was more successful with flexible EU coalition-building. Two major EU crises – the Covid-19 pandemic and the invasion of Ukraine – provided significant, though complex, opportunities for the president. However, the advances connected with Macron's leadership are either – as are those in the defence field – lacking in substance or – as in the case of the 'Next Generation EU' budgetary debt-funding – have major problematic aspects. In addition, for a president posturing as a European game-changer, many of those advances have had a rather distinct French national-interest dimension, and he has struggled to convince French citizens of his European vision.

Introduction: a European hymn appropriately played

One of the images of the Macron presidency that may stay in the French collective memory is that of the newly elected president's solitary walk around the effectively illuminated Louvre Pyramid in the late evening of 7 May 2017 before addressing his supporters, a scene reminiscent of François Mitterrand's walk up to the Panthéon in May 1981, an event also staged to the European anthem, Beethoven's *Ode to Joy*. Macron had fought his entire presidential campaign, starting with the much-cited 'We love Europe! We want Europe' of his December 2016 Porte de Versailles speech, on a distinctly pro-European platform. In so doing, he had benefitted considerably from *Front National* leader Marine Le Pen's negative positioning on European matters, especially her advocacy of France leaving the Eurozone, which Macron could effectively present as a danger to French savings, jobs, salaries and price stability – in contrast with his own as a safer and more competent choice. While it may be a step too far to assert that Macron's strongly pro-European agenda won him the 2017 election (as argued in Grillmeyer, Keller and Seidendorf, 2018), it certainly attracted some of the centrist voters in elections rightly qualified as the 'most Europeanised' until then in terms of Europe as a political cleavage-defining subject (Schön-Quinlivan, 2017, p. 301). Macron's pro-European profile surely also helped with his re-election in 2022, although less so, since Le Pen had, by then, dropped more extreme parts of her European agenda, and a succession of crises had generated some convergence between candidates on the centrality of EU membership to French national interests (Bertoncini, 2022).

Beyond contributing to his election, Macron's European commitment also came with political opportunities at the EU level: still reeling from the shock of the British Brexit vote of June 2016, pro-European continental elites had been deeply scarred by a potential Le Pen victory with possible 'Frexit' implications. There was a palpable sense of relief after Macron's victory, with unusually warm congratulations to the president-elect from other EU leaders – including Angela Merkel – and from EU institutions (*Touteleurope*, 2017). Macron therefore entered his high office with more initial political capital on the European policy side – at both the national and the European level – than any of his predecessors.

This chapter examines how Emmanuel Macron used his considerable initial political capital on the European policy side. It first analyses the president's conceptualisation of Europe and major European policy objectives, then reviews his search for EU-level allies and assesses the results achieved (or not) in terms of crisis management (the Covid-19 pandemic and Ukraine) in the security, economic and financial domains. Finally, it provides an evaluation and outlook for the remaining years of the Macron presidency.

Claiming the conceptual high ground – and an avalanche of proposals

Of all the presidents of the Fifth French Republic – with the exception of Charles de Gaulle's concept of a Europe of nation-states – Macron has made the most sustained and distinctive effort to re-conceptualise 'Europe' as a political project. This has served two primary purposes. The first is the president's interest in shoring up domestic support for a European project, which only a minority of French citizens, at the time, considered beneficial to them, many mistrusting it and some even seeing it as an agent of destructive globalisation (Eurobarometer, 2016, p. 2). Conceptualising Europe differently and more positively than his predecessor – François Hollande – and constructing a new narrative around it, responded to a domestic political and electoral objective. At the same time, casting himself as the bearer of a renewed dynamic view of European construction provided him, at least initially, with political leadership potential in an EU shaken by self-doubt after the British Brexit vote, the destabilising migration emergencies of 2015–2016 and bad memories of the 2009–2012 debt crisis. Claiming the conceptual high ground on Europe promised benefits at both the national and the European levels.

Macron accompanied his re-conceptualisation of 'Europe' by a long list of proposals aimed at reinforcing EU policies and structures both before and after his election. These can all be related to two core elements: 'Europe' – which, in his public statements, generally equals the EU – has to be a 'sovereign Europe' (*une Europe souveraine*) and one which protects (*une Europe qui protège*). As first clearly stated in his speech at Humboldt University in Berlin in January 2017[1] and reaffirmed in his electoral programme, only a 'sovereign' Europe can, for Macron, respond effectively to the multiple security, economic, ecological and societal challenges its countries are facing; only a 'sovereign' Europe can therefore also be a 'protective' one, shielding citizens against a whole range of risks stemming from these challenges (*En Marche!*, 2017).

The significance of the terminology used by Macron cannot be overstated. Well beyond the purely legal and constitutional dimension of 'sovereignty' – which, according to a 1976 landmark judgement of the French Constitutional Council 'can only be national' (*Conseil constitutionnel*, 1976) and which has necessitated a series of constitutional amendments in order to protect its 'essential conditions' against a potential infringement by EU law (Gaïa, 2013) – the term itself carries considerable political weight in French political culture and discourse as an affirmation of national authority, autonomy and even identity. Its emotive appeal across party boundaries – *souverainistes* are found on both left and right – may to some extent be compared to the salience of 'sovereignty' as an issue in the British Brexit referendum campaign. By applying the attribute of 'sovereign' to Europe, Macron has broken – at least in his public discourse – the traditional exclusive ideational link between sovereignty and the (French) state and transferred much of the positive connotation of sovereignty from the national to the EU level. Without suggesting any formal transfer of sovereign powers to the European level, the president simply projected the EU into a 'sovereign' role and status formerly only associated with the nation-state. The 'protective' dimension of the EU is a key component of this (mini) Copernican revolution of a 'sovereign' Europe, as it corresponds to another major element of French political culture regarding the state: if the state is traditionally, in France, most associated with 'power', the power of the state is essentially there to protect (Birnbaum, 2021), and French citizens expect much protection from their state, both on the social side and beyond. By assigning to the EU a strongly protective function – and even defining it as essentially protective – Macron not only transferred the most positive French connotation of the state to the European level but also provided a powerful justification for a 'sovereign' Europe because only such a Europe can be 'protective'.

To be effective, political concepts need to be substantiated. It was in his September 2017 'initiative for Europe' speech in the great amphitheatre of the Sorbonne that Macron fleshed out his re-conceptualisation of the EU with extensive programmatic substance. He identified six 'keys' to a 'sovereign Europe' (Élysée, 2017): the need to guarantee all dimensions of security, to respond to the challenge of migration, to turn itself towards Africa and the Mediterranean, to become a model of sustainable development, to be a leader in innovation and regulation in digital transformation and, finally, to be an economic and monetary 'power'. In a panel debate in March 2017 in Berlin, with philosopher Jürgen Habermas and German Finance Minister Sigmar Gabriel, Macron as a candidate had criticised – with a cavalier disregard for the many European Commission initiatives – the absence at the EU level of any proposals 'for ten years'.[2] In the Sorbonne speech, he cast himself as a true game-changer by linking several proposals to each of his 'keys' to European sovereignty, ranging from the fairly obvious – such as a more efficient management of EU external borders and more investment in sustainable development – over the more ambitious, such as the creation of a common military intervention force, a European Defence Fund and an EU border carbon tax – to the more controversial, such as a separate Eurozone budget, new EU financial resources and EU minimum-wage legislation. Macron completed his list of political prescriptions by declaring that the EU would also need to become more 'democratic', by the convocation of 'European conventions', to give citizens a chance to discuss key questions of a 'refoundation of Europe' and by the introduction of transnational party lists in European Parliament (EP) elections. Some of the proposals, such as those on the intervention force, the Defence Fund, the Eurozone budget, the carbon tax and more focus on the Mediterranean and Africa were old (and mainly French) wine in new bottles. Yet, the bottles came with a new shape and shine and, in conjunction with the re-conceptualised 'sovereign' and 'protective' Europe, they made for an innovative and dynamising mix with which to address the ills of a Europe threatened, according to the president, by stagnation and nationalist revival.

Macron added further to the 49 proposals of his Sorbonne speech in an open letter addressed to the citizens of Europe on 4 March 2019, timed to influence the upcoming 2019 EP elections, under the heading 'For European

Renewal' (Élysée, 2019). This letter, which re-emphasised the EU's protective role, added to the earlier objectives – *inter alia*, the creation of a European Council for internal security, a European agency for the protection of democracies, a European climate bank and a European food safety force, the introduction of a European preference in strategic industries and public procurement, a complete reform of the Schengen system and the convocation of a 'Conference for Europe' engaging with 'citizens' panels' … 'in order to propose all the changes our political project needs'. While some of these were subsequently modified, the president's European policy has remained systematically connected with his vision of a sovereign and protective Europe, reaffirmed, again, at the presentation in December 2021 of the French EU Presidency's programme for the first half of 2022 (Élysée, 2021a). With Macron's forceful European leadership role legitimated as part of the *domaine réservé* of French presidents in the foreign policy domain, rooted in the constitution and confirmed by institutional practice, it comes as no surprise that Europe ministers in their successive governments have been unable to develop strong policy profiles of their own.

European coalition-building: beyond the Franco–German tandem

As a candidate, Macron twice chose Berlin to publicly state key elements of his project for Europe, leaving no doubt that he regarded a major relaunch of the European 'motor' role of the Franco-German tandem as crucial to his EU plans. However, the intended partnership with Germany turned out to be a struggle: there was considerable unease amongst Merkel's coalition partners regarding some of his objectives, especially the massive reinforcing of Eurozone governance and expansion of EU policies, which raised the spectre of substantial fiscal transfers and the loosening of budgetary restraints. A further complicating factor arose when the new German coalition government of March 2018 revealed internal tensions over EU policies between Chancellor Merkel and Social-Democratic Finance Minister Olaf Scholz. While German support was essential for Macron's October 2017 success regarding the revision of EU rules on the posting of seconded workers (Directive (EU) 2018/957), limiting secondments to other Member States to 12 months, Macron's vying for German support had generated, one year after his Sorbonne speech, nothing more strategic than the June 2018 Franco-German 'Meseberg Declaration', a sort of bilateral European wishlist without commitments to concrete action.

With Germany proving a somewhat reluctant partner, Macron went in search of broader European support. In October 2018, he began relaunching EU-level French cooperation with the Benelux countries – with a summit meeting at Bourglinster Castle – and reinforcing French links with Central and Eastern European countries through visits to Bratislava and Prague. He also started to adopt positions openly diverging from German interests: from February 2019 onwards, he became increasingly critical of the German–Russian North Stream II pipeline project – a stance that appealed to Poland and other Central and Eastern European countries – and he put the brakes on and, in October 2019, finally blocked the opening of accession negotiations with Albania and Northern Macedonia, which Germany had strongly favoured. He also shocked German political elites with his famous remarks about the 'brain death' of NATO in November 2019. Having, meanwhile, also sought more common European ground with Italy, by autumn 2019, he had clearly moved towards flexible European coalition-building – away from his initial focus on a strategic partnership with Germany, which was anyway undermined by the increasing French budgetary deficit following concessions to the Yellow Vests, which had renourished German concerns about French overspending habits.

In 2019, the president also sought support for his European agenda among EU institutions, particularly the creation of a potential power base in the EP through the May 2019 European elections. Macron went to great lengths to present the elections – using the nationalist right, again, as a convenient bogeyman – as 'decisive for the future of our continent' (Élysée, 2019) and to push the electoral chances of his party, *La République en Marche!* (LREM) by, *inter alia*, reverting back from an electoral system of multi-regional to national lists thought to favour his relatively new party. Yet, LREM was narrowly beaten by Le Pen's *Rassemblement National* (RN), with 22.4 against 23.3 per cent of the votes, and it subsequently struggled to exercise a major influence within the liberal 'Renew Europe' EP political group. However, Macron was more successful in expanding his support among new leaders of the EU institutions: he played a key role in the appointment of reform-oriented Belgian liberal Prime Minister Charles Michel – widely seen as a European ally of the president – as the new President of the European Council, and he used some rough manoeuvring (discussed later) to secure the selection of Ursula von der Leyen as the new president of the European Commission.

From 2020 onwards, Macron succeeded in building sufficiently broad and flexible EU-level coalitions, for example, in the negotiations on the 'Next Generation EU' (NGEU) recovery package, an unprecedented breakthrough towards intra-EU emergency fiscal transfers and a 'federal' type of debt via European Commission borrowing on the capital markets. With the Covid-19 crisis putting considerable pressure on national finances, Macron assumed a lead role in a group of nine Member States – including heavily indebted Italy and Spain as his main partners – calling for the issuing of joint EU *corona-bonds* to help Member States to tackle increasing budgetary difficulties (*Financial Times*, 2020a). Debt mutualisation had traditionally been staunchly opposed – especially by Germany. However, in the context of the Covid-19 crisis and of German fears of a destabilising economic slump and a new Eurozone debt crisis, Macron convinced Merkel to endorse a joint proposal for an EU recovery fund of €500 billion. This became the basis of a compromise on the NGEU recovery facility of €750 billion (at 2018 prices) approved by the European Council in July 2020 (Becker, 2021), with Macron playing a key role in overcoming the resistance to the so-called 'Frugal Four' (Austria, Denmark, the Netherlands and Sweden).

Another example of flexible coalition-building was the negotiations on the 2022 EU Directive on adequate minimum wages in the EU (Directive (EU) 2022/2041), during which staunch resistance from Central and Eastern European and Scandinavian Member States had to be overcome by concessions and sustained support from Mediterranean and Benelux countries. The directive helped the president to enhance his domestic credentials as a defender of workers' rights in a 'protective Europe', though the granting of concessions – such as the exemption of Member States without statutory minimum wages – indicated Macron's willingness to sacrifice substance in return for advancing his EU agenda.

Overall, however, despite some successes, Macron's coalition-building has thus far failed to generate any stable coalition supporting his 'sovereign Europe' vision. He has struggled, for example, with Central and Eastern European scepticism regarding his emphasis on EU (rather than NATO) defence capabilities and his long-sustained dialogue with Russia, as well as the opposition of the so-called 'New Hanseatic League' countries (the Nordic-Baltic 'Six', Ireland and the Netherlands) to his economic and financial plans (Schulz and Henökl, 2020). Domestic factors such as the 2018–2019 Yellow Vests crisis and the loss of his parliamentary majority in 2022 have also negatively affected his political weight in European negotiations.

Navigating and using EU crises: Covid-19 and the Russian invasion of Ukraine

Jean Monnet had been convinced that 'Europe will be forged through crises' (Monnet, 1978, p. 488). The two major and unprecedented crises that the EU has had to face (thus far) during Macron's period in office – the Covid-19 pandemic and the Russian invasion of Ukraine – have offered him commensurate, if complex, opportunities.

When the Covid-19 pandemic started filling hospital wards throughout Europe, Macron was at the forefront of European leaders declaring it to be a European challenge requiring European responses. On 14 April 2020, he asserted that this was to be Europe's 'moment of truth' concerning its capacity to deliver effective solidarity (*Financial Times*, 2020b). His primary focus was on EU action addressing the financial consequences and, in this respect, he achieved a major success with the NGEU funding package. Yet, his image as a protagonist of European solidarity was tainted by the French decision in March 2020 to requisition all protective masks for distribution to French medical personnel and citizens infected with Covid-19.[3] Given the severe mask penury across the EU, this blatant reassertion of national interests resulted in the requisition of 4 million masks stored in the Lyon warehouse of Swedish company Mölnlycke, a major Swedish supplier to other EU countries. The ensuing 'war of masks', involving diplomatic tensions with Sweden and criticisms of the French policy in Italy and elsewhere, was subsequently defused by a French donation of 1 million masks to Italy and personal intervention by Macron in April deblocking the Mölnlycke stocks; however, France's credibility as a leader on EU solidarity never entirely recovered.

The effective production and distribution of Covid-19 vaccines could have shown Macron's 'sovereign' and 'protective' Europe at its best, but the EU's performance was somewhat underwhelming: ministers were slow to agree on the principle of the joint procurement of any vaccines and more precious time elapsed before, from 18 June onwards, the Commission was allowed to negotiate for the member states' advance vaccine purchase contracts with companies (Della Corte, 2023). By then, the EU was already lagging more than two months behind the United States and the United Kingdom (European Court of Auditors, 2022). The contracting process was later accelerated, but the eventual rollout of the vaccines was delayed both by a longer EU approval process and by insufficiently defined delivery obligations for pharmaceutical companies (Hyde, 2021). Commission President von der Leyen, who had received such decisive backing from Macron when appointed, came under fierce criticism and had finally to admit before the EP in February 2021 that 'We were late in granting authorisation. We were too optimistic about mass production. And maybe we also took for granted that the doses ordered would actually arrive on time' (European Parliament, 2021, p. 4). There is no indication that Macron took any action to accelerate the EU-wide rollout of the vaccines in the crucial period from November 2020 to January 2021. It appears that he personally – as always sure of his own judgement – was sceptical of the effectiveness of the new vaccines. As late as 4 December 2020, more than two weeks after the breakthrough of the Pfizer and BionTech vaccines had been announced, Macron declared that he wished to be 'very careful' and that vaccinating the population was not a priority in the French strategy against the pandemic,[4] a position that also resulted in a much-criticised delay in the preparation for the vaccine rollout in France itself.[5]

'Sovereign' and 'protective' Europe has been challenged in a very different way by the Russian Federation's military aggression against Ukraine since February 2022. Before the Russian invasion, the French president had gone to great lengths to avert it through his dialogue with President Vladimir Putin, starting with a reception in the splendours of Versailles in May 2017. Macron persisted with his efforts despite mounting criticism from Central and Eastern European and Baltic and Nordic EU Member States, even at the risk of embarrassment when Putin received him in February 2022, at the opposite end of an improbably long marble table, for five (eventually fruitless) hours of bilateral talks. This persistence (while France was holding the rotating EU presidency at the beginning of 2022) indicated that, unlike many other Western leaders and, apparently, even Ukraine itself, Macron judged military action by Russia to end Ukraine's independence to be a distinct possibility. An invasion would not only wreck his intention, perfectly compatible with the Gaullist tradition, to establish a constructive partnership between the EU and its most powerful neighbour – still described by Macron as 'profoundly European' – at his August 2019 meeting with Putin at Briançon (*Le Monde*, 2019) but would also inevitably relaunch a debate about further EU enlargement, about which he was clearly not enthusiastic. Once the Russian tanks started rolling in, the French president then gradually – but substantially – changed his strategy.

While keeping communication channels with Putin open, Macron not only fully backed successive EU sanctions packages against Russia – and EU economic, financial and military aid to Ukraine – but also gradually became a protagonist of further EU enlargement. On 9 May 2022, he launched his initiative of a 'European Political Community' (EPC), an intergovernmental policy coordination platform involving the EU and other neighbouring countries sharing its values, including the United Kingdom. This was seen by many as a concealed alternative to EU membership for Ukraine and other candidate countries since he also declared at the time that Ukraine's accession to the EU would take 'probably several decades' (see Mucznik, 2022). However, in June 2022, he fully supported the decision of the European Council – which also approved his EPC initiative – to grant EU accession candidate status to Ukraine and Moldova, the acceleration of the accession process of Western Balkan countries and the recognition of a 'European perspective' for Georgia. His policy change was completed by his call at the Bratislava GLOBSEC summit in May 2023 for the entry to the EU of Ukraine, Moldova and the Western Balkans 'as quickly as possible' (Élysée, 2023) and his major contribution to the European Council's December 2023 decision to open accession negotiations with Moldova and Ukraine. What has been described as a turning point in French EU policy (de Weck, 2023) can best be explained as Macron making a virtue of necessity by using the renewed pro-enlargement dynamic in the EU as a new element of his 'sovereign' Europe strategy and narrative. Having already stressed, in his Bratislava speech, necessary parallelism between further EU enlargement and EU governance reforms, he emphasised in his post-European Council press conference in December 2023 that further enlargement should be conditional upon prior major reforms enhancing the EU's 'sovereignty' and effectiveness, adding that the EU was still 'far away from an effective membership of the Ukraine'.[6]

Macron's Ukraine-crisis–induced strategy change linking enlargement with his EU reform agenda came with a much-needed new opening for Franco-German cooperation. This had come under strain, most notably because of a rift, defused only in October 2023, over the French insistence on including nuclear energy as a 'clean technology' under the EU's 'Green Deal'. Since December 2021, German Chancellor Olaf Scholz has constantly backed further EU enlargement whilst also linking it with the need for institutional reforms. This provided common ground for Macron and Scholz on an enlargement-related EU reform agenda. The main result (thus far) has been the presentation, in September 2023, of a report by a joint ('independent') Franco-German expert group on EU institutional reform that, *inter alia*, advocates a major extension of qualified majority voting and EU budgetary resources as well as a model of differentiation of Europe in four concentric circles (France Diplomacy, 2023). The report's bewildering range of proposals, the dramatisation of Europe's situation (sailing in high seas) and concern about Europe's 'overall sovereignty' suggests a strong influence of Macron's European narrative. Yet, the report has had a mixed reception in other capitals – and has so far generated only a vaguely phrased December 2023 commitment of the European Council to address internal reforms 'with a view to adopting, by summer 2024, conclusions on a roadmap for future work' (European Council, 2023, p. 6).

European 'sovereignty' in the security domain – and French national interests

On Macron's European reform agenda, security has ranked the highest. The international context has provided major tailwinds: in 2017, Member States were still under the shock of US President Donald Trump's 'America First' unilateralism and unsettling pronouncements on NATO, which made the US security commitment to Europe look increasingly uncertain. If the new Biden administration considerably allayed European security fears, the Russian invasion of Ukraine generated a new dramatic European perception just as Macron was seeking re-election in 2022.

In his 2017 Sorbonne speech, Macron had identified a joint intervention force, defence budget and doctrine for action as strategic objectives for European 'sovereignty' in the security domain (Élysée, 2017). In November 2018, he went even further by advocating a 'real European army' capable of defending Europe 'alone, without depending only on the United States and in a more sovereign manner'.[7] Whereas some critics have dismissed the reference to a 'European army' as a mere political slogan (Soutou, 2019), others have seen it as aiming at a fully fledged European military alliance, though not necessarily based on a federal EU army model (Keohane, 2017). The president's major emphasis on enhanced European security capabilities corresponds to a long-standing French interest in 'European strategic autonomy', which was first publicly formulated in the 1994 French White Paper on security (Ministère de la Défense, 1994, p. 139) but which originates with de Gaulle's emphasis on a 'European Europe' during the Cold War (Mélandri, 1985). Macron's European 'sovereignty' in the defence domain serves manifest political and economic interests. With France's military capabilities (since the United Kingdom's withdrawal) because of its nuclear weapons surpassing those of any other EU Member State, the country will necessarily be a key player in any move towards more integrated European defence structures, compensating, *inter alia*, for its weaker economic position *vis-à-vis* Germany. There is also a specific French economic-interest dimension, as European defence 'sovereignty' may well serve France's large share in EU defence industries and the development of critical military technologies (Bora and Schramm, 2023, pp. 15–16).

Despite the favourable exogenous factors, Macron has remained vague on the concrete action to be taken to achieve European defence 'sovereignty', such as the joint defence doctrine, with implementing proposals overall falling short of his conceptually ambitious reform discourse (Vallée, 2022). Inevitably, Macron has struggled with scepticism or even outright opposition regarding European strategic autonomy, mainly among Central and Eastern European Member States, which still regard more assertive EU defence moves as potentially undermining essential NATO and US security guarantees (Franke and Varma, 2019). Consequently, Macron's advances have been patchy rather than system-changing.

The 'joint intervention force' of the Sorbonne speech has taken the form of a 'European Intervention Initiative' (EI2). According to the letter of intent of June 2018, signed initially by 9 and currently by 13 European countries, EI2 has the primary objective of developing a 'shared strategic culture' through strategic foresight, intelligence sharing, scenario development and planning and lessons learned from operations and doctrine (Ministère des Armées, 2018, p. 2). The EI2 would not have come into being without Macron's initiative and tenacity. Nevertheless, it is unclear how much progress it brings towards a more 'sovereign' Europe: thus far, only 11 Member States have joined, and there is ample room for competition, duplication and complexity (two non-EU countries, Norway and the United Kingdom, are also participating) in relations with the 'Permanent Structured Cooperation' (PESCO) of the EU's 'Common Foreign and Security Policy' (CFSP). Macron may well have intended to bypass the various dysfunctionalities of the larger PESCO by regrouping, under the EI2 umbrella, only the more politically willing and more militarily capable (such as the United Kingdom) to increase European force projection capability (van Eekelen, 2018). Yet, it is uncertain whether the addition of another differentiated European defence cooperation framework to an already rather crowded and complex European security landscape will make a positive difference. Given that the EI2 has thus far generated mainly ministerial meetings, various working parties and conferences, sceptics labelling the EI2 as an 'Erasmus for soldiers' (Witney, 2018, p. 1) and/or a 'politically inflated talking shop' (Koenig, 2018, p. 6) may eventually not be proven wrong. If Macron had any hopes – as many have suggested (Cánovas, 2019) – to use the EI2 as a vehicle to secure support for French security concerns in Africa and the Sahel, the progressive crumbling of French African policy through the military coups in Mali in 2021, Burkina Faso in 2022 and Niger in 2023, without any discernible reaction by the EI2, should by now have put those to rest (see Chapter 13).

The 'joint defence budget' advocated by Macron in his Sorbonne speech has seen a first concretisation with the 2019 agreement on the innovative 'European Defence Fund' (EDF), which uses, for the first time, the EU budget for coordinating, supplementing and amplifying national investments in defence research, the development of prototypes and the acquisition of defence equipment and technology. Although the EDF goes back to a 2016 proposal by Commission President Jean-Claud Juncker, it owes much of its final establishment and funding line of €7.9 billion for the 2021–2027 Multi-Annual Financial Framework (MFF) to Macron's strong support. While the strengthening of the fragmented Research and Development (R&D) capabilities of European defence industries is surely the EDF's primary strategic objective, specific French interests have not been far behind, given the aforementioned strong French defence sector. According to EDF implementation figures for 2021 and 2022, 31 and 32 per cent, respectively, of coordinators of EDF projects have been French (Masson, 2023, p. 15), making for an impressively large national share in the EU-27. A similarly major convergence between EU and French national interests can be identified in the strong emphasis on collaborative investments in joint projects and the joint procurement of defence capabilities in the European Council's 'Versailles Declaration' of March 2022 (European Council, 2022, p. 4), unsurprisingly highlighted on the Élysée website as one of the President's European achievements (Élysée, 2024).

The creation of a 'Security and Defence' section in the EU's 2021–2027 MFF – agreed by the December 2020 European Council – might seem like a decisive breakthrough of Macron's 'joint defence budget' objective – and, indeed, is presented as such on the Élysée website (Élysée, 2024). Yet, the €14.9 billion covers not only spending on defence but also expenditure on internal security and nuclear safety, leaving for actual defence merely the €7.9 billion of the EDF and €1.7 billion for enhancing military transport mobility within the EU (European Commission, 2021). With only €9.6 billion over seven years and a total of just 0.79 per cent of the total MFF, this EU 'defence fund' verges on the merely symbolic. Although MFF defence spending has been complemented, with strong French support, by another funding instrument – the 'European Peace Facility' (EPF) – for actions with CFSP defence implications, this is an intergovernmental instrument outside the EU budget and – with €12 billion for the period 2021–2027 – financially only marginally more substantial. Given this rather modest financial framework, it is no surprise that the president has recently – at the World Economic Forum in Davos in January 2024 – advocated the issuing of Eurobonds for EU defence industries and military assistance to Ukraine.[8]

Regarding the third strategic defence objective identified in the Sorbonne speech, a 'joint doctrine of action' – thus far the only concrete advance achieved apart from the nebulous EI2 framework – is the adoption by the European Council in March 2022 of a 'Strategic Compass' of the EU (Council of the European Union, 2022). Championed by Macron, this policy document provides a fairly comprehensive assessment of the strategic security challenges that the EU faces, ranging from more conventional threats in its neighbourhood over a destabilised multilateral system to transnational threats in cyberspace, terrorism, climate change and environmental degradation. Yet, the imbalance between the identified threats and the capabilities that the 'Compass' proposes to deploy is both obvious and striking (Perissich, 2021). For example, one of the key action points – the creation of an 'EU Rapid Deployment Capacity' of up to 5,000 troops by 2025, falls size-wise well short even of the EU's Corps of Border and Coast Guards, scheduled to reach a personnel strength of 10,000 by 2027. With unresolved key issues of the EU's security relationship with the United States and NATO carefully avoided and most of the 40 pages of the 'Compass' taken up by analysis and issues for further deliberation, one commentator saw the document as just another example of the EU's 'unfortunate habit of wanting to drape the most banal political and administrative activity in the clothes of a major reform' (Santopinto, 2022, p. 5).

European 'sovereignty' in the economic and financial domain and French national interests

In his 2017 Sorbonne speech, Macron defined a 'stronger budget ... at the heart of the Eurozone' in order to fund more investments and 'provide stability in the face of economic shocks as essential to European "sovereignty"'. It took the president until October 2019 – after much working on his German partners and struggling with 'frugal' Member States, especially the Netherlands – to achieve a first success with the agreement of Eurozone finance ministers on a 'Budgetary Instrument for Convergence and Competitiveness' under the 2021–2027 MFF, with up to €30 billion for loans to Member States to enable them to better respond to changing economic circumstances and large asymmetric shocks. However, this instrument of relatively modest size fell well short of Macron's ambitions. It was ultimately superseded, before even being implemented, by the much larger NGEU, declared by the Elysée to be 'the greatest relaunch plan of European history' (Élysée, 2024).

Complementing the 2021–2027 MFF to tackle the adverse economic and financial consequences of the Covid-19 crisis, the bulk of the NGEU – €723.8 billion out of a total of €806.9 billion (at 2023 prices) – is allocated to a 'Resilience and Recovery Facility' (RRF). Up to €338 billion of the RRF is provided to Member States as non-repayable grants and up to €385.8 billion in repayable loans. Member States can apply for this funding based on national project-based 'Recovery and Resilience Plans' (RRPs), which serve a number of defined objectives, amongst which green transition, digital transformation and smart, sustainable and inclusive growth are ranked first (Council Regulation (EU) 2021/241). With economically and financially weaker Member States benefitting from the highest funding levels, the NGEU is a real instrument of solidarity, and it has been estimated that transfers – net of expected repayments to those Member States projected to benefit the most – are likely to significantly exceed the aid worth 2.6 per cent of recipients' GDP that the United States granted to Europe under the Marshall Plan (Pisani-Ferry, 2020). The NGEU is funded by the European Commission's issue of EU-Bonds on the capital markets, secured against an EU budget with a raised ceiling and with repayments to take place from 2028 to 2058.

The NGEU is as unprecedented as it is problematic: it has set a precedent both for massive EU-level borrowing and its use for off-setting crisis effects and related net transfers between Member States. Amongst others, the German Court of Auditors has warned that the result could be both an increased moral hazard – with some Member States incurring higher debts in the expectation of further 'next-generation' EU solidarity – and more EU extensive borrowing in the advent of other (surely inevitable) crises (*Bundesrechnungshof*, 2021). The NGEU is also an 'emergency' temporary instrument whose funding stimulus will run out in 2026. If the RRPs underperform – and certain quality assurance gaps in the implementation process have already become apparent (European Court of Auditors, 2023) – the EU could, from 2027 onwards (when Macron will no longer be in office), face the unpleasant prospect of having to reimburse long-term debts for an underperforming former instrument. Meanwhile, the costs of a greater European economic 'sovereignty' funded by debts are already mounting, as the estimated borrowing cost of the NGEU instrument proposed in the draft estimates for the 2024 EU budget has increased by 53.6

per cent compared to initial financial programming (European Parliament, 2023).

Macron has consistently supported an expansion of EU 'own-resources' revenue. In December 2020, a new own resource based on non-recycled plastic waste (Council Decision [EU, Euratom] 2020/2053) was introduced with full French support and, in December 2021, the Commission proposed additional own resources deriving from an extended emissions trading scheme (ETS), the EU's new carbon border adjustment mechanism (CBAM) – proposed in Macron's Sorbonne speech – and a share of the profits of large multinational companies. However, at the time of writing, approval of the Commission proposals by the Council was still pending because of disagreements over details.

Macron's 'whatever it costs' approach to limit the Covid-19–related socioeconomic damage through various income support measures during 2022 was broadly welcomed in France and possibly helped with his re-election. Yet, these measures contributed to a drastic increase in the national debt which, by late 2023, had made France the third most indebted Member State after Greece and Italy (Eurostat, 2024) and an unprecedented debt total of €3,088 trillion (INSEE, 2023). France therefore came under pressure to avoid an infringement of the Stability and Growth Pact (SGP) debt rules, potentially resulting in an excessive deficit procedure, with EU-imposed fines and a significant loss of credibility. This accelerated French efforts, backed by Italy and other highly indebted Member States, to reach a deal with Germany, backed by a coalition of 'frugals', on a revision of the SGP rules. Negotiations between the French Finance Minister and his German counterpart proved difficult, as Germany – after a temporary relaxation of the SGP rules because of the Covid-19 crisis – wanted a return to their rigorous application. Eventually, a compromise was reached reconfirming the SGP rules with a temporary loosening of conditions. France won, in particular, a 'resilience margin' for all countries to create 'buffers', enabling them to cope with economic shocks without painful cuts to essential spending and a transition period until 2027 (the final year of Macron's presidency), taking into account rising interest rates in the calculation of debt-reduction efforts (Council of the EU, 2023). This raises the wider issue of whether a Member State that has budgetary discipline problems may well see a longer-term advantage in the precedent set by the NGEU for EU-level borrowing, as it may have to rely on this source of additional income stream at some time in the future.

'Sovereign' Europe: a 'democratic power'?

In his 2017 Humboldt University speech, Macron had stated that 'sovereign' Europe 'must rely on a true democratic revival'[2] and, in his Sorbonne speech a few months later, he had proposed both transnational electoral lists for EP elections and the organisation of 'European conventions' to associate citizens with the 'refoundation' of Europe. After the transnational list proposal was rejected in February 2018 by the EP and later shelved by the European Council, the president was left with his idea of 'European conventions'. Other capitals were initially unenthusiastic, not only because Macron had made neither the conventions' format nor their eventual objective entirely clear but also because the 2002–2003 'Convention on the future of Europe' – with the subsequent failure of its 'Constitutional Treaty' – had not left unclouded memories. In March 2019, Macron relaunched the idea, in an open letter to European citizens, of a citizens' convention to 'propose all the changes our political project needs, with an open mind, even to amending the treaties' (Élysée, 2019). Endorsed by the Commission President and supported by the EP but with only a lukewarm endorsement by the European Council, Macron's initiative resulted in the convocation and opening on 9 May 2021, delayed by the Covid pandemic, of the 'Conference on the Future of Europe'.

The conference involved 800 randomly selected citizens from all 27 Member States, who discussed among themselves and with political representatives the policy challenges and reform needs, with an online platform for citizens' input and a conference plenary of 449 members – bringing together representatives of European institutions, national parliaments, social partners, civil society and citizens – tasked to draw up recommendations. The conference concluded on 9 May 2022 with the adoption of a 333-page final report comprising 49 'proposals' and 326 'proposed measures', ranging from comparatively minor policy recommendations to more fundamental EU system changes requiring treaty reforms (Conference on the Future of Europe, 2022). At the closing ceremony, Macron hailed this 'unprecedented democratic exercise' and – without taking up any of the conference's recommendations – praised 'our ambition' of 'acting decisively, moving swiftly, dreaming big' (Élysée, 2022). Yet, the same day, Sweden – holding the EU Council Presidency – and the governments of the 12 Members States having acceded since 2004 – moved to curb any further acting, moving or dreaming: they published a 'non-paper' on the conference's outcome, rejecting any 'unconsidered and premature attempt to launch a process towards treaty change' and stating that recent crises had 'clearly shown how much the EU can deliver within the current treaty framework' (Swedish Presidency of the Council of the EU, 2022). Neither the European Council nor the French president – the spiritual father of the whole exercise – has made any real effort since then to introduce the conference's proposals into the EU policy-making process. The imbalance between the declared purpose and the tangible results of the whole venture reminds us of Macron's domestic 'National Refoundation

Council' (*Conseil national de la refondation*) initiative of 2022 (discussed in Chapter 3).

At the launch of the conference in 2021, Macron stated that 'our European democracy is a democracy of compromise, of balance, which is a virtue that we must protect, but it is also a weakness when it suffocates in its own procedures' (Élysée, 2021b). This seemed to suggest that European democracy occasionally needs a bit of management in order not to be 'suffocated in procedures'. Macron's handling of the appointment of the new Commission President in 2019, mentioned earlier, showed how this can work in practice.

According to the precedent set after the 2014 EP elections and based on a (contested) interpretation of Article 17(7) of the Treaty establishing the European Union, the lead candidate (*Spitzenkandidat*) of the political group having gained the highest number of votes in the EP elections had been widely expected to become the candidate proposed by the European Council to the EP as the new president of the Commission. Yet, this European People's Party (EPP) candidate, the German Christian-Democrat Manfred Weber, was strongly disapproved of by Macron, who regarded him as lacking in experience and too conservative in his EU agenda. Taking the lead of an anti-Weber coalition in the European Council and rejecting the principle of the *Spitzenkandidaten* process, the president effectively blocked the appointment of Weber, despite the latter's initial backing by Merkel and other governments. After other *Spitzenkandidaten* had also been ruled out by the Council, Macron proposed, on 1 July 2019, German defence Minister Ursula von der Leyen, although she had been neither a candidate for the presidency nor was a primary choice of her party colleague, Merkel. With this surprise move, the president was not oblivious to French interests, since the appointment of a German president of the Commission could (and eventually did) clear the way for the appointment of French International Monetary Fund Director, Christine Lagarde, as the new head of the European Central Bank. Faced with deadlock after days of acrimonious negotiations, the other EU heads of state and governments followed Macron's lead on a German Christian-Democrat candidate lacking both democratic legitimacy and a European profile but with years of governmental experience and the prospect of being the first woman ever appointed to the job (Meissner, Schoeller and Moury, 2021). Widespread criticisms of her record as Defence Minister in Germany were vigorously brushed aside by the French president, who praised, *inter alia*, her commitment to enhanced EU military capabilities. Irrespective of von der Leyen's qualifications, the fact that Macron did not hesitate to secure the appointment of a candidate at the top of the EU's executive, who European citizens in the preceding elections had neither known to be a candidate nor had had an opportunity to vote for, can be taken as an indication that the president's more 'sovereign' Europe may not necessarily also mean a more 'democratic' one.

Conclusions

Given Macron's conceptual fireworks surrounding a 'sovereign' and 'protective' Europe and his avalanche of reform proposals, the balance sheet – after two-thirds of his presidency – while certainly not empty, is hardly impressive, all the more so as two major EU crises – Covid-19 and the invasion of the Ukraine – have provided forceful tailwinds. Thus far, the advances connected with Macron's leadership are either – as in the defence field – lacking in substance or – as with NGEU debt-funding – have their problematic side. Furthermore, many of these advances have a distinct French national-interest dimension. This is usual business in the EU, but, for a leader posturing as a European game-changer, it has been rightly said that 'this point deserves to be stressed' (Bora and Schramm, 2023, p. 19).

Macron's presidency cannot be connected to any breakthrough moments in the process of European integration comparable to those of his predecessors: Valéry Giscard d'Estaing (introduction of the European Council and direct Europe elections), François Mitterrand (launch of the Single Currency project) or Nicolas Sarkozy (passing of the Lisbon Treaty after the Constitutional Treaty debacle). Macron may have made a number of tactical mistakes, such as investing initially too much in an elusive grand alliance with Germany, taking up the fight for European reforms on too many issues at the same time and constantly seeking the maximum limelight for his European agenda rather than trying to further it through quiet background diplomacy and consensus-building. However, more importantly, Macron's reform plans have run up against a wide range of well-entrenched interests and, simply, different visions of Europe among diverse Member States, rendered all the more formidable by the enhanced diversity generated by successive EU enlargements. As these obstacles were perfectly predictable, one may ask why a president whose speeches are rich in logical argumentation has pushed his conceptualisation of Europe and his reform agenda well beyond the realistically attainable. Personal conviction – always difficult to ascertain with serving politicians – may have played its part; an overestimation of his own powers of persuasion another. Nevertheless, there is also a considerable element of political 'spin' in the mantra-like usage of the image of a 'sovereign' Europe (which legally remains as non-sovereign as ever), the talking up of threats facing Europe, the systematic over-representation of advances (however modest) and the non-acknowledgement of fundamental obstacles.

As mentioned earlier, Macron's discourse about a 'sovereign' and 'protective' Europe has also been aimed at increasing support for the European project amongst mostly unenthusiastic French citizens. *Eurobarometer* opinion polls indicate that, thus far, the president has failed to fundamentally change the prevailing attitude in his country: according to the December 2016 *Eurobarometer*, the last edition before Macron's election, 65 per cent of

French citizens polled tended not to trust the EU compared to 29 per cent trusting it and 9 per cent not knowing (Eurobarometer, 2016, p. 2). In the December 2023 *Eurobarometer* – after more than six years of sustained pro-European discourse by the president and his governments – these figures had not fundamentally changed, with 55 per cent of French citizens still not trusting the EU compared to 35 per cent trusting it and 10 per cent having no opinion, making France, alongside Cyprus, the EU Member State whose citizenry has the least trust in the EU (Eurobarometer, 2023, p. 10). While a number of EU incidents, such as the ongoing EP Quatar corruption scandal, have surely not helped the EU's public image in recent years, the president's vision of Europe is apparently failing to convince the majority of his fellow citizens. Opinion polls at the time of writing suggest that support for Macron's 'Besoin d'Europe' list in the June 2024 EP elections could be less than half that for Le Pen's party, headed by the young and charismatic Jordan Bordella.

Prospects for major advances of the president's European agenda thus hardly look promising: even in the (unlikely) case of the European Council's mandated 'roadmap' for EU reform opening a path towards an EU treaty reform, the president would enter probably conflictual negotiations with a much-weakened domestic position, the end of his term in sight and the usual ratification risks. With his presidency fast running out, Macron's frustration over what he has recently called 'the disastrous stupidity' (*Le Point*, 2023) of his being constitutionally prevented from seeking a third mandate in 2027 may also result from his thus far unfulfilled European plans. It will be up to future historians to judge whether Macron's departure in 2027 will be as great a loss for the European construction as the president himself may think.

Notes

1 A speech all the more aimed at a European audience as it was given in English, available at: https://www.rewi.hu-berlin.de/de/lf/oe/whi/FCE/2017/rede-macron.
2 Video of the debate 'Gabriel–Macron–Habermas: Which future for Europe?', Hertie School of Governance: https://www.youtube.com/watch?v=OZRE3P3z_jA.
3 Décret n° 2020-190 relatif aux réquisitions nécessaires dans le cadre de la lutte contre le virus Covid-19.
4 Interview given to *Brut*, 4 December 2020 (available at https://www.midilibre.fr/2020/12/04/suivez-en-direct-linterview-demmanuel-macron-sadressant-aux-jeunes-sur-le-media-en-ligne-brut-9238156.php).
5 Critics have not provided estimates of the number of French lives possibly lost because of initial presidential doubts about the effectiveness of the new vaccines.
6 No transcript available. Video: https://www.youtube.com/watch?v=o6uVHhr5wOg
7 *Public Sénat*: Macron propose '*une vraie armée européenne*', 6 November 2018.
8 Video: https://www.elysee.fr/emmanuel-macron/2024/01/17/54eme-edition-du-forum-economique-mondial-de-davos

References

Becker, P. (2021) 'Haushaltspolitik', in Weidenfeld, W. and Wessels, W. (eds) *Jahrbuch der Europäishen Integration 2021*. Baden-Baden: Nomos, pp. 245–250.

Bertoncini, Y. (2022) 'Les candidats-présidents et "l'Europe": une convergence en trompe l'œil ?' *La Grande Conversation*, 31 March. https://www.lagrandeconversation.com/politique/les-candidats-presidents-et-leurope-une-convergence-en-trompe-loeil/

Birnbaum, P. (2021) 'La force de l'État à la française', *Pouvoir*, 177, pp. 17–24.

Bora, S.I. and Schramm, L. (2023) 'Toward a more "sovereign" Europe? Domestic, bilateral, and European factors to explain France's (growing) influence on EU politics, 2017–2022', *French Politics*, 23, pp. 3–24.

Bundesrechnungshof (2021) *Bericht nach § 99 BHO zu den möglichen Auswirkungen der gemeinschaftlichen Kreditaufnahme der Mitgliedstaaten der Europäischen Union auf den Bundeshaushalt (Wiederaufbaufonds)*. Bonn: Bundesrechnungshof.

Cánovas, L.E.M. (2019) *The European Intervention Initiative, Permanent Structured Cooperation and French Institutional Engineering*. Madrid: Instituto Español de Estudios Estratégicos, Opinion Paper 79/2019.

Conference on the Future of Europe (2022) *Report on the Final Outcome*, May 2022. The report on the final outcomes of the Conference on the Future of Europe is now online | Knowledge for policy (europa.eu).

Conseil Constitutionnel (1976) 'Décision n° 76-71 DC du 30 décembre 1976 (élection de l'Assemblée des Communautés au suffrage universel direct)', *Journal officiel* du 31 décembre 1976, p. 7651.

Council of the European Union (2022) *A Strategic Compass for Security and Defence*. Brussels: Council of the European Union, Council document 7371/22, 21 March.

Council of the EU (2023) *Presidency Revised Compromise Text on Commission Proposal for a Regulation [...] on the Effective Coordination of Economic Policies and Multilateral Budgetary Surveillance*. Brussels: Council of the EU, Council document 15874/1/23 REV 1, 8 December.

Della Corte, F.S. (2023) 'The EU vaccines strategy: A missed opportunity for EU public health?', *European Journal of Risk Regulation*, pp. 1–13.

De Weck, J. (2023) 'Why Macron is now embracing EU and NATO enlargement', *Internationale Politik Quarterly*, 4.

Élysée (2017) 'Initiative pour l'Europe: discours d'Emmanuel Macron pour une Europe souveraine, unie, démocratique', 26 September. https://www.elysee.fr/emmanuel-macron/2017/09/26/initiative-pour-l-europe-discours-d-emmanuel-macron-pour-une-europe-souveraine-unie-democratique

Élysée (2019) 'Lettre d'information: pour une renaissance européenne', 4 March. (https://www.elysee.fr/emmanuel-macron/2019/03/04/pour-une-renaissance-europeenne).

Élysée (2021a) 'Présentation de la Présidence française du Conseil de l'Union européenne', 9 December. https://www.elysee.fr/emmanuel-macron/2021/12/09/presentation-de-la-presidence-francaise-du-conseil-de-lunion-europeenne

Élysée (2021b) 'Discours du Président de la République à l'occasion du lancement de la Conférence sur l'avenir de l'Europe', 9 May. https://www.elysee.fr/emmanuel-macron/2021/05/09/lancement-de-la-conference-sur-lavenir-de-leurope

Elysée (2022) 'Discours du Président de la République à l'occasion de la Conférence sur l'avenir de l'Europe'. https://www.elysee.fr/emmanuel-macron/2022/05/09/cloture-de-la-conference-sur-avenir-de-europe

Élysée (2023) 'Sommet Globsec à Bratislava: discours de clôture du Président de la République', 31 May. https://www.elysee.fr/emmanuel-macron/2023/06/01/sommet-globsec-a-bratislava

Élysée (2024) 'Bilan de l'action européenne du Président de la République'. https://www.elysee.fr/emmanuel-macron/bilan-de-laction-europeenne-du-president-de-la-republique

En Marche! (2017) *Le programme d'Emmanuel Macron pour l'Europe*. Paris.

Eurobarometer (2016) *Standard Eurobarometer 86, The Key Indicators, France, Autumn 2018*. Luxembourg: Eurobarometer.

Eurobarometer (2023) *Standard Eurobarometer 100, First Results Report*. Luxembourg: Eurobarometer.

European Commission (2021) *Multiannual Financial Framework 2021–2027 (in commitments): current prices*. Brussels: European Commission.

European Council (2022) 'Informal meeting of the Heads of State or Government. Versailles Declaration 10 and 11 March 2022'. Press release, 11 March.

European Council (2023) 'European Council meeting (14 and 15 December 2023) – Conclusions, EUCO 20/23', 15 December.

European Court of Auditors (2022) *Special Report 19/2022: EU Covid-19 Vaccine Procurement*. Luxembourg: Publications Office of the European Union.

European Court of Auditors (2023) *Special Report 07/2023: Design of the Commission's Control System for the RRF*. Luxembourg: Publications Office of the European Union.

European Parliament (2021) *Verbatim Report of Proceedings*. Wednesday 10 February, CRE-9-2021-02-10_EN, p. 29.

European Parliament (2023) *Long-Term EU Budget for 2021 to 2027: State of Play, EPRS Briefing*, June.

Eurostat (2024) 'Government debt down to 89.9% of GDP in euro area', *Euroindicators*, 12/2024.

Financial Times (2020a) 'Nine eurozone countries issue call for "coronabonds"', 25 March.

Financial Times (2020b) 'Emmanuel Macron: "We are at a moment of truth"' (French), 14 April.

France Diplomacy (2023) *Report by the Independent Franco-German Group of Experts on EU Reforms: Sailing on High Seas. Reforming and Enlarging the EU for the 21st Century*. Paris-Berlin, 18 September.

Franke, U. and Varma, T. (2019) *Independence Play: Europe's Pursuit of Strategic Autonomy*. London and Berlin: European Council on Foreign Relations.

Gaïa, P. (2013) 'Le Conseil constitutionnel et le droit de l'Union européenne', *Annuaire international de justice constitutionnelle*, 28, pp. 547–599.

Grillmeyer, D., Keller, E. and Seidendorf, S. (2018) *Ein Jahr Macron. Reformen, Regierungsstil, Herausforderungen. Aktuelle Frankreich Analysen, no. 32*. Ludwigsburg: Deutsch-Französisches Institut.

Hyde, R. (2021) 'Von der Leyen admits to Covid-19 vaccine failures', *The Lancet*, 397(10275), pp. 655–656.

INSEE (2023) 'À la fin du troisième trimestre 2023, la dette publique s'établit à 3 088,2 Md€', *Informations rapides*, 331, 22 December.

Keohane, D. (2017) 'Macron's European Defense Doctrine', *Carnegie Europe*, 28 September (https://carnegieeurope.eu/strategiceurope/73246).

Koenig, N. (2018) *PESCO and the EI2: Similar Aims, Different Paths*. Berlin: Hertie School Jacques Delors Institute, Policy Brief. (https://www.delorscentre.eu/en/publications/detail/publication/pesco-and-the-ei2-similar-aims-different-paths).

Le Monde (2019) 'A Brégançon, Emmanuel Macron tend la main à la Russie, "profondément européenne"', 20 August.
Le Point (2023) '"Une funeste connerie": Macron regrette la limitation des mandats présidentiels', 31 August.
Masson, H. (2023) *European Defence Fund. EDF 2022 Calls Results and Comparison with EDF 2021*. Levallois-Perret: Fondation pour la Récherche Stratégique.
Mélandri, P. (1985) 'Le Général de Gaulle, la construction européenne et l'Alliance atlantique', in Barnavi, É. and Friedländer, S. (eds) *La Politique étrangère du général de Gaulle*. Paris: Presses Universitaires de France, pp. 87–111.
Meissner, K., Schoeller, M. and Moury, C. (2021) *The European Parliament and the Investiture of the Commission*. Vienna: Centre for European Integration Research, Working Paper No. 03/2021.
Ministère de la Défense (1994) *Livre Blanc sur la Défense*. Paris: Ministère de la Défense.
Ministère des Armées (2018) *Letter of Intent between the Defence Ministers of Belgium, Denmark, Estonia, France, Germany, The Netherlands, Portugal, Spain and the United Kingdom Concerning the Development of the European Intervention Initiative*, 25 June.
Monnet, J. (1978) *Mémoires*. Paris: Fayard.
Mucznik, M. (2022) 'The European (geo)political community and enlargement reform', *European Policy Forum*, 14 July https://www.epc.eu/en/Publications/The-European-geopolitical-community-and-enlargement-reform~49e404
Perissich, R. (2021) *Europe's Strategic Compass: Merits and Shortcomings*. Rome: Istituto Affari Internazionali, IAI Commentaries, 10 December.
Pisani-Ferry, J. (2020) *Europe's Recovery Gamble*. Brussels: Bruegel, 25 September.
Santopinto, F. (2022) 'The new Strategic Compass leaves the EU disoriented', *IPS-Journal*, 22 March 2022.
Schön-Quinlivan, E. (2017) '"The elephant in the room" no more: Europe as a structuring line of political cleavage in the 2017 presidential election', *French Politics*, 15(3), pp. 290–302.
Schulz, D. and Henökl, F. (2020) 'New alliances in post-Brexit Europe: Does the New Hanseatic League revive Nordic political cooperation?', *Politics and Governance*, 8(4), pp. 78–88.
Soutou, G.-H. (2019) 'L'Armée européenne: une gageure historique et structurelle', *Revue Défense Nationale*, 4, pp. 15–21.
Swedish Presidency of the Council of the EU (2022) 'Non-paper [...] on the outcome of and follow-up to the conference on the future of Europe', Brussels, 9 May.
Touteleurope (2017) 'Emmanuel Macron président: soulagement et espoir chez les Européens'. https://www.touteleurope.eu/vie-politique-des-etats-membres/emmanuel-macron-president-soulagement-et-espoir-chez-les-europeens/.
Vallée, S. (2022) 'Why Macron's European policy keeps failing, *Foreign Policy*, 18 August.
Van Eekelen, W. (2018) 'Too many ways of European defense cooperation', *Atlantisch Perspectief*, 42(6), pp. 24–29.
Witney, N. (2018) *Macron and the European Intervention Initiative: Erasmus for Soldiers?* London/Berlin: European Council on Foreign Relations.

8
MACRON AND THE ECONOMY: A LABOUR-MARKET PERSPECTIVE

Brigitte Granville

Abstract

In this chapter, the author discusses economic performance under President Macron from a labour-market perspective, aimed at those without specialist knowledge of economics. While the French economy has performed close to the average of its OECD peer group based on core indicators such as GDP growth rates and real household incomes, the country has been a notable relative underperformer when it comes to unemployment and labour participation rates, with negative impacts on overall welfare. This makes the extent of progress towards a healthier labour market a key criterion for assessing the Macron presidency in the economic sphere – as implicitly acknowledged by Macron's own consistent prioritisation of economic reform policy efforts related to employment. The assessment in this chapter relates Macron's reforms to an analysis of the structural causes of the French labour-market problem and finds substantial progress – particularly as regards bringing about more efficient industrial relations and implementing active labour-market policies designed to reduce skills mismatches and promote full employment. At the same time, several important challenges, notably relating to competitiveness, have been side-stepped. This analysis also casts light on broader obstacles to structural reform embedded in the French model of top-down technocratic action and its vulnerability to the leader's character.

Introduction

Developments on the French labour market offer an excellent vantage point for assessing the country's economy during Emmanuel Macron's presidency and evaluating the impact of his policies on economic outcomes. One pivotal

DOI: 10.4324/9781003323259-8

reason for this perspective is Macron's self-imposed challenge during his 2017 presidential campaign, where he placed substantial emphasis on the broad set of questions relating to employment, labour-market regulation and industrial relations. His manifesto book *Révolution* (Macron, 2016) notably highlighted a series of structural reforms aimed at addressing the substantial human and economic toll of high unemployment. Macron's deliberate focus on the theme of work was not merely a strategic move to differentiate himself from François Hollande, his predecessor, who – despite making the reduction of unemployment the primary objective of his presidency – fell short of that goal (see Figure 8.1); rather, Macron's attention to the labour market stemmed from the chronic nature of high unemployment that had persisted long before Hollande's tenure and, notably, represented a distinctive weakness of the French economy.

Concerning other conventional measures of economic performance, such as the real GDP (gross domestic product) growth rate or real disposable income per person, France – by the time Macron came to power – was generally aligned with its peer group of advanced industrial nations within the Organisation for Economic Co-operation and Development (OECD). For instance, between 2012 and 2016, the OECD area saw an average annual real GDP growth rate of 1.7 per cent, closely comparable to France's rate of 1.6 per cent during that period. Likewise, the average annual growth rate of real disposable income per person in the OECD from 2012 to 2016 stood at 0.8 per cent, while France's rate for that period was 0.7 per cent. While these metrics place France in the middle of the pack, the country's comparative standing had been declining in the period preceding Macron's presidency. Over the years, France's GDP *per capita* in relation to that in the United States dropped from 71 per cent in 1995 to 64 per cent in 2016.[1] This trend indicates that France was failing to keep pace with its key peers as regards growth rates of output and incomes; however, when it comes to employment indicators, France's performance was worse than just a relative decline leaving the country in the middle of the peer-group pack for, in this area, with all its importance for overall welfare, France was persistently among the worst-performing countries.

For over 50 years, following the prosperous 'Thirty Glorious Years' of robust post-war growth and full employment, France has grappled with the problem of persistently high unemployment that has significantly marked its economic landscape. Economist Edmond Malinvaud (1986, p. S197) highlighted this shift in the mid-1980s, noting a stark rise in the unemployment rate from under 2 per cent in 1967 to 7.3 in 1981 (annual averages, using ILO definitions). Despite varying economic conditions during the following four decades, unemployment remained entrenched within the 8–10 per cent range, notably exceeding rates in neighbouring Germany. This prolonged high unemployment in France was not merely a temporary phenomenon

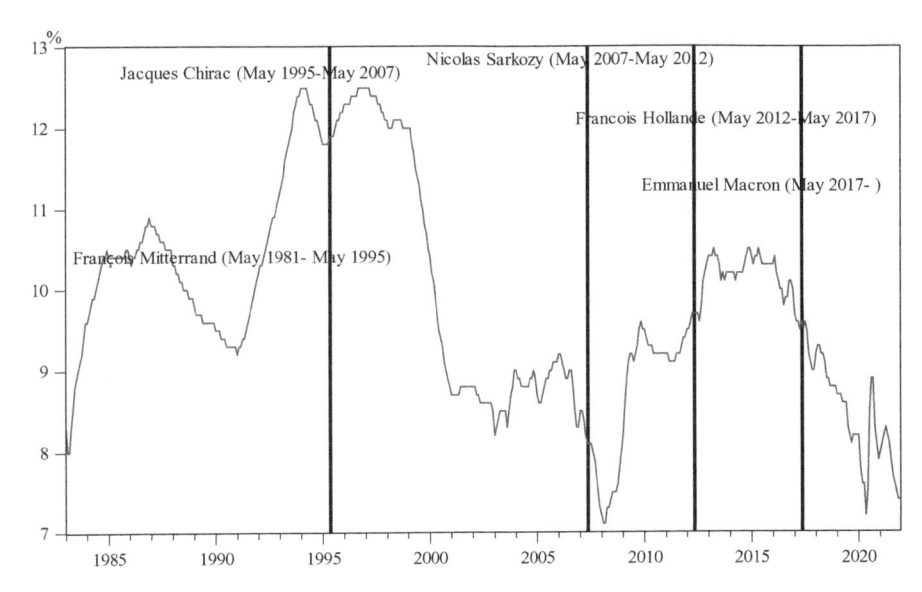

FIGURE 8.1 Monthly unemployment rate, total, % of labour force, January 1983–December 2021

Source: OECD (2022). *Notes:* The unemployed are people of working age who are without work, are available for work and have taken specific steps to find work. The uniform application of this definition results in estimates of unemployment rates that are more internationally comparable than those based on national definitions of unemployment. This indicator is measured in numbers of unemployed people as a percentage of the labour force and is seasonally adjusted. The labour force is defined as the total number of unemployed people plus those in employment. Data are based on labour-force surveys (LFS). For European Union countries where monthly LFS information is not available, the monthly unemployed figures are estimated by Eurostat.

tied to external shocks like the oil crises of the 1970s or the 2008 Global Financial Crisis (GFC). It was fundamentally structural, persisting even during periods of favourable global economic conditions and demonstrating that the problem was more inherent than cyclical in nature.

Alongside this problem of chronic structural unemployment, France has also underperformed its peers in its employment or 'participation' rate. Lower 'participation', in this context, means more people having dropped out of the labour market altogether – that is, they are neither employed nor seeking work (in contrast to active job seekers who constitute the number of unemployed people in official statistics). As of December 2021, France's employment rate stood at 67.7 per cent, below the OECD average of 68.6 per cent and notably lower than the rates in the Netherlands (80.6 per cent), Germany (76.6 per cent) and the United Kingdom (75.7 per cent) (see Figure 8.2). This trend of weak labour-market participation is particularly visible among younger individuals entering the job market and those nearing retirement age. As economist Thomas Philippon (2007) has highlighted, France's

158 Revolution Revisited

relatively low labour-participation rate signifies millions of underutilised workers. This results in economic loss since overall output would otherwise be higher; it also carries a human cost. Even if labour-market dropouts are somewhat protected by France's relatively generous welfare state, given the importance of work for dignity and purpose (Collier, 2018), it is reasonable to suppose that many of them would flourish much more if they saw accessible employment opportunities (Philippon, 2007).

The importance of these labour-market themes for both material and non-material welfare outcomes is the reason for this chapter's focus on Macron's reformist endeavours to improve matters in this area. Additionally, Macron's determination to tackle such a vast and intricate economic and

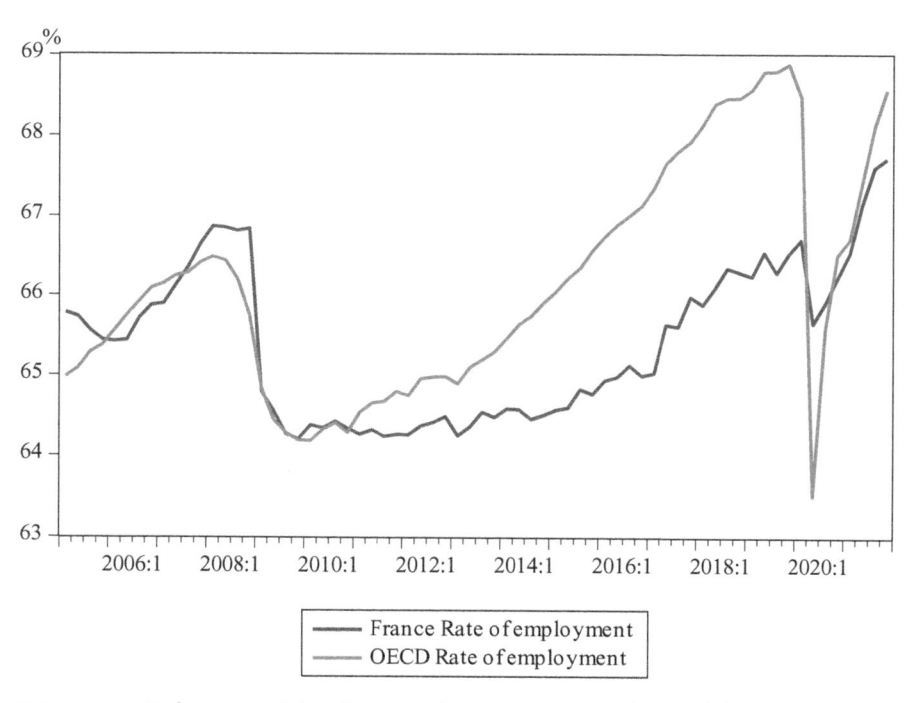

FIGURE 8.2 Labour participation: employment rate total, % of the working-age population

Notes: Employment rates gauge the utilisation of available labour resources by measuring the ratio of the employed population to the working-age population. These rates fluctuate with economic cycles but are notably influenced by government policies concerning higher education, income support and initiatives promoting the employment of women and disadvantaged groups. The employed are individuals aged 15 and above who worked in gainful employment for at least one hour in the previous week or had a job but were absent. The working-age population comprises individuals aged 15 to 64. This indicator, seasonally adjusted, is measured in thousands of persons aged 15 and over, presented as the number of employed individuals aged 15 to 64 as a percentage of the working-age population.

Source: OECD (2022).

social dilemma has the potential to shed light on the broader political obstacles associated with implementing structural changes in France.

Following this introduction, I examine three key causes of the peculiar French labour-market dysfunction: the erosion of external competitiveness (resulting from exchange-rate rigidity and high payroll taxation), rigid and intrusive regulation, and skills mismatches. This analysis of causes provides an essential background for understanding and evaluating the various policy responses undertaken during Macron's presidency that are surveyed in the second section, which distinguishes measures implemented during Macron's first term (the key items being the September 2017 'Macron ordinances' overhauling labour relations and the September 2018 'LCAP' law, focused mainly on skills and other labour supply improvements) from follow-up measures in progress during the second five-year term to which he was re-elected in May 2022 – and which, at the time of writing, had not yet reached its half-way mark. The concluding section draws up a scorecard of achievement that is substantial while, at the same time, falling short of a 'sea change' – and speculates about the causes of that shortfall, both structural and specific to the figure of Macron himself.

Causes of France's dysfunctional labour market

A prime method to unearth the causes behind French underperformance in the areas of unemployment and labour-market participation involves heeding the insights of employers. In a survey by INSEE (the national statistics agency) in 2017, skills shortages emerged as the foremost hurdle – cited by 32 per cent of respondents – in hiring employees for both permanent (CDI) and temporary fixed-term (CDD) contracts (Dortet-Bernadet, 2017). General economic uncertainty was the second most prevalent concern for 25 per cent of respondents. High taxation and social-security contributions were identified by 22 and 17 per cent of respondents, respectively. Only 12 per cent expressed worries about regulatory obstacles hindering labour reduction when firms needed to trim costs due to unfavourable business conditions. Subsequently, a *France Digitale* survey of 356 companies conducted in 2019 echoed these findings. Over half of the respondents emphasised the mismatch between the skills they required and those provided by the French education system. The main reasons for this major social and economic problem besetting France are all reflected in these survey findings: the rest of this section examines each one more closely.

Poor external competitiveness

Since the end of the Cold War, a significant catalyst propelling globalisation has been the inclusion of China – and other previously closed, poor nations

– into the global workforce. This integration, alongside job displacements caused by technological advancements – primarily the IT revolution – has had a negative impact on employment, particularly in the manufacturing sector, across advanced industrial nations, where worker wages lost competitiveness against counterparts in China and emerging economies due to this global shift. Economies more 'open' in terms of substantial external trade relative to their output – specifically, the relatively affluent ones – have been notably susceptible to this trend. France mirrors these vulnerabilities, sharing with other medium-sized developed economies a high degree of economic openness. Between 2018 and 2022, France's trade-openness ratio averaged around 64 per cent – that is, exports and imports together accounted for that percentage of the country's GDP. In contrast, the United States, characterised by a continental-sized economy, had a trade-openness ratio of 26 per cent during the same period.[2]

France and comparable nations have seen a decrease in their share of global exports, a process often termed 'de-industrialisation'. This shift is evident in the diminishing contribution of the manufacturing sector to the economy, a sector that had previously been a primary source of steady and relatively well-remunerated employment. According to the International Labour Organization (ILO), the proportion of employment in industry relative to total employment in France stood at approximately 28 per cent in 1991 but dwindled to merely 19.5 per cent by 2021.[3] Since these vulnerabilities are by no means unique to France, they cannot explain how deteriorating external competitiveness contributed to the inferior French labour-market performance compared to peer-group countries in Europe and the wider OECD area.

The Economic and Monetary Union (EMU)

One crucial method for relatively more open economies to alleviate, if not reverse, any impact on their external competitiveness involves exchange-rate devaluations, which have the effect of reducing the price of a country's exports in the global market – that is, making exports more competitive. Since the introduction of Europe's monetary union in 1999, France has given up the advantages of flexible exchange rates, hindering its ability to reduce wages and other costs in comparison to the outside world and thereby decreasing competitiveness (Bliek and Parguez, 2008). With fixed exchange rates as the irrevocable norm, the sole alternative to counteract competitiveness losses is cost reduction – primarily through restraining wages, the largest expense for firms – an approach termed as 'internal devaluation'. However, slashing wages, particularly in nominal terms, poses practical challenges for social and political reasons. Consequently, employers have responded by either relocating their manufacturing operations to cheaper countries (commonly in Asia or Eastern Europe) – known as *délocalisation* – or by investing in labour-saving machinery. The latter approach, substituting labour with capital, has led to France achieving relatively robust growth in labour productivity. This achievement, albeit somewhat diminished in recent years, is occasionally cited as a testament to France's economic strength. However, this gain has been accompanied by persistently high unemployment rates, translating into reduced aggregate hours worked and bearing negative implications for welfare (Weisbrot and Ray, 2011). Differences – between countries – in productivity levels based on working hours might be explained by the characteristics of the available labour supply. France's elevated productivity levels per hour worked could be linked to the 'composition effect' of a smaller presence of low-skilled workers in its workforce. Compared to key peer-group countries such as Germany, the United States or the United Kingdom, France has not only experienced a higher unemployment rate but also a lower employment rate among individuals aged 15 to 64. As those unemployed or inactive individuals generally exhibit lower average productivity than their employed counterparts, their exclusion might contribute to the observed productivity variations between countries (Martin *et al.*, 2019, p. 26).

The primary blow to France's external competitiveness triggered by Europe's monetary union did not stem from the terms of trade with countries beyond Europe. The euro could always – and did – depreciate against currencies like the US dollar or the Chinese *yuan*. Instead, the most substantial impact arose in relation to France's major trading partners within the Eurozone, notably Germany. A study by the IMF of the exchange rates that were irrevocably fixed with the launch of the euro in 1999 found that it was Italy rather than France that gained an initial competitive advantage relative to the currency bloc as a whole and Germany in particular (Garcia Cervero, Lopez, Alberola Ila and Ubide, 1999). Whatever explanations for this may come to light from future archival research (perhaps French officials were too proud to enter the euro at anything other than an 'equilibrium' exchange rate), this inherent competitive edge for Germany, baked into the monetary union, meant that any depreciation of the euro against other major global currencies favoured Germany more than France.

France's vulnerability to the erosion of its competitiveness was demonstrated in 2002 when Germany implemented an internal devaluation through stringent wage compression under the Hartz employment reforms aimed at bolstering German competitiveness (Cesaratto and Stirati, 2010). This German decision has been criticised as contradictory to the ethos of the monetary union (Flassbeck, 2019). Since this damage to French competitiveness had an external source (Germany), it may be seen as a misfortune over which the French government had little or no control. Nevertheless, just two years before this, under a socialist-led government, French policymakers had

TABLE 8.1 Unit labour cost, percent change between Q3 1999 and Q4 2008

	France	*Germany*	*Greece*	*Italy*	*Portugal*
ULC	5.2	−15.94	19.79	12.54	10.03
Relative to Germany	21.14	0	35.73	28.48	25.98

Source: Authors' calculation in Granville and Nagly (2015) on data from OECD Economic Outlook.

Note: Competitiveness indicator, relative unit labour costs, overall economy, Index: 2005 = 100, price index, seasonally adjusted.

ULC is a measure of how much it costs to produce one unit of output, such as a product or service. It is calculated by dividing the total wage costs by the number of units of output produced.

themselves dealt an additional – and this time self-inflicted – blow to the country's competitiveness by introducing the 35-hour working week. The overall deterioration of the French economy's external competitiveness is visible in the widening gap between unit labour costs (ULC) in France and Germany during the euro's initial years (Table 8.1).

High 'tax wedge'

The single currency's adverse impact on French competitiveness extended to other significant French trading partners, such as Italy; however, another factor that impaired competitiveness to the detriment of the labour market uniquely pertains to France. This factor revolves around taxation – not only its magnitude but also its fundamental structure. During Macron's initial presidential term, France carried the highest tax burden among OECD nations, with tax revenues hitting 45.43 per cent of GDP in 2021. By comparison, Italy stood at 42.91 per cent and Germany at 38.34, while the OECD averaged at 33.51 per cent of GDP. Research highlights the detrimental effects of elevated taxes on economic activity, particularly payroll taxes directly influencing employment (Romer and Romer, 2010). France's tax system, while featuring lower average marginal rates for personal income tax, VAT and corporate profit tax compared to the OECD average, heavily burdens payrolls. The financing of France's social-security system mainly relies on compulsory levies imposed on firms as a proportion of their employees' wages, resulting in the highest relative contributions from companies within the EU. These charges, intricate and burdensome, apply regardless of a company's profitability and vary across industry sectors, company sizes, job roles, remuneration levels and job statuses (Paya and de Greef-Madelin, 2020). In 2021, employers' contributions to social security and related charges represented 26.63 per cent of labour costs. This 'payroll tax' burden exceeds that of all other OECD countries. In Germany, for instance, payroll taxes account for 16.65 per cent of labour costs, while the OECD average was 13.46 per cent (OECD, 2022). Elevated payroll taxes in France have increased the cost of French labour relative to corresponding costs in the country's trading partners. This comparatively high payroll tax burden has magnified the negative impact of the single currency on competitiveness, incentivising businesses to shift jobs and production to countries with lower wage rates and less burdensome payroll tax structures. Comparisons of relative tax burdens between countries can be challenging owing to the varied complexities of different countries' tax systems, but any doubts about the reality of taxation making labour more expensive in France than peer countries in Europe and elsewhere were dispelled by an OECD study published in 2022 that computed the tax wedge – a gauge of how much tax on firms' payroll costs discourages employment (see Figure 8.3).

This OECD study mentions that the tax wedge for the average single worker in France increased by 0.4 percentage points from 46.6 per cent in 2020 to 47.0 per cent in 2021. The OECD average tax wedge in 2021 was 34.6 per cent (2020 = 34.6 per cent). In 2021, France had the fourth-highest tax wedge among the 38 OECD member countries, up from fifth position in 2020.

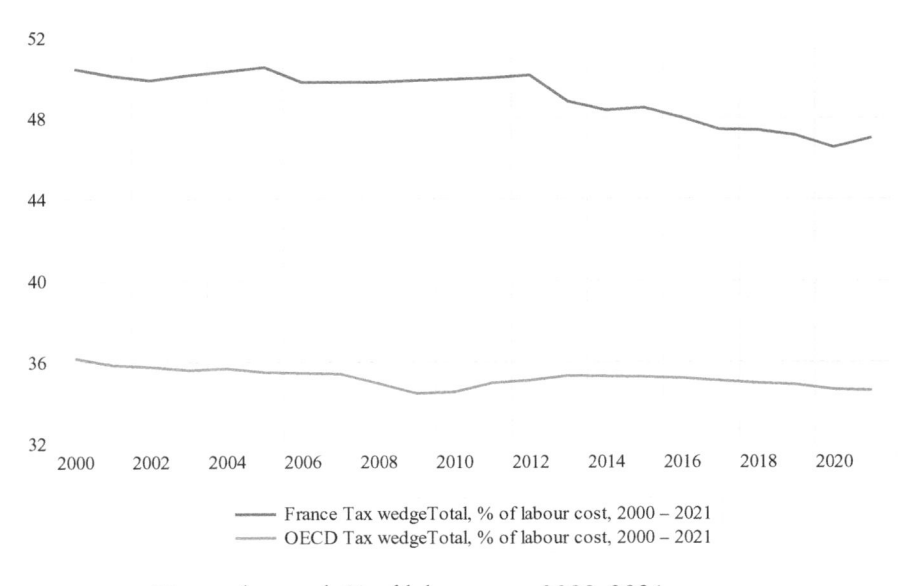

FIGURE 8.3 Tax wedge total, % of labour cost, 2000–2021

Notes: The tax wedge is defined as the ratio between the amount of taxes paid by an average single worker (a single person at 100 per cent of average earnings) without children and the corresponding total labour cost for the employer. The average tax wedge measures the extent to which tax on labour income discourages employment. This indicator is measured in percentage of labour cost.

Source: OECD (2022).

Counter-productive pro-labour regulation

The spirit of French labour regulations has long been to surpass the standards of peer-group countries on safeguarding workers' rights, producing a regulatory framework that is more 'pro-worker' and less 'pro-business'. However, much of this regulation exacerbates the impact of high payroll taxes, making it excessively costly for employers to hire staff. Examples of such regulations include rules regarding redundancies when companies reduce the size of their workforce, and until the 2010s (as detailed below), the requirement for all employers within a specific industry to adhere to wage settlements determined through heavily state-influenced centralised collective bargaining. The weight of inflexible and intrusive labour regulations not only discourages initial hiring but also encourages companies to circumvent these regulations by increasingly employing a larger portion of their workforce on temporary contracts. Consequently, this has led to an overall decrease in worker security and well-being, aggravating the problem of low labour-market participation.

Since the 1970s, France has grappled with a growing prevalence of precarious temporary employment, a trend confirmed by the ILO's 2015 research conducted across 119 nations (Méda, 2016). Those engaged in temporary contracts face job insecurity and notable negative wage disparities (Kahn, 2015). Despite the different labels – French 'CDD' (contract of limited duration) and 'CDI' (contract of unlimited duration) – they function similarly to temporary and permanent roles elsewhere.[4] Temporary employment in France surged from 3.34 per cent of the total workforce in 1983 to 15.7 per cent in 2021, significantly impacting on women and the 15–24 age bracket. Despite increased female labour participation, women encounter relative disadvantages, being involuntarily over-represented in part-time roles and facing double the under-employment rate of men (COR, 2019, p. 4). Within the 15–24 age group, half are on fixed-term contracts, compared to 24 per cent across the broader OECD area. Outside this age group, however, only 12 per cent of French workers are on temporary contracts (INSEE, 2018), revealing a more-pronounced trend in France among young labour-market entrants. This 'dualisation' of the French labour market – based on the distinction between CDI and CDD contracts – has diminished overall job security, with temporary workers being six to ten times more likely than permanent employees to end up unemployed (Charmettant, 2017). This insecurity amplifies the appeal of public-sector roles enjoying the enhanced job security provided by civil-service regulations (Frey and Stutzer, 2000; Saint-Paul, 2010). However, the issue of dualisation persists even within the public sector, where 'outsider' employees like substitute schoolteachers are regularly dismissed and rehired to circumvent EU directives on permanent contracts (Audier, Bacache, Courtioux and Gautié, 2012).

Skills mismatch: failure of the education system and social relations within firms

Extensive research on the causes of persistently high unemployment in France highlights shortcomings within the education system and their social repercussions. As already noted, business surveys consistently reveal concerns about the difficulty of finding adequately skilled individuals to fill job vacancies despite high unemployment rates. This mismatch between labour supply and demand is attributed to the interlinked problems in the French education system of centralised governance structures and learning environments. Writing in 2016, journalist Peter Gumbel underscored the immense scale – 1,162,650 employees in 2021, comprising 866,500 teachers with the remainder being administrators – and rigid management structures of France's education system. Educational reforms often stem from fiscal constraints or hurried strategies to tackle unemployment, neglecting comprehensive consultations with educators and stakeholders and resulting in ineffective reforms (Gumbel 2016). Algan, Cahuc and Zylberberg (2012) attribute France's low societal trust to school culture, highlighting how rote learning stifles initiative and risk-taking. Criticism extends to negative portrayals of entrepreneurship in textbooks, discouraging young people from pursuing business careers to the detriment of commercialised innovation and economic growth (Noé, 2013).

Philippon (2007) notes that labour laws and social charges explain only 30 per cent of variations in countries' labour-market participation rates, with the remainder stemming largely from the quality of social relations within firms, the importance of which has increased in the post-industrial growth model reliant on effective cooperation. Studies indicate that French workers feel undervalued, leading to stress, absenteeism and burnout (Eurofund, 2016; Fourquet, Mergier and Morin, 2018). French management often emphasises top-down control to the detriment of employee empowerment, exhibiting poorer records in career development and internal promotions compared to Germany and the United Kingdom (Garicano, Lelarge and van Reenen, 2013). Large French companies demonstrate a relatively poor track record in terms of career development and internal promotions – only 21 per cent of executives in France have experienced internal career growth, a stark contrast to the 66 and 51 per cent of senior management in large companies in Germany and the United Kingdom, respectively (Algan *et al.*, 2012). Promotion policies in firms tend to favour educational backgrounds and governmental connections over expertise or performance (Bloom, Genakos, Sadun and van Reenen, 2012). Irrespective of company ownership (the most common forms being control by the state, private families or collective investment structures), corporate-leadership appointments often hinge on inheritance (family ties) or the so-called 'parachuting' into top industry jobs of (former) civil servants with similar educational and social backgrounds rather than internal promotions (Philippon, 2007).

Macron's labour-market reforms

The gravity of such labour-market–related issues has steered much of the economic reform policymaking during Macron's presidency. Assessing these reform endeavours in the perspective of their main causes reveals an uneven landscape. Like his predecessors, Macron looked to the Scandinavian model for inspiration (Aukrust and Weiss-Andersen, 2019). Emulating this model was seen as the optimal path to address structural unemployment, bolster economic performance and, consequently, strengthen France's positioning alongside Germany in advancing towards a more-unified monetary union and a more-vibrant Europe. Lefebvre (2018) highlights that the core of the Scandinavian 'flexicurity' model, blending worker protections with economic efficiency, lies in prioritising worker training and skills development.

From this standpoint, a positive aspect of Macron's initial term was a substantial legislative initiative aimed, in part, at addressing the issue of skills mismatches – a frequent complaint among employers. However, the primary focus of the first significant reform in 2017, known as the Macron Ordinances,[5] centred on labour-market regulation with the goal of easing rigidities. As regards the other main obstacle to hiring revealed by surveys of employers – unfavourable economic conditions – the significance of global demand for an open economy like France limits the impact of domestic policymaking. Nonetheless, domestic policies can still enhance firms' relative capacity to access external demand through measures geared at improving competitiveness. Effective policies in this context would, at least, slow down France's declining share of global export markets, as reflected in a deteriorating balance of payments that hampers businesses' ability to invest, innovate and generate jobs.

Competitiveness brakes beyond the scope of reforms

Reforms addressing the critical challenge of boosting competitiveness had results so limited as to border on the negligible. The desire to replicate Scandinavian countries' success falls short of following the paths of Denmark and Sweden, which remain outside the EMU. For France, venturing down this route to bolster competitiveness is considered taboo. France not only joined the newly formed Eurozone but also played a pivotal role in initiating the entire project when broader negotiations surrounding German reunification in 1990 opened a window of opportunity for this monetary union initiative that was finally agreed the following year in the Treaty of Maastricht. In addition to establishing a reserve currency with the potential to rival the US dollar, the French political motive was to achieve 'co-manager' status with Germany of the European project by taking a formal share in what had, until then, been the Bundesbank's *de facto* controlling influence over the monetary policy of France (Feldstein, 1997). French policymakers counted on achieving a substantial degree of control over the new single central bank – an assumption based on the country's track record of exercising strong influence in European institutions (Granville, 2021). Consequently, the French political establishment invested significant political capital in the monetary union. Its fundamental importance for the country's identity and global standing is perceived as outweighing any economic costs – those few openly acknowledged are relegated to the status of manageable expenses (Granville, 2019). This approach avoids addressing a major underlying cause of the country's competitiveness problem by sidestepping the option of withdrawing from Europe's single-currency area.

If leaving the monetary union has not been a realistic policy to address competitiveness problems, the same goes for another hypothetical strategy – emulating the Scandinavian model as a way of dealing with the other cause of poor external competitiveness to do with the significant French labour 'tax wedge'. This 'Scandinavian' solution is scarcely more accessible than leaving the EMU. One key relevant aspect of that model involves funding a comprehensive welfare system – a cherished French ideal – through a transparent and accountable mechanism of heavy direct taxation. In contrast, France emphasises payroll taxation, which shifts the visible burden from citizens to employers. However, citizens end up bearing the brunt through wage compression and, notably, higher unemployment. Various French governments, including the Macron administration, have displayed a degree of awareness regarding this issue. Efforts have been made to alleviate the payroll tax burden, especially on small- and medium-sized enterprises (SMEs), which employ nearly half of the active workforce (when considering part-time SME jobs as full-time equivalents), contribute 43 per cent of the economy's value added and account for 15 per cent of export turnover. Measures in this domain have included reductions in charges for salaries of minimum-wage earners, payroll tax incentives to encourage hiring younger employees or apprentices and support for employers in economically disadvantaged regions. However, the administrative intricacies associated with these measures prevent firms from fully capitalising on their benefits. A more drastic overhaul of the tax system in line with Scandinavian practices remains evidently beyond the current political horizon and the capabilities of even a determined reformist administration like Macron's.

Reform of labour regulation: trust in firms

Instead of concentrating on a radical tax overhaul, reformist efforts have pivoted towards empowering enterprise management to bolster efficiency. Macron built upon a pioneering reform initiated during Hollande's single-term presidency. This relatively less-ambitious yet still contentious measure

– the El Khomri Law passed in 2016 and supported by then-Economics Minister Macron – eased several provisions within the Labour Code regarding working hours, overtime, company-level bargaining on wages and redundancy terms. While maintaining the legal working week at 35 hours, the law permitted increases of up to 44 or 46 hours within a 12-week span if mutually agreed upon at the company level.

In the five Ordinances encompassing 36 alterations to the Labour Code, which constituted the first major reform of his presidency in 2017, Macron extended this shift toward company-level collective bargaining. This move steered away from the previously entrenched system of centralised bargaining within each industry sector. Emphasising firm-level agreements on wages and conditions over individual employment contracts, Macron's reforms prioritised collective agreements within individual companies. Moreover, by introducing the provision for collective agreements to be validated by a majority vote (referendum) among employees, the reform aimed to safeguard these agreements, in turn strengthening business stability and certainty. Such measures align with research indicating the significance of fostering quality relationships within firms to cultivate trust, thereby benefiting both the firm and overall economic performance (Blanchard, Jaumotte and Loungani, 2014; Philippon, 2007). This research underscores the idea that successful labour-market reform hinges on decentralised negotiations between firms and their workforce. In a repeat of the public reaction to the El-Khomri Law, these Macron Ordinances sparked repeated and frequently violent street protests coordinated by trade-union organisations, which stood to lose influence as a result of these reforms. The protests against the Ordinances were, however, the milder of those two episodes, despite Macron's measures being a determined extension of the agenda that had been more tentatively broached by the El-Khomri Law towards the end of the Hollande presidency. This contrast may reflect Macron's clear mandate for carrying out such reforms at the outset of his presidency, but this political 'honeymoon' proved short-lived – as shown by the Yellow Vests protests that erupted the following year and subsequent more-serious protest movements against pension reforms in 2019 and 2023.

The increased flexibility introduced by the 2017 Ordinances reform was complemented subsequently by the 2019 Dussopt Law (named after the then-Employment Minister), which aimed to simplify the hiring of contract workers. Additionally, it curtailed unions' capacity to intervene in decisions concerning employee relocations. An associated initiative aimed to alleviate the burden of labour-relations regulation on firms by consolidating the array of employee representative bodies into a unified 'Social and Economic Committee' (CSE) for companies with over 11 employees. However, a study conducted in 2022 by the Labour Ministry's research arm, Dares, offered a mixed verdict on this reform, indicating a net reduction in employee representation and an increase in firms violating these regulations (Pignoni, 2022). In the broader context of labour-market challenges and overall economic performance, reforms like these appear to be ineffective adjustments (Heyer, Méda and Lokiec, 2018).

In the more-critical aspect of facilitating hiring by easing firing processes, the Ordinances established a framework of rules for companies that decide to shed labour. These rules subject any such mandatory company downsizing to a new 'collective contractual termination' procedure. Additionally, they clearly define and cap the scale of damages payable by employers in cases deemed as unjustified dismissals (i.e., without a 'real and serious' cause). This measure had an immediate impact, making redundancy procedures more predictable and manageable for employers. The maximum cost of dismissal now stood lower in comparison with the results of recent similar reforms in Spain and Italy. In specific cases, this cost became even less burdensome than in Germany, where lawsuits are rare but can be highly expensive for employers (Heyer *et al.*, 2018).

The streamlining of collective redundancy procedures, coupled with the admissible grounds for redundancies being based on national rather than global comparisons of business conditions, aimed to boost investor confidence – particularly among foreign investors – by mitigating concerns about returns on capital being excessively damaged during periodic economic downturns.

Enhancing the quality of labour supply

A year after the 2017 Ordinances, the French parliament introduced a law encompassing a comprehensive array of 'active labour-market' policies geared towards empowering individuals and fostering lifelong learning. The *Loi pour la liberté de choisir son avenir professionnel* (LCAP) marked an ambitious overhaul of France's approach to professional training, facilitating access to it and enhancing individuals' ability to exercise control over their professional development. The aim was to correct the shortcomings in training that had become apparent during the past four decades of rising youth unemployment and that largely stemmed from insufficient workplace experience.

France's education system traditionally segregates into vocational and general tracks, often directing children from working-class backgrounds toward vocational paths perceived as less prestigious, offering limited social mobility (Schleicher, 2019). Despite initiatives in the 1960s and the introduction of the *Bac Pro* diploma in 1985 to enhance vocational education, these efforts have not notably improved the status of vocational training nor adequately prepared students for the job market. Subsequent measures to improve the situation have focused on promoting German-style apprenticeships, combining classroom instruction with practical training within private companies. This LCAP reform prioritises vocational training, empowering individuals to choose their future careers and providing support through career guidance. The simplification of funding regulations for professional development aims to streamline the process for businesses. Macron initiated a significant shift by dismantling the traditional trade-union–controlled professional-training system, replacing it with a universal mechanism termed 'Individual Professional Training Accounts' (CFPs). Implemented via the mobile app *MonCompteFormation* launched in 2019, this reform has resulted in over 2 million new training contracts. The growth has been rapid, with 675,000 contracts signed in 2021, marking a 32 per cent increase from 2020, itself 40 per cent higher than in 2019. This liberalisation has been lauded as 'undoubtedly the great economic success' of Macron's first term (Challenges, 2022).

Concurrently, regional administrations relinquished their authority over establishing apprenticeship training centres, allowing major companies like L'Oréal, Accor and Total to establish their own *Centres de formation d'apprentis* (CFA) since 2018. To encourage this transition, the government offered tax-free grants of €5,000 and €8,000 for each person (under and over 18, respectively) enrolled on these apprenticeships. This reform yielded significant success, with the number of apprenticeship and professionalisation contracts increasing from 494,000 to 799,000 between 2018 and 2021 (approximately 18 per cent annually). Over three years, this resulted in around 336,000 additional students, predominantly driven by apprenticeship contracts, the primary focus of the reform. In June 2022, the government reaffirmed its commitment to fostering apprenticeships, aiming for 1 million contracts annually by the end of the presidential term in 2027. By the second quarter of 2022, the unemployment rate among individuals aged 15–24 decreased to 17.8 per cent,[6] marking a 6.8 percentage point decrease compared to Q2 2017.[7]

However, a significant drawback emerged, as this initiative caused a substantial financial deficit for *France Compétences*, the agency overseeing vocational training, estimated at €6 billion for 2022 (Ruello, 2022a). In June 2022, the Court of Auditors highlighted concerns about shortcomings in meeting the needs of vulnerable young people and companies encountering recruitment challenges. It recommended reorienting subsidies toward educating young people outside the higher-education system and addressing inflated course costs to enhance the efficacy of apprenticeship programmes (Cour des Comptes, 2022).

In Macron's second term, the reform of vocational education in high schools has emerged as a significant priority. The primary goal is to enhance the employability of high-school-level (*lycée*) vocational graduates, aligning their skills more effectively with the demands of various industries (Battaglia and Bissuel, 2022). Addressing the issue of low esteem associated with vocational education is crucial, as it has pushed a growing number of young people towards higher education with escalating grade inflation. A central focus is on *alternance* training, encouraging a blend of classroom learning and practical work experience. This approach aims to make vocational studies more appealing to students and simultaneously more advantageous for potential employers (Troger, 2018).

Another key element of the LCAP revolved around the reform of the unemployment-insurance system. In July 2019, two decrees were issued containing new regulations on eligibility for unemployment benefits and detailed measures on job searches – all aligned with the LCAP's principles. This facet of the LCAP reform had three objectives. Firstly, it aimed to extend eligibility for unemployment benefits to self-employed individuals, though not universally. It also targeted specific categories of individuals leaving their jobs voluntarily. Concerning the widened eligibility, those who voluntarily left their jobs could potentially qualify for benefits if they had previously held a permanent contract for at least five years and had a professionally endorsed retraining project approved by a regional joint inter-professional commission, Transitions Pro. This adjustment sought to encourage risk-taking and support individuals transitioning to jobs requiring some re-skilling, with potential productivity gains. By the end of 2021, the opportunities offered by this reform had been taken up by 65,200 people, resulting in approximately €150 million in cumulative benefits. This outcome exceeded initial estimates derived from the impact study that had been carried out in advance of the reform's implementation. The second aim focused on ensuring accountability by scaling back unemployment benefits for high-income job-seekers after eight months, with additional reductions as labour-market conditions improved.[8] The reform also aimed to address abuses linked to short-term employment contracts. Modifications in benefit entitlements for individuals switching between short-term work contracts and unemployment led to a 17 per cent decrease in benefits for 1.15 million beneficiaries. Finally, this adjustment extended the average duration of benefits from 11 to 14 months (Unédic, 2021).

The pandemic disrupted the implementation of several aspects of this reform. Unédic (*Union nationale interprofessionnelle pour l'emploi dans l'industrie et le commerce*), the agency responsible for administering unemployment benefits, estimated that, post-pandemic, the reform, upon full implementation, would reduce unemployment-related expenses by about €2.3 billion annually, projecting a surplus in the unemployment-insurance scheme from 2022 onwards (see Figure 8.4).

In Macron's second term, the focus on reforming the unemployment-benefits system persisted, marked by two changes implemented in late 2021. The first involved revising how benefit amounts are calculated, while the other

172 Revolution Revisited

tightened eligibility criteria, extending the necessary period of prior employment from four to six months. At the heart of this second-term agenda is the principle of aligning benefits with the economic cycle. This strategy aims to provide greater assistance to job seekers during economic downturns while reducing support as the economic situation improves. The reform blueprint acknowledges the current pro-cyclical nature of unemployment benefits in France, where benefits are somewhat more generous during periods of low unemployment compared to economic downturns when more workers get maderedundant and new jobs are harder to find (Cahuc, Carcillo and Landais, 2021). The intended changes in benefits aim to reverse this trend, seeking to adjust payouts in a more rational, counter-cyclical manner, with the most-flexible variable being the duration rather than the amount of unemployment-benefit payments. Regarding eligibility for unemployment benefits, one of Macron's pivotal proposals would make receiving such benefits contingent upon engaging in an approved activity for a minimum of 15–20 hours per week. Approved activities encompass participation in training programmes, the completion of internships or company immersion periods or involvement in workshops. The underlying principle aims to foster a culture of rewarding engagement rather than passive reliance.

Another major effort in this field entailed a restructuring of *Pôle emploi* into *France travail*, a change officially launched on 1 January 2024. *Pôle emploi*, the public employment service, emerged from the merger of two other agencies, the National Employment Agency (ANPE) and the Association for Employment in Industry and Commerce (*Assédic*), back in December 2008. However, this merger left behind a fragmented landscape

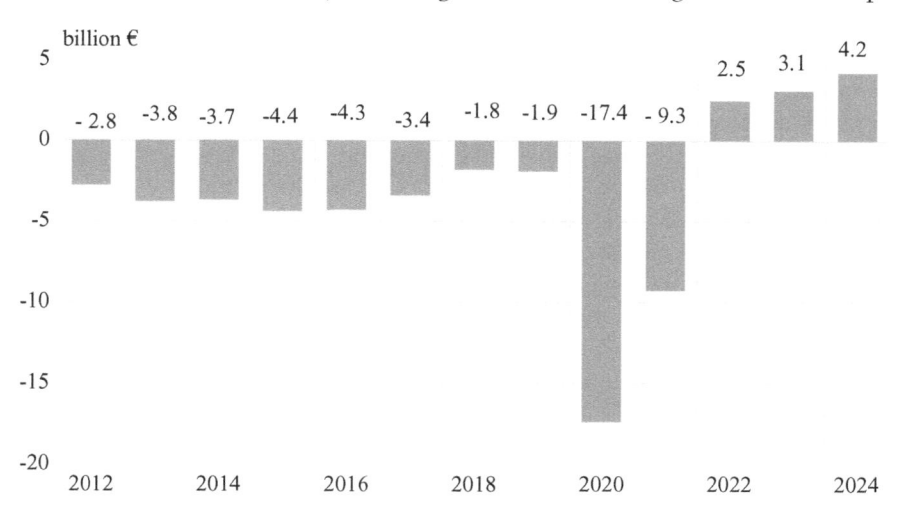

FIGURE 8.4 Financial balance of the unemployment insurance in € billions
Source: Unédic (2021, 2022).

of employment-related public-service provisions, including *Cap emploi* (for the disabled) and various scattered associations alongside public authorities at different levels (regional and sub-regional). These fragmented entities were therefore consolidated into a single institution to optimise support for job seekers, help with skills assessment, gaining access to training opportunities and overcoming barriers (such as housing-related challenges) to finding work (Ruello, 2022b). The resulting *France travail* agency is thus designed to enhance overall effectiveness in reducing unemployment rates. Further efficiencies and synergies could be attained by merging Unédic, which shares some of the same functions, into this consolidated body (Cahuc *et al.*, 2021).

In Macron's second term, a key focus on unemployment insurance pertained to its governance. This reform, which had already been set as a first-term goal, revolves around resurrecting the original 'horizontal' essence of unemployment-insurance governance from its inception in 1958. Initially, social partners established funding and benefit parameters every few years across sectors, subject to the Ministry of Labour's final approval. However, LCAP introduced heightened centralised government control by offering framework guidance to social partners' discussions, including a time constraint. Failure to meet this limit could lead to the government unilaterally making decisions by decrees (*décrets de carence*). The drawback of such government interventions lies in their lack of coordination with other benefits, levies and unemployment policies. Moreover, these decisions exclude various stakeholders, missing opportunities to integrate a broader array of professions and sectors into unemployment-insurance funding and benefit provisions (Cahuc *et al.*, 2021).

The LCAP legislation included a significant initiative to promote gender equality within the workforce that had a substantial effect on the labour market. This initiative, known as the Index of Professional Gender Equality, was endorsed by the LCAP to serve as the primary tool for enhancing company performance in this domain. The index consolidates multiple indicators to evaluate a company's performance regarding gender equality, including factors such as the gender pay gap, discrepancies in pay rises and promotions based on gender, the reintegration rate of female employees after maternity leave and the representation of women among a company's top-ten earners. During the initial three years of implementing this facet of the LCAP, the mean ratings for Professional Gender Equality have consistently risen each year. By 2022, companies with over 1,000 employees achieved an average score of 86 out of 100, up from 83 in 2019. Similarly, those with 250 to 1,000 employees increased from 82 to 85 and companies with 50 to 250 employees averaged 83 compared to 82 in 2019. Notably, all these scores comfortably exceed the minimum requirement of 75 out of 100 to avoid penalties. Only 2 per cent of companies managed to attain a flawless score of 100 (DREETS, 2022).

Conclusion

Measuring the effectiveness of structural reforms typically requires time, often extending well into the future. The long-term impact of Macron's labour-market reforms may only become fully apparent in the 2030s. Distinguishing the direct influence of reform policies on near-term shifts in crucial labour-market and broader economic indicators from unrelated factors is a challenging task. For instance, France experienced a decline in the unemployment rate from 9.6 to 7.8 per cent[9] between Macron's inauguration in May 2017 and February 2020 (pre-pandemic). This improvement no doubt owed more to this being a period of relatively strong global growth than to the employment-related reforms towards the end of the Hollande presidency, let alone Macron's first set of reforms, which could not plausibly have had such a rapid impact. In any case, this positive development still left France ranked among the second-highest quartile for unemployment rates among European countries.

Assessing the impact of these reforms faces complications, particularly because the period that might have revealed their effectiveness was overshadowed by the significant economic disruption caused by the Covid pandemic. During this time, the pandemic prompted substantial measures to assist companies and preserve jobs, as large sectors of the economy shut down. Measures like subsidising youth recruitment and normalising remote working during the pandemic could have contributed to net job creation and the overall stability of the labour market. Nevertheless, external macroeconomic influences, rather than government policies, might have played a more significant role in the observable outcomes thus far – such as the vibrant labour-market recovery post-pandemic, as labour-supply distortions gradually corrected themselves. Looking ahead beyond the Covid aftermath into the next decade, demographic shifts like an ageing population and societal resistance to sustained mass immigration could reduce the working-age population: any resulting decline in labour supply might contribute to lower unemployment rates, irrespective of the success or failure of the ongoing reform policies.

These caveats notwithstanding, significant lessons can be drawn from the labour-market reforms carried out during the Macron presidency, shedding light on both the potential and the constraints of the French-style technocratic administration. The potential is evident in decisive policymaking, displaying clarity, dynamism and determination to address persistent hurdles and imbalances. The emphasis on labour-market reforms, particularly in the early phase of Macron's tenure, before facing challenges like the *gilets jaunes* (Yellow Vests) protests, the Covid pandemic and the subsequent economic strain, resulted in two pivotal achievements: the 2017 Ordinances and, notably, the active labour-market initiatives introduced within the LCAP legislation in 2018. Yet, these accomplishments also highlight limitations, exposing situations where even a sophisticated technocratic approach might fall short in evidence-based decision-making. The problem here does not stem necessarily from a misjudgment of issues but, rather, from a misunderstanding of their relative importance. The focus on facilitating labour-shedding rather than alleviating the payroll tax burden stands out as an example.

This instance underscores two more significant constraints on the effectiveness of structural reform in bringing about sustained long-run improvements in economic performance, both of which lie largely beyond the scope of this chapter. The first is France's deteriorating public finances, leading to high budget deficits. These fiscal challenges intersect with the labour-market agenda in various ways. Attempts to reduce the labour 'tax wedge' face significant hurdles due to the fragility of public finances. Furthermore, some labour-market reforms seem to serve as a cover for fiscal adjustments. For instance, tightening unemployment-benefit rules not only helps to improve labour-participation rates and other labour-market indicators but is also clearly motivated by the goal of reducing public deficits. The most notable example is the increase in the pensionable age decreed in 2023 amid political turmoil and street protests. Although aligned with Macron's goals for his second term, particularly around achieving full employment and a higher participation rate, this reform was mainly designed to bolster public finances by limiting pension liabilities and supporting government revenue by slowing the decline in the working-age population. This link between labour-market and fiscal challenges was made strikingly explicit in Macron's remarks at the major press conference he held in January 2024 after appointing Gabriel Attal as prime minister and in which he outlined policy priorities for the remainder of his presidential term. One of Macron's core goals emerged as being to increase the number of people in work: more workers would mean higher output and, therefore, healthier public finances. Referring to employers' increasing difficulties in finding suitably qualified workers, he promised further reform efforts in the area of vocational education and making unemployment benefits ever-more-strictly conditional on recipients undertaking training courses, which the state would facilitate. Macron summed all this up with the stated aim of achieving full employment by the end of his term in 2027. The outcome of this self-imposed test will be aided by the effect of demographic trends (population ageing) in reducing the supply of labour and the unemployment rate regardless of further reforms. Nevertheless, the extent of progress towards this goal defined as an unemployment rate of 5 per cent of the active workforce (the 2023 rate being 7.5 per cent) will be a revealing indicator of the overall effectiveness of Macron's economic reform efforts.

The second constraint has to do with the ingrained top-down technocratic approach to carrying out reform. This approach contrasts starkly with

Macron's theoretical reform strategy outlined in his 2016 book *Révolution*, intending to replace vertical regulation with more horizontal action and initiative. However, the existing instrument for reform – the vertical technocracy – often results in intricate measures imposed from above that fail to yield the desired effects. The analysis of labour-market reforms in this chapter underscores how technocracy struggles to reshape culture, particularly in fostering increased citizen participation and more constructive social relationships. Instead, it mirrors the centralised, hierarchical structure ingrained in the recruitment, practices and operations of the policymaking elite at the pinnacle of the civil service.

Macron himself was a product of this hierarchical system, occasionally exacerbating its inherent flaws with a noticeable absence of a 'common touch' – further straining the political climate with his periodic expressions of impatience and even disdain towards ordinary citizens. These personal characteristics might have accelerated the erosion of his initial political capital and limited the extent to which his stock of political capital was regenerated by his re-election in 2022. This constraint will weigh against Macron's persistent determination when it comes to the outcome of his full employment project and other aspects of the overall record of his presidency. In any case, more profound transformations, such as correcting resource mismanagement perpetuated by deeply rooted interest groups – particularly within the layered state administration – or nurturing more effective social dynamics rooted in trust and collaboration from early education, demand cultural generational shifts. Such substantial changes probably surpass the capacity of any single leader to achieve through conventional top-down reform efforts, especially one with Macron's shortcomings.

Notes

1 World Bank national accounts data and OECD National Accounts data files.
2 World Bank national accounts data and OECD National Accounts data files.
3 International Labour Organization, 'ILO modelled estimates database'.
4 OECD (2022), Temporary employment (indicator): doi: 10.1787/75589b8a-en (accessed 17 January 2024).
5 These Ordinances – consisting of five documents comprising 36 measures and all dated 22 September 2017 – were executive orders or decrees promulgated on the president's authority pending the adoption of parliamentary acts enshrining exactly the same measures in law – a process that was completed in March 2018.
6 Fiches - Chômage – Emploi, chômage, revenus du travail – Insee Références - Édition 2017 – Emploi, chômage, revenus du travail | Insee (accessed 18 January 2024).
7 https://www.lek.com/insights/edu/eu/ei/apprenticeship-france (accessed 18 January 2024).
8 Unemployment benefits in France are still income-related.
9 OECD (2022), Unemployment rate (indicator). doi: 10.1787/52570002-en (accessed 19 July 2022).

References

Algan, Y., Cahuc, P. and Zylberberg, A. (2012) *La fabrique de la défiance… et comment s'en sortir*. Paris: Albin Michel.

Audier, F., Bacache, M., Courtioux, P. and Gautié, J. (2012) *The effects of pay reforms and procurement strategies on wage and employment inequalities in France's public sector*. Manchester: Manchester Business School, EWERC Working Paper.

Aukrust, K. and Weiss-Andersen, C. (2019) 'Is France becoming more Scandinavian? The utopia of Scandinavian virtue in France from Chirac to Macron', *Utopian Studies*, 30(2), pp. 146–173.

Battaglia, M. and Bissuel, B. (2022) 'Comment la réforme du lycée professionnel se prépare', *Le Monde*, 30 July.

Blanchard, O., Jaumotte, F. and Loungani, P. (2014) 'Labor market policies and IMF advice in advanced economies during the Great Recession', *IZA Journal of Labor Policy*, 3(2), pp. 1–23.

Bliek, J.-G. and Parguez, A. (2008) 'Mitterrand's turn to conservative economics: a revisionist history', *Challenge*, 51(2), pp. 97–109.

Bloom, N., Genakos, C., Sadun, R. and van Reenen, J. (2012) *Management practices across firms and countries*. Cambridge MA: National Bureau of Economic Research, Working Paper 17850.

Cahuc, P., Carcillo, S. and Landais, C. (2021) 'Repenser l'assurance chômage: règles et gouvernance', *Les Notes du Conseil d'Analyse Économique*, 61(1), pp. 1–12.

Cesaratto, S. and Stirati, A. (2010) 'Germany and the European and global crises', *International Journal of Political Economy*, 39(4), pp. 56–86.

Challenges (2022) 'Quel bilan pour Macron? Neuf sujets phares passés au crible', *Challenges*. https://www.challenges.fr/politique/bilan-de-macron-neuf-sujets-phares-passes-au-crible_796526 (accessed 17 January 2024).

Charmettant, H. (2017) 'État des lieux de la protection de l'emploi en France: l'essentiel préservé… jusqu'à maintenant', *Halshs-01616862f*.

Collier, P. (2018) *The future of capitalism: facing the new anxieties*. London: Allen Lane.

COR (2019) 'Evolution des inégalités intragénérationnelles', paper given to the Conseil d'Orientation des Retraites conference in Paris, 11 July 2019.

Cour des Comptes (2022) *La formation en alternance: une voie en plein essor, un financement à définir*. Paris: Cour des Comptes.

Dortet-Bernadet, V. (2017) 'La moitié des entreprises signalent des barrières à l'embauche', *Insee Focus* 106.

DREETS (2022) *Les résultats de l'index de l'égalité professionnelle 2022*. Paris: Directions régionales de l'économie de l'emploi du travail et des solidarités.

Eurofund (2016) *Sixth European working conditions survey: overview report*. Luxembourg: Publications Office of the European Union.

Feldstein, M. S. (1997) 'The political economy of the european economic and monetary union: political sources of an economic liability', *Journal of Economic Perspectives*, 11(4), pp. 23–42.

Fourquet, J., Mergier, A. and Morin, C. (2018) *Inutilité ou absence de reconnaissance: de quoi souffrent les salariés français?* Paris: Fondation Jean Jaurès.

Flassbeck, H. (2019) 'Hartz IV and matching efficiency – or what is the purpose of economics?' *Flassbeck Economics International*, blog: flassbeck economics international - Economics and politics - comment and analysis (flassbeck-economics.com) (accessed 17 January 2024).

Frey, B.S. and Stutzer, A. (2000) 'Happiness, economy and institutions', *The Economic Journal*, 110(466), pp. 918–938.

Garcia Cervero, S., Lopez, J.H., Alberola Ila, E. and Ubide, A.J. (1999) *Global equilibrium exchange rates: euro, dollar, 'ins', 'outs' and other major currencies in a panel cointegration framework*. Washington DC: International Monetarty Fund, Working Paper 175.

Garicano, L., Lelarge, C. and van Reenen, J. (2013) *Firm size distortions and the productivity distribution: evidence from France*. Cambridge MA: National Bureau of Economic Research, NBER Working Paper Series 18841.

Granville, B. (2019) 'The euro is doomed', *Inference*, 4(3).

Granville, B. (2021) *What ails France?* Montreal: McGill-Queen's University Press.

Granville, B. and Nagly, D. (2015) 'Conflicting incentives for the public to support the EMU', *The Manchester School*, 83(S2), pp. 142–157.

Gumbel, P. (2016) 'Ten ways France must fix its "failing" school system', *The Local*, 30 August.

Heyer, É., Méda, D. and Lokiec, P. (2018) *Une autre voie est possible*. Paris: Flammarion.

INSEE (2018) *France, social portrait*. Paris: Institut national de la statistique et des études économiques.

Kahn, L.M. (2015) 'The structure of the permanent job wage premium: Evidence from Europe', *Industrial Relations*, 55(1), pp. 149–178.

Lefebvre, A. (2018) *Macron le Suédois*. Paris: PUF.

Malinvaud, E. (1986) 'The rise of unemployment in France', *Economica*, 53(210), pp. S197–S217.

Martin, P., Bénassy-Quéré, A., Blanchard, O., Boone, L., Cette, G., Criscuolo, C., Epaulard, A., Jean, S., Kyle, M., Ragot, X., Roulet, A. and Thesmar, D. (2019) *Productivity and competitiveness: where does France stand in the Euro zone?* Paris: Conseil National de Productivité.

Méda, D. (2016) *The future of work: the meaning and value of work in Europe*. Geneva: International Labour Organization, ILO Research Paper No. 18.

Noé, J.-B. (2013) 'La vision de l'entreprise dans les manuels scolaires', *Contrepoints*, 21 August.

OECD (2022) *Taxing wages 2022. Impact of COVID-19 on the tax wedge in OECD countries*. Paris: OECD.

Paya, F. and de Greef-Madelin, M. (2020) 'Agnès Verdier-Molinié: "Macron, le flou et l'incertitude permanents"', *Valeurs Actuelles*, 2 January.

Philippon, T. (2007) *Le capitalisme d'héritiers: la crise française du travail*. Paris: Seuil.

Pignoni, M.T. (2022) *Les instances de représentation des salariés dans les entreprises en 2020: la baisse du taux de couverture se poursuit bien qu'à un rythme plus lent*. Paris: Dares, 32: 12 July.

Romer, C.D. and Romer, D. (2010) 'The macroeconomic effects of tax changes: Estimates based on a new measure of fiscal shocks', *American Economic Review*, 100(3), pp. 763–801.

Ruello, A. (2022a) 'Une hausse spectaculaire des crédits pour l'emploi et la formation', *Les Echos*, 9 August.

Ruello, A. (2022b) 'Pourquoi Macron veut transformer Pôle emploi en France travail', *Les Echos*, 18 March.

Saint-Paul, G. (2010) 'Endogenous indoctrination: occupational choice, the evolution of beliefs, and the political economy of reform', *The Economic Journal*, 120(544), pp. 325–353.

Schleicher, A. (2019) *Pisa 2018. Insights and interpretations*. Paris: OECD.

Troger, V. (2018) 'L'enseignement professionnel en attente d'un projet politique', *Revue Politique et Parlementaire*, 1089.

Unédic (2021) *Réglementation d'assurance chômage applicable au 1er octobre 2021*. n° 2021–13. Paris: Direction des Affaires Juridiques et Institutionnelles, Sous-Direction Juridique.

Unédic (2022) *Situation financière de l'assurance chômage pour 2022–2024. Prévisions financières*. Paris: Unédic.

Weisbrot, M. and Ray, R. (2011) *Latvia's internal devaluation: a success story?* Washington DC: Center for Economic and Policy Research.

9

EMMANUEL MACRON'S REFORM OF THE HIGHER CIVIL SERVICE: TRANSFORMING THE STATE NOBILITY INTO 'CAN-DO MANAGERS'?

Jean-Michel Eymeri-Douzans

Abstract

This chapter presents President Macron's reform of the French higher Civil Service and analyses its underlying logic, which can be summarised as transforming the French 'state nobility' into 'can-do managers'. This reform is neither as new in its inspiration nor as disruptive as claimed but is the French avatar of a common trend observed in many post-modern democracies towards what was identified, as early as the 1980s, as a growing 'functional politicisation' of top bureaucrats who are increasingly summoned to be more docile to increasingly 'presidentialised' executives and much more committed to the enforcement and success of the current political masters' policies. To reach that conclusion, the chapter first shows how Emmanuel Macron, himself a pure product of technocracy, broke away from the 'state nobility' once in power. To do so, he put the top civil servants 'under pressure' to quickly take political control over the central state apparatus. Such a 'disruption' has gone as far as imposing a 'refounding of the system' of the higher civil service, including its recruitment, initial training, careers and system of promotions. That undertaking, somewhat discontinuous in time, is consistent in its very substance with the acceleration of the French higher bureaucracy's 'functional politicisation'.

Introduction

Each country has its own trajectory of state-building. France has followed a state-building path where the imposition of a state apparatus preceded the invention of a consequently more political nation than in other cases, where a common culture and national sentiment preceded the late creation of a state. As de Tocqueville (1856) first pointed out, there are undeniable continuities in French history marked by so many revolutions and episodes of social unrest, often ending in changes of regimes and constitutions. While, in the United Kingom, the Crown symbolises and embodies such continuity, in French culture, this role is played by a 'strong state' (Badie and Birnbaum, 1979) or, better said, 'State-in-majesty' (Eymeri-Douzans, 1999), which all French pupils are taught to spell with a capital 'S'. The socio-political, economic and cultural prominence of the 'tutelary state' (Rosanvallon, 1990) *in* and *over* the French society and the economy, first 'Colbertist' then *'dirigiste'*, defined by Schmidt (2003) as a type of 'state-centred capitalism', has long been a major feature of French culture compared to Anglo-American or North European cultures.

Nevertheless and 'at the same time' – to borrow Macron's favourite expression to show that he always considers both sides of a coin – France has been profoundly transformed since the 1980s by the effects of the end of the Cold War and the collapse of the Soviet bloc, combined with the repercussions of increased Europeanisation and Anglo-Saxon, neo-liberal globalisation, triggering financialisation and deindustrialisation of our economies and creating mass unemployment. As regards the state and the public sector, France has been following the global movement of institutional reformism – but in its own way and at its own pace. This ongoing national trajectory of reform follows a peculiar combination of three related yet distinct streams of 'constitutive' reform policies (in the sense of Ted Lowi, 1964) that have been taking place at the multiple levels of power of the French politico-administrative system. These include reforms of both the central and the 'territorial' state ('administrative deconcentration' of the vast web of state services working in the provinces and overseas, coordinated by the state-appointed 'prefects') and of the waves of 'political decentralisation' and 'territorial reforms' aimed at devolving competencies and powers to regional, meso-local (*départements*), metropolitan and municipal elected authorities. These reforms represent a never-ending and major process that is resistant to political shifts and crises, marked by some key moments: the 'modernisation' then 'renewal of Public Service' under the Rocard Government in 1988–1991; the 'state reform memorandum' of Prime Minister Juppé (1995–1997); the LOLF (*Loi organique sur les lois de finances*), a cross-party, unanimous reform of the public budgeting and accounting system under socialist Prime Minister Jospin (1997–2002); President Sarkozy's 'General Review of Public Policies' (RGPP; 2007–2012) and President Hollande's 'Modernisation of Public Action' (2012–2017) 'disruptively' upgraded by President Macron to become 'Public Transformation', since when it is handled by a Ministry and Interministerial Delegation (DiTP) bearing the same name. These reforms have produced a vast academic literature in both French and English, best synthesised in *Réinventer l'Etat* by Bezes (2009). Considering this long trend of state reform in a wider comparative perspective (Eymeri-Douzans and Pierre, 2011), it can be analysed as a form of contextualised appropriation, embedding and layering, a French 'acclimatisation' of the neo-managerialist, ideological and praxeological repertoire of reform ideas and recipes circulating globally since Reagan and Thatcher, known as 'New Public Management' (Eymeri-Douzans, 2011).

The current magnitude and complexity of French public administration, the sheer size of the civil service *stricto sensu* (5.6 million civil servants) and the wider public-sector workforce (25 per cent of the country's total workforce), together with the major responsibilities and prestige retained by senior civil servants, all constitute a major legacy of French history. As Macron himself, endorsing many historians, wrote in his election campaign book: 'Our history has made us children of the state [and] it is around the state that our common project brings us together' (2016, pp. 39–41). Indeed, this historical legacy is now embedded in a political regime created in 1958 – the Fifth Republic – whose leader, bearing the official title of President of the Republic, is also known as the 'Head of the State'.

In such a specific national context, the 'Elected One', invested as the 'Republican monarch' (Duverger, 1974) who aims – and is expected – to rule a traditionally turbulent nation and to introduce major reforms, needs first to govern the state bureaucracy and, especially, to impose their political domination over the administrative elite of top civil servants (*hauts fonctionnaires*) at the apex of a very distinctive statutory civil service built on a 'career system': any public agent entrusted with a permanent post, after meritocratic recruitment by *concours* (competitive exam), becomes a *fonctionnaire titulaire* – that is, they are tenured, for life, at a given grade of a given *corps* (an administrative body of civil servants entrusted with the recruitment and regulation of categories of posts, such as teachers, tax officers and police officers) to which they can belong until retirement. Heading this populous civil service is a prestigious and powerful socio-professional group of senior civil servants (*hauts fonctionnaires*) – a custom-defined elite of a few thousand – from which academia, the judiciary, the military and the high officials serving regional, meso-local and local governments are *de facto* excluded. In this respect, France differs from other European countries where young university graduates joining the civil service are first appointed to middle-rank positions, then make a career and eventually reach what is considered as the 'senior' civil service. Against such a positional definition of the top bureaucracy, France has a more essentialist definition: by virtue of their initial recruitment through the *concours* of a very few *grandes écoles* (very select and prestigious initial selection and training schools controlled by the state elite), the 27-year-old generalist civil servants graduating from ENA, the National School of Administration founded in

1945 by General de Gaulle and Michel Debré to train the higher 'State's Guards' (Eymeri-Douzans, 2001) and young state engineers from the École Polytechnique, are immediately considered as *hauts fonctionnaires* – a sort of state nobility (Bourdieu 1989) whose members enjoy a lifelong passport to quick and (usually) successful careers. This is especially true for the super-elite among them who join the three state administrative bodies known as the *grand corps* (the Finance Inspectorate, the Council of State and the Court of Accounts) since the effective solidarity and *esprit de corps* of these old and venerable institutions has long guaranteed a status of 'high-flyers' to their members (Kessler, 1986). French political science qualifies these *hauts fonctionnaires* as true 'policists' (policymakers) who co-govern the country (Eymeri-Douzans, 2019; Offerlé, 2004) alongside their political masters and their powerful *entourages* of special advisors – the *cabinets* (Eymeri-Douzans, Bioy and Mouton, 2015). Many of them often share the same profile as *énarques* – the ENA alumni. At the same time, party politics are weaker in France (except on the extremes) than in neighbouring parliamentary democracies, and party professionals are much less influential. Such a political landscape is often typified by prominent foreign scholars seeing France as 'technocratic' (Cole, 2008). Compared to the United States, for instance, what is remarkable is the quasi-absence of business leaders or academics gaining access to the Core Executive, combined with a regular flux of top civil servants who, after serving in the grey zone of ministerial *cabinets*, enter politics and often become ministers. Such a 'technocratisation' of French politics has existed since the 1960s: no fewer than five presidents out of eight (Pompidou, Giscard d'Estaing, Chirac, Hollande and Macron) were top civil servants who served in major ministerial cabinets before entering politics and reaching the presidency. Many (prime) ministers followed the same path, often passing, like Emmanuel Macron, directly from a *cabinet* to a ministerial portfolio without ever running for parliament.[1] For decades, ENA alumni have thus been populating not only the administrative elite – which is normal – but also the political elite.

Moreover, if one considers (after Wright Mills, 1956) that the 'power elite' of a country also includes top business representatives, it is noteworthy that a constant osmosis between the French administrative, political and business elites (Birnbaum, 1977; Suleiman, 1974) is ensured through the traditional practice of *pantouflage* (revolving doors), whereby usually middle-aged *hauts fonctionnaires* – either specialists or generalists – leave public administration for much-better-paid executive positions in the semi-public or private sector, whilst retaining the right to return to a post with their *corps*. This practice started in the mid-nineteenth century amongst the 'elites of the republic' (Charle, 1987) and has since been perpetuated by various revolving-doors practices with investment banks, insurance companies or consultancies (France and Vauchez, 2017). Bourdieu (1989) has shown how the *habitus* and behaviour of these happy few are deeply rooted in their common initial socialisation through the highly selective recruitment processes (*grands concours*) to the *grandes écoles* and how their *esprit de corps* and 'old-boy networks' ensure lifelong privileges to this 'state nobility'.

However, the inherited domination of this power elite (Birnbaum, 1977; Suleiman, 1974) is now increasingly contested, and its legitimisation by the 'meritocratic' initial selection of its members – assumed to guarantee their 'technocratic' competence – has been undermined by several developments. First, there have been too many scandals relating to managerial errors committed by *énarques* appointed as CEOs of major state-run businesses (such as Jean-Yves Haberer leading the major Crédit Lyonnais bank to near bankruptcy or Jean-Marie Messier doing the same with Compagnie Générale des Eaux, transformed into Vivendi) or conflicts of interest due to personal interconnections within that small elite. Second, there has been recurrent criticism of their supposed *pensée unique* (shared mindset) by extreme-right and extreme-left populist leaders, tabloids and social networks. Third, factual evidence produced by social scientists has shown that their supposedly 'meritocratic' selection is biased in many regards, is globally unfair and favours well-born candidates. Finally, observers have pointed out that this rather arrogant elite is not doing any better than more modest ones in other countries in tackling the major 'wicked problems' of our time. Indeed, the government's increased use of consultancy under Macron – especially in response to the Covid pandemic (and although 'consultocracy' has been increasing in influence since the end of the Chirac presidency) – was the subject of a media controversy and a parliamentary enquiry which questioned why the state needed to resort to 'outsiders' on such a grand scale if the administration was as well-qualified and competent as it was alleged to be.[2] All these developments have tarnished the golden image of these happy few and given rise to very strong anti-elite feelings amongst the French citizenry.

In sum, this is the context in which Emmanuel Macron – himself a pure product of that segregated educational background and a high-flyer already at the top of the technocratic elite at an early age – decided to run for the presidency without any affiliation to – or support from – the two dominant parties of the Left (PS) and Right (LR). For his 2017 campaign, he published a book significantly entitled *Revolution* (Macron, 2016), in which he argued that the main political cleavage was no longer between Left and Right but between the 'old world' – whose cynical elites claim to pursue so-called 'reforms' but who, in reality, only 'manage' the French decline – and a new generation of 'disruptive' leaders of a 'new world' represented by himself and his supporters, *les marcheurs*, whose ambition was no less than to profoundly 'transform' France into a 'start-up nation,' propelled into the twenty-first century. Clearly, such a political narrative was, from the very start, a strong symbolic attack against the elites in charge, including the state nobility from which Macron emerged.

Whereas many (cynical?) observers thought that such an electoral discourse would soon be forgotten, President Macron, throughout his first presidency (interrupted twice by the Yellow Vests and the Covid pandemic), took some decisive initiatives to shake up the state nobility, challenging its domination and privileges. First, after the Yellow Vests movement, which was provoked by a decision to enforce an eco-tax on fuel prices (denounced as emblematic of a very 'technocratic', 'Parisian' neglect of the disproportionate probable impact on the working poor in rural and peri-urban areas with little access to public transport), the president announced, in April 2021, the 'sacrifice' of ENA, this very 'fabric' of the French elite, as an expiatory victim. He then followed up with measures hastily imposed on his government (especially a reluctant Prime Minister, Edouard Philippe, himself an *énarque* who was more in favour of keeping the *status quo*) to produce a far-reaching 'rebuilding' of the system of selection, training and careers of the senior bureaucracy, condemned for its narrow social base and 'conformist' ethos. This 'most important reform of the higher civil service since the Liberation' (as proudly described to me by a minister's Chief of Staff), whose basic text is the Presidential Ordinance (a French form of decree-law) of 2 June 2021, has now been completed by the adoption of the necessary secondary legislation under the governments of Elisabeth Borne, Gabriel Attal, and Michel Barnier. At the time of writing, it is still too early to assess what will be the long-term outcome, given that public administration is always very skilled at 'digesting' reforms.

Nevertheless, the rest of this chapter analyses the underlying logic of this major reform, which can be summarised as transforming the 'state nobility' into 'can-do managers'. I argue that Macron's reform of the French top civil service is neither as new in its inspiration nor as disruptive as claimed but is the French avatar of a common trend observed in many post-modern democracies towards what two prominent German scholars (Mayntz and Derlien, 1989), identified as early as the 1980s as a growing 'functional politicisation' of top civil servants, who are increasingly summoned to be more docile towards ever-more-'presidentialised' executives (Poguntke and Webb, 2009) and more committed to the enforcement of the current political masters' programme. To reach this conclusion, the next section shows how Macron broke away from the 'state nobility' once in power. The following section explains that he did this by deciding to put the top civil servants under pressure to quickly take political control over the central state apparatus. The penultimate section 4 argues that this 'disruption', somewhat discontinuous in time but consistent in substance, represents a genuine 'refounding of the system' of the higher civil service, while the final section concludes that this can be understood as the acceleration of the French higher bureaucracy's 'functional politicisation'.

Emmanuel Macron, a technocrat *par excellence* who publicly broke away from the 'state nobility' once in power

Without reopening the classic debates on technocracy (Dubois and Dulong, 1999; Meynaud, 1964), I adopt here a flexible definition of the 'technocrat' as someone who takes an active part in the governing processes of a given public or private organisation, policy field, territory or polity, whose selection in the art of governing is based not on the exercise of elective mandates but on a distinctly French form of highly competitive exam, the *concours* (Dreyfus and Eymeri-Douzans, 2012). Thus, the technocrats' entitlement to participate in governing processes does not come from democratic legitimisation but from their legitimisation by the knowledge, skills and competencies recognised or claimed by their peers. Using this definition, the dazzling trajectory that propelled Emmanuel Macron to become the youngest president ever at 39, is indeed that of a technocrat who became president. This statement can be substantiated by his own social background, typical of those who achieve the level of academic success that delivers access to the *Grandes Écoles* (Eymeri-Douzans, 2001; Larat, 2015). After two years of 'preparatory classes' at the elite Parisian Lycée Henri-IV, he studied at Sciences Po Paris, before being accepted into ENA on his first attempt (while many other brilliant candidates need two or even three attempts). Young Macron graduated in the top five ENA students in 2004, which enabled him to choose to join the very prestigious Finance Inspectorate – which, of the three *Grands Corps*, had the strongest elite and business-friendly reputation,[3] an itinerary well in line with the French model of selection of adolescent elites (Eymeri-Douzans, 2005).

Macron's subsequent career combined personal distinctiveness with features typical of all those in the *Grands Corps*. In 2007, he joined the very influential 'Attali Commission for the Liberation of French Growth', and from 2008 to 2012, he worked at the Rothschild Bank. This was certainly a personal choice to leave public service (a choice that 80 per cent of *énarques* never make), though this variant of *pantouflage* is a tradition at the Finance Inspectorate (Rouban, 2002). What was more unusual with Macron was the precocity of his moving into the private sector, whereas, typically, *pantouflage* takes place in mid-life. Yet, he was not alone in taking this path: Edouard Philippe, his future prime minister, left the Council of State to become a business lawyer before entering politics and Sébastien Proto, his classmate at ENA and colleague as Finance Inspector, who became President Sarkozy's special advisor, joined Rothschild's just after Macron (Jauvert, 2018; Larnaudie, 2018). Such itineraries (much quicker than traditionally) are marked by early access 'at the same time' to the heart of the state and to the top business world. This allows a rapid accumulation of important assets that constitute financial (housing in select neighbourhoods), social (networks, clubs, etc.) and symbolic capital ("I succeeded in business!"), which, in return, makes these individuals stand out as what HR jargon describes as 'high-potential talents'. Macron's itinerary is truly emblematic of that new generation of postmodern technocrats who navigate with ease the former boundary between public and private (France and Vauchez, 2017). In 2010, only six years after graduating from ENA, Macron was offered (but declined) the prestigious position of deputy director of staff of the right-wing Prime Minister François Fillon: this shows the level of esteem he had quickly built up. It was Jacques Attali (former special advisor to socialist President François Mitterrand) who then invited him, in 2011, to join the campaign of socialist presidential candidate François Hollande – which would lead to his appointment as the newly elected president's Deputy Secretary General at the Elysée in 2012.

Macron's trajectory towards eligibility for the presidency thus conformed to a classic pattern in the Fifth Republic of 'access to the centre' (Gaxie, 2003). Like four of his predecessors and many prime ministers, he entered politics via the ministerial *cabinets*, these spaces of socialisation in the exercise of state power which are like an extension of ENA's training, since the prince is no longer an individual person but a collective brain with special advisors (Eymeri-Douzans, 2015). Having learned the practical art of governing at the Elysée as head of the pool of advisors in charge of economic and financial matters for two years, Macron was then appointed as Minister for the Economy in 2014, a position from which he would launch his presidential bid. Without the existence of ENA and the *cabinets*, Macron would never have been in a position to become president so soon – he would have had to take the traditional route of elections and climb the party ladder, which takes time. Macron is, even more than Giscard d'Estaing, with whom the stereotype was often associated, the Technocrat-President *par excellence*.

Considering that technocrats, especially *énarques*, are seen in a negative light in France, denigrated daily by humourists and essayists denouncing the 'deep state' (Morin, 2020) – a notion at times used by Macron and his lieutenants – was it a Machiavellian motive that pushed candidate Macron, in 2016–2017, to adopt an electioneering stance and language that advocated a fundamental upheaval of the state technocracy to which he owed so much? Or was he genuinely convinced that this ruling 'caste' that he knows as an insider is detrimental to the country and must be weakened to allow the 'disruptive transformation' necessary to put France back on the right track? Maybe both, since a smart tactician can also be a man of strong vision and *vice versa*.

Let us recall a few significant facts. In his campaign book *Revolution*, candidate Macron distanced himself from his *milieu* to the point of appropriating the populist critique: recognising that senior civil servants constitute a 'caste', allegedly running the country's affairs from the shadows, he argued for the need to modernise the upper ranks of the civil service in two ways. First, by opening up far more management positions to non-career civil servants hired on contracts (*contractuels*), which would depend on the state becoming an employer capable of attracting different and new 'talents' and, second, by challenging the traditional protection offered to top civil servants, whose life-long membership of a *corps* with an unlimited 'right to return' to a post is no longer in step with the practices of the rest of society (Macron, 2016, p. 250). Matching actions to words, when announcing his candidacy on 17 November 2016, Macron resigned from the civil service – which meant having to reimburse €50,000 to the state – commenting: 'I am in favour of reform for the civil service, in particular the *corps* I belong to, which is not a judicial body and does not justify having lifelong protection and a permanent right to return'. In so doing, prior to a very uncertain electoral contest, he was giving up a formidable safety net that has so often benefited many French politicians after their electoral misfortunes. Beyond the calculation of (dis)interest, this strong gesture signified that being a civil servant was only one stage in his life and not the essentialised identity, experienced as belonging to an order, described by Tönnies' (1957) as a *Stand* and by Weber (1978) as a 'status group', which it is (still) for most *énarques*. Thus, there was no reason to expect from this prince, disaffiliated from his professional group, any particular loyalty to the '*esprit de corps*' and objective interests of the group. To make things even clearer to his former colleagues, he later referred, in several interviews, to the US 'spoil's system' – an *horresco referens* for French bureaucrats. He warned them that, during his first semester in office and against all French administrative customs, all positions at the top of the administrative hierarchy of the ministerial departments would be submitted to a 'Review of directors' aimed at individually asking them to pledge allegiance to the new government and its policy objectives or to leave.

A new president who intends to take political control over the state by putting the top civil servants under pressure

Once elected – and mindful of the intrigues that characterise the corridors of power – the new president and his close advisors wanted to take a stand against what was often described as the crisis of authority suffered by his predecessor, François Hollande. This is why President Macron and his first Prime Minister, Édouard Philippe, strongly insisted upon the primacy of the political will of a 'Jupiterian' Head of State – anointed with universal suffrage – over technocratic or bureaucratic demands. To ensure his hold over ministers, their *entourages* and the state apparatus more generally, Macron, at the first meeting of the Council of Ministers (*Conseil des Ministres*) on 18 May 2017, resolutely put two coordinated innovations on the table: first, a drastic limitation on the size of ministerial *cabinets* and, second, a decision to submit the holders of the 250 highest administrative positions, the *Directeurs d'Administration Centrale* (hereafter DACs) to a 'review' procedure within six months.

The first of the two innovative measures, the downsizing of ministerial *cabinets*, had in fact been attempted several times before by newly elected presidents but with little success, since the limited number of 'official' advisors, the ones appointed by decree, are surrounded by many 'unofficial' members, whose names do not appear on the decrees. For instance, the total number of advisors amounted to 650 at the end of Hollande's presidency, of whom a third were 'unofficial' (Eymeri-Douzans *et al.*, 2015). Against these laxist habits, Article 1 of the Decree of 18 May 2017 set very strict quotas: ten advisors for a full Minister, eight for a Delegated Minister (equivalent to UK mid-level Minister of State) and five for a Secretary of State (equivalent to a British junior minister). Article 2 removed any room for manœuvre: 'Appointments of ministerial *cabinet* members are made by ministerial order after being submitted to the Prime Minister, who ensures compliance with the provisions of Article 1'.[4] Above all, the last sentence – 'No-one may carry out tasks in a ministerial *cabinet* unless he or she appears on this decree' – was written to mark the end of the epoch of 'unofficial' advisors and huge *cabinets*. The aim of this reduction in members of *cabinets* was to fluidify and accelerate governmental work by reducing rivalries between ministers' staff members and by forcing each minister and their *cabinet* to work closely with the top departmental administrators.

The initial result was impressive: on 1 August 2018, even including the unlimited prime minister's *cabinet* (56 civilian advisors plus 11 military officers), the Philippe government employed no more than 300 advisors: this was a huge contraction, by almost two-thirds, compared to the Sarkozy and Hollande periods. However, the initiative did not stand the test of time. The pace of work within the *cabinets*, already excessive, became unmanageable for such reduced teams. As soon as the 'one-hundred-days' milestone was reached, the press reported many cases of advisors' exhaustion, followed by a series of resignations. The situation worsened the following year: regular interviews, conducted anonymously with 'insiders' within the Core Executive, revealed stories of frequent burnouts and excessive staff turnover within the *cabinets*. The Yellow Vests movement, which started in autumn 2018 and only dissipated with the onset, in early 2020, of the Covid pandemic, put the government and ministers under such constant pressure that the president allowed them, on a case-by-case basis, to hire extra advisors. Then, in July 2020, with a new prime minister, Jean Castex, a new decree authorised ministers once again to employ 15 personal advisors. This provision, combined with an increase in the number of delegated and junior ministers, increased the total number of *cabinet* members to 570 in 2022.

The rationale behind Macron's second innovation – the DACs 'review', carried out in the second half of 2017 – was set out in the 'Circular' Memorandum[5] of 24 May 2017, which the prime minister sent to his ministers; it related to an exemplary, collegial and efficient method of government work, as follows:

> The French administration is competent, neutral and loyal. It is one of our country's strengths. I ask you to rely on it. The DACs are appointed by decree taken in the Council of Ministers. It is up to you to work closely with them. [...]. You are the heads of the administrations under your authority. [...] On the one hand, your *cabinets* must focus on political missions and ensure that our action is well explained and communicated. On the other hand, the DACs are responsible for carrying out the public policies within the frame of the government's action. Simply put, it is now necessary to avoid duplicating the functions of the administration in the *cabinet*. [...]. The administration of your ministry must commit itself to the implementation of the political priorities determined by the government with the Head of the State. You must therefore organise effective working arrangements with your DACs – all of whom will be appointed or confirmed within six months – to take charge of those public policies under your authority. Short decision-making channels and a good flow of information should make the working methods more efficient. You need to meet with your directors very regularly and to rely fully on the administrative services [...]. You will set the roadmap for each DAC.

In martial style, this was a real attempt to put the highest public servants under more direct command and control and thus under more pressure from the political masters.

To better understand what was at stake in spring 2017, it is important to know that the highest administrative positions are defined by the French Council of State case law as being 'at the discretion of the government'. They include the DACs, the prefects, the ambassadors and the heads of many public entities, organisations and agencies with national jurisdiction: in all, more than 700 positions, all of which are also revocable at the weekly Council of Ministers' meeting. Far from illustrating the theory of a spoils system almost more radical than in the United States (where the Senate has to endorse appointments), a civilised administrative alternation of power or *alternance* had, in fact, developed since 1981, when the Left first came to power under the Fifth Republic, whereby two politico-administrative teams of senior officials, one closer to the Left, the other closer to the Right (but without explicit party affiliation), alternate at a faster or slower pace, with a constant concern from the Executive to avoid a 'witch hunt'. The incumbents 'complete the three years' of their appointment (except in rare cases) and, when replaced, are 'resettled' in other suitable positions – prestigious and well-paid but with much less involvement in policymaking (Eymeri-Douzans, 2006).

Macron's decision to proceed, *ab initio*, to a 'review of directors' was thus, if not illegal, a clear rupture with what had become an established tradition. The Elysée staff even spread the rumour that the president would convoke to the Palace those lucky ones, newly nominated or confirmed in their posts, thereby playing with the archaic image of a personal allegiance to him. Six months later, one of our interviewees (male, 57, Finance Inspector, former DAC) said:

> The pressure put on the DACs was effective in the first few months. There were reviews until Christmas. However, frankly, we did not get rid of many directors. As for the president receiving candidates in person, this happened at the beginning but the presidential agenda is such that it is no longer the case today. We have returned to previous practices: recruitments are delegated to the prime minister's office and the presidency has its word to say.

It is thus no surprise that an assessment of the six-month 'review' period, reported in three articles by Pierre Laberrondo (2018), came to mixed conclusions: after the six-month review, only 49 DACs of the 240 targeted had been replaced – comparable to the beginning of Sarkozy and Hollande's presidencies. There were contrasts between ministries, with Education Minister Jean-Michel Blanquer removing all the directors at the Ministry of Education while Culture Minister Françoise Nyssen maintained the *status quo*. Moreover, despite candidate Macron's plan to recruit a quarter of the directors from 'outside' the administration, the 49 promoted were as much civil servants as their predecessors. One interviewee (male, 44, editor-in-chief of a specialised magazine) confirmed: 'There are no disruptive profiles among the new appointments'.

Nevertheless, throughout his first term in office, interviews confirmed that President Macron and his two prime ministers 'put everyone under pressure. Those who don't like it get themselves thrown out and the rest of them stand to attention' (male, 44, DAC). This shared feeling is fostered by well-orchestrated episodic shows of force: for instance, in mid-summer 2020, the removal of Marc Guillaume – the far-too-influential secretary-general of the government inherited from Hollande – which caused uproar amongst the administrative elite and many subsequent dismissals. As an interviewed prefect (male, 59) commented: 'The president wants to be obeyed and he takes a very hard line with people who do not understand that!'

Indeed, even more than by such individual sanctions, it was by attacking ENA and the *Grands Corps* to impose a 'genuine refounding of our system, affecting the recruitment, the training as well as the careers of top civil servants' (Macron, 2019) that the president intended to maintain sustained collective pressure on senior administrators urged to become 'State entrepreneurs' (Macron, 2017).

A 'refounding of the system', discontinuous in time but consistent in substance

Emmanuel Macron, like Margaret Thatcher during her 'Next Steps Initiative' in the mid-1980s, believes that bringing outsiders' fresh blood into public administration greatly helps to 'debureaucratise' bureaucracy – that common dream of all neoliberals. Accordingly, he tasked junior minister Olivier Dussopt to terminate the oligopoly of ENA alumni over the appointments in ministerial hierarchies, which dated back to a decree from 1955. Using the effect of surprise, three government amendments opening all civil-service posts to contractual workers were introduced in the 'Law for the Freedom to Choose One's Professional Future' and adopted by the National Assembly, in five minutes, on Saturday 16 June 2018 at 3.20 a.m., with only 40 deputies present. Following a parliamentary appeal, the Constitutional Council censured the relevant articles on procedural grounds. However, Macron reaffirmed that he would continue to open all posts, particularly in the senior civil service, to people of talent and merit from other backgrounds. Consequently, Dussopt ensured that the 'Law of Civil Service Transformation' bearing his name contained provisions opening up recruitment for all permanent administrative positions to civil servants from all *corps* and careers as well as to contractual workers from outside. Thus, the 775 top positions under the direct authority of DACs, responsible for the senior management of French ministries, are no longer a closed shop. This is a real cultural revolution, and a clear message sent to the *énarques*: the state's higher bureaucracy is no longer your 'private hunting ground'.

The same year, the president committed the most symbolic ritual crime imaginable against the state nobility: on the very mediatised occasion of the post-Yellow Vests 'Great National Debate' press conference (25 April 2019), without any prior consultation (even the prime minister was only informed a few minutes before), he announced his intention to, *inter alia*, close ENA and put an end to the *Grands Corps* – that is, the Finance Inspectorate, the Council of State and the Court of Accounts. This was a traumatic moment for *énarques*: anonymous witnesses of the event have recounted to me how an emergency meeting of the ENA alumni association's governing board was convened, where its incredulous members watched the president's video three times, repeating in disbelief: 'But he didn't say that! It's impossible!'. Then, the president announced his unusual choice of Frédéric Thiriez (a former top civil servant with an atypical career, having moved into the world of football) to conduct a consultation and produce a report. The Thiriez Report was delivered in February 2020 to a reluctant prime minister – himself an *énarque* and proud member of the *corps* of the Council of State who did not share the anti-ENA views of the president. The prime minister's office intimated that the many disruptive proposals in the Thiriez Report would not be binding for the drafting of the reform, thus opening a window for compromise. However, the issue then quickly disappeared from the political agenda because of the Covid pandemic. Nevertheless, specialists noted that, in the summer of 2020, in Prime Minister Jean Castex's new government, a separate Ministry for Public Transformation and Public Service (detached from the Ministry of Economy and Finance) was reinstated and placed in the hands of a close presidential ally, Amélie de Montchalin. Her staff worked in the shadows towards a clear deadline of June 2021, set by the Dussopt Law, when the period allowing the delegation of legislative power to the executive to legislate using 'ordinances' ('*Ordonnances*' – a type of legislation bypassing parliamentary discussion) would run out.

Between the end of the last lockdown and the prologue to the presidential campaign of 2022, a decisive acceleration was imposed: in March 2021, a new and specific recruitment *concours* to ENA – *Talents concours* – was introduced, designed to promote 'diversity' by means of positive discrimination in favour of students with lower social backgrounds or rural origins. This went against all French traditions of supposed equal treatment between candidates on strict lines of meritocracy. In April, the president summoned hundreds of top officials and, to everyone's surprise, once again repeated his intention to close ENA and replace it by an 'Institute of Public Service' (ISP). He also confirmed the rapid adoption by 'ordinance' of the main proposals from the Thiriez Report. The sequence was so sudden that no-one in the ministerial *cabinets* had checked the legal availability of the acronym ISP, which happened to be an existing registered trademark: the adjective 'national' was therefore added after another detailed report, and the National Institute for Public Service (INSP) was born on 1 January 2022.[6]

A lack of space here prevents the narration of the palace war, with all its dramatic twists and turns, triggered by the writing, adoption and enforcement, over the final months of Macron's first presidency, of an impressive series of legal texts implementing the detail of this reform; this continued, after his re-election, into 2022 and 2023, regulating the INSP, creating a new *corps* of general state administrators to replace the three *grands corps* and transforming the Finance Inspectorate from a *grands corps* into a functional department of the Finance Ministry. This major reform is a combination of Macronian 'disruption' together with path-dependent measures under consideration for decades. Amongst the real innovations are, first, the real-fake 'end of ENA', replaced, in the same buildings and with the same personnel, by the INSP; second, the addition of a new *Concours talents* based on positive discrimination; third, the creation of a few, mainly online, teaching modules common to the 13 training institutes within the French public administration to give their students a 'common culture' and 'shared values' (rather than being in separate *corps* as before); fourth, the abolition of the *corps* of ministerial Inspectorates-General as administrative bodies but the maintenance of their missions on a functional basis (the so-called 'functionalisation of inspectorates-general'); fifth, the surprising abolition of the prefectoral and diplomatic *corps*, which provoked such an outcry that the government wisely recognised the specificities of these distinct professions and finally maintained them with specific working conditions with derogatory rules; finally, the opening up of the senior civil service positions to contractual outsiders, as discussed above.

However – and 'at the same time' – the current transformation encompasses reform ideas that had already been envisaged for some time. First, the elimination of the 'general culture' dissertation in the ENA/INSP entrance exam – long denounced as a test of belonging to the bourgeoisie – had been under discussion for two decades and was abolished by Sciences Po Paris in 2013. Likewise, the abolition of the 'exit ranking' (*classement de sortie*) referred to earlier had been proposed by Human Resources practitioners and specialised academics for 20 years and had almost been accepted under President Hollande and Prime Minister Valls; however, the lobbying of the Council of State within the government's Secretariat-General had succeeded in blocking it. Similarly, the creation of a vast inter-departmental *corps* of 'state administrators' (consistent with the abolition of ENA's *classement de sortie*) is an upgraded version of the 1945 goal of setting up a body of civil administrators, which was, *de jure*, interdepartmental but ended up being *de facto* managed on a departmental basis: such a merger had been an ongoing request from the Union of Civil Administrators (USAC). The same is true of the re-creation, inspired by the *Ecole de guerre* (the war college which trains military officers), of an advanced-level programme of study, *Cycle des hautes études du service public* (CHESP) operated by the INSP for the selection and training of future administrative high-flyers – a new version of the stillborn 'Centre for Advanced Administrative Studies' of 1945. Finally, with regard to the new strategy aimed at better connecting the INSP with academia and research, including the recruitment of a few researchers and PhD/post-doctoral students, this has been under consideration since 2002, when ENA absorbed the IIAP (International Institute of Public Administration, a survival of the former Colonial School) and the French Review of Public Administration (RFAP), creating a small research centre and signing agreements with a few universities to establish dedicated Masters' programmes offering a formal diploma to the many foreign students from all continents who come and study at ENA/now INSP. It is too early to say in which research activities the INSP will invest its new financial and human resources in the years to come, but a dedicated division has been established, assisted by a committee to provide some guidance, and has recruited several academics.

The creation in December 2021, under the prime minister's direct authority, of an inter-ministerial delegation (DIESE) with, amongst other roles, that of supervising the INSP, deserves a paragraph *per se*. The Elysée presented it as 'the inter-ministerial HR directorate for state managers, designed to accompany and build the careers of senior civil servants over time, to regularly evaluate them and to decide on their career reorientations'.[7] It started its activity in January 2022, with Emilie Piette as its founding head, a state engineer who graduated from two *grandes écoles* – Polytechnique and the *Ecole des Mines* – and who had served as Secretary-General of the huge block of Ministries for Ecological Transition: Transport, Infrastructure and Territorial Cohesion. The DIESE is a much stronger incarnation of a venture established in 2014 within the Secretariat-General of the government and whose head, Florence Méaux, was the co-author of the Thiriez Report – which recommended empowering the state to centrally control its senior managers. This idea dates back to the early 2000s: substituting the inherited 'statutory' approach by *corps*, ranks and grades with a new *approche métiers* (approach by profession) favoured by Human Resource Management (HRM) specialists, based on occupations, 'job families', generic and specific job descriptions, skills and competencies for all the A+ category of public servants. For the higher echelons, this means a 'functionalisation' of the top managers appointed by ministers (*encadrement supérieur*) and those appointed by presidential decree (*encadrement dirigeant*). It was a Circular Memorandum issued by Prime Minister Fillon in 2010 that created the *Mission Cadres Dirigeants*, a special service dedicated to detecting the best 'potential talents' and putting them into a 'talent pool' (*vivier*), managed in a somewhat opaque manner. Since 2016, this service also organises the 'audition committees', which interview candidates and produce the short-lists of the happy few proposed to the president and prime minister as new general secretaries, inter-departmental delegates and DACs. The DIESE will pilot the new HR policy for the state's top civil service in coordination with all HR departments in the ministries, with a special focus on equal opportunity and diversity. More individually, the DIESE selects and mentors (future) high-flyers, distributed according to their seniority into two broader 'talent pools', offering them tailor-made training, skills and competence assessments, individualised career coaching, etc. It is far too early to predict how this new ecosystem will develop and stabilise, especially regarding the degree to which the HR departments of the strongest and biggest ministries – especially those of Economy and Finance or the Interior – will accept – and to what extent – the coordination from the prime minister's office by the DIESE. If top careers and appointments at the Ministry of Economy and

Finance continue to be handled in a 'closed-shop' manner, the DIESE's room for manœuvre will be significantly reduced.

Finally, what happened to the two remaining *grands corps*: the Council of State and the Court of Accounts? These prestigious, powerful institutions saved themselves due to their specific legal status and following tough negotiations that ended in a compromise: a regular flux of newcomers from the INSP has been maintained, preventing them from becoming, like the Court of Appeal (*Cour de Cassation*), a club of old judges. Yet, these new recruitments are somewhat delayed: INSP alumni will start their first position, mainly with the new status of 'state administrator'. After serving two years, those who dare will compete for the few positions vacant in each institution. If selected, they will be hired first for three years before an 'integration commission' decides whether they join the Council or the Court, although still for life. To prevent co-optation, each commission is composed of three members of the *corps* and three outsiders (chosen by the President of the Republic, and presidents of the Senate and National Assembly), with no chairperson or preponderant vote. Once again, it is too early to assess the long-term impact that such an innovation in their recruitment will have on the two remaining *grands corps* and their *esprit de corps*. What is obvious, however, is that the *aggiornamento* imposed on them by Macron does not undermine their power or their grandeur, derived not only from their core missions but also from the opportunity for their members, over three decades of a career, to enter and leave the Council and the Court and occupy the highest positions in the state apparatus (Kessler, 1986) – an opportunity that remains almost unchanged, with integration into these *corps* simply delayed by five years.

How do the main protagonists perceive this package of measures adopted in such a rapid burst of activity? The combination of opening the top managerial posts to contractual workers and the functionalisation of all senior positions is what shakes everything up. From now on, there are no more life-long careers for top civil servants except those in the Council or the Court: this is what Macron is aiming at when he says he wants to put an end to 'rent-seeking'. However, as one deputy director declared: 'Of course, as I have a three-year post and I want the minister to renew it, I am servile'. 'This reform dangerously threatens the impartiality of the senior civil service and exposes it to the risk of unhealthy politicisation', declared the ENA alumni president (at the ENA Council of Administration meeting, 5 May 2021). A right-wing male prefect aged 59, declared:

> This affair is to justify destroying the *corps* and move towards a logic of generalised functional positions in the entire state hierarchy. The models are the positions of directors-general of the services in the regions, the *départements* and the big municipalities. And it will produce the same effects: politicisation, politicisation, politicisation!'

The FGF-Force Ouvrière union, in its press communiqué (6 May 2021) commenting on the draft ordinance, said:

> Behind the epiphenomenon that constitutes the name change of ENA hides a completely different reality: the transformation of a statutory system of civil service into a position system of civil service. This means, as the minister explained, that 'the government will be able to choose its recruits'. Thus, the president would obtain the spoils system that he wanted for the senior management of the state – i.e., a senior administration at the service of the political masters and no longer at the service of the nation and its citizens.[8]

This is a rare convergence of analyses between people with such diverse backgrounds and worldviews! However, the meaning of some words needs clarification: the 'politicisation' in question here is certainly not the partisan patronage on appointments and clientelism observed in many countries, based on the enrolment of those concerned into governmental parties – this would make no sense in a *Macronie* (Macron's world) that has not really tried to build a traditional partisan organisation. Of course, what is at stake is 'functional politicisation'.

Conclusion: the underlying logic of Macron's reform as an acceleration of the higher bureaucracy's 'functional politicisation'

'Functional politicisation' is neither new nor specific to the France of today. Identified as early as the 1970s in Germany (theorised by Mayntz and Derlien, 1989), and spreading in France since the banalisation of political alternations of power in the 1980s, it differs essentially from traditional partisan patronage, in that it selects the most talented people capable of ensuring the success of reforms that are conceived 'in project mode'. Thus, it requires from them a new form of loyalty that has little to do with classic loyalty, understood as the neutral duty of obedience of Weberian bureaucrats. Such post-Weberian loyalty requires the total dedication of the individual – what the neo-managerial discourse calls 'strong commitment' – to the success of the reforms and projects of those in power at the time (Eymeri-Douzans, 2003). Similarly, Minister de Montchalin said, when interviewed by *Acteurs publics* (No. 2554, 27 May 2021):

> I reject this Anglo-Saxon concept of a spoils system for our country. The president has always openly said that those who are responsible for implementing the public policies of a democratically elected government must share its ambition, spirit and objectives. It is, indeed, a question of loyalty and neutrality – values that are at the heart of the civil service statute – and of respect from those who are appointed to implement the roadmaps given to them. It is not about party affiliation.

It could not be better said!

This increased functional politicisation will undoubtedly be fostered by the 'managerialisation' and 'functionalisation' of the highest appointments and careers under the auspices of the DIESE, combined with the competition orchestrated between career civil servants and high-flying contractual outsiders. This should tend – in the grey zone where ministers, their *entourages* and the top 'policists' daily interact – towards a sort of symbiotic collaboration in the strategic steering of reforms. Such a symbiosis, already observed for a long time in the Ministry of Finance fortress between ministers, *cabinets* and the Treasury and Budget Directorates, was experienced by Macron when he was minister there … and he also enjoys it as president in his direct piloting of the country's European policy (Eymeri-Douzans, 2022). It is thus no surprise that he wanted to expand this symbiotic *modus operandi* throughout the entire state apparatus. Indeed, this was already the very purpose of the 2017 Philippe Circular Memorandum. The higher civil-service reform, including the highly symbolic degradation imposed on the 'state nobility' by the abolition of the ENA 'brand', the end of 'ranking', etc., is fully consistent with its inspiration.

Ensuring that this newly born reform and the non-stabilised new balance of powers between political masters and senior bureaucrats that it has created becomes an irreversible transformation is a main – yet undercommented – motivation as to why, after his semi-defeat in the legislative elections of June 2022, Macron confirmed an almost minority – but cohesive and submissive – government instead of opening up to a coalition government with *Les Républicains*. This was a scenario that would have obliged him to dangerous compromises in writing the decrees still to come on DIESE and INSP, as in the highest appointments to be made in the Council of Ministers. Amongst ministers and top civil servants, President Macron has always wanted to be obeyed. In the end, while he is often compared to Tony Blair because his *en même temps* rhetoric seems to take some inspiration from the social-liberal 'third way', Macron's style of leadership is more that of a Thatcherite with a young and smiling face who wants to be relieved of 'wait-a-minute advisors' and supported by docile 'can-do managers' – to borrow, at some distance, the words of the Iron Lady. Will this have been Macron's downfall? His failed dissolution of the National Assembly in the summer of 2024, and its resulting fragmentation marked the end of such hyper-personal exercice of power, with President Macron now forced to share executive power with the old centrist leader, Prime Minister François Bayrou, and a very minority government with very little room for manoeuvre. Only time will tell.

Notes

1 Members of the government in France do not have to have a seat in parliament since the Constitution establishes a strict separation of powers between the

Executive and Legislature. Any MP who is appointed as a minister must abandon their seat to the 'replacement' (*suppléant*) who stood with the main candidate on a 'double ticket' at the election.
2 Senate Report No. 578, March 2022.
3 The ENA training used to end up with a *classement de sortie*, a final exit ranking of the whole cohort, according to their marks achieved: the top graduates were able to choose the most prestigious posts. This system of ranking is one of the main victims of Macron's reform.
4 All translations of official documents are by the author.
5 'Circulaire' is the name given to an administrative document setting out details of how particular decisions should be implemented.
6 https://insp.gouv.fr/
7 As defined by the president himself: https://www.elysee.fr/emmanuel-macron/2021/04/08/intervention-du-president-de-la-republique-emmanuel-macron-a-loccasion-de-la-convention-manageriale-de-letat (consulted 21 August 2023).
8 As defined by the president himself: https://www.elysee.fr/emmanuel-macron/2021/04/08/intervention-du-president-de-la-republique-emmanuel-macron-a-loccasion-de-la-convention-manageriale-de-letat (consulted 21 August 2023).

References

Badie, B. and Birnbaum, P. (1979) *Sociologie de l'Etat*. Paris: Grasset.
Bezes, P. (2009) *Réinventer l'Etat. Les réformes de l'administration française (1962–2008)*. Paris: PUF.
Birnbaum, P. (1977) *Les sommets de l'Etat*. Paris: Le Seuil.
Bourdieu, P. (1989) *La noblesse d'État*. Paris: Minuit.
Charle, C. (1987) *Les élites de la République, 1880–1900*. Paris: Fayard.
Cole, A. (2008) *Governing and governance in France*. Cambridge: Cambridge University Press.
De Tocqueville, A. (1856) *The ancien régime and the French revolution*. Cambridge, New York: Cambridge University Press (Jon Elster, ed., 2011).
Dreyfus, F. and Eymeri-Douzans, J.-M. (2012) 'Les concours administratifs en questions', *Revue Française d'Administration Publique*, 142(2), pp. 305–306.
Dubois, V. and Dulong, D. (eds) (1999) *La question technocratique*. Strasbourg: Presses Universitaires de Strasbourg.
Duverger, M. (1974) *La monarchie républicaine*. Paris: Robert Laffont.
Eymeri-Douzans, J.-M. (1999) *Les gardiens de l'Etat. Une sociologie des énarques de ministère*. Paris: Université Paris 1, PhD thesis.
Eymeri-Douzans, J.-M. (2001) *La fabrique des énarques*. Paris: Economica.
Eymeri-Douzans, J.-M. (2003) 'Frontière ou marches? De la contribution de la haute administration à la production du politique', in Lagroye, J. (ed.). *La politisation*. Paris: Belin, pp. 47–77.
Eymeri-Douzans, J.-M. (2005) 'La machine élitaire. Un regard européen sur le modèle français de fabrication des hauts fonctionnaires', in Joly, H. (ed.). *Formation des élites en France et en Allemagne*. Cergy-Pontoise: CIRAC, pp. 101–128.
Eymeri-Douzans, J.-M. (2006) 'Comparer les hauts fonctionnaires en Europe. Variations sur le thème de la carrière', in Dreyfus, F. and Eymeri-Douzans, J.-M. (eds) *Science politique de l'administration. Une approche comparative*. Paris: Economica, pp. 28–46.
Eymeri-Douzans, J.-M. (2011) 'NPM reforms legacy. A common praxeologic, a variety of acclimatizations, a renewed bureaucratization', in Eymeri-Douzans, J.-M. and Pierre J. (eds) *Administrative reforms and democratic governance*. London: Routledge, pp. 9–26.

Eymeri-Douzans, J.-M. (2015) 'Le ministre n'est plus une personne physique. Sur la collectivisation de la fonction ministérielle', in Eymeri-Douzans, J.-M., Bioy, X. and Mouton, S. (eds) *Le règne des entourages. Cabinets et conseillers de l'Exécutif*. Paris: Presses de Sciences Po, pp. 553–597.
Eymeri-Douzans, J.-M. (2019) '"Policistes" ou "fonctionnaires gouvernants"?', in Michel, H., Lévêque, S. and Contamin, J.-G. (eds) *Rencontres avec Michel Offerlé*. Paris: Editions du Croquant, pp. 339–344.
Eymeri-Douzans, J.-M. (2022) 'Déterminer et conduire la politique européenne de la France. Un modèle de symbiose du pouvoir présidentiel et du pouvoir administratif', *Revue Française d'Administration Publique*, 181(1), pp. 13–40.
Eymeri-Douzans, J.-M. and Pierre, J. (eds) (2011) *Administrative reforms and democratic governance*. London: Routledge.
Eymeri-Douzans, J.-M., Bioy, X. and Mouton, S. (eds) (2015) *Le règne des entourages. Cabinets et conseillers de l'Exécutif*. Paris: Presses de Sciences Po.
France, P. and Vauchez, A. (2017) *Sphère publique, intérêts privés. Enquête sur un grand brouillage*. Paris: Presses de Sciences Po.
Gaxie, D. (2003) *La démocratie représentative*. Paris: Montchrestien.
Jauvert, V. (2018) *Les intouchables d'Etat. Bienvenue en Macronie*. Paris: Robert Laffont.
Kessler, M.-C. (1986) *Les grands corps de l'Etat*. Paris: Presses de la FNSP.
Laberrondo, P. (2018) 'Enquête sur le spoils system version Macron', *Acteurs publiques*, https://acteurspublics.fr/articles/enquete-sur-le-spoils-system-version-macron-1-3
Larat, F. (2015) 'Le dernier maillon dans la chaîne des inégalités? Les particularités du profil des élèves de l'ÉNA', *Revue Française d'Administration Publique*, 153(1), pp. 103–124.
Larnaudie, M. (2018) *Les jeunes gens*. Paris: Grasset.
Lowi, T.J. (1964) 'American business, public policy, case studies and political theory', *World Politics*, 16(4), pp. 677–715.
Macron, E. (2016) *Révolution*. Paris: XO.
Macron, E. (2017) 'Presidential address to the annual meeting of Prefects, 05 September.
Macron, E. (2019) 'Press conference', 25 April.
Mayntz, R. and Derlien, H.-U. (1989) 'Party patronage and politicization of the west German administrative elite 1970–1987. Towards hybridization?', *Governance*, 2(4), pp. 384–404.
Meynaud, J. (1964) *La technocratie. Mythe ou réalité?* Paris: Payot.
Morin, C. (2020) *Les inamovibles de la République: Vous ne les verrez jamais, mais ils gouvernent*. Paris: Editions de l'Aube.
Offerlé, M. (2004) *Sociologie de la vie politique française*. Paris: La Découverte.
Poguntke, T. and Webb, P. (2009) *The presidentialisation of politics: A comparative study of modern democracies*. Oxford: Oxford University Press.
Rosanvallon, P. (1990) *L'état en France de 1789 à nos jours*. Paris: Le Seuil.
Rouban, L. (2002) 'L'inspection générale des finances, 1958–2000: Quarante ans de pantouflage', *Cahiers du CEVIPOF*, 31, pp. 2–76.
Schmidt, V. (2003) 'French capitalism transformed, yet still a third variety of capitalism', *Economy and Society*, 32(4), pp. 526–554.
Suleiman, E. (1974) *Politics, power and bureaucracy in France*. Princeton: Princeton University Press.
Tönnies, F. (1957) *Community & Society*. East Lansing: Michigan State University Press.
Weber, M. (1978) *Economy and society*. Berkeley, Los Angeles, London: University of California Press (G. Roth and C. Wittich, eds).
Wright Mills, C. (1956) *The power elite*. Oxford: Oxford University Press.

10
EDUCATION UNDER EMMANUEL MACRON: SOME MARKET-INSPIRED CHANGE AND MUCH CONTINUITY

Nicolas Charles and Andy Smith

Abstract

As a candidate and as president, Emmanuel Macron announced significant changes to the French education sector. Specifically, he promised to radically improve schooling, increase equality and modernise 'access to higher education'. However, it remains uncertain whether deep change has actually been brought about. This chapter analyses this outcome from two angles. The first entails an analysis of the institutional ordering in place in 2017. Although this sector is best known internationally for the reputed top-down power of the French Ministry of Education, this source of policy impulsion has always been tempered, on the one hand, by the autonomy of its teachers and, on the other, by the multiple effects of a singular national approach to 'meritocracy'. The second angle concerns initiatives undertaken under the first Macron presidency to foster institutional change. Overall, the authors find relatively little transformation – institutional continuity has tended to prevail. Nevertheless, through various revised policy instruments, seeds have been sown for re-institutionalising the French approach to meritocracy in the name of 'choice' for pupils, students and educational establishments. Explanation of this shift lies in top-down measures undertaken to introduce market mechanisms into the education sector in the name of competition and a corresponding approach to social justice.

Introduction

As a presidential candidate, Emmanuel Macron announced various ambitions for education in his 2016 book *Revolution* and in his 2017 manifesto. In the former, he clearly framed education as being central to the transformation of French society, which he promised to bring about if elected. He focused especially on how inequalities, which he claimed were largely maintained or exacerbated by France's educational sector, needed instead to be reduced by that very system (Macron, 2016, chap. 8). Indeed, in the 2017 manifesto, he even went so far as to place education at the top of his list of promises:

> The first issue area to be tackled will be that of education and culture (...). This is why I want to put the transmission of fundamental knowledge of our culture and our values at the centre of our project for schools and universities.[1]

Given his other priorities and commitments, to translate the vision of education publicised during the campaign into concrete policies, President Macron obviously had to enrol a set of like-minded collaborators. This was achieved firstly through the nomination of two ministers, Jean-Michel Blanquer for Education and Frédérique Vidal for Higher Education and Research, both of whom already possessed considerable experience in their respective sub-sectors: Blanquer had been a *recteur* in charge of an educational region then Director General of the Ministry of Education, whilst Vidal had chaired a university.[2] Moreover, whilst French education ministers typically change every two to three years, these two remained in post throughout Macron's first term in office. Their loyalty to their president was also shared by the advisors in their respective *cabinets*, where there are usually frequent changes in personnel. In these instances, significant change only occurred in 2021, since when there have, by contrast, been several changes.

Together with senior officials from their respective ministries, Blanquer and Vidal, along with their *cabinets*, then spent much of their five years in office developing and implementing a range of education[3] policies discussed in this chapter. Put simply, the central research question addressed is: *What has the educative dimension of Macron's first presidency actually changed?* We tackle this question head-on by framing it in the language of historical (Hall and Taylor, 2009) and sociological (March and Olsen, 1989) institutionalism. These theoretical strands first guide research to develop a critical distance from the policies through which governmental actors understandably claim that they have made changes. Whilst, of course, taking policy content and discourse seriously, conducting analysis within these institutionalisms is, unsurprisingly, centred instead upon the institutions that structure the sector under study. Defined as sets of rules, norms and expectations that have developed over time, institutions structure thought and practice through constructing 'the normal' within organisational and sectorial cultures. Moreover, far from being politically neutral, each institution is created, reproduced or replaced as a result of 'powering' between actors with asymmetrical resources (Bourdieu, 1992). Since any sector is deeply structured by a singular configuration of institutions and power relations, these are what constitute the primary focus of what follows, rather than the often misleading and transient features of officially presented public policy *per se*.

Indeed, the second contribution of historical and sociological institutionalism drawn upon here is its capacity to guide research in order to clearly set out both what it seeks to explain and, on the basis of the data it generates, the main explanation it then proceeds to develop. What is to be explained in this chapter is quite simply the extent of institutional change within France's education sector. As regards this chapter's explanation of change or continuity, we focus upon powering that is conceptualised as the 'political work' undertaken by a range of politicians, civil servants, trade unions and interest groups all specialised in the sector in question. Specifically, the concept of 'political work' (Smith, 2019; 2021) disciplines research such as ours to focus upon the three processes – problem definition, policy instrumentation and legitimation – through which institutional change is either worked for or resisted.

Based upon our original research on the education sector (Charles, 2014; 2015a; Charles and Delès, 2020), together with syntheses of other research in this issue area (Smith, 2021), the first part of this chapter describes the institutions and power relations which, together, had structured France's education sector before Macron took office. The aim here is to set out the political challenge of change which they faced from the outset by focusing upon how, until 2017, education had been framed as 'a public problem' in France – that is, what arguments and symbols justified the state's very involvement in education, its policy instruments and its priorities.[4] Indeed, through analysing the instruments used to both tackle and shift the very definition of this problem, the second part then examines the content of education-policy initiatives launched over the course of the following five years and, above all, what became of them and why. Throughout, we show how problem definitions and policy instruments have been legitimised over time, through discourse in general and appeals to certain values and symbols in particular.

Overall, the chapter makes three claims. First, the fundamentals of French education did not change during the period studied: these continue to feature a diploma-centred approach to a distinctively republican concept of meritocracy, the centrality of the *grandes écoles* and relatively low levels of average spending per pupil or student compared to other countries. The second claim is that, since 2017, some significant changes in policy instruments have, nevertheless, taken place. Third, this change has been driven by top-down policy work that has vaunted 'freedom of choice' and competition whilst ensuring that the French state remains firmly in control of the government of education. We argue that, if 'social justice' has certainly featured highly in the discourse used by Macron and his allies to justify policy and institutional change, it has generally played only a supporting role for an overall strategy centred on competition and 'choice', both of which are indeed part and parcel of the Macronian approach to social justice itself.

The challenge of changing France's educational meritocratic institutional order: educational justice in discourse and actual practice

As numerous scholars have underlined, since the 1789 revolution and, in particular, following deep conflicts over its social meaning in the late-19th century, education has been both a central plank of French republicanism and a frequent source of societal tensions (Dubet, 2018). Specifically, transforming a monarchy into a republic was largely motivated and justified by the rejection of rights to positions of power on the basis of one's family. Instead, all citizens of the Republic were to be treated as equal and, consequently, to rise or fall within it through efforts made to improve their respective positions. For extreme liberals, of course, such efforts were simply up to individuals to choose to make or not. For actors further to the centre or left, however, a national education system was seen as the vehicle through which all citizens, regardless of their social origins, should be given the tools with which to improve their respective socio-economic statuses. In parallel to several changes of regime that favoured either change or continuity, over the 19th century, debate raged as to whether state schools or Church-sponsored private entities should dominate this system. In 1833, under the July Monarchy (a liberal constitutional monarchy), a decree had forced each municipality to provide at least one primary school. However, it was only after the 1866 Education Act under Emperor Napoleon III that the secularisation of teaching and curricula began to institutionalise. Indeed, when compulsory schooling for children between 7 and 13 years of age was introduced under the Third Republic in 1881–1882 by the-then Education Minister, Jules Ferry, dissension between Church and State remained rife in many regions. Nonetheless, over the course of the end of the 19th and the first decades of the 20th centuries, the pre-eminence of the state within both the provision of schooling and its national governance generated and normalised a stabilised and standardised set of rules and practices ranging from the recruitment, training and career paths of teachers to compulsory usage of the French language (Weber, 1976). Notwithstanding the continued importance of private (mostly Catholic) schooling, bolstered by the 1959 Loi Debré and further legislation in 1984, these institutions have largely been rolled on, despite the challenges of expanding secondary schooling and higher education since World War II.[5]

Consequently, from the point of view of the education sector's institutions as they stood in 2017 – and with a view to determining what the first Macron presidency has or has not changed – a set of rules, norms and expectations will now be described in order to capture the 'public problem' definition behind educational 'meritocracy' in France, born of the 1789 Revolution. Used in this country to encapsulate an approach to equality within the country's entire educational sector (and beyond), as a principle, meritocracy has rarely been contested directly. However, transforming it into practice within the educational sector has frequently proved to be highly contentious. Indeed, by the mid-2010s, in this context, meritocracy had largely become reduced to a set of procedures ostensibly designed to equalise competition between pupils and students (Charles, 2015a, p. 68). By then, three institutions in particular were central planks of the approach: an emphasis placed upon national schooling policy and on teaching programmes, together with a higher-education system legitimised paradoxically by both universalism and elitism.

A national school system and mode of teacher recruitment

Within a commitment to public schooling, equivalent amounts of resources ostensibly have to be attributed to schools and higher-education establishments on the basis of supposedly objective and neutral criteria (such as school numbers and local demographics). Consequently, apart from some introduction of educational priority areas discussed below, very little reference to other sources of inequality (e.g. poverty rates, ethnic diversity and discrimination) has ever officially been authorised.

This policy has gone hand-in-hand with another concerning the recruitment of teachers. Theoretically, all the nation's teachers are selected on the basis of the same entry requirements and examinations. In practice, however, these *concours* (competitive exams) are organised on a regionalised basis, and certain regions – in particular, the Île de France region, which includes Paris – tend to soften their entry requirements because, otherwise, they simply cannot attract sufficient candidates.

Just as importantly, the longstanding system of central allocation of teachers to schools has produced a situation where the newest recruits are sent to the most disadvantaged (and least desirable) establishments.[6] This system has endured despite abundant evidence that the most experienced teachers are the most likely to enable pupils in such schools to actually learn. Moreover, once young teachers have spent a few years in schools of this type they are allowed to leave, thereby generating considerable turnover and instability amongst teaching teams, which is also detrimental to the pupils concerned. For some years now, teachers in such schools have been paid bonuses, but these are too weak to constitute genuine incentives. Indeed, because most teachers in these schools are so young, they are actually cheaper to staff than most other schools (Benhenda, 2020).

National programmes of teaching: a national curriculum?

The second plank in the French approach to educational meritocracy is an emphasis laid upon national 'programmes' of teaching content – that is, ones that ostensibly apply equally to all pupils across the nation. Developed through a nationwide process of consultation with teacher representatives, then 'corrected' and validated by the Ministry of Education, in practice, these programmes are top-down directives transmitted to schools and policed by the bureaucratic powers of rectors and their staff (regional Ministry of Education field officers) and inspectors (Van Zanten, 2006). As historians have highlighted (Weber, 1976), educating children in a similar way via a body of teachers employed as national civil servants was used both to consolidate the republican approach to citizenship and to deepen identifications with France 'the nation' (as opposed to its regions) and the principle of meritocracy itself. One of the major consequences of this statist policy has thus been to strongly develop a closed profession of teachers within the system of French public administration and to systematise their methods. Although at its outset this institutional change was radical in many ways, over the decades, it also frequently became a force for educational conservatism. Three strands of research have revealed the causes and consequences of this trait.

The first strand concerns the posture of teachers as regards knowledge and its transmission. This is particularly evident for post-primary schooling, where different disciplines are the core building blocks of curricula and their implementation. As in many, if not most, other countries, nearly all teachers at this level are specialists in a limited range of subjects. However, their methods are essentially centred upon the top-down transmission of knowledge as 'truth' rather than as groupings of information and propositions that are open to interpretation and thus discussion. Consequently, during the training of teachers, little emphasis is placed upon inciting children to discover things for themselves (Dubet *et al.*, 2010). More profoundly still, rather than a primary focus upon the acquisition of skills, emphasis is placed instead upon the learning and testing of facts and, more generally, conforming to the norms of interpretation and reasoning held by each disciplinary segment of the teaching profession (Dubet and Duru-Bellat, 2015).

Secondly, research has shown that, as a profession, teachers in France have long been relatively well-organised and politically represented. Unsurprisingly, one of the keys to their collective action is the strength of teaching unions. If actual membership of these unions is fragmented and no longer that high (around 30 per cent), these organisations are still always consulted by the Ministry of Education. Indeed, at least until the 1990s, many specialists concluded that education in France was governed by a form of neo-corporatism, and this mode of governing deepened during the 1980s while François Mitterrand was in power, when 34 per cent of the socialist MPs elected in 1981 were teachers (Ambler, 1985).

Moreover, the power of teaching unions has also had deeply institutionalising effects upon how each school is staffed and run. Due to their influence and the centralised character of the Ministry of Education, the power of head teachers in France has long been relatively weak. Meanwhile, this distribution of power has also played a role in keeping parents out of school governance. Encouraged to organise end-of-year parties and, increasingly, to raise money for extra-curricular activities, the parent organisations that do exist have no formal access to decision-making arenas (Van Zanten, 2006). Indeed, the closed character of French educational establishments – and of teaching more generally – is also reflected in their relationship to research on education. When this is firmly linked to teacher training, such research is given some credence. However, studies that maintain more critical distance with the teaching profession, especially those that dare to question the beliefs and methods of actual teachers, are generally ignored or treated with disdain – an attitude that is also shared by many officials within the Ministry (Dubet and Duru-Bellat, 2015).

Thirdly, French junior high schooling from 11–15 (*le collège unique*) is ostensibly based upon an institutionalised rejection of streaming within each year group. In practice, many – if not most – *collèges* have informally reintroduced streaming via self-selecting language streams and/or 'European' sections. More fundamentally still, in terms of actual practices, over the last 20 years, the right of pupils to succeed at this level of schooling has progressively been transformed into an individualised duty (Dubet, 2014). More generally, despite the fact that no less than 10 per cent of each annual cohort leave school without any qualifications, as an institution *le collège unique* remained relatively uncontested until the arrival of Gabriel Attal as Minister of Education in July 2023; Attal advocated the establishment of 'level groups' (streaming) in French middle schools.

Higher education: the paradoxical mix of universalist principles with tough selection mechanisms

A third plank in French educational meritocracy concerns a mode of access to higher education that is curiously both universal *and* selective. This logical contradiction reflects the existence in this country of two parallel but unequal systems. On the one hand, the first three years of university studies remain relatively easy to get into and cheap. On the other hand, to enter a range of *grandes écoles*,[7] marks from a candidate's *lycée*, exams and/or interviews, as well as dedicated fee-paying 'preparatory classes' usually lasting two years, are all part of a competitive selection process (*les concours*). Presented as enhancing equality, this mode of selection has, for decades, invariably favoured candidates with the most social, cultural and economic capital (Allouch, 2017).

More generally, contemporary educational research has highlighted two aspects of how meritocracy has shaped education in France. Firstly, it has shaped the 'Darwinian' character of much of the French educational system. Indeed, Charles (2015a: p.164) underlines that the cumulative result has been profoundly dualistic. On the one hand, those who can work the system end up being protected from arbitrariness, usually for life; those who cannot, however, end up losing everything, including hope – thus adding to the growing problem of *l'échec scolaire* (educational failure). Secondly, educational meritocracy's formalised character has meant that emphasis has always been placed upon procedures and principles rather than on actual results for pupils and students. What has counted has been to aim for *un collège unique*, a national programme, a single *concours* for teachers, etc – all this despite the fact that actually making the education system work necessarily requires flexibility (Charles, 2015a).

By 2017, for Emmanuel Macron, his collaborators, his supporters and large swathes of the population in general, it had become obvious that this approach to merit was in difficulty. More generally, it had become widely admitted that the Republican ideal of educational justice for all had simply not been achieved. Without ever going so far as to question the very principle of meritocracy, during the 2017 election campaign, Macron's manifesto clearly emphasised issues of inequality and social justice:

> This is not a matter of knowledge but one of justice. Because our Republic's very mission is to put each of its members on the same starting line.[8]

Similarly, often using 'poor' results from the OECD's PISA league table of international educational performance, increasing numbers of actors began to question the standard of teaching in France, a trend picked up on and reiterated by Macron and his supporters. Indeed, Macron's 2017 election manifesto put this bluntly and linked it to the country's problems more generally: 'Ever since the performance of our schools has dropped, our country has been in difficulty'.[9] Indeed, both these motivations for change in this sector implicitly challenged the longstanding definition of education as a public problem that had, until then, so deeply marked the institutionalisation of France's educational sector. In short, its institutional order was clearly marked by a framing of what should be taught and how that owed more to the path-dependent continuity of institutions than it did to a myriad of ultimately transient and isolated policy initiatives. Consequently, the commitment to change made before and during the 2017 election campaign renders particularly relevant to analyses of these years in office the question of what Macron actually did 'for education' during his first presidency.

Explaining variable outcomes to Macron's key policy initiatives

As emphasised above, many aspects of the educational institutional order were largely rolled on under the first Macron presidency. Notwithstanding this power of path dependency within the French education sector, together with the impact of minor reforms that only reinforce it, two sets of deeper changes were nonetheless introduced during this term in office. Taking the shape of new or revitalised policy instruments, the first destabilised the principle of meritocracy within education in the name of individual freedom and competition. Meanwhile, the second targeted the very political economy of the education sector from the angle of marketisation. As will be highlighted, both these deeper reforms were driven by a commitment of Macron and his ministers to introduce more competition and 'choice' into the education system. Indeed, far from being at odds with their vision of social justice, we argue that these principles actually lie at the heart of what they consider to be socially just – and therefore right – for France and the French.

Institutional continuity: schooling still at the heart of the lives of French individuals

A striking feature of the Macron first presidency's approach to education is that at no point did it question one of the central dimensions of longstanding national policy in this field – the hold that schooling has upon the whole lives of the individuals who make up the population of France. Firstly, as studies have shown (Charles, 2015a), compared to their opposite numbers in most other developed countries, very few French adults above the age of 25 study at university. *Formation continue*, as adult education is called in France, is predominantly very short and entails strictly skill-based training. If a person does not go straight into higher education upon leaving school, there are few options for trying again later in life. In a sense, such a person is cast as a failure. Secondly, qualifications earned during initial schooling strongly affect the employment prospects of young adults (Chevalier, 2016): in France, an 'adequationist' obsession has fuelled a dominant theory of action, wherein each type of education must lead to employment as quickly as possible (Charles, 2015b). Consequently, schooling and access to a first job are intense sources of stress for a large proportion of French youth. Indeed, this obsession with initial diplomas goes hand-in-hand with a conception of social justice, where school result–based merit strongly trumps any dimension of social worth relating to extra-curricular or work-linked activities (Charles and Deles, 2020). Indeed, this chimes with a low level of public importance given to youth in general, a period in life that many specialists see as largely being 'sacrificed' in France (Chevalier and Loncle, 2021).

Analytically, continuity in all these respects can best be captured through the institutionalist concept of 'path dependency' (Pierson, 2000). During the first Macron presidency, three series of relatively minor reforms and modifications fit smoothly with this model of institutional reproduction. On the one hand, schooling has largely reinforced its hold on France's youth: a law adopted in July 2019 entitled *Pour une école de la confiance* (for a school based on trust) reduced the compulsory schooling age to three years old (previously six) and restricted possibilities for home-schooling, thereby continuing the trend set by previous public policies (Bongrand, 2016). Indeed, this legislation on home-schooling was introduced after a period, during which this practice had increased considerably and was legitimised as part of a drive against alleged 'separatism' and the concern that mainly Muslim home-schooled children were not being educated in republican values of citizenship. Moreover, the same act also extended an obligation for young persons to remain in education from the ages of 16 to 18. Even if, in practice, this change constituted more the bestowing of a right than the imposition of a duty, it further reinforced a pre-existing trend towards the vast majority of each cohort leaving school with senior high school's final diploma (*le baccalauréat*) – a ratio that had risen to a record 87 per cent by 2021.[10]

Meanwhile, during this presidency, the proportion of young persons in post-obligatory education also rose. Here, even more importance was given to linking classroom teaching to 'integrating' students into the world of work. The 'adequationist' obsession mentioned above took the form of renewed state support being given to apprenticeships. Whereas, hitherto, they had been restricted to linking secondary schooling to professional training, under Macron apprenticeships were suddenly extended to the world of higher education, including in universities across most disciplines, starting with business administration. Essentially stable between 2013 and 2017, the number of apprentices in France rose from 305,000 in 2017 to 732,000 in 2021 (two-thirds in higher education). Often presented by the presidency and the government as the vindication of a policy aimed at linking young people with the world of work and employment, once again this shift – above all – actually reveals the extent to which schooling in France has a hold over the lives and opportunities of its inhabitants.

Disturbing the roots of French educational meritocracy as equality of treatment in the name of freedom and competition

Structured for so long by quests for the strictest equality of treatment given to students and candidates for places on courses, educational meritocracy under the first Macron presidency began to change in at least five ways in order to increase competition and freedom of choice – which, from Macron's own perspective, is consistent with focusing on social justice as fairness more than simply upon a formal educational meritocracy.

Firstly, in 2017, Macron advocated an evidence-based policy to halve class sizes in certain education investment areas (called *éducation* prioritaire[11] in France). For the two first years of primary school, about 20 per cent of such schools had their classes split in two, with some positive results in terms of pupils' success but less in terms of the renewal of teachers' practices (DEPP, 2021). This initiative was essentially legitimised by the argument that fairness could not be achieved if all pupils, seen as competitors, did not share the same starting line.

Secondly, at the level of primary schools, some significant experiments were introduced – notably the launching of 50 'laboratory' schools in Marseille. This experiment entailed the introduction of US-type 'charter schools', funded publicly but pedagogically and organisationally autonomous (thus resembling the 'academies' introduced in England since 2000). There is no intention here of shifting the legal status of primary schools in France towards that of a charity, as in the United States or England. Nevertheless, launched in 2021 and set to expand as of 2022–2023, these schools were authorised to develop their own 'pedagogical projects' and recruit their own staff. The government's aim here was to test how far French public primary schools can be decentralised from a pedagogical point of view. More generally, in line with OECD evidence-based recommendations, this decentralisation has been presented by Macron and his ministers as a path to improving pupils' success. Many teachers, however, strongly challenge the notion of competition which lies at the centre of this model.

Thirdly, the end of *lycée* qualification, the *baccalauréat* exam or '*bac*', so long a bastion of equal-treatment meritocracy, has been made more flexible through the introduction of continuous assessment which, since 2018, is applied to 40 per cent of pupils' results. Moreover, since 2021, individual *lycées* have been accorded leeway to formulate their own 'local evaluation projects', which can include different types of testing and marking and flexible exam dates. This clearly introduces a level of inequality between pupils that did not exist previously. Beyond the question of assessment, the *baccalauréat* as a whole was reformed by the Minister, Jean-Michel Blanquer, then applied as of 2021–2022. In particular, the three broad 'sections' that had structured this level of examination since 1968 – *économie et social* (ES), *littéraire* (L), *scientifique* (S) – were replaced by a system distinguishing between obligatory subjects and optional ones. This shift was justified as giving pupils more choice and as a means of moving away from homogeneity by 'section'. French teachers, not surprisingly, have mostly seen this change as a direct challenge to the equal treatment of pupils. Moreover, they often criticise the fact that pupils can now choose most of their subjects and see it as a way of undermining the cohesiveness of pathways that teachers felt best able to recommend to each pupil they followed. As for the pupils themselves, most have grasped the notion of choice as a means of dropping mathematics. In so doing, they collectively started a trend that, in 2022, the Ministry of Education was already seeking to reverse by reinstating maths as an obligatory subject.

Fourthly, concerning access to higher education, other changes were introduced, all tending to weaken the equality-of-treatment approach to meritocracy. One of the most publicised examples concerns the competitive procedure (*concours*) that applicants to Sciences Po Paris and Bordeaux must now follow. Whereas these *concours* had previously taken the form of written exams, since 2020, they now include the re-coding of academic results by *lycée* (so as to reduce the impact of schools that mark their pupils too highly) and an interview that lays emphasis upon personal qualities and achievements – similar to those once practiced widely within the British university system (Charles, 2015a). Moreover, in the Parisian case, forms of positive discrimination were introduced to ensure that at least part of each year's student intake comes from lower-income backgrounds. Here, it is important to note that such positive discrimination had no history in France until the 2000s when Sciences Po Paris first introduced this. Since 2021, it has also been introduced in top-ranked business schools such as HEC (*Hautes Etudes Commerciales*), whose *concours* now has a system of extra points for candidates who received grant aid for 'social' reasons during their secondary schooling. Meanwhile, ESSEC (*L'Ecole Supériuere des Sciences Economiques et Sociales*) now gives such candidates an extra oral exam in cases where they are close to passing the entrance exam. However, only Sciences Po Paris has gone as far as to organise two such exams in parallel. This said, all these systems have only slightly modified the academic dimension and standardised nature of such exams (Oberti and Pavie, 2020). Moreover, they have only been introduced in a handful of 'top schools', each of which has responded to pressure from the state to 'diversify the nation's elites'.

Finally, and above all, a new web portal procedure called *Parcoursup* was introduced to systematise the regulation of access to most French higher-education establishments, especially all its university departments. The policy goals are twofold: to reinforce the place of merit instead of equality in higher-education access and to initiate more systematic modes of competition between institutions and between students. Initially introduced under the Hollande presidency but completed under Macron, this procedure is essentially based upon a matching of candidates to all courses using a computerised, algorithm-based selection device that affects meritocracy directly. Firstly, all candidatures are now evaluated, whereas, beforehand, obtaining a *baccalauréat* ostensibly guaranteed access to university-level education (even if, in practice, physical limits on places meant that a form of lottery allocated actual places on specific courses). Now, such easy access has been restrained, which constitutes deep institutional change because, until now, social mobility in France has been structured by qualifications obtained at school, a trait reinforced by low numbers of mature students, as explained earlier (Charles and Delès, 2020). By making access to higher education more dependent on educational achievement, *Parcoursup* has strongly challenged the principle of social justice that previously predominated. It has been received very negatively in the higher-education sector for numerous reasons: it is said to lead to higher stress for candidates – the algorithm plays out from April to September; students are sometimes informed at the last minute of their allocated course; and all courses are now considered selective – and less accessible to underprivileged pupils. A sizeable proportion of higher-education teaching staff went on strike over this initiative and/or refused to take an active part in its administration.

Moreover, *Parsoursup* has not just had a strong impact on meritocracy. It has also been seen by its critics as a vector for a liberal logic of action, according to which each educational organisation must now be ranked to enable the highest number of students of the same 'quality' to choose their place of study (previously, rankings existed only for business and engineering schools). Whereas most university courses were not selective before *Parcoursup*, the reform has created competition between universities. Over the last few years, the ranking of Master's courses, in particular, has increased (Blanchard *et al.*, 2020). This, in turn, has increasingly transformed students into market-driven agents and universities into bodies that have systematically adopted modes of recruitment – derived from other parts of the higher-education system – that were already selective, as described above (Frouillou *et al.*, 2020).

The reforms described above have been legitimised in several different ways. Most present themselves as evidence-based policies but are based essentially on international benchmarking, wherein liberal educational systems are over-represented. These narratives, notably emanating from the OECD (Kallo, 2021), have pushed forward a conception of fairness that is very different from French views on meritocracy. More precisely, this legitimising rhetoric considers that enhancing the freedom of education establishments to choose their respective pupils or students or enabling head teachers to recruit their respective pedagogical teams will improve the realisation of social justice goals. In particular, it is argued that these changes will make underprivileged children more successful because they will have greater choice over their own education. Indeed, the same line of argument underpins the increased choice of subjects within *lycées* as well as within different initiatives introduced to reduce discrimination in access to higher education. Indeed, ultimately all these changes constitute a generalised means of inciting pupils to compete 'equally' against one another, thereby encouraging them to take ownership of the pathways that they respectively choose.

Increased marketisation of education

A second major way through which the first Macron presidency sought to strongly reform the education sector has been through encouraging marketisation. In the secondary-school system, the longstanding pauperisation of state education can be seen through the declining percentage of Gross Domestic Product (GDP) devoted to it over the last 20 years – and this despite the fact that the number of pupils and students has risen during this time. In contrast to many other countries, in France, the private sector is fully funded by the state.[12] The latter has also, for decades and this time unofficially, limited the role of private schools within secondary education to approximately 20 per cent of all pupils. However, increasing social inequalities between public and private schools (the proportion of pupils in private schools from middle- and upper-class families has risen from 41.5 per cent in 2000 to 55.4 in 2021) has implicitly been reinforced by several trends,[13] including the ever-increasing number of temporary staff in the public sector: between 2015–2016 and 2020–2021, while the number of tenured personnel remained stable, the number of non-tenured staff working for the Ministry of Education rose by 107,243, representing a rise from 14.5 to 22 per cent of total staff over this period. Nevertheless, in the secondary-school system, the government has no clear-cut financial interest in running down the state schools so that more parents will move their children to private schools since, as stated above, the state heavily subsides any such schools that are 'under contract'.

What about higher education? As with the school system, the number of higher-education students in France rose between 2010 and 2018 from 2.32 to 2.68 million. In contrast, public expenditure per higher-education student fell over the same period by 3.7 per cent (from 11,910 euros per student to 11,470 euros – i.e. well below the OECD average). Pauperisation is thus quite similar in higher education to that which has occurred in schools. However, the case of higher education is radically different on one point: at this level, the private sector is almost never subsidised by the state. This has encouraged a quest by the state – or at least certain powerful actors within it – to marketise the higher-education sector more strongly than the rest of the education system. This said, one needs to bear in mind that the actual concept of marketisation has little legitimacy in France (Ansaloni and Smith, 2017). Consequently, public policies that take the path of the market almost invariably do so in the form of undercover operations which, in the case of education, has generated two trends.

The first trend concerns encouraging the private sector. The Ministry of Education has progressively and implicitly externalised part of higher education to the private sector (notably the business and engineering schools discussed earlier). Whilst this sector only represented 13.5 per cent of all students in 2001, by 2017, it had already risen to 18.6 per cent – and 20.6 per cent in 2019. That year, private engineering schools took on 2.3 times as many students as they had in 2000 – despite the fact that, during this period, the total number of engineering students was only multiplied by 1.8. Meanwhile, the number of business studies students in private schools increased threefold to a total of 199,000 in 2019. As stated above, because private higher education is barely subsidised, its growth has constituted a means of increasing student numbers but not public expenditure.

A second trend in marketisation can be seen in the rise in fees for public higher-education establishments that are not universities (Charles, 2014). In this way, public institutions that have long been more autonomous than universities (e.g. Sciences Po) or are independent from the Ministry of Higher Education (e.g. many engineering schools) have increased their annual fees to several thousand euros (though sometimes accompanied by big fee reductions for students from low-income families). Here, the role of public authorities has been crucial: in exchange for the stagnation – and sometimes even cuts – in public expenditure, they have opted for a policy of *laissez-faire* when *grande écoles*, including those managed by the state, have sought to increase their respective fees. Under the first Macron presidency, this policy was even reinforced in the case of fees for non-EU students (allowed to rise to 2,770 euros per year for undergraduates and 3,770 euros for Master's students[14]) in the name of what it depicted as a 'crisis' in public-sector finances. Once again, this policy stemmed from a liberal postulate, according to which France should compete with other large, more-developed countries in order to attract foreign students and improve its comparative advantage, particularly by bringing in higher numbers of students from more-developed countries.

Conclusion

Writing in early 2024, it would be imprudent to conclude that Emmanuel Macron's first presidency either changed little or radically the priorities and government of education in France. As we saw above, during this period, a number of policy instruments were introduced or recalibrated, which have certainly shaken up the practices of many specialised actors. In so doing, some of them have been empowered (e.g. head teachers), whilst others have experienced reductions in their respective stocks of resources (e.g. tenured teaching staff). However, it is still too early to evaluate whether these policy instruments have either modified pre-existing definitions of public problems or constituted the policy results of shifts made earlier in problem definitions. More fundamentally, one still needs more evidence before concluding that key institutions, notably those linked to meritocracy (e.g. student selection and teacher allocation), have changed considerably since 2017.

Nonetheless, this chapter has shown that, during the first Macron presidency, education was clearly a space heavily invested in by the president and his closest political allies. If these modifications are fully implemented over the medium term and their market-based logic of action continues to be promoted consistently, they do contain the potential for deep change in the very structuring of France's educational sector. Indeed, although detailed research on this point still remains to be done, the political work of problematisation, instrumentation and legitimation – undertaken to introduce the changes described above – appears to have stemmed from a relatively coherent political enterprise: a highly liberal one driven from the top down that has certainly contained a commitment to achieving greater social justice for pupils and students. Nevertheless, this has essentially been framed around a combination of two liberal postulates: by inciting schools, higher-education establishments and pupils to compete more amongst themselves, as well as to develop greater choice in their courses of action, the national education system will be both more successful and more just.

Initially, at least, the departure of Macron's ministers from the government formed after the 2022 elections seemed to add another twist to 'the tale' told here. In particular, the replacement of Jean-Michel Blanquer by a Minister for Education plucked from academia and previously close to the *Parti Socialiste* – Pap Ndiaye – seemed for a time to indicate a change in presidential policy preferences and priorities. However, Ndiaye's sidelining within the government, then replacement in mid-2023 by a committed Macronist (Gabriel Attal) and subsequently by a member of *Les Républicains* (Amélie Oudéa-Castéra), strongly suggests instead that the presidential approach to education developed during his first term in office has been rolled on and even deepened. This observation in turn speaks to a more fundamental question whose 'surface' has only been scratched by this chapter: Do presidents and ministers actually matter when it comes to education in France? Or is this sector steered and structured by pressures and forces that have deeper, longer-lasting roots and causal effects? We should be better positioned to answer that question once Macron's second term has ended.

Notes

1 *Programme En Marche !*, p. 2.
2 Specifically, after obtaining a diploma in philosophy, a Master's from Sciences Po Paris and a doctorate in law, Blanquer became a lecturer and then a professor in public law. As of the mid-2000s, he moved into the governance of education by successively becoming a *recteur*, a member of the Minister for Education's cabinet, a senior civil servant within the Ministry of Education and director general of a large business school (ESSEC). As for Frédérique Vidal, having obtained

a doctorate in biology, she subsequently became a lecturer and then a professor in this discipline. Immediately before becoming minister, she was president of the University of Nice Sophia-Antipolis.
3 For the purposes of this chapter, the term 'the education sector' will encompass schooling, higher education and academic research. It should be noted that, within political sociology, each is generally analysed separately.
4 As most sociologists and policy analysts concur, societal frictions only generate durable public policies once they have been defined, through argumentation and debate, as 'public problems', that is, as issues meriting intervention by public authorities (Gusfield, 1981).
5 Expansion first began in the 1950s via a raising of the leaving age to 16 in 1959 and the mass building of junior high schools (*les collèges*). It was followed in the 1970s and 1980s by a dramatic enlargement of access to senior high schools (*les lycées*). Today more than 75 per cent of children in France become *lycéens*, whereas this figure was less than 30 per cent in the 1950s. As for higher education, it spread first after 1968, then subsequently during the presidencies of François Mitterrand from 1981 to 1995.
6 After this initial allocation of positions, teachers earn 'points' based on years of seniority and family status. The more points one has, the more chances one has of being allowed to move to a more favoured school. Therefore, teachers with several years of experience leave the disadvantaged school, and new, inexperienced teachers arrive. This is why the most disadvantaged students are faced with teaching teams who are not only the least experienced but also the least stable over time.
7 The term *Grandes écoles* encompasses a select band of higher-education establishments, most of which were set up in the early-19th century. Designed originally to train specialised state civil servants (e.g. civil engineers at *Polytechnique*), these *écoles* have subsequently come to include a large number of business schools (from which HEC, ESSEC and ESCP are the most highly ranked) and engineering schools (from which *Polytechnique*, *Télécom*, *Centrale Supelec*, *Ecole des Ponts* and *Ecole des Mines* are the most highly ranked). Other disciplines – such as political science within the 10 Sciences Po establishments and the state's higher administration itself (*Institut national du service public* since 2022, formerly ENA, *Ecole nationale d'administration*), architecture and design – are less represented. According to their representative association (*Conférence des grandes écoles*), there are 218 *grandes écoles* in France, of which 64 per cent are public and 66 per cent are engineering schools. Overall, this category encompasses about 400,000 students – 15 per cent of French students in any one year.
8 *Programme En Marche !*, op. cit., p. 9. As the sociologist and specialist of education, François Dubet, has put it, ultimately the question posed by the primacy of meritocracy in the structuring of French education policymakers and citizens alike is: What inequalities are actually 'tolerable'? (Dubet et al., 2010, p. 74).
9 *Programme En Marche !*, op. cit., p. 9.
10 In total, 46.3 per cent of these pupils obtained a *baccalauréat général*, 18 per cent a *baccalauréat technologique* and 22.8 per cent a *baccalauréat professionnel*.
11 First named ZEP (Priority Education Zone), then REP (Priority Education Network) and REP+ (Reinforced Priority Education Network).
12 The 1959 Debré Law established a system enabling private schools at primary and secondary levels to be granted government funding if they adhere to the terms of a contract with the state to deliver the national programmes defined by the Ministry of Education. Teachers in private schools are not civil servants (*fonctionnaires*) as they are in the public sector. A report by the Cour des Comptes (equivalent of UK National Audit Office) in 2023 established that, in

2022, there were 2 million pupils in private education, representing 17.6 per cent of all pupils spread across just over 7,500 schools: 7,056 Catholic, 134 Jewish, 10 Muslim, 21 Protestant and 352 'other'. Most parents choose Catholic schools less for religious reasons than for the supposed better conditions, standards and discipline that they offer. Private schools have the freedom to select their pupils and charge fees, but these are very much lower than in the United Kingdom and can be indexed to parental income.

13 The issue of social inequalities relating to private education was propelled to the forefront of the political agenda in January 2024 when a new Minister of Education, Amélie Oudéa-Castéra, was appointed to replace Gabriel Attal (after his promotion to prime minister): press reports revealed that her own children attended highly élitists private schools that, moreover, were using questionable methods to help their pupils by-pass the *Parcoursup* procedure. This controversy also re-ignited long-standing debates over the funding of private schools by the state and the under-funding of public schools.

14 In practice, each higher-education establishment has been left relatively free to charge these higher fees or not.

References

Allouch, A. (2017) *La société de concours: L'empire des classements scolaires.* Paris: Seuil.

Ambler, J. (1985) 'Neocorporatism and the politics of French education', *West European Politics*, 8(3), pp. 23–42.

Ansaloni, M. and Smith, A. (2017) 'Le marché comme instrument d'action publique', special issue of *Gouvernement et Action Publique*, 6(4), pp. 1–178.

Benhenda, A. (2020) *Tous des bons profs: un choix de société.* Paris: Fayard.

Blanchard, M., Chauvel, S. and Harari-Kermadec, H. (2020) 'La concurrence par la sélectivité entre masters franciliens', *L'Annee Sociologique*, 70(2), pp. 423–442.

Bongrand, P. (2016) '"Compulsory schooling". Despite the law: How education policy underpins the widespread ignorance of the right to home educate in France', *Journal of School Choice. International Research and Reform*, 10(3), pp. 320–329.

Bourdieu, P. (1992) 'The logic of fields', in Bourdieu, P. (ed.) *An invitation to reflexive sociology.* Chicago: University of Chicago Press, pp. 94–114.

Charles, N. (2014) 'France: a low fee, low aid system challenged from the margins', in Ertl, H. and Dupuy, C. (eds) *Students, markets and social justice: Higher education fee and student support policies in Western Europe and beyond.* Providence: Symposium Books, pp. 67–83.

Charles, N. (2015a) *Enseignement supérieur et justice sociale: sociologie des expériences étudiantes en Europe.* Paris: La documentation française.

Charles, N. (2015b) 'When training is not enough: Preparing students for employment in England, France and Sweden', *Sociologie du Travail*, 57(1), e1–e21.

Charles, N. and Delès, R. (2020) 'Les conceptions de la justice sociale en Europe. Le cas de l'accès aux études supérieures', *L'Année Sociologique*, 70(2), pp. 313–336.

Chevalier, T. (2016) 'Varieties of youth welfare citizenship: Towards a two-dimension typology', *Journal of European Social Policy*, 26(1), pp. 3–19.

Chevalier, T. and Loncle, P. (2021) *Une jeunesse sacrifiée?* Paris: PUF.

Cour des Comptes (2023) *L'Enseignement privé sous contrat. Rapport public.* Paris: Cour des Comptes.

DEPP (2021) *Evaluation de l'impact de la réduction de la taille des classes de CP et de CE1 en REP+ sur les résultats des élèves et les pratiques des enseignants*. Paris: Direction de l'Evaluation, de la Prospective et de la Performance, Document de travail n°2021.E04, https://www.education.gouv.fr/media/94352/download

Dubet, F. (2014) 'Préface', in Berthet, T. and Zaffran, J. (eds) *Le décrochage scolaire: enjeux, acteurs et politiques de lutte contre la déscolarisation*. Rennes: Presses Universitaires de Rennes, pp. 9–17.

Dubet, F. (2018) 'Durkheim et les questions scolaires: hier et aujourd'hui', in Cuin, C. and Hervouet, R. (eds) *Durkheim aujourd'hui*. Paris: Presses Universitaires de France, pp. 48–66.

Dubet, F. and Duru-Bellat, M. (2015) *10 propositions pour changer l'école*. Paris: Seuil.

Dubet, F., Duru-Bellat, M. and Vérétout, A. (2010) *Les sociétés et leur école. Emprise du diplôme et cohésion sociale*. Paris: Seuil.

Frouillou, L., Pin, C. and van Zanten, A. (2020) 'Les plateformes APB et Parcoursup au service de l'égalité des chances?', *L'Année Sociologique*, 70(2), pp. 337–363.

Gusfield, J. (1981) *The culture of public problems. Drinking-driving and the symbolic order*. Chicago: University of Chicago Press.

Hall, P. and Taylor, R. (2009) 'Health, social relations and public policy', in Hall, P. and Lamont, M. (eds) *Successful societies. How institutions and culture affect health*. Cambridge: Cambridge University Press, pp. 82–103.

Kallo, J. (2021) 'The epistemic culture of the OECD and its agenda for higher education', *Journal of Education Policy*, 36(6), pp. 779–800.

Macron, E. (2016) *Révolution*. Paris: Editions XO.

March, J. and Olsen, J. (1989) *Rediscovering institutions*. New York: Free Press.

Oberti, M. and Pavie, A. (2020) 'Les paradoxes d'un programme d'ouverture sociale: les conventions éducation prioritaire à Sciences Po', *L'Annee Sociologique*, 70(2), pp. 395–422.

Pierson, P. (2000) 'Increasing returns, path dependence, and the study of politics', *American Political Science Review*, 94(2), pp. 251–267.

Smith, A. (2019) 'Travail politique et changement institutionnel: une grille d'analyse', *Sociologie du Travail*, 61(1).

Smith, A. (2021) *Made in France: Societal structures and political work*. Manchester: Manchester University Press.

Van Zanten, A. (2006) 'La construction des politiques d'éducation. De la centralisation à la délégation au local', in Culpepper, P., Hall, P. and Palier, B. (eds) *La France en mutation 1980–2005*. Paris: Presses de Sciences Po, pp. 229–262.

Weber, E. (1976) *Peasants into Frenchmen: The modernization of rural France 1870–2014*. Stanford: Stanford University Press.

11
A PALER SHADE OF GREEN: EMMANUEL MACRON'S POLICIES ON THE ENVIRONMENT AND CLIMATE CHANGE

Charlotte Halpern

Abstract

This chapter explores President Macron's record on policies designed to address the many problems relating to the environment and climate change. When President Trump announced that he would take the United States out of the Paris Agreement on Climate Change, Macron pledged to 'make our planet great again', promising investment support for US climate scientists and warning the US Congress that 'there is no Planet B'. He pledged to put environmental concerns at the heart of societal change, not only in France but also in the EU. The green economy would play an important part in transforming France, its agriculture and the way of life of all its residents. However, fewer than 18 months after his election, his Minister of Ecology had resigned, the carbon tax project had sparked major protests and the executive backtracked on several campaign promises. So, halfway through President Macron's second term, how much progress has been made in pursuit of the 'ecological imperative'? Focusing on the discrepancy between environmental and climate (EC) discourses and policy processes, this analysis highlights the role of climate delaying and how the politics of small steps does not make it possible to deliver an ambitious environmental and climate agenda.

Introduction

Since the election of President Macron in 2017, his pledge to address the climate crisis has been the subject of much scrutiny (Halpern, 2023).[1] His ambition maintains France's ambivalent position on the environmental and

DOI: 10.4324/9781003323259-11

climate agenda compared with other European countries (Szarka, 2001). To be fair, environmental and climate policy (ECP) issues did not hold a prominent role in Macron's 2017 campaign. Nevertheless, his election raised high expectations, in view of his understanding of environmental and climate (EC) concerns as being, above all, a political struggle (Macron, 2016, p. 93), his personal commitment to the 2015 Paris Agreement and his 2017 programme's opening statement that 'climate change forces us to rethink our organisation and our lifestyles'.[2] A few days after President Trump announced that he would take the United States out of the Paris Agreement on Climate Change, Macron followed this rather vague and ambiguous statement by a declaration, in which he addressed the American people in English, urging them to 'make our planet great again', promising investment support for US climate scientists and warning the US Congress that 'there is no Planet B' (Abrams, 2017). His desire to put EC concerns at the heart of societal change, not only in France but also in the EU, was reasserted following his re-election for a second term, as he warned of 'the end of abundance' (Le Monde/AFP, 2022).

Eight years later, in a rapidly evolving geopolitical context and having faced massive protests in France, Macron is far from having lived up to his EC ambitions. Focusing on the discrepancy between ambitious discourses and policy processes, this chapter examines ECP developments under the Macron presidency since 2017. EC policy processes refer to all public interventions that address, sometimes in relationship with non-state actors, an ever-increasing number of issues that are considered as problematic for the state of the environment – such as ensuring the sufficient provision and distribution of energy supplies, managing ecological resources (water, soil, etc.), monitoring the level of environmental protection and mitigating and adapting to climate change. Previous efforts to review the achievements of presidential mandates have highlighted the discrepancy between the 'heroic rhetoric' that characterises political discourses about environmental protection and the ability to make these political goals operational. Such discrepancy is often accounted for in comparative political research by the tension between politics and policies (Lowi, 1964). Reflecting on Macron's three predecessors, the use of EC rhetoric served the candidates' and later, the presidents' efforts to assert their leadership and governing capacity both within and outside France.

In this regard, Macron's use of EC rhetoric has been instrumental in promoting his agenda for modernising the French economy and strengthening his leadership. Bold discourses and ambitious pledges helped to reach out to specific segments of the electorate and forge new alliances in a rapidly evolving political-party system. Furthermore, by emphasising the ability to innovate in governance and public policy, EC rhetoric was instrumental in his distancing himself from the outgoing majority and taking a leadership role outside France. This chapter argues that the fight against climate change has been impeded by climate delaying (Lamb *et al.*, 2020) and the politics of small steps, which hinder the achievement of the objectives initially set. The chapter begins by characterising ECP developments in the pre-2017 period and continues with the expectations raised during the 2017 campaign before exploring the discrepancy between discourses and actions by focusing on ECP initiatives and processes since then.

Environmental and climate policy processes in the pre-2017 period

Some contextual elements are needed to make sense of the developments taking place in ECP under the Macron presidency. These are partly accounted for through long-term policy dynamics and pre-existing forms of collective action. In this section, the trajectory of the French case is discussed in relation to other EU countries and major drivers for policy change.

Characterising ECP in the Fifth Republic

Environmental and climate policies are often considered a challenge for classic models of the functioning of the state and policymaking in France (Muller, 2018). The study of ECP's origins, when examined as part of the comparative political research agenda, often led to portraying France as an outlier (Hayes, 2002). In the Fifth Republic, 'political opportunity structures' – that is, the nature of political institutions and processes (Kriesi *et al.*, 1995) – have shaped the ability of policy challengers to impact on policymaking. Access to 'policy venues' (institutional arenas where policy decisions are formulated) is highly dependent on strategic alliances, mainly with left-wing political parties and the top echelons of the civil service or *grands corps de l'Etat* (see Chapter 9) and less so on the movement's characteristics. Moreover, the country's unique position as a nuclear state often justified the need for in-depth, issue-specific, monographic explorations (Brouard and Guinaudeau, 2015; Topçu, 2013).

When compared with other policy areas in France, ECP is considered a case of failed institutionalisation (Lascoumes, 2022). Unlike other policy domains, where close relationships between specific corporations and specialised segments of the administration played a critical role in shaping policy preferences and outcomes, ECP processes resemble other transversal policy issues (such as gender) that emerged in the 1970s closely connected to social movements (Grossman and Saurugger, 2012). Policy developments resulted from strong within-state activism – higher civil servants and experts (Boy *et al.*, 2012; Charvolin 2003) – as well as from continual mobilisation from outside the state apparatus, notably through a dense grassroot movement consisting of more than 5,000 organisations spread across the territory (Ollitrault, 2008; Villalba, 2022). This policy's long-term trajectory was shaped by the proliferation of non-state actors, the poor ability of State authorities to effectively structure activities and groups and the structural role of conflicts, all of which contributed to this policy area's institutional instability (Cohen, 2022; Lascoumes, 1994, 2022).

Together, these alternative institutionalisation mechanisms fostered an all-out process of policy expansion, by which policy resources and governing capacities were accumulated over time (Lacroix and Zaccaï, 2010). In a context in which the Ecology Ministry's authority to claim leadership over ECP formulation and monitoring was regularly challenged from both within and outside the state apparatus (Lascoumes *et al.*, 2014), ECP processes did not automatically lead to the centralisation of resources within this administration, since when its name, perimeter and powers have changed frequently.[3] Over the years, it rarely had the upper hand in inter-partisan and departmental negotiations. The creation of many specialised agencies and expert bodies, especially the ADEME (Agency for Ecological Transition) in 1991, further contributed to organisational and policy fragmentation at the state level. Successive decentralisation reforms, while adding to ECP resources by transferring new and pre-existing powers towards subnational levels of government, have resulted in high levels of differentiation. This transfer was neither homogeneous nor systematic; it often failed to provide clear leadership over ECP issues or to reorganise/dismantle pre-existing arrangements. As of today, ECP processes in France are characterised by high levels of thematic and territorial diversity (SDES, 2022).

Heroic rhetoric as the privilege of weak political leadership

Particular attention has been given to examining drivers of ECP change in France, including political leadership. While there is some consensus about the role of European and international regulations as a major driver for ECP developments in France (Berny, 2011), the country still holds an ambivalent position in comparative policy research when it comes to its leadership. Depending on the issue, the indicator or the period under scrutiny, it is sometimes classified as a leader (Knill *et al.*, 2012) or 'fence-sitter' (Liefferink *et al.*, 2009). This confirms the role of other factors in shaping ECP developments in France (Evrard, 2012), such as strong levels of misfit between European ECP and domestic political and institutional settings or different capacities, according to issues and territories, to challenge corporatist arrangements and bureaucratic routines. The role of conflicts and multiple forms of resistance is repeatedly highlighted to account for the Ecology Ministry and its allies being unable to impose its preferred policy instruments, resulting in the further locking of power relations and problem settings (Boy *et al.*, 2012). Unless the proposed measures are aligned with industrial policy preferences (e.g., the nuclear or the agriculture industries), they are likely to meet with strong resistance from within the state administration and national champions.

ECP study thus suggests that the 'clichéd' view of France – that is, an archetypically strong, centralised and unified state – should be reconsidered in the light of broader state-restructuring dynamics in this policy domain (Hayes, 2002). Indeed, the development of ECP over time highlights the role of alternative institutionalisation policy mechanisms (Lascoumes, 2022). In a context of increased fragmentation and spatial differentiation, both political alliances and corporatist arrangements are being reconfigured, offering multiple opportunities to shape the selection of ECP priorities and solutions through processes of policy innovation as well as through strong resistance, including the reproduction of existing oligarchies. This has strong implications in the context of this chapter, with the presidency (and the executive branch more generally) only holding limited capacity to drive change on its own ... should it wish or declare the wish, to do so (Guinaudeau and Persico, 2018).

The strategic uses of ECP to raise expectations

From an early stage, Macron drew on EC concerns to distance himself from the outgoing Socialist–Green majority and forge a new political majority. EC issues were singled out as a cornerstone of his modernisation agenda and his efforts to reassert France's leadership in Europe and globally.

Stepping away from the Hollande presidency's legacy

During the 2017 election campaign, Macron benefited from ambivalent views towards the outgoing majority's achievements: while acknowledging its ability to set long-term goals through major pieces of legislation, as well as the success of COP 21 – and the Paris Agreement – in asserting France's climate leadership, prominent members of the ecologist-green party (Europe Ecology – The Greens, EELV) questioned the Hollande presidency's lack of vision when it came to translating long-term goals into concrete policy strategies.

The case of energy transition, undoubtedly the most salient EC issue on the agenda, is particularly representative of such ambivalence. The Socialist–Green agreement, adopted in 2011, promised to cut the share of nuclear power in electricity production from 75 to 50 per cent by 2025 and to take the necessary measures to achieve this goal, including the closure of 24 nuclear plants. During the 2012 campaign, Hollande committed to the former but distanced himself from the latter except for France's oldest nuclear plant at Fessenheim. A large-scale consultation, the National Debate on Energy Transition, was organised in 2013 to engage major stakeholders; long-term goals were formally adopted under the 2015 Law on Energy Transition for Green Growth (LTECV), resulting in more than 100 enforcement decrees and measures. In addition, new planning tools were introduced to foster consensus and clarify responsibilities between public authorities and the industry and between levels of government. This includes, at the national level, the National Low-Carbon Strategy (SNBC) adopted in 2015, which identifies the main drivers and levers for the climate change mitigation policy in transport, housing and industry, as well as the multi-year energy programme (PPE). At the local level, regional and inter-municipal leadership was strengthened for energy efficiency through climate air energy plans (PCAET). However, in the absence of large-scale programmes, dedicated resources and EC-issue ownership to champion renewable energy and sufficiency, new layers were added, but no transformative change took place in existing policy arrangements (Aykut and Evrard, 2017). The closing of the Fessenheim nuclear plant was postponed on several occasions (Deront et al., 2018).

Beyond the case of energy, limited progress was achieved on issues like strengthening ecological democracy or addressing major flagship projects such as the Notre Dame des Landes airport near Nantes and the nuclear-waste landfill in Bure. Several explanations were put forward, including the organisational and political weakness of EC champions within the government, with a number of different ministers in succession. On several occasions, with the exception of the ban on shale gas (Chailleux and Zittoun, 2021), tensions within the Socialist Party and the Socialist–Green majority accounted for the limited capacity (or will) to oppose lobby groups – representing economic, professional or territorial interests. Minister Bricq was replaced in 2012 following her attempts to freeze oil-drilling permits in French Guyana and to reform the mining code. Resources available to support organic agriculture or land sufficiency were too limited to effectively challenge dominant policy solutions. The Red Caps movement which developed in Brittany in 2013 to oppose the introduction of an ecotax (or 'truck tax') and the death of Rémi Fraisse, (an environmental activist killed during the demonstration against the Sivens Dam in 2014), marked a turning point in the Hollande presidency's environmental ambitions in terms of state–civil society relations. By contrast, EC concerns were instrumental in enabling other prominent figures in the Socialist Party – such as Foreign Minister Fabius and Finance Minister Moscovici – to strategically draw on EC concerns to raise the country's profile internationally in preparation for COP 21 (reform of the Foreign Office) and to improve the representation of green business interests (the creation of Business France).

In other words, a significant number of milestones were reached during the Hollande presidency through consensus-building and goal-setting, but, when it came to implementation, it followed a classic 'pass the buck' strategy – that is, to deflect blame by forcing others to make costly political choices. In this context, expectations regarding the future president's ECP agenda were particularly high in all the areas in which the Hollande presidency had failed.

Pragmatism and ecological reality

Having played a prominent role in that outgoing government, Macron sought to distance himself by putting the green economy at the heart of his plans to transform French society – this would play an important part in transforming France, its agriculture and its residents' way of life. Emphasis was put on pragmatism, resource-seeking and a selective number of strategic levers. Yet, the promises made in *Révolution* (Macron, 2016) remained quite vague and were not reflected in his 2017 electoral manifesto[4] where climate change is briefly mentioned in the opening statement in relation to modernising the economy, followed by a few concrete policy proposals (see Box 11.1). This approach did, however, enable him to successfully reach out to parts of the centre (Bayrou's MoDem), the centre-left and, to a lesser extent, the EELV electorate and some of their leading figures. First, by referring to the notion of ecology rather than climate, he marked his ambition to also address biodiversity and the environment at large; second, despite calling for a changed relationship to ecology and the environment, the programme remained grounded in a green growth perspective, with particular attention paid to mitigating health impacts, creating jobs and speeding up implementation through domestic or European policy initiatives.

BOX 11.1: A SELECTIVE OVERVIEW OF MACRON'S PLEDGES FOR ADDRESSING EC CONCERNS SINCE 2016

Révolution, Chapter 7, "Produce in France and save the planet". Commitment to:

- Support the 2015 Paris Agreement on climate change
- Be exemplary by reconciling the economic imperative with the ecological imperative
- Invest in cleantech to achieve energy transition, restore ecosystems, explore opportunities to develop feedback loops, develop green finance, expend the smart and green urban agenda in rural areas, reorganise production lines, transform practices and make the environment everyone's business

> 2017 Election manifesto, section "Invent a new growth model"
>
> - Research and development in industry
> - The fight against pesticides, the renovation of old housing
> - Making France a world leader in environmental transition research
> - Incentives to replace old and polluting vehicles
> - A 5 billion euros fund for agricultural transition
> - Ensuring a 50% share of organic, ecologically or locally produced food in collective catering by 2022
>
> Other sections
>
> - Not adding domestic to European regulations for agriculture and fisheries
> - At the EU level: a single carbon price
>
> 2022 Electoral manifesto, section "Plan the ecological transition"
>
> - By 2050, build 6 new nuclear power plants, multiply solar power by 10, install 50 offshore wind farms, and develop the French sector for renewable energy production
> - 700,000 housing units renovated each year, with solutions for all, some without upfront costs
> - Affordable electric vehicles for all through a 100% French industry
> - Plant 140 million trees by the end of the 2020 decade and invest in the wood sector.

However, most of the EELV electorate did not espouse this model of 'chosen, selective growth', which explains the strong support for them in the 2019 European and 2020 municipal elections rather than for *En marche*. Since then, Macron's electorate and his party have shifted increasingly towards the right to ensure support from those segments of society with high levels of income as well as from rural areas and small and medium towns.

When the promise of systemic change fails against the limitations of *realpolitik*

Although not reflecting the preferences of the EELV electorate, Macron's election raised high expectations at first. In addition to his bold reaction to President Trump's decision to leave the Paris Agreement, the appointment of the hugely popular journalist and environmental activist Nicolas Hulot as 'Minister for Ecological and Inclusive Transition', ranked third in the official order of importance of government ministers, vouched for the newly elected president's EC ambitions. Several environmentally controversial projects were abandoned during the first 18 months, such as Notre Dame des Landes airport near Nantes, the Montagne d'Or gold mining project in French Guyana[5] or the Europa City commercial 'hyper-place' north of Paris. Yet, just over a year later, having already acknowledged that cutting nuclear power to 50 per cent by 2025 was unrealistic, Hulot resigned, saying that he had 'a little influence but no power' to resist powerful lobbies protecting vested interests (*Le Monde*, 2018).

Socioecological justice as the missing link: the Yellow Vests movement and the Citizens Convention for Climate (CCC)

This section examines how the Yellow Vests movement and the Covid-19 pandemic fostered the reshuffling of EC priorities to help Macron forge new alliances and ensure governing capacity in certain areas. The Yellow Vests movement represented an important setback in rolling out the government's initial EC agenda; yet, it also presented a major opportunity for Macron to reshuffle ECP issues. The protests were sparked in November 2018 by a climate policy instrument (carbon tax proposal) and a reduced speed limit on the departmental road network. Despite being often depicted as anti-climate (Driscoll, 2023), the demands stemming from this heterogenous movement (Collectif d'enquête sur les Gilets Jaunes *et al.*, 2019, p. 881) went far beyond EC concerns to address institutional reforms and did not systematically oppose ECP measures. Rather, it called for an alternative approach – to add a robust socio-ecological justice component to the EC agenda, using the slogan: 'End of the month, end of the world, same fight'. This was confirmed during the subsequent 'Great National Debate' (Mission du Grand Debat National, 2019) orchestrated by Macron, and the alternative 'Real Debate' organised by the Yellow Vests to generate their own input (L'Observatoire de Triangle, 2019). To find both the right rhythm and the right solutions on the ground, Macron and the Philippe government addressed these demands in two different ways.

On the one hand, the protests provided new opportunities and enhanced legitimacy for postponing EC action. Conflict avoidance and the urge to enhance social acceptability were put forward to justify the prevalence given to small steps, incentivising and local experiments. Highly controversial decisions, such as the use of pesticides (Dedieu, 2022) and new petrol and non-electric cars, were transferred to the EU level; expert groups within and outside the state were urged to step away from carbon taxing or any other mandatory type of measure and to explore alternative policy tools aimed at generating support. In several policy areas – such as energy, agriculture or transport – meaningful action was postponed or replaced with non-transformative solutions, in alignment with those advocated by target groups across policy sectors. On the other hand, flagship initiatives in governance were introduced, such as the Citizens Convention for Climate (CCC) (October 2019–July 2020) and the High Council on Climate (*Haut Conseil pour le Climat*) created in November 2018 to, respectively, reach out to citizens and scientific knowledge in a bid to overcome barriers and resistance to climate action.

The proposal to set up a citizens' convention stems from the Yellow Vests movement, the greens and ecologists, and expert groups advocating an institutional reform rooted in ecological democracy. Drawing lessons from past initiatives, notably the *Grenelle de l'environnement* (a national debate held in 2007 on a wide range of environmental issues), this highly innovative initiative brought together 150 citizens (chosen at random by a professional sampling organisation) with the support of an independent governance committee and logistical support from the Economic, Social, and Environmental Council (CESE) to develop 'a set of structural measures to achieve, in a spirit of social justice, a reduction in greenhouse gas emissions by at least 40 per cent by 2030 compared to 1990'.[6] The CCC covered a wide range of EC issues, submitting 149 policy proposals in total. Whilst it was undoubtedly an innovative experiment in democratic engagement (or in crisis management), the CCC did not fully meet expectations. First, apart from a few exceptions, the proposed measures offered few surprises. Rather, they recycled solutions that pre-existed among experts and NGOs, focusing on their feasibility and leaving aside radical and constraining implementation options. Second, despite its careful design and efforts to avoid radical proposals, the CCC was seen as more of a presidential public-relations exercise. Indeed, throughout the process, the organisers refuted the accusations of being instrumentalised by maintaining pressure on the government and by repeatedly referring to Macron's promise that the CCC's measures would be submitted 'without filter'.[7] Yet, the president immediately rejected three of the proposed measures: a tax on dividends, a 110 km/h speed limit on motorways and a proposal to include an article on environmental protection in the constitution. Just as a decade before with *Grenelle de l'environnement*, the formal adoption and implementation of the 146 remaining policy measures was fragmented, depending on the issue, on whether the State had full authority and on the politics of tool selection at both national and EU levels. In other words, the implementation of CCC measures did not take place in a vacuum. This, in turn, provided additional room for manoeuvre for shaping implementation processes, including for Macron, as he sought to regain the upper hand on the governmental agenda. It also confirmed the need to consider EC policy processes in their entirety.

Ecological transition in the time of recovery: 'pragmatism' against 'dogmatism'

While becoming hugely divisive politically, economically and socially, EC issues also benefited from unprecedented levels of attention and fierce competition in agenda-pushing in the context of the 2019 European elections and the first round of the 2020 municipal campaign. In this context, polls showed that Macron, his government and the state level were far from being perceived as frontrunners. By contrast, other levels of government reasserted their roles: the European Green Deal was launched by the EU to become 'the first climate-neutral continent by 2050'; subnational authorities, notably the newly elected mayors, promoted their transformative EC agendas and blamed national governments' inability to advance ambitious policy measures. Within the climate movement and akin to developments observed in other European countries, action repertoires were being reconfigured through the arrival of new organisations such as Alternatiba and Extinction Rebellion as well as the creation of joint platforms with youth and anti-poverty organisations such as Youth for Climate and Oxfam. While the former pushed for the use of radical and targeted actions, the latter opted for a socio-ecological transformative agenda and successfully sued the state for climate inaction (*Affaire du siècle*) through the Paris Administrative Tribunal,[8] though this judgement was later revised in favour of the government.[9] 'Youth for Climate' and other ecologist organisations accused Macron of environmental indifference. All political parties addressed EC concerns – discourses that emphasised the role of local politics and 'territories' were particularly dominant: conservative groups, including the *Rassemblement national* (RN), denounced decades of neglect of small- to medium-sized cities and rural communities, whereas the left highlighted growing inequalities and the urban world's ecologically unsustainable lifestyles.

Does this mean that nothing was achieved during the first Macron presidency? Certainly not, but, in a changing political context and following the Covid-19 pandemic, EC concerns became instrumental in drafting the recovery agenda, while policy processes were increasingly shaped by climate delaying and blame-avoidance strategies. First, this provided an opportunity for Macron to reassert his preference for technological innovation and investments and to strengthen his ties with techno-optimists within and outside government while clearly distancing himself from post- and de-growth agendas, both in his speeches and in successive governmental agendas. 'Pragmatism', 'feasibility' and 'reason' were opposed to 'dogmatism', as illustrated in his critique of 'the Amish model' when referring to demands to put a hold on deploying the 5G.[10] Demands to radically transform the agriculture system were targeted by prominent members of the government as 'agribashing'. Second, several initiatives were introduced from autumn

2020, selectively drawing on already planned measures and the Covid-19 recovery agenda while, at the same time, drawing lessons from the Yellow Vests movement and subsequent electoral campaigns. The National Low-Carbon Strategy (SNBC) was revised in 2020. Progress was made to enhance and expand the climate and resilience policy framework (law adopted in 2021), covering new issues such as soil protection (discussed below) and setting new targets for the circular economy, anti-waste and enhanced food quality for school catering. New administrative structures were created, including OFB, the French Biodiversity Agency. Monitoring tools, such as environmental budgetary reviews and impact assessments, were introduced. Drawing on the EU Green Deal agenda, new planning, contracting and financing tools, such as the Recovery Plan and the Recovery and Ecological Transition Contracts (CRTE), were introduced to engage subnational levels of government – notably the classic duo of mayors and prefects – and to increase their role in territorialising the goals set at national/EU levels (Mazeaud et al., 2022). Following the nomination of Prime Minister Castex in June 2020, the shift away from the metropolitan discourse was confirmed, and increased attention was given to advancing the ecological transition agenda in medium- and small-sized towns. Third, despite EC concerns being dominant in discourse, both policy processes and outcomes suggest that they were often combined with climate-delaying and blame-avoiding rather than advancing the climate and environmental agenda. The addition of new policy layers (targets, venues, organisations, etc.) did not strengthen political capacity but, rather, contributed to exacerbating the fragmentation of the climate governance system. Organisations that were responsible for ensuring compliance were not provided with sufficient clout to dismantle pre-existing policies and overcome institutional resistance, bureaucratic routines and corporatist arrangements. Throughout the first mandate, the Ecology Ministry lacked strong political leadership, with no fewer than four ministers, three of whom were members of EELV, succeeding one another. By aligning their demands with Macron's search for pragmatism, professional organisations and interest groups – in the agriculture, transport and energy sectors more specifically – successfully obtained the postponement of carbon-emission reduction targets and proposals to ban harmful products and activities.

Several examples are illustrative of this broader trend, which also shows strong continuity with long-term policy developments in EC. First, the fate of the proposals stemming from the CCC: most notably, the selection of policy tools highlights the prevalence given to initiatives aimed at incentivising and experimenting, whilst other levels of government were left with the responsibility of adopting unpopular measures on a larger scale. In the case of policy measures targeted at the aviation and advertising industries, the regulatory and legislative venues offered many opportunities to obstruct the policy process through classic climate-delaying strategies such as questioning the relevance of these measures or discussing whether other authorities (often the EU) should act first. In other cases, ensuring the buy-in from specific target groups justified the prevalence given to short-term measures. This was particularly the case with polluting vehicles and sustainable mobility more generally. Additional support was provided to specific target groups – for example, low-income households, employees and employers from the private sector (sustainable mobility package) and zero-rate loans to purchase clean vehicles – while metropolitan authorities were left with the responsibility of regulating the use of cars within low-emission zones. Food provides another example, with vouchers being given to low-income households to purchase quality products, as opposed to long-term measures such as taxing ultra-processed food, reducing the use of pesticides (or banning the most dangerous ones), increasing the number of vegetarian meals and cutting the share of meat and dairy products. Overall, claims about the adoption of the CCC's measures remain a hotly debated issue, depending on whether one considers those implemented or adopted as fully, partially or forthcoming. Following the end of the CCC, the press and environmental NGOs regularly published their own estimates. In September 2022, the government's spokesperson, Oliver Véran, claimed that 8 per cent had been adopted,[11] contradicting the Ecology Ministry, which claimed that 100 measures were implemented – about 67 per cent.[12]

Beyond CCC measures, other paradigmatic cases are illustrative of the shift observed from autumn 2020 onwards. As with former ruling majorities, successive governments under Macron chose to shift the burden of introducing unpopular measures regarding, for example, agriculture transition and air quality to European institutions. This provided an opportunity to delay implementation while shifting blame. In the case of glue-traps hunting, for example, a ban was proposed to make France compliant with the EU Birds Directive. Ecology Minister Pompili was violently accused by the powerful hunters' lobby of being dogmatic and by regional hunters' associations of acting 'in the name of ideological motivations having nothing to do with the protection of animal species'. She received little support from within the government and political elites more generally, with several prominent politicians and Macron himself calling for the protection of traditional forms of hunting as part of the country's heritage and way of life. Following months of procrastination, the Council of State eventually confirmed the legality of the ban in 2021, following a court action initiated five years earlier by the Birds Protection League (LPO).

In the case of energy transition, France still failed to achieve EU targets to develop renewable energies, and no clear decision was made to close its coal mines. However, Macron singled out nuclear power as being key to achieving goals for the reduction of carbon emissions. The deadline to reduce the share of nuclear power in the energy mix from 75 to 50 per cent was postponed from 2025 until 2035. Both within and outside the state apparatus, pro-nuclear discourses gained a new momentum after Russia's invasion of Ukraine – and nuclear energy was reframed as a major asset to limit the country's energy dependence on importing and consuming carbon energies. A major investment programme in nuclear power was announced with the support of business organisations, senior echelons of the civil service and leading figures in the climate movement.

Finally, institutional reforms to advance the ecological democracy agenda were delayed or transferred to subnational levels of government. By contrast, surveillance mechanisms were introduced to monitor ecologist activism – understood in the broadest sense to include symbolic actions – and criminal charges were systematically applied (Comby and Dubuisson-Quellier, 2023; Sommier, 2021). The Demeter Unit[13] was set up nationally in 2019 by Interior Minister Christophe Castaner under the authority of the *gendarmerie* for monitoring attacks on agriculture. In its initial brief, this surveillance mechanism extended to 'acts of an ideological nature', even the symbolic ones. The limitations set on journalistic investigations, environmental activism and any other critique against the dominant agricultural model were repeatedly highlighted (Collombat, 2021; Massiot, 2020). Following legal action led by several NGOs, the administrative judge put an end to the surveillance of acts of an ideological nature in early 2022. In its 2020 and 2021 reports, the High Council on Climate highlighted France's delay in achieving its climate objectives by 2030, pointing specifically to insufficient efforts to reduce emissions in road transport and agriculture. It also pushed for a more ambitious agenda to be adopted, should the country want to play a leading role internationally.

Advancing the country's 'sovereignty agenda' through ecological planning

Solely focusing on domestic politics to make sense of ECP processes would be misleading. Several exogenous factors shaped, unexpectedly and dramatically, domestic EC politics and policy processes during this period, including the European Green Deal, the Covid-19 pandemic, the war in Ukraine and the international EC agenda. Both the COP 26 in Glasgow and the French EU presidency of the Council of the EU (January–June 2022) had been initially identified as major opportunities for Macron to strengthen the country's green leadership. It did, however, confirm France's ambivalent position about EC issues.

When it comes to the climate-change agenda and notwithstanding Macron's clear commitment to the European integration process, France's support for 'a sovereignty agenda' for France in Europe and Europe in the world is primarily guided by the promotion of its strategic interests and more marginally shaped by its climate ambitions or efforts at supporting enhanced integration in this area (see Chapter 7). Several examples are illustrative of this: France aggressively pushed for nuclear energy to be labelled as a green investment under the EU taxonomy.[14] During the French presidency, although attention was on Ukraine, Macron nevertheless pushed his EU climate agenda – including the adoption at the end of 2022 of a carbon border tax – and worked towards increased cooperation to reduce energy dependence. In addition to committing to the achievement of 40 per cent of renewable energy by 2030, France exhorted the German government to support the adoption of the ban on new fuel and diesel cars by 2035 (adopted in 2023) but was only able to convince a minority of states to adopt Nutriscore as a common scoring system in the face of fierce opposition from the Italian government.

Macron also drew strategically on the EU Green Deal agenda to realign his domestic EC agenda. His plan to reindustrialise France relies on EU funds and the Climate Bank (EIB), and the development of new technologies, such as hydrogen, is being fostered, alongside exploring scope for innovative processes in the industry with the support of regional authorities. Although not particularly salient in political debates during the 2022 campaign, his election manifesto proposed to make France 'a great ecological nation, the first to phase out petrol, gas and coal'.[15] Once re-elected, he singled out the importance of ecological transition in transforming the country's economy, highlighting innovation, new technologies and investments as the main levers and calling for a temporary stop to EU environmental constraints in order not to hamper reindustrialisation efforts:[16] his claim that the EU had done 'more than its neighbours' reminded his EU allies of the limits of his European commitment while also addressing the concerns of specific target groups at home. Since then, major legislative proposals under discussion in Parliament (Law on the Green Industry, Farm France, etc.) aim to contribute to the greening of the economy with limited measures to enhance ecological democracy and social-justice issues.

ECP developments reflect the constant back-and-forth between efforts to actively shape governing capacity at the state level in order to advance the green economy agenda and reactive discourses and measures. Regarding the former, it should be noted that, despite addressing new issues, policy processes show some level of continuity with classic EC forms of policy-making while also seeking to enhance coordination, as illustrated by organisational reforms. Many proposals to achieve a significant reform of the climate governance system were laid out during the 2022 campaign, opposing a technocratic model to those favouring a parliamentary or ecological democracy model.[17] The former clearly won out, at the expense of the ministry: although the new Ecology Minister, Christophe Béchu, appointed in July 2022, was given authority over both Ecological Transition and Spatial Cohesion, he is challenged politically, institutionally, and administratively since ecological planning activities were put under the responsibility of Prime Minister Borne through a newly created General Secretariat for Ecological Planning (SGPE) aimed at 'coordinating the development of the national climate, energy, biodiversity and circular economy (and ensuring) the proper execution of the commitments made by all ministries'.[18] Building on administrative developments taking place during the first presidency, the Finance Ministry significantly enhanced its expertise and authority across all EC issues,[19] notably the industry portfolio, and a separate Ministry for Energy transition was set up.[20] While Béchu's role is to ensure the territorial deployment of the EC agenda in coordination with subnational administrative and political authorities, traditional elite groups and technocratic forms of expertise have regained the upper hand on planning activities and policy formulation at the state level, including scenario building, target setting, budgetary planning and tools selection.

Yet, Macron's EC agenda also was reactively shaped by social demands, natural disasters and the international agenda. This has been the case with the 'sufficiency' strategy,[21] in which the Borne government addressed the energy crisis sparked by the war in Ukraine, the 'Zero Net Artificialisation' goal (to suspend any net increase in the total amount of artificial surfaces) and the water crisis. In parallel to speeding up on Macron's promise to build six new-generation nuclear reactors by 2028, a patchy list of short-term measures was set up 'to get through the winter', that is, to reduce energy demand by 10 per cent to prevent shortages in the context of the war in Ukraine. The set targets were unexpectedly met, without sparking new protest, as this was also considered a timely opportunity for households, the industry and subnational authorities to reduce their spending. A large-scale consultation was set up to develop a fully-fledged strategy for energy sufficiency while pushing for a similar approach at the EU level under the REPower EU legislative proposal (Boasson *et al.*, 2020).

'Zero Net Artificialisation' (ZNA) provides another example. Targets were set under the 2021 Law on Climate and Resilience, as one of the CCC's149 measures requiring a 50 per cent reduction in the rate of consumption of natural, agricultural and forest areas between 2021 and 2031. Sparking massive opposition from inter-municipal authorities, a new bill was adopted in July 2023 to accommodate their demands for increased support (e.g., expertise and planning tools) throughout implementation. By contrast, the need for a holistic and multilevel approach to soil protection has been advocated (Offner, 2022), highlighting the focus on urban land (or adjacent to urbanised areas) – while agricultural land was left out – and criticising the bill's vagueness with regard to schedule setting and monitoring, as well as for the large number of exceptions allowed. This is to be clarified through implementation decrees, which traditionally leave considerable room for manoeuvre to weaken a bill's effective implementation, as observed on many occasions in the past, notably with the coastal and mountain laws (Lascoumes, 2022).

The case of water is the most contentious. While Macron's promise for a 'nuclear renaissance' sparked some concerns but little protest, the case of water developed into a major conflict. High levels of funding are needed to achieve large-scale network maintenance, to deploy countrywide re-use technologies and to develop water-adaptation measures.[22] Urban authorities have led the way, examining a wide range of solutions and governance arrangements. Yet, the share of water resources, whether withdrawn or consumed, by the agriculture sector and industry, are being questioned. The project to develop a large-scale water reservoir at Sainte-Soline sparked a violent confrontation with the police in March 2023, only seven years after the protest against the Sivens Dam. Several prominent members of the government used the notion of 'ecoterrorists' and the decision was made in June 2023 to shut down *Soulèvements de la Terre* (Earth Uprisings) – an umbrella organisation bringing together various climate activist groups – though this decision was later suspended by the Council of State in an emergency procedure.[23]

Conclusion

Since his election in 2017, Emmanuel Macron's proactive political declarations about climate and the environment have raised as much expectation as frustration. ECP developments confirm that these issues have been instrumental in advancing his agenda to modernise the French economy and strengthen his leadership both at home and abroad. Although acknowledged as a top priority, with the results of the European, municipal and, to a lesser extent, the legislative elections bearing witness to this, EC concerns also are hugely divisive when it comes to the allocation of costs (Hamdi-Cherif et al., 2022; Rouban, 2023). As such, they constitute a major opportunity to forge alliances and enhance leadership in a rapidly evolving political system. Whether through his speeches or his successive governments' actions, Macron strategically exacerbated divisions about EC concerns to secure his government's capacity and re-election in a highly unstable political context. To do so, he reached out to climate and environment organisations and technocratic elites within and outside the state, as well as to a selected number of interest groups (hunters, dominant farmers' unions, etc.). In this regard, ECP discourses and measures have been instrumental in securing these clienteles. Following the Covid-19 crisis, some efforts were made to accommodate the demands of subnational authorities.

Overall, ECP issues that aligned best with sovereignty issues and greening – and, later, reindustrialising – the economy were considerably enhanced, whereas, for others, climate and environmental action were slowed down by climate delaying and the politics of small steps. In this context, proactive political declarations and the permanent search for innovation and coordination, often highlighted as a characteristic of EC rhetoric, reflect Macron's attempts to maintain the upper hand and avoid blame. Yet, in delaying transformative actions and paying lip service to demands for a strong socio-ecological justice component to the EC agenda, it is unlikely that his legacy will match the climate emergency.

Notes

1 This chapter benefited from LIEPP's support, which is funded under the France 2030 investment plan through IdEx Université Paris Cité (ANR-18-IDEX-0001).
2 All quotations translated by the author. 'En Marche ! Élections présidentielles 23 avril et 7 mai 2017'. https://www.aefinfo.fr/assets/img/modules/comparateur/docs/6/Programme-Emmanuel-Macron.pdf (last accessed 17 May2023).
3 Because of these many changes, the ministry is referred to throughout this chapter as the 'Ecology Ministry'. A detailed overview of these changes is provided on the Ministry's website: https://www.ecologie.gouv.fr/lhistoire-des-ministeres
4 'En Marche ! Elections présidentielles 23 avril et 7 mai 2017'. https://www.aefinfo.fr/assets/img/modules/comparateur/docs/6/Programme-Emmanuel-Macron.pdf (last accessed 17 May 2023).
5 Following a failed at attempt at relaunching the project in a different form, this decision was confirmed by the Constitutional Court in 2022.
6 Briefing letter signed by Prime Minister Philippe, 02 July 2019, https://www.conventioncitoyennepourleclimat.fr/wp-content/uploads/2019/09/lettre-de-mission.pdf (last accessed 12 March 2023).
7 In his speech concluding *Le Grand Débat* on 25 April 2019, he declared that 'what comes out of this convention will be submitted without filter, either to the parliamentary vote, or to a referendum, or to direct regulatory application'. https://www.elysee.fr/emmanuel-macron/2019/04/25/conference-de-presse-grand-debat-national (last accessed 12 March 2024).
8 http://paris.tribunal-administratif.fr/Actualites-du-Tribunal/Espace-presse/L-Affaire-du-Siecle-l-Etat-devra-reparer-le-prejudice-ecologique-dont-il-est-responsable
9 http://paris.tribunal-administratif.fr/Actualites-du-Tribunal/Espace-presse/L-Affaire-du-Siecle-la-reparation-du-prejudice-ecologique-bien-que-tardive-est-complete
10 https://www.elysee.fr/emmanuel-macron/2020/09/14/discours-du-president-emmanuel-macron-aux-acteurs-du-numerique
11 Interview with *France Inter*, 12 September 2022.
12 https://www.ecologie.gouv.fr/suivi-convention-citoyenne-climat/
13 Press release 13 December 2019: https://mobile.interieur.gouv.fr/Archives/Archives-ministres-de-l-Interieur/Archives-Christophe-Castaner/Dossiers-de-presse/Presentation-de-DEMETER-la-cellule-nationale-de-suivi-des-atteintes-au-monde-agricole

14 This was adopted in 2020, with a list of criteria established in October 2022 to specify which investments would qualify, namely those of France, Estonia, Finland, and Sweden.
15 '*Emmanuel Macron avec vous, Élections présidentielles, 10 et 24 avril 2022*' https://avecvous.fr/wp-content/uploads/2022/03/Emmanuel-Macron-Avec-Vous-24-pages.pdf (last accessed 25 May 2023).
16 Speech on reindustrializing France, 11 May 2023: 'We don't need small measures but big changes. ... We must forge a new production model and invent new ways of moving, feeding ourselves and producing. The proposed model brings solidarity, jobs, competitiveness for our businesses, renewal for our farmers, health and a better quality of life for citizens'. https://www.gouvernement.fr/actualite/accelerer-la-reindustrialisation-de-la-france (last accessed 12 March 2024).
17 Report by France Stratégie (2022), proposals formulated by think tanks and NGOs - Amorce, Fondation de la Mer, I4CE, Association Biodiversité, L'affaire du siècle, FNE, WWF France, Patrimoine nucléaire et Climat France, The Shift Project.
18 Decree establishing the SGPE, 7 July 2022.
19 A dedicated sub-unit for ecological transition was set up during summer 2023 to strengthen the Ministry's economic analysis across all EC issues.
20 A dedicated sub-unit for ecological transition was set up during summer 2023 to strengthen the Ministry's economic analysis across all EC issues.
21 As per the IPCC, sufficiency policies are 'a set of measures and daily practices that avoid demand for energy, materials, land and water while delivering human well-being for all within planetary boundaries' (Cabeza et al., 2022).
22 The EU Commission launched an action against France in 2021 for failure to fulfil its obligations. Levels of water reuse are among the lowest in the EU, only 1 in 2022.
23 https://www.conseil-etat.fr/actualites/le-conseil-d-etat-suspend-en-refere-la-dissolution-des-soulevements-de-la-terre

References

Abrams, A. (2017) 'French President Emmanuel Macron trolls Donald Trump: "Make our planet great again"', *Time Magazine*, 1 June.
Aykut, S. and Evrard, A. (2017) 'Une transition pour que rien ne change? Changement institutionnel et dépendance au sentier dans les "transitions énergétiques" en Allemagne et en France', *Revue internationale de politique comparée*, 24(1–2), pp. 17–49.
Berny, N. (ed.) (2011) 'Special issue: Intégration européenne et environnement: vers une union verte?', *Politique européenne*, 33(1), pp. 7–36.
Boasson, E.L., Banet, C. and Wettestad, J. (2020) 'France: from renewables laggard to technology-specificity devotee', in Boasson, E.L., Leiren, M.D. and Wettestad, J. (eds) *Comparative renewables policy: Political, organizational and European fields*. London: Routledge, pp. 149–169.
Boy, D., Brugidou, M., Halpern, C. and Lascoumes, P. (eds) (2012) *Grenelle de l'environnement. Acteurs, discours, effets*. Paris: Armand Colin.
Brouard, S. and Guinaudeau, I. (2015) 'Policy beyond politics? Public opinion, party politics and the French pro-nuclear energy policy', *Journal of Public Policy*, 35(1), pp. 137–170.
Cabeza, L.F., Bai, Q., Bertoldi, P., Kihila, J.M., Lucena, A.F.P., Mata, É., Mirasgedis, S., Novika, A. and Saheb, Y. (2022) 'Buildings', in Shukla, P.R., Skea, J. and Slade, R. et al. (eds) *IPCC Sixth assessment report. Working group III: Mitigation of*

climate change. Cambridge, UK and NY: Cambridge University Press, pp. 953–1048. https://doi.org/10.1017/9781009157926.011 Available at: www.ipcc.ch/report/ar6/wg3/chapter/chapter-9/

Chailleux, S. and Zittoun, P. (2021) *L'Etat sous pression*. Paris: Presses de Sciences Po.

Charvolin, F. (2003) *L'invention de l'environnement en France*. Paris: La Découverte.

Cohen, L. (2022) *800 jours au Ministère de l'impossible*. Paris : Les petits matins.

Collectif d'enquête sur les Gilets jaunes, Bedock, C., Bendali, Z. et al. (2019) 'Enquêter *in situ* par questionnaire sur une mobilisation: une étude sur les gilets jaunes', *Revue française de science politique*, 69(5–6), pp. 869–892.

Collombat, B. (2021) Radio France. https://www.radiofrance.fr/franceinter/les-opposants-a-l-agriculture-intensive-dans-le-viseur-de-la-cellule-demeter-2852919

Comby, J.B. and Dubuisson-Quellier, S. (2023) *Mobilisations écologiques*. Paris: Le Seuil, La vie des idées.

Dedieu, F. (2022) *Pesticides, le confort de l'ignorance*. Paris: Le Seuil.

Deront, E., Evrard, A. and Persico, S. (2018) 'Tenir une promesse électorale sans la mettre en œuvre: le cas de la fermeture de Fessenheim', *Revue française de science politique*, 68(2), pp. 265–289.

Driscoll, D. (2023) 'Populism and carbon tax justice: The Yellow Vest movement in France', *Social Problems*, 70(1), pp. 143–163.

Evrard, A. (2012) *Contre vents et marées*. Paris: Presses de Sciences Po.

Grossman, E. and Saurugger, S. (2012) *Les groupes d'intérêt*. 2nd ed. Paris: Armand Colin.

Guinaudeau, I. and Persico, S. (2018) 'Tenir promesse: les conditions de réalisation des programmes électoraux', *Revue française de science politique*, 68(2), pp. 215–237.

Halpern, C. (2023) 'France: not living up to its ambition', in Kaeding, M., Pollak, J. and Schmidt, P. (eds) *Climate change and the future of Europe*. Cham: Springer, pp. 39–43.

Hamdi-Cherif, M., Touzé, V., Reynès, F., Malliet, P. and Landa, G. (2022) 'Enjeux socio-économiques de l'action pour le climat', *Revue de l'OFCE*, 176, pp. 5–12.

Hayes, G. (2002) *Environmental protest and the state in France*. New York: Palgrave Macmillan.

Knill, C., Heichel, S. and Arndt, D. (2012) 'Really a front-runner, really a straggler? Of environmental leaders and laggards in the European Union and beyond', *Energy Policy*, 48, pp. 36–45.

Kriesi, H., Koopmans, R., Duyvendak, J.W. and Giugni, M.G. (eds) (1995) *New social movements in Western Europe*. Minneapolis: University of Minnesota Press.

Lacroix, V. and Zaccai, E. (eds) (2010) 'Quarante ans de politique environnementale en France', *Revue Française d'Administration Publique*, 134(2), pp. 205–232.

Lamb, W., Mattioli, G., Levi, S., Roberts, J., Capstick, S., Creutzig, F., Mix, J.C., Müller-Hansen, F., Culhane, T. and Steinberger, J. (2020) 'Discourses of climate delay', *Global Sustainability*, 3, p. E17.

Lascoumes, P. (1994) *L'Eco-pouvoir*. Paris: La Découverte.

Lascoumes, P. (2022) *Action publique et environnement*. 3rd ed. Paris: Presses Universitaires de France.

Lascoumes, P., Bonnaud, L., Le Bourhis, J.P. and Martinais, E. (2014) *Le développement durable. Une nouvelle affaire d'État*. Paris: PUF.

Le Monde (2018) 'Démission de Nicolas Hulot : ce que l'ex-ministre a dit en direct', 28 August.

Le Monde/AFP (2022) 'Emmanuel Macron appelle à "l'unité" face à "la fin de 'abondance" et "de 'insouciance", 24 August.

Liefferink, D., Arts, B., Kamstra, J. and Ooijevaar, J. (2009) 'Leaders and laggards in environmental policy: A quantitative analysis of domestic policy outputs', *Journal of European Public Policy*, 16(5), pp. 677–700.

L'Observatoire de Triangle (2019) 'Le Vrai débat – éléments de synthèse', https://triangle.ens-lyon.fr/spip.php?article8544, (last accessed 13 March 2024).

Lowi, T.J. (1964) 'Four systems of policy, politics, and choice', *Public Administration Review*, 32(4), pp. 298–310.

Macron, E. (2016) *Révolution*. Paris: XO Editions.

Massiot, A. (2020) 'Fil vert', https://www.liberation.fr/terre/2020/09/08/enquete-sur-la-cellule-demeter-un-dispositif-politique-contre-une-menace-fantome_1798524/

Mazeaud, A., Aulagnier, A., Smith, A. and Compagnon, D. (2022) 'La territorialisation de l'action climatique', *Pôle Sud*, 57(2), pp. 5–20.

Mission du Grand Débat National (2019) 'Traitement des données issues du Grand Débat National, « La transition écologique »', April. https://granddebat.fr/ (last accessed 23 May 2023).

Muller, P. (2018) *Les politiques publiques*. 12th ed. Paris: Presses Universitaires de France.

Ollitrault, S. (2008) *Militer pour la planète*. Rennes: Presses Universitaires de Rennes.

Offner, J.M. (2022) 'ZAN, contre-enquête: de l'impasse légaliste de l'arithmétique foncière à l'ambition régulatrice de la gouvernance des sols', *Urbanisme*, ZAN, contre-enquête De l'impasse légaliste de l'arithmétique foncière à l'ambition régulatrice de la gouvernance des sols - Urbanisme (accessed 8 January 2024).

Rouban, L. (2023) 'La transition écologique au risque de la cohésion sociale en France', *Note de recherche: Le baromètre de la confiance politique, vague 14. Paris: Sciences Po Cevipof.*

SDES (Unit for Data and Statistical Analysis) (2022) *Bilan environnemental de la France*, édition 2022. Paris: Ministère de la transition écologique et de la cohésion des territoires.

Sommier, I (2021) '"Les sociétaux": une violence en devenir?', in Sommier, I., Crettiez, X. and Audigier, F. (eds) *Violences politiques en France*. Paris: Presses de Sciences Po, pp. 135–156.

Szarka, J. (2001) *The shaping of environmental policy in France*. New York: Berghahn.

Topçu, S. (2013) *La France nucléaire*. Paris: Seuil

Villalba, B. (2022) *L'écologie politique en France*. Paris: La découverte (Repères).

12
PROTEST AND REPRESSION DURING EMMANUEL MACRON'S PRESIDENCY

Olivier Fillieule, Fabien Jobard, and Anne Wuilleumier

Abstract

This chapter explores the paradox that although Emmanuel Macron campaigned as a police reformer, his presidency was marked by a wave of repression unprecedented since the 1945–1948 wave of protests. Although numerous cases of police violence and racism led him to vow on three occasions to reform police ethics, each time was to no avail. Some 50 years ago, the American criminologist, Lawrence Sherman, explained that police corruption scandals offer a unique window of opportunity for police reform – however, while this diagnosis is true in the United States, it is clearly not true in France. This chapter explains why not, by looking at the repression of the Yellow Vests movement, the pressure of terrorism and the power of the police unions, as well as President Macron's commitment to an authoritarian liberalism that has made him dependent on – or even a prisoner of – those police forces that are the most hostile to change.

Introduction

When running for election, Macron boldly called his presidential 'manifesto', sold in bookshops across the country, *Revolution* (Macron 2017). Eighteen months after celebrating his election victory to the strains of Beethoven's *Ode to Joy* – the anthem of the European Union – and parading down the Champs-Elysées in a military vehicle, the spirit of revolt was certainly alive in the crowds that would soon occupy the same hallowed avenue, at times attempting to storm the Elysée Palace, through unprecedented clouds of tear gas and often to the tune of the *Marseillaise*, the national

DOI: 10.4324/9781003323259-12

anthem symbolising the 1789 Revolution. The movement, which came to be known as the Yellow Vests, was a motley, unorganised and disruptive one that would punctuate Macron's first presidency from mid-November 2018 until (at least) the spring of 2019. The government's response was particularly brutal. By the time France was locked down in March 2020, according to the Ministry of Justice, 12,000 protesters had been arrested by the police, 11,000 were in police custody and 3,000 verdicts had been handed down by judges, including 1,000 prison sentences (440 of which were immediate remands in custody). In terms of police tactics, the figures speak for themselves: 1,800 police and *gendarmes* and 2,500 demonstrators were injured. The president himself is said to have feared being lynched by angry demonstrators. The most serious violence (maiming, crippling, death) was recorded among demonstrators or ordinary passers-by: an 80-year-old woman, Zineb Redouane, died in Marseille after a tear-gas grenade was fired through her apartment window by police officers; six people had their feet or hands torn off by the explosion of grenades fired by police officers or *gendarmes* and 30 people lost an eye to rubber bullets fired by the police. Some 19,000 rubber bullets and 5,420 fragmentation and explosive grenades were fired in 2018 by the *Police Nationale*.[1] The number of serious injuries (those crippled or maimed for life) significantly exceeds that recorded for the entire month of May 1968, a particularly brutal high point of protest policing (Davis, 2018).

This chapter examines the logic of what happened: how did a candidate who professed liberalism become the president of one of the most repressive governments in contemporary history? To answer this question, we first recall some salient features of the organisation of the French police before looking at the specific dynamics of the policing of the Yellow Vests uprising and, finally, proposing some more general lines of interpretation of authoritarian liberalism.

Policing in France: an old and deep-rooted public problem

Emmanuel Macron's first statement as a presidential candidate on policing issues was in a Facebook post on 8 February 2017: 'The authority of the police is never given, it is earned, day by day ... it is earned by being a good example'. The date of the post speaks volumes: a few days earlier, during an operation in Aulnay, a northern suburb of Paris, a police unit had held down a 19-year-old black man, Théo Luhaka, and maimed him for life. When one of the officers' retractable batons penetrated his rectum, it caused a ten-centimetre tear in his anus. In the same Facebook post, Macron added: 'What happened in Aulnay is an illegitimate use of force by the state, which violated the dignity of a young man, his family and his neighbourhood'. As a presidential candidate, Macron thus demonstrated a resolutely progressive position on policing in an area with a history of violence, marked by recurrent and intense expressions of what has long been seen as the 'police problem' in France (Fassin, 2013; Mouhanna, 2009). It is therefore necessary to recall some historical milestones in order to shed light on the pressures that all French governments have faced in dealing with the issue of law and order.

In all respects, the French police system differs profoundly from the common law systems of the United Kingdom or the United States (Emsley, 1999; Lévy, 2012). France has a dual police system: a national police force – the *Police Nationale* – and a military police force – the *Gendarmerie Nationale*, formerly attached to the Ministry of Defence. The *Police Nationale* operates in densely populated urban areas, and the *Gendarmerie Nationale* in smaller towns and rural areas. Since 2008, both forces have been under the authority of the Interior Ministry, making it a highly centralised system without any real checks and balances. Indeed, in a general context of weak parliamentary power, both forces continue to be controlled from within by the ministry, although a 2008 reform established the constitutional authority of an ombudsman, the *Défenseur des droits* (de Maillard, 2022, pp. 42–45). In addition, there is a *Prefect* who represents the state in the *départements*, who reports directly to the Interior Ministry and who 'directs the action of the national police and the national gendarmerie in matters of public order' (Article L. 122-1 of the Interior Security Code). However, since 2009, there is also a Police Prefect with extended powers over public order in Paris and the three neighbouring *départements*, which gives him/her considerable powers (Mouhanna and Easton, 2014; Renaudie, 2008). More generally, policing in France remains an institutional domain whose officers are at first sight perceived as, in the words of the American, David Bayley (1975, p. 337), 'brutal and aloof ... armed, feared and unpopular'.

Without going into the causes of this situation (see Fillieule and Jobard, 1998; Fillieule and Della Porta, 2004), it is worth recalling here that, at the end of the Second World War, the Parisian police succeeded in imposing the narrative that they had played an important role in the street battles that led to the liberation of Paris from German occupation, thus erasing the French police's involvement in the Jewish deportation policy (Anderson, 2011, pp. 116–120). A decade later, the decision of the Algerian liberation movements to extend their struggle to metropolitan France gave the *Police Nationale* – and the Paris police in particular – a central role in the Algerian War of Independence (1954–1962), in the protection of the Parisian population and, above all, in the harsh police control of the Arab population living in the Paris region (House and McMaster, 2006). At the end of the war, large numbers of migrant workers from North African countries were housed in shantytowns on the outskirts of major cities, where order was maintained by a small number of police officers, trained and supervised by police officers who had, for the most part, practised policing in Paris during the Algerian

War or who had provided colonial policing in Moroccan, Tunisian or Algerian territories (Blanchard, 2012; Jobard, 2021). The policing of immigrant populations and second-generation immigrants has, therefore, always been particularly brutal, aimed at protecting wealthy city centres from poor minority populations living on the outskirts.

From the late 1970s, many riots broke out in the suburbs for this reason and became more frequent in the 1990s, usually following fatal encounters with police officers, the vast majority of whom were not convicted or even charged (Jobard, 2014). The media and public opinion began to focus on the issue of policing, particularly in relation to immigrants and minorities. When he returned to power, Prime Minister Lionel Jospin (1997–2002) proposed the creation of an independent body to monitor the police, the *Commission nationale de déontologie de la sécurité (CNDS)* – which became part of *Le Défenseur des droits,* a constitutional authority created in 2008 – and a move towards 'proximity policing' (bobbies on the beat). This term is more or less analogous to an idea, then in vogue around the world and popularised by American reformers, known as 'community policing' (de Maillard and Zagrodzki, 2020), which aims to reinstate foot patrols and encourage contact with citizens, providing support rather than repression. However, the reform was poorly implemented and met with hostility from conservative police forces, leading to a massive street protest in 2001 by police officers and *gendarmes*, despite their status prohibiting them from demonstrating. At the turn of the millennium, the politicisation of police and crime issues reached its peak, contributing to Lionel Jospin's electoral defeat when National Front candidate Jean-Marie Le Pen beat him into the second round of the presidential election, leading to the re-election of the conservative Jacques Chirac and the appointment of the hardliner Nicolas Sarkozy as Interior Minister from 2002 to 2007 (Monjardet, 2008).

Sarkozy successfully used his police minister status as part of a plan to win the next presidential election in 2007. He adopted a strategy similar to the 'governing through crime' approach described, for example, by Simon (2007) in relation to California: focusing the public agenda on crime, making a lot of noise about minor street crime, scapegoating delinquent immigrant groups, promoting a style of policing that maintains order and managing the police by statistics and results while overlooking white-collar crime. This permanent tension led, in the autumn of 2005, to the largest wave of riots that France had ever seen and lasted three weeks, during which more than 300 towns were affected by urban violence involving the destruction of vehicles and public buildings and clashes with the police or *gendarmes*, causing several hundred million euros' worth of damage (Jobard, 2014; Moran and Waddington, 2016; Roché and de Maillard, 2009). At another level, Sarkozy significantly increased police salaries and reorganised the police unions, thereby significantly strengthening their power. This hard line, which appealed to National Front voters, contributed significantly to his election as president in 2007. However, the strategy ran out of steam during his presidency and his Socialist opponent, François Hollande, won the 2012 election.

Policing issues were less central to Hollande's presidency than previously, and the 'governing through crime' approach lost momentum (Drenkhahn, Jobard and Singelnstein, 2023). However, two events quickly brought policing issues back to the forefront of the public agenda. The first was the series of terrorist attacks that struck France from 2015 onwards: the massacre at the editorial offices of the satirical magazine *Charlie Hebdo* (12 killed), the massacre at the kosher supermarket in Paris in January 2015 (5 killed), the massacres on café terraces and at the Bataclan concert hall in November 2015 (130 killed) and the massacre at the 14 July festival in Nice in July 2016 (86 killed). These attacks, which placed France in a state of emergency from November 2015 to October 2017 and gave the police exceptional powers (notably to search homes), were compounded by the murders or attempted murders of police officers by so-called 'radicalised' youth (often young Frenchmen of Arab origin from the *banlieues*): two police officers had their throats slit in their homes in June 2016, a police officer was shot dead on the Champs-Elysées in April 2017 and more would be killed during the Macron presidency. Under constant terrorist pressure, the police became an essential part of everyday life in France and used this pivotal position to push through their demands (particularly on pay), considering themselves beyond the reach of criticism from non-police actors (ombudsmen, parliamentarians, journalists, citizens, etc.). However, criticism of the police increased again in 2016, when a labour law reform proposed by Hollande (but actually introduced and carried by his Economy Minister, Emmanuel Macron) sparked a major public uprising. Macron, believing that President Hollande had not been firm enough, stepped down from the government in the summer of 2016 to prepare his bid for the presidency; however, these protests in spring 2016 were the scene of numerous clashes with demonstrators, journalists or passers-by (Fillieule and Jobard, 2016). The renewed popularity of the police after the attacks of 2015 and 2016 seemed to dissipate, and public attention returned to policing issues, scrutinising police brutality during demonstrations as well as their treatment of young people in the *banlieues*. Indeed, the death in police custody of a young man of African origin, Adama Traoré, in July 2016 led to a significant public mobilisation that lasted several years and continued to focus journalists' attention on police behaviour towards ethnic-minority youth.

It was precisely in response to a particularly violent act committed against a young black man that candidate Macron took a stand on police issues in the Facebook post mentioned earlier. This post suggested a return to the policy of opening up the police, initiated by the Jospin government in 1997:

'I believe in the need to create a police force for everyday security (...), a police force better rooted in the territories ... (that) knows the population (to) be able to solve local problems', he wrote. This was a particularly courageous position at the time, given the context just described: the police were in a strong position, given both the terrorist threat and their role in policing crowds in a context of renewed social unrest. This context largely explains the intellectual transition from Macron the candidate to Macron the president.

The repression of the Yellow Vests movement (2018–2020)

When the Yellow Vests movement broke out, its main characteristic was that it was completely unpredicted by the police intelligence services or by society more generally (Fillieule and Dafflon, 2022). The movement was born out of a call by unknown people on Facebook to occupy roundabouts across France in protest against an additional tax on fuel proposed by the Macron government. From the outset, the movement was made up of employees of small businesses – and especially self-employed people who were totally dependent on their cars to get to work or to carry out their trade (Fillieule, Dafflon, Bendali, Beramendi and Morselli, 2022). It broke out on 17 November 2018 with the occupation of hundreds of roundabouts and undeclared demonstrations without a pre-established itinerary in city centres, where the first violent clashes with the police had already taken place, particularly in Paris and Bordeaux. Two weeks later, on 1 December, the demonstrations were particularly violent. In Paris, demonstrators fought pitched battles (though without firearms) with the police, particularly on the Champs-Elysées. Very violent confrontations also took place in Bordeaux and Marseille: Zineb Redouane died the next day in Marseille, a man in Bordeaux was left hemiplegic after being shot in the head with rubber bullets by the police and the prefecture building in Puy-en-Velay was set alight. Violence continued, albeit at a lower level, until March 2019 and then again on 1 May 2019, in July and again at the end of November and beginning of December, when a protest movement against the pension reform began. Only the Covid lockdown in March 2020 finally put an end to the movement.

President Macron's management of the Yellow Vests protests was based on the mobilisation of almost all police resources. However, due to the changes in crowd policing that had taken place between 2000 and 2010, Macron was, in fact, calling on destabilised police resources. In the name of rationalising costs in the context of strong political pressure, these changes had actually favoured the emergence of a dangerous and inefficient low-cost crowd policing.[2] As a result, criticism of crowd policing during the Yellow Vests crisis was fuelled both by the demonstrators – whose initial political protest against their impoverishment was transformed into a protest against 'police violence' – and, at some distance from public opinion, by the police themselves, particularly within the *gendarmerie*, as discussed below.

Reduced reliance on specialised units

One of the cornerstones of the management of demonstrations in France is the use of specialised police and *gendarmerie* units: the *Compagnies Républicaines de Sécurité* or CRS (French riot control units) – part of the *Police Nationale* – and the *Escadrons de Gendarmeries Mobiles* or EGM (Mobile *Gendarmerie* Squadron), part of the *Gendarmerie Nationale*. As far as possible, the prefect in charge relies on these mobile units when dealing with crowds of people (whether revellers or demonstrators). In fact, these formations have a military character (in terms of their chain of command, equipment, barracks, etc.) and devote most of their time to training, cohesion and discipline. These troops are specialised in crowd management and are called upon to intervene in cities or areas far from their garrisons. From the point of view of the French authorities, the advantage of this is that the officers remain impervious to the political and social context of the cities in which they intervene. As one CRS manager put it in 2019:

> We arrive, we have a mission to fulfil... we don't have any qualms about negotiating here or turning a blind eye there and then being able to intervene at a certain moment, it's just material for us... We don't have any emotional attachment to the city.

This emotional neutrality is in line with the objective pursued when the mobile *gendarmerie* was created in 1921: to have police forces operating far from their place of residence in order to avoid both the risk of officers fraternising with the population and the tensions that could arise from personal ties within the community. Another feature of these mobile forces is that they are very close-knit. The CRS and EGM squadrons are made up of four sections or platoons that move and intervene together according to the orders that the section or platoon commander receives from the unit commander. Individual initiative is forbidden so as not to hinder the overall manoeuvre.

However, these units were severely disrupted between 2010 and 2012: 15 EGMs were closed, while CRS units were reduced in size, complicating manoeuvres in the field by preventing them from splitting up, as one police chief explained in 2019:

> The CRS companies have been reduced, so where you had a company with four sections, now you have a company with three. And as the CRS[3] say, 'With three sections, we can't split in two'. They'll send you two

companies, so you'll have six sections but you only need four to hold two positions. So, in a way it's a false economy. I mean, it's not a good economy.

The CRS believes that an isolated section (consisting of only 15–20 peacekeepers) is too vulnerable if taken over by a hostile crowd.

There are several reasons for these changes in crowd control. Since the early 2000s, French governments have suffered from a kind of Fukuyama syndrome (a pacifist belief in the end of history) and, believing that large-scale social movements were a thing of the past, have downsized these specialised units. Moreover, public spending cuts, which intensified after the 2008 global financial crisis, made it difficult to maintain forces that spent most of their time training in their garrisons. From the end of the 1990s, these CRS and EGM units found themselves carrying out day-to-day policing tasks, sent out in their paramilitary gear to patrol sensitive areas in the *banlieues* that they knew nothing about. Finally, security concerns shifted from social protests to urban riots. As a result, governments favoured the creation of small paramilitary anti-riot squads, trained not to deal with protesting masses but with small groups of highly mobile suburban youths, against whom they are taught to act quickly and violently in order to make as many arrests as possible and secure convictions in court. More recently, the specialised units have also been involved in the fight against terrorism and illegal migration in border areas. A CRS trainer interviewed in spring 2018 admitted, for example, that counter-terrorism training was so important in the CRS training curriculum that he sometimes no longer had time to organise advanced training in crowd management.

When the Yellow Vests protests broke out, the specialised police forces were reduced, less organised and in competition with the anti-riot units. Moreover, almost half of the specialised forces available for this type of event were already allocated to the Paris police prefecture. The reserve forces available at very short notice were few, which meant that, during the Yellow Vests movement, some prefects could not count on mobile units to monitor demonstrations of several thousand people. When the government did send these units to a given city, it was so late that the final adjustments were often made on Friday evening, with the rallies generally taking place on Saturday morning, thus limiting the tactical capacity of the police and *gendarmes*.

This inability to anticipate was exacerbated by the reorganisation of the police's domestic intelligence services between 2000 and 2010. In 2008, the age-old Domestic Intelligence Service (*Renseignements généraux*) was closed down and merged into a large department focused on counter-terrorism and the fight against jihadism, thus neglecting the monitoring of social-protest movements. This process of reorganisation, again based on budget cuts, continued until 2014, profoundly destabilising the police's ability to analyse French society. The intelligence services had traditionally been responsible for the continuous monitoring of movements at the forefront of French public opinion, particularly in the labour sector. As a former agent told our colleague, Laurent Bonelli, in 2007: 'Reform means doing more or better with less money. But in this case, they found a rhetorical sledgehammer: Terrorism. Terror simply smashes the last remaining psychological or administrative barriers to reform' (Bonelli, 2021, p. 239). In addition to these elements, which changed the nature of the units sent to police demonstrations from 2016 and, even more so, from 2018, there was also a shift in the strategic purposes for which governments used them.

From crowd management to arresting troublemakers

A new phrase has become common in crowd policing and is omnipresent in the discourse of key stakeholders: the 'judicialisation of protest policing'. Traditionally, police interventions in protesting crowds were aimed at reducing crowd violence and not at making arrests. Pragmatism dictated this practice: rather than risk going into the crowd to pursue the perpetrators of crimes committed during a protest and potentially aggravating the situation, the police preferred not to risk individual confrontations. Priority was given to crowd control and the safety of individuals (police, demonstrators and the public); the apprehension of offenders was secondary.

The judicialisation of protest policing can be explained in social and historical terms as well as in relation to the changes in police forces described earlier. The main exogenous factor was the disruption of (mainly student) protests by groups of rioters or perpetrators of various crimes, often from the deprived areas of the Paris suburbs. The protest of 12 November 1990 (with the looting of a youth clothing store) was a milestone in this trend, followed by the student and high-school protests of 1994, the high-school protests of 1999 and 2005 and, most notably, the 2006 protests against the government's attempt to reform a youth-labour law (the CPE), during which young Parisian high-school and university students were robbed and beaten by youths from the tough banlieues. In this context, it was difficult to defend a 'crowd management' approach and not intervene to help those in danger by arresting the perpetrators.

However, this judicialisation is also a political strategy of 'governing through crime', in which the government (especially the Interior Minister) wants to demonstrate to public opinion that crime does not go unpunished. In the name of what he called a 'culture of results and performance', Sarkozy used arrest and conviction figures as indicators of the success of police operations, borrowing heavily from the 'policing by numbers' approach adopted by the N.Y.P.D. under Bratton-Giuliani (Douillet, de Maillard and

Zagrodzki, 2016). The number of people arrested, detained or convicted is one that can be easily aggregated and communicated, and their growth continues to be encouraged. Moreover, this judicialisation of protest policing also meets the professional objectives of local police chiefs, who are responsible for policing crowds in their areas. Indeed, reporting figures to central management in Paris is a regular part of the police work of these senior chiefs, who are not experts in crowd policing. As a result, protest policing is not given any special consideration, as this 2020 comment by the Chief Police Officer illustrates:

> In my opinion, public security cannot be guaranteed only on the streets, it also needs the courts. The court's action, which is more balanced than other parts of the system, provides a conclusion and, in any case, a more lasting response to the problem of crime. It's the same with protest policing.

This judicialisation also reflects a desire to align protest policing with crime control. However, implementing this goal of prosecuting offenders in crowds is difficult for some police officers, especially some *gendarmes*, who are used to a more pacifying relationship with crowds. The legal work involved in prosecuting a 'looter' is indeed complex:

> You have to provide traceability and proof that it was really the right person who was seen at such and such a time breaking such and such a billboard, such and such a shop window, or throwing such and such a projectile from such and such a place that landed in such and such a place, but also finding the victim who might help the police to identify the person who picked up the cobblestone, etc. It's extremely complicated and technical. It's very complicated, very technical.
> *(Direction Départementale de la Sécurité Publique, interview 2020)*

Technically, the arrest is fraught with risks and dangers:

> If you want to arrest someone, you have to break through 15 metres of crowd to go and arrest a guy who is going to resist. You need two people to arrest him, plus a third to protect the two who are doing the arresting, and you have to be ready to fire quickly behind you because a bunch of people will be coming at you. If you don't want to light everyone up with a flash-ball gun to make an arrest, you have to mobilise a team (…) [to] get him back behind the line of police officers who will advance with shields and take the blows (…) there will be resistance, adversity.

However, arrest to convict is, indeed, the direction that has been taken, as shown by the instructions given since 2016 by the ministers of justice to prosecutors, who are asked to show good figures and find perpetrators, whatever the risks. This explains the very high figures for judicial repression reported in the introduction. Sometimes, police officers have even been instructed to 'preventively' arrest demonstrators, even before any offence has been committed, in order to keep them in the police station for the duration of the protest (as in Paris, following an order from the public prosecutor, dated 22 November 2018, before the second Yellow Vests protest). Or, as in the case of an order received by all the public prosecutors in France to arrest people going to a demonstration with simple goggles to protect themselves from tear gas or to arrest people on grounds buried deep in the penal code, such as insulting the national anthem or on the basis of a law adopted in 2010 in response to problems of violence between football fans or between rival gangs. This law (No. 2010–201) allowed the police to stop and search groups of young people (a few dozen people) travelling on public transport and, if they were carrying certain items (a knife, pepper spray, etc.), to take them to court for 'participating in an assembly with the aim of committing a crime'. It had been criticised for allowing convictions on the sole basis of an intention to commit an offence rather than on the basis of an *actual* offence. Rarely applied before 2018, it was used opportunistically by the courts on the recommendation of the Ministry of Justice against groups of demonstrators heading towards protest sites: 1,192 convictions were handed down on these grounds in 2019 compared to between 203 and 439 in 2016–2018 (AN 2020, p. 40). Another rarely used provision was a conviction for unregistered demonstrations. In 2019, 42 convictions were handed down on these grounds compared to between 6 and 19 in 2016–2018 (AN 2020, 40).

For all these reasons, a repressive paradigm took hold under Emmanuel Macron when faced with the Yellow Vests protests. This was made possible by using a legal repertoire mainly designed to combat urban violence, which testifies to the very low tolerance for disorder and the increasingly disorderly nature of protests, urban riots and common crime. However, this quest for maximum arrests and convictions does not, in itself, explain police brutality.

Low-cost crowd control

Faced with the reduction in the number of mobile police officers described earlier and with the proliferation of simultaneous protests in dozens or even hundreds of locations, the authorities massively called on local police forces to rebuild their crowd-control units. To have a sufficient number of peacekeepers, some directorates decided to mobilise all their staff, including those who normally worked in offices and 'who had never worn a helmet before' (interview DDSP, 2020). The massive nature of the movement, combined with the attrition of the specialised forces, led to a very unprofessional management of the crowds.

In addition, all the units created in the 1990s and 2000s to control and repress – somewhat brutally – the youth of the suburbs, such as the plainclothes policemen of the notorious *Brigades Anti-Criminalité (BAC)*, were called up for the Yellow Vests protests, given the simultaneity of these large and undeclared protests across the country. In Paris, from March 2019, a new police prefect – appointed by President Macron for his reputation for toughness (he was the prefect who had overseen the interventions in Bordeaux, which were unusually brutal) – even used units with a professional culture quite distinct from that of specialised law-enforcement units to make contact with the police more brutal. This inevitably affected the quality of the police interventions. The *gendarmes*, more used to military discipline, abhorred the use of these forces and tactics (Fillieule and Jobard, 2020). Even police chiefs doubted that these BACs could properly replace the specialised units.

> What they do in the BAC, the force they use, they do it on their own initiative, it's all about initiative. There's no room for initiative in a protest policing unit. There's a chain of command in the police force that decides what effect they want to have and how they're going to do it. If people start to take individual initiatives within the unit, sooner or later there will be disastrous consequences.
> *(interview with Police Chief, 2020)*

Forcing these officers to adapt to a working environment other than one of petty crime and zero tolerance for disorder while, at the same time, getting them to follow orders from a chain of command is no easy task:

> In other words, someone who is used to taking the initiative has to understand that they are being told: 'So what, they're throwing stones at you. I can see they're throwing stones at you, but don't move'. [You don't have to explain that to a CRS: he knows how it's done].
> *(interview with Police Chief, 2019)*

The mismatch between the BAC's working habits and the basic principles of crowd policing in practice puts both police and protesters at real risk. Because some interventions are made at inopportune times or without an overall view of the march, a BAC unit can sometimes find itself surrounded by protesters and feel the need to use their LBD riot guns or rubber-bullet grenades, putting protesters at risk of physical harm. Significantly, according to a parliamentary report based on police and *gendarmerie* data, almost 80 per cent of LBD shots fired at the beginning of the Yellow Vests movement (from

17 November 2018 to 5 February 2019) were attributed to non-specialised units (Sénat, 2019, p. 16). In contrast to the mobile units that sometimes monitor relatively peaceful demonstrations – sometimes without helmets or with their weapons holstered – the BAC and other small anti-crime units appear only as repressive forces, never as forces that monitor or accompany the demonstration.

Why, then, should these violent units be deployed at the expense of specialised units? To answer this question, we need to recall the very specific context of the Yellow Vests movement: dozens of simultaneous protests across the country, alongside the occupation of roundabouts or actions in rural areas against private companies (e.g. supermarkets and logistics warehouses). The ransacking of the buildings of a motorway concessionaire in the south of France in December 2018, which led to the conviction of 21 people, is just one of many such examples. Moreover, these units, trained to arrest and pursue criminals, are perfectly suited to a strategy that prioritises convictions over crowd management. Finally, local police chiefs like to have units they are used to working with under their command, and these units certainly know the city they are working in – they can move around very quickly if necessary. Less heavily equipped and more flexible than specialised units, anti-crime units can move more easily to arrest demonstrators. Their increased involvement in crowd policing was thus not only a consequence of the cutbacks in specialist personnel but also helped to implement the new goal of judicialising protest policing. Catching a protester in the act of throwing a projectile or insulting the police was favoured. This form of policing, which is known to be a constant source of conflict with the population in the context of crime control, especially in the poor and immigrant neighbourhoods of the *banlieues* (Fassin, 2013; Jobard, 2005), was thus extended to the lower-middle classes, which made up the bulk of the Yellow Vests protesters.

These three elements (the reduction in the number of specialised units, the policy of chasing judicial statistics and the use of anti-crime and anti-riot units) are the key factors that explain the repressive turn seen during the Yellow Vests movement. A crucial question remains: was the brutalisation of the police that occurred inextricably linked to the Yellow Vests – a movement so particular that it could be called a historical accident – or was the construction of a strong police force a lasting political decision by President Macron?

President Macron: authoritarian liberalism or policing trap?

It is impossible to understand Macron's action in the face of the Yellow Vests upsurge without recalling its exceptional nature. Without warning, dozens or even hundreds of sites (city centres and roundabouts in rural areas) were occupied or taken over by disorganised crowds, without leaders, without banners or signs, refusing any form of negotiation with the authorities – as is customary in protests – regarding marching routes, assembly and dispersal points. The movement took the police by surprise and, if there is one thing that police all over the world have in common, it is that they hate uncertainty and often respond to it with excessive force. These situational dimensions are critical. However, we want to draw attention here to two contradictory elements that are structural. The first is that protest and repression have played out in a kind of mirror image of the 'French neoliberal turn' embodied by Macron. We have already mentioned this in relation to the notion of 'low-cost protest policing' but would like to theorise this dimension. The second element is quite simply the space that policing occupies in French politics. According to this second line of analysis, Macron found himself trapped by the police, to whom he and his predecessors had conceded too much.

Authoritarian liberalism

Emmanuel Macron came to power in France with a plan: to bind France to a neoliberal agenda by destroying social policies (in his own words, by waging a 'relentless fight against rent-seekers'[4]). However, unlike his predecessors, Chirac, Sarkozy and Hollande, Macron declared that he was 'open to disruption' and reaffirmed his unwavering determination not to give in to protests because 'democracy is not the streets'. Macron already used this turn of phrase as a warning in September 2017, on the eve of a day of protest against a labour law reform. Let us recall that, when Macron resigned as economy minister under Hollande in the summer of 2016, he had accused the president of giving in to the street after a labour-law reform bill proposing to cap unemployment benefits that he had inspired and supported had triggered widespread street protests that spring, already marked by violent clashes with the police. As soon as he was elected president with an extremely small majority (only 15 per cent of registered voters opted for him in the first round), he had the same measure passed by 'ordinance' (a type of decree), immediately provoking the wrath of the unions. His Prime Minister, Edouard Philippe, then declared, on 9 September 2017: 'The protests are not going to change the content of the ordinances' and the President reiterated, in a tone reminiscent of Margaret Thatcher, that he would 'not give in to cynics, idlers or extremists' (Godin, 2019, p. 166). In the spring of 2018, with the same inflexibility, Macron opposed the strikes of the SNCF railway workers (36 days of strike since the beginning of April and the end of June) and succeeded.[5]

As a result, when the Yellow Vests movement broke out, the trade unions were no longer able to mobilise workers for whom negotiations and traditional demonstrations – and even trade union membership – were bringing fewer tangible benefits. Moreover, a general trend that underpinned the social reality of the Yellow Vests protest was that the movement was the result of years of labour liberalisation policies in France, which, alongside deindustrialisation in favour of a service society, had significantly reduced salaried employment and led to the development of precarious work: short-term contracts, casual work and self-employment – all characteristic of a gig economy. These were the social categories that made up the Yellow Vests: private nurses, small-business owners with one or two employees or the self-employed, delivery drivers, temporary and zero-hours workers, etc. While union demonstrations follow accepted traditions (e.g. no demonstrations on the Champs-Elysées), the Yellow Vests sought 'disruptive' strategies, reminiscent of the 'poor people's movements' in the United States in the 1930s, based on 'disruption', as described by Frances Fox Piven and Richard Cloward (1977). In a way, these unorganised movements perfectly reflect the society that Emmanuel Macron, the presidential candidate, called for in his aptly named book *Revolution* (2017): a society freed from the constraints of labour laws and labour contracts.

Thus, the brutalisation of the relationship between the government and the street during Macron's presidency was not a new departure. Rather, it is the expression within policing of what has been called the 'neoliberal turn' in public policy since the 1990s. The economist Godin (2019) has compared this brutalisation to the repression of unrest that resulted from the implementation of so-called structural adjustment programmes in South America. The comparison is not unfounded, except for two major differences. Firstly, because the police in France have never used firearms in response to collective protests, it is much less lethal than in South America – in Chile or Venezuela – to take three countries that have been marked by violent protests in recent years. Second, the French 'neoliberal turn' followed decades of deindustrialisation and the subsequent loss of employment opportunities for unskilled young men in the *banlieues*, whom the police were then called upon to discipline (Fassin, 2013). The current brutalisation of protest policing is thus the product of two economic trends whose effects have proved explosive: long-term deindustrialisation and, in the last five years, the radicalisation of Macron's neoliberal agenda, first in response to the union-led protests of spring 2016 when he was economy minister and then intensified in the face of the Yellow Vests movement of 2018–2020, which was independent of the unions. This analysis is, of course, reminiscent of the authoritarian liberalism championed by Margaret Thatcher: freeing the economy from the constraints of labour law and the protections it provides, intolerance of political dissent on the grounds that it interferes with the conduct of economic policy and the subsequent strengthening of police capacity (Jessop, 2015). According to this analysis, the radicalisation of the police can be seen as part of Macron's political agenda. However, in the following analysis, Emmanuel Macron is, on the contrary, its prisoner.

President Macron's policing trap

We remember how moved candidate Macron was by the violence inflicted on a young black man from the *banlieues* and how he called on the police to set an example. Nevertheless, two years later, in March 2019, when around 20 protesters had lost an eye to rubber bullets and images of police brutality were broadcast on the news and social media, Macron responded to a woman who challenged him on the issue: 'Don't talk to me about police violence, these words are unacceptable in a state of law'.[6] Taking this denial even further, in January, his Interior Minister claimed not to know 'a single policeman or *gendarme* who attacked the Yellow Vests'. The bold candidate Macron, who had called for an in-depth reform of police practices, gradually lost control as president in the wake of the Yellow Vests movement in the face of growing pressure from the police unions. The latter had not failed to make a series of professional demands (for bonuses, allowances, etc.) from the first weeks of the movement, all of which had been met by the end of December 2018. Throughout the Yellow Vests mobilisation, police officers were not the subject of any criticism from the government or the president.

However, a series of police scandals forced them to speak out, albeit timidly, against police abuse. In late June 2019, a particularly violent police raid on a party on the banks of the Loire in Nantes pushed a dozen people into the water, one of whom, a 24-year-old childcare worker, could not swim and drowned. Following this incident, the Interior Minister claimed, contrary to what he had been arguing for months, that it was necessary to rethink the doctrine of crowd control.

Yet, this led, a year later, to a highly controversial document,[7] which essentially endorsed the low-cost policing discussed earlier. The government was clearly not backing down from its hard line on protests. However, the move was the first sign of politicians distancing themselves from the police. The document – and the debates that led to it – were very poorly received by the police trade unions, who saw it as an apportioning of blame and a public questioning of the need to reform the protest policing techniques that had, in their view, saved the Republic from insurrection. On 9 October 2019, with police suicides back in the spotlight (60 since the beginning of the year), a 'police anger march' saw around 12,000 police officers of all ranks on the streets of Paris (Noûs, 2019). The collateral benefit of these demonstrations was that the special police pension scheme was protected from the pension reform proposed by Macron in December 2019, even though the aim was precisely to abolish France's special pension schemes.

The confrontation between the police unions and the government intensified in the following months. In January 2020, a motorbike courier, Cédric Chouviat, died of asphyxiation while being held down by a police officer, in a similar way to George Floyd a few weeks later in the United States.

The scandal was immediate, especially as the victim was a white family man, the embodiment of the French middle class, working for the just-in-time service economy. Macron then took a stand in line with his position as a presidential candidate: he officially asked the police to present him with measures for more ethical behaviour. However, Covid put the issue on the back burner. During the lockdown, the police were given increased powers to stop and fine people who flouted the rules – and cases of blatant violence and racism once again made the headlines, notably when a police officer told an Arab man he had just saved from drowning that 'Bicots can't swim'[8] (his words were captured on a viral video) and when a WhatsApp group of 80 racist police officers was discovered in Normandy.[9] However, the end of the lockdown coincided with the global eruption of the Black Lives Matter movement and the activists, in the case of Adama Traoré mentioned earlier, relaunched their campaign with great success – tens of thousands of demonstrators, mainly young black people, gathered in front of the courts at the Palais de Justice in Paris (Beaman, 2022). President Macron again asked the police to propose measures to improve police ethics. His Interior Minister called for the abandonment of the 'chokehold' and the 'systematic consideration of suspension for any justified suspicion of racist acts or statements' (Focraud, 2020). This proved too much for the police, who organised protests in Marseille, Bobigny, Nice, Bordeaux, St Etienne and Lille, while the director general of the national police force declared that he 'shares with (the police officers) the feeling of a profound injustice', and the Police Prefect sent a letter of support to the officers under his command entitled 'Do not doubt'.[10]

The police unions showed their strength. They managed to get a promise from the president that there would be a new Interior Minister when the government was reshuffled the following June. The new minister, Gérald Darmanin, then implicated in a rape case (later dropped by the courts), was a loyal supporter of Sarkozy. He supported a bill on security (called *Loi Sécurité Globale*) aimed at improving cooperation between the various security forces – in particular, the national police and the *gendarmerie* – and presented by a deputy and former police officer; controversially, in September, he accepted an amendment – demanded by the police unions – aimed at prohibiting citizens from diffusing images of police interventions during protests. This particular proposal (originally Article 24) triggered a wave of protests from mid-November 2020: every Saturday, people marched in several French cities against the law, which had also provoked the anger of journalists, who denounced its encroachment on the freedom of the press, enshrined in law since 1881. The protests turned violent, particularly in Paris. The government's attempt to quell the anger of the police with this and other measures to give them legal protection failed miserably. Although the bill was passed by parliament, some of its most controversial articles were condemned by the Constitutional Council, including the diffusion of images identifying individual police officers.

Alongside the street protests, another event was to have a significant impact: Michel Zecler, a black music producer in his 30s, was severely beaten by three policemen who followed him into his home in Paris while his colleagues looked on passively. The videos of this beating went viral and, for a third time, Macron called for measures on police ethics.[11] A few weeks later, during a dialogue with journalists on the website *Brut*, he went so far as to admit the established existence of police violence and racial profiling (Jobard and de Maillard, 2021). Tensions with the unions then rose sharply, while police officers continued to be the target of murderous attacks by jihadists, as described earlier. The police unions organised a high-profile demonstration in Paris on 19 May 2021, during which the name of the Minister of Justice was publicly booed[12] in the presence of the Interior Minister, illustrating the notorious weakness of the political leadership *vis-à-vis* police unions.

Like Peter at the rooster's crowing, by the end of his first term, Macron had not received a single proposal worth mentioning to improve police ethics, despite three public requests. The police unions had been remarkably successful in protecting their institution and the traditions of French policing, in a context where, since spring 2016, the police, rather than offering a solution to the problems of violence and crime, had themselves become a public problem, a problem hotly debated by journalists, researchers and associations but one that the political leadership – under Macron and his predecessors – had failed to mobilise sufficient resources to tackle. In this sense, none of Macron's declared good intentions on policing, either as a candidate or as president, have ever been followed through by his government. On the contrary, the president found himself trapped by the unbounded dependence he had placed on the police and their unions in the face of social unrest, a trap from which he has since not been able to escape.

Conclusion

To understand President Macron's position on the police, it is important to bear in mind that France is one of the few European countries where the police are a permanent 'public problem' in the sense that Gusfield (1981) gave to this term – policing is constantly on the political and media agenda, with one 'police scandal' after another. President Macron's second term has confirmed this dubious quality of the French police: the violence of its officers and the dangerous nature of its weapons make it a constant problem for the executive. The protests against the 2023 pension reform, marked by Macron's authoritarian move to strip parliament of its power to pass the law, saw the huge mobilisation that supported the parliamentary debate turn into smaller demonstrations marked by (small-scale) destruction and clashes with police and *gendarmerie* forces. During these movements, the police motorbike units in particular, which had been trained during the Yellow Vests movement, could be seen on many videos indulging in excesses (clubbing, racist insults, using the motorbike as a weapon, using mutilating grenades, etc.). During the same period, in February 2023, a rural mobilisation against the construction of a huge water reservoir led to a massive operation by the *gendarmerie* (around 300 explosive grenades and 4,800 tear-gas grenades fired in less than three hours), which left many demonstrators injured, including two demonstrators who remained in a coma for several days and even weeks. A few months later, on 27 June, a video showing a police officer shooting a young man in the chest from a few centimetres away triggered a wave of rioting the likes of which France had not seen since 2005. Some 200 police stations were attacked, along with around 100 town halls and dozens of public buildings (including schools), while thousands of businesses were also attacked and looted. The damage was such that, in mid-July, the government proposed a special law to provide public funds to support insurance companies. Repression was intense, with – by the end of July – 4,200 prosecutions (two-thirds of them adults), 60 per cent of them sentenced to prison with an average time of nine months (IGA-IGJ, 2023, pp. 16–22). In the weeks following these events, there were numerous reports of police violence (one death by a rubber bullet, mutilations with weapons, beatings, etc.). One of these cases was so serious that a judge remanded a Marseille police officer in pre-trial custody for firing a rubber bullet into the head of a young man who was found unresponsive at the scene (surgeons will have to trepan him to remove the bullet lodged between his brain and skull). The detention led to a strong mobilisation of police hostility towards the judiciary and the government, demonstrating once again President Macron's inability to discipline his police force.

According to Sherman (1978), police scandals can provide an opportunity for governments (in the United States, municipalities) to attempt to reform the police. However, in France, police scandals never seem to open a window of opportunity for major reforms. The reason for this is the growing weakness of governments, including Macron's, towards the *Police Nationale* and its unions. The 2023–2022 security law, passed in February 2023, is a clear sign of this, since it provides for a 22 per cent increase in the police and *gendarmerie* budget and the recruitment of 8,500 police and *gendarmerie* officers by 2027, without the slightest attempt to change the organisation of the police. As such, this 'great law for security', as the Interior Ministry was keen to call it, is a blank cheque for the *Police Nationale*, as it has always been. Together with the terrorist threat, the dissent generated by Macron's brutal social reforms and also, paradoxically, the major disruptions caused by police scandals such as those of June and July 2023 make the police indispensable while making the president institutionally weak in the face of police abuse of force, thus perpetuating – under his government and for the future – the French tradition of Napoleonic statism in which the police are central.

Notes

1 Ministry of the Interior, https://medias.vie-publique.fr/data_storage_s3/rapport/pdf/194000511.pdf
2 Between 2019 and 2021, we conducted research on the management of protesting crowds in Europe in cooperation with the French police, which provides much of the material for this chapter.
3 By a semantic shortcut, an officer who is part of a CRS company is known as 'a CRS'. This metonymy does not, however, apply to mobile *gendarmes*.
4 These were the words reported by his two advisors, David Amiel et Ismaël Emelien, cited in Godin (2019, p. 147). Rent-seeking is an economic concept involving the pursuit of wealth without creating any benefits for society, discussed in the Introduction to this volume.
5 https://www.lepoint.fr/economie/la-greve-a-coute-790-millions-d-euros-a-la-sncf-20-07-2018-2237903_28.php
6 https://www.francetvinfo.fr/economie/transports/gilets-jaunes/video-gilets-jaunes-macron-juge-inacceptable-dans-un-etat-de-droit-de-parler-de-violences-policieres_3222835.html
7 https://www.lemonde.fr/societe/article/2020/09/23/le-nouveau-schema-national-du-maintien-de-l-ordre-
8 Old-fashioned racist term, often used during the Algerian War of Independence, to refer to someone of North African origin.
9 https://www.lemonde.fr/societe/article/2021/11/05/propos-racistes-dans-un-groupe-whatsapp-cinq-policiers-de-rouen-condamnes-a-des-amendes_6101100_3224.html
10 https://www.leparisien.fr/faits-divers/ne-doutez-pas-la-lettre-du-prefet-didier-lallement-a-ses-policiers-11-06-2020-8333763.php
11 https://www.leparisien.fr/video/video-paris-michel-frappe-par-des-policiers-sous-l-oeil-d-une-camera-26-11-2020-8410748.php
12 https://www.alternativepn.fr/intersyndicale-rassemblement-le-19-mai-2021

References

AN (2020) *Rapport n° 3786 relatif à l'état des lieux, la déontologie, les pratiques et les doctrines de maintien de l'ordre*. Paris: Assemblée Nationale.
Anderson, M. (2011) *In thrall to political change. Police and Gendarmerie in France*. Oxford: Oxford University Press.
Bayley, D. (1975) 'The police and political development in Europe', in Tilly, C. (ed.) *The formation of national states in Western Europe*. Princeton: Princeton University Press, pp. 328–379.
Beaman, J. (2022) 'Black feminism and transnational solidarity: Mobilization against police violence in France', *Esclavages & Post-Esclavages*, 6 online. URL: http://journals.openedition.org/slaveries/6563 (accessed 20 October 2022).
Blanchard, E. (2012) 'The police and the "Algerian medinas" in France. Argenteuil, 1957–1962'. *Métropolitiques.eu*, 2012, translated by O. Waine. Available at: http://www.metropolitiques.eu/The-police-and-the-Algerian.html

Bonelli, L. (2021) 'Domestic intelligence and counterterrorism in France', in de Maillard, J. & Skogan, W. (eds) *Policing in France*. London: Routledge, pp. 234–252.
Davis, O. ed. (2018) 'The anti-police of mai '68 fifty years on', special issue of *Modern & Contemporary France*, 26(2), pp. 107–207.
De Maillard, J. (2022) *Comparative policing*. London: Routledge.
De Maillard, J. and Zagrodzki, M. (2020) 'Community policing initiatives in France', in de Maillard, J. and Skogan, W. (eds) *Policing in France*. London: Routledge, pp. 294–309.
Douillet, A.-C., de Maillard, J. and Zagrodzki, M. (2016) 'Do statistics reinforce administrative centralisation? The contradictory influence of quantified indicators on French national police', in Hondeghem, A., Rousseau, X. and Schoenaers, F. (eds) *Modernisation of the criminal justice chain and the judicial system*. Berlin: Springer, pp. 65–77.
Drenkhahn, K., Jobard, F. and Singelnstein, T. (2023) 'A strained restraint: The ambivalences of penal moderation in Germany and France', in Drenkhahn, K., Jobard, F. and Singelnstein, T. (eds) *Impending challenges to penal moderation in France and Germany: A strained restraint*. London: Routledge, pp. 249–272.
Emsley, C. (1999) 'A typology of nineteenth-century police', *Crime, Histoire & Sociétés*, 3(1), pp. 29–44.
Fassin, D. (2013) *Enforcing order. An ethnography of urban policing*. Cambridge: Polity Press.
Fillieule, O. and Dafflon, A. (2022) 'Yellow vests movement in France 2022', in Snow, D. Della Porta, D., Klandermans, B. and McAdam, D. (eds) *The Wiley-Blackwell encyclopedia of social and political movements*. 2nd ed. London: Blackwell, pp. 1–6.
Fillieule, O. and Della Porta, D. (2004) 'Policing social protest', in Snow, D., Soule, S. and Kriesi, H. (eds) *The Blackwell companion to social movement*. Oxford: Blackwell, pp. 217–241.
Fillieule, O, and Jobard, F. (1998) 'The maintenance of order in France. Towards a model of protest policing', in Della Porta, D. and Reiter, H. (eds) *Policing protest. The control of mass demonstrations in western democracies*. Minneapolis: University of Minnesota Press, pp. 70–90.
Fillieule, O. and Jobard, F. (2016) 'A splendid isolation. Protest policing in France', *Books & Ideas*, 10 October. Available at: https://booksandideas.net/A-Splendid-Isolation.html
Fillieule, O. and Jobard, F. (2020) *Politiques du désordre*. Paris: Le Seuil.
Fillieule, O., Dafflon, A., Bendali, Z., Beramendi, M. and Morselli, D. (2022) 'From uprising to secession: A plea for a localized and processual approach to the avatars of the yellow vests movement', *French Politics*, 20, pp. 366–394.
Focraud, A. (2020) 'Fin de la technique "de l'étranglement", sanctions: les réponses de Castaner face aux violences policières', *Le Journal du Dimanche*, 8 June.
Godin, R. (2019) *La guerre sociale en France. Aux sources économiques de la démocratie autoritaire*. Paris: La Découverte.
Gusfield, J. (1981) *The culture of public problems: Drinking-driving and the symbolic order*. Chicago: University of Chicago Press.
House, J. and MacMaster, N. (2006) *Paris 1961. Algerians, state terror, and memory*. Oxford: Oxford University Press.
IGA–IGJ (2023) *Mission d'analyse des profils et motivations des délinquants interpellés à l'occasion de l'épisode de violences urbaines (27 juin–7 juillet 2023)*. Paris: Inspection générale de la Justice; Inspection générale de l'Administration.

Jessop, B. (2015) 'Margaret Thatcher and Thatcherism. Dead but not buried', *British Politics*, 10, pp. 16–30.
Jobard, F. (2005) 'Le nouveau mandat policier. Faire la police dans les zones dites "de non-droit"', *Criminologie*, 38(2), pp. 103–121.
Jobard, F. (2014) 'Riots in France. Political, proto-political, or anti-political turmoils?', in Pritchard, D. and Pakes, F. (eds) *Riot, unrest and protest on the global stage*. Basingstoke: Palgrave, pp. 132–150.
Jobard, F. (2021) 'Policing the *banlieues*', in de Maillard, J. and Skogan, W. (eds) *Policing in France*. London: Routledge, pp. 187–201.
Jobard, F. and de Maillard, J. (2021) 'Identity checks as a professional repertoire', in de Maillard, J. and Skogan, W. (eds) *Policing in France*. London: Routledge, pp. 202–218.
Lévy, R. (2012) 'About the proper use of policing "models"', *Champ pénal/Penal field* [online], 9, uploaded 12 May 2012, accessed 19 October 2022. http://journals.openedition.org/champpenal/8276
Macron, E. (2017) *Revolution*. London: Scribe UK. (French edition (2016) *Révolution*. Paris: XO Editions.
Moran, M. and Waddington, D. (2016) '"France in flames": the French riots of 2005' in Moran, M. and Waddington, D. (eds) *Riots: an international comparison*. London: Palgrave Macmillan, pp. 39–65.
Monjardet, D. (2008) 'Assessing a policing policy: The first Sarkozy ministry (May 2002 through March 2004)', *Sociologie du Travail*, 50(1), pp. e30–e49.
Mouhanna, C. (2009) 'The French police and urban riots. Is the national police force part of the solution or part of the problem?', in Waddington, D., Jobard, F. and King, M. (eds) *Rioting in the UK and France. A comparative analysis*. Culompton: Willan, pp. 173–182.
Mouhanna, C. and Easton, M. (2014) 'Policing Paris: "Out of" or "still in" Napoleonic time?', *European Journal of Police Studies*, 2(1), pp. 94–109.
Noûs, C. (2019) 'Mobilisations policières', *Sociétés contemporaines*, 116, pp. 51–69.
Piven, F.F. and Cloward, R. (1977) *Poor people's movement. How they succeed, how they fail*. New York: Vintage Books.
Renaudie, O. (2008) *La Préfecture de police*. Paris: LGDJ.
Roché, S. and de Maillard, J. (2009) 'Crisis in policing: The French rioting of 2005', *Policing: A Journal of Policy and Practice*, 3(1), pp. 34–40.
Sénat (2019) *Rapport n°345 sur la proposition de loi visant à interdire l'usage du LBD*. Paris: Sénat, Proposition de loi visant à interdire l'usage de l'écriture inclusive – Sénat (senat.fr), accessed 9 December 2023.
Sherman, L. (1978) *Scandal and reform. Controlling the police corruption*. Berkeley: University of California Press.
Simon, J. (2007) *Governing through crime. How the war on crime transformed American democracy and created a culture of fear*. Oxford: Oxford University Press.

13

MACRON'S AFRICA POLICY: PROMISES, PRACTICES AND PATH DEPENDENCIES

Tony Chafer

Abstract

After granting political independence in 1960, France established a model of neo-colonial relations with its former colonies frequently referred to as la Françafrique. French presidents since François Mitterrand have promised to change this relationship, to break with its neo-colonial practices and to establish a new partnership with Africa. President Macron is no exception. This chapter explores his promise of change against the historical legacy bequeathed to him by his predecessors and against his own declared intentions, in a context where the historical French presence is increasingly challenged by other countries – notably China and Russia – and where domestic public opinion in Africa is increasingly vocal in its hostility to France. After outlining Macron's promises of change, the chapter examines three major policy areas – military cooperation, economic and business policy and political relations – and reviews the 'dependent pathways' that inhibit change in this uniquely French area of presidentialised policymaking. It concludes by showing that policy errors and a high-handed approach to policymaking by the Macron presidency have further stoked anti-French feelings on the continent and made the ambition to establish a new relationship with Africa even more unachievable.

Introduction

Following the independence granted to its African colonies, France established a model of neo-colonial relations with them, which became known as '*Françafrique*' after the publication of a book by Verschave (1998) called *La Françafrique: le plus long scandale de la République*. The *Françafrique*

DOI: 10.4324/9781003323259-13

relationship was based on the goal of preserving exclusive rights to developing resources and markets in its former colonies, maintaining close relations with African political leaders and asserting the right to use military intervention to protect its interests. Economic control over these former colonies was further embedded through the maintenance of a common currency, the CFA franc, a legacy of the colonial period and managed by France (Pigeaud and Sylla, 2021; Taylor, 2019).[1] When Charles de Gaulle became president of the new Fifth Republic in 1958, he created a special unit in the Elysée Palace to manage these relationships; subsequent presidents maintained this model, which, over the years, became increasingly criticised for fostering corruption and supporting despotic regimes in Africa.

President Macron's predecessors, Nicolas Sarkozy and François Hollande, announced plans to transform this unhealthy relationship, as had François Mitterrand before his election in 1981. However, in the view of most commentators, they all failed to deliver substantive change in the nature of the relationships and the deeply embedded ties between France and its former colonies in Africa. In keeping with this tradition, Macron reiterated the promise of a break (*'rupture'*) with past practices – specifically, an end to *la Françafrique* – and the establishment of a new partnership with Africa.

This chapter explores Macron's record in Africa against the historical legacy of his predecessors and against his own declared intentions in a context where domestic public opinion in Africa is increasingly vocal in its hostility to France and where the historical French presence is increasingly challenged by other countries, notably China and Russia, which present themselves as potential liberators from French neo-colonial rule and which are increasingly rivalling French intervention and investment. The chapter first outlines Macron's promises of change, then examines three major policy areas – military cooperation, economic and business policy and political relations – and reviews the 'dependent pathways' that inhibit change in this uniquely 'French' area of presidentialised policymaking, where domestic and international interests are closely enmeshed. It concludes by showing that policy errors and a high-handed approach to policymaking have further stoked anti-French feelings on the continent and made the ambition to establish a new relationship with Africa even more unachievable.

Promises of change

During his election campaign, Macron sought to project himself as a transformative president, who would break with the past (Hewlett and Kuhn, 2022, p. 394). Africa policy was no exception. Thus, in April 2017, he promised to act 'transparently – far away from the shady networks (*'réseaux'*) of *Françafrique'* – and to create a 'new partnership' with Africa (Ben Yahmed, 2017). With its population set to double in the next 30 years,

Africa represented, for him, a 'continent of opportunities' – but this would mean addressing 'the elements of fragility' of African development, notably insecurity, insufficient training for young people, inequalities, degradation of the soil and global heating. He also stated that, in this new relationship, the French language and the African diaspora in France would play a key role, and he created a new body, the *Conseil Présidentiel pour l'Afrique* (Presidential Council for Africa: CPA), to advise him on reshaping France's Africa policy. He claimed that his youth – he was born after the colonial period – meant that he was well-placed to drive forward a new Africa policy. However, he also noted that there would be some continuity with his predecessor: counterterrorism would remain a priority, and he recognised that it would be impossible for France to withdraw from Mali in the short term due to the seriousness of the security situation there. Although France is not a member, he also promised to call a meeting of the G5 Sahel[2] – an organisation created in 2014 by five Francophone countries (Mauritania, Mali, Burkina Faso, Niger and Chad) to promote regional cooperation in development and security – as a first step towards resolving problems in the western Sahel (Dossier Emmanuel Macron et l'Afrique, 2017).

Reflecting his focus on Africa's youth, Macron fleshed out his plans in an important speech to students at the University of Ouagadougou in November 2017. He started by stating that France 'no longer has an Africa policy', by which he meant that France would henceforth have a policy *for* Africa – just as it did for the other continents of the world – but not an 'Africa policy'. The clear message from this was that he wanted to 'normalise' French policy towards the continent. He also outlined measures intended to mark this break with the past (Macron, 2017) including a promise to release the French archives relating to the 1987 assassination of former Burkinabè President, Thomas Sankara, who had been a vocal critic of French neo-colonialism; the restitution to Africa of cultural objects taken from the continent during colonisation; rapprochement with Rwanda; greater cooperation in the fields of education, entrepreneurship, sustainable development and culture and a renewed emphasis on economic relations, in particular with the continent's large economic powers such as Nigeria, Ghana and Ethiopia. The Ouagadougou meeting marked a significant break with past presidential practice, as his speech was followed by an unscripted question-and-answer session with university students, in which he responded to questions on contentious issues such as the future of the CFA franc and France's continuing military presence on the continent. However, there were widespread doubts about whether he would deliver on his promises, particularly in Africa. One local newspaper commented: 'There is great scepticism when you know that Macron's predecessors all distinguished themselves by making similar speeches but, in the end, changed nothing in the relationship between France and Africa' (Faivre, 2017).

Military cooperation

Shortly after his election in May 2017, Macron visited French troops in Mali to reaffirm France's commitment to its ongoing military action there, Operation Barkhane, comprising some 4,500 troops. Barkhane (2014–2022) was the successor to Operation Serval, launched in Mali in 2013 by President Hollande and aimed at driving out Islamic militants from the north of the country who were pushing south towards the capital, Bamako. Barkhane was a much more ambitious regional operation, whose aim was to support the armed forces of the G5 Sahel countries in their struggle against armed terrorist groups, whose attacks had spread beyond Mali to neighbouring countries. Underlining the continuity with his predecessor, he paid tribute to President Hollande's efforts to combat terrorism and prevent the Sahel from becoming a sanctuary for terrorists. At the same time, concerned that a credible exit strategy had not been put in place, Macron promoted the creation of the G5 Sahel Joint Force (G5SJF) in the hope that it would eventually be able to take over counterterrorism operations from Barkhane; he also played a key role in lobbying the international community to provide financial support (Desgrais 2018; Dieng, Onguny and Ghouenzen Mfondi, 2020). This resulted in the EU and Saudi Arabia both pledging 100 million euros, the United Arab Emirates 30 million and the United States, Japan and Norway also promising support (Barma, 2017), although it is unclear how much of this money actually materialised. Despite the creation of the G5SJF, the international pledges of support and the presence of Barkhane and of a large UN peacekeeping force, by 2019 the security situation had worsened in central Mali, insecurity had spread to Burkina Faso, and there was no realistic prospect that Macron would, in the short or medium term, be able to claim success, withdraw French troops and transfer responsibility for security to the G5SJF. By the end of the year, French public opinion was increasingly sceptical about the French military presence in the region and the death of 13 French troops, after two helicopters of Operation Barkhane crashed on 25 November 2019, increased domestic pressure on Macron to show that France's military efforts were delivering positive results. He was also angered by the growing expressions of anti-French sentiment on the streets of Bamako (Mali), Ouagadougou (Burkina Faso) and Niamey (Niger) and on social media (D'Alançon, 2019).

Recognising the need for a new approach, Macron summoned the G5 Sahel leaders to a summit meeting in Pau, France, at the end of the year. The summit was postponed after an armed attack on the Nigerien military base at Inates on 10 December – resulting in the death of 71 Nigerien soldiers – but eventually took place on 13 January 2020. With the violence escalating, Macron decided that the military effort needed strengthening but also recognised that the complex nature of the security problems facing the region could not be resolved by a military-focused response, as pursued up to this point. Alongside the announcement of a 'troop surge' of 600 extra troops for Operation Barkhane, bringing its total complement to 5,100, he therefore announced a major new initiative – the creation of the international Coalition for the Sahel – aimed at ensuring that the military operations would be accompanied by renewed international efforts to improve governance, restore government services and promote development (Macron, 2020).

The Coalition comprised four 'pillars': the fight against armed terrorist groups; building the capacities of the armed forces of the region; supporting the return of the state and its administrations and improving access to basic services; and assisting development. A central element of the first pillar was the launch of Takuba, a European (but not EU) military task force composed of European special forces under French leadership. Its role would be to advise and accompany the Malian armed forces, in coordination with their G5 Sahel partners, in their fight against armed terrorist groups, with a particular focus on the 'Three Frontiers' Liptako-Gourma area that borders Mali, Niger and Burkina Faso. The second pillar was essentially a fleshing out of the Partnership for Security and Stability in the Sahel (P3S), launched at the 2019 Biarritz G7 summit and designed to coordinate all the defence and security capacity-building actions for the armed forces of the G5 Sahel countries. Within the framework of the P3S, the third pillar aimed to coordinate the training and equipping of national internal security forces (police, *gendarmerie* and national guard) and to help to bolster the sovereign function of the state, including rebuilding the legal capacities and local administrations of the G5 countries. Finally, the fourth pillar centred on the Sahel Alliance: launched on 13 July 2017 by France, Germany and the EU, its aim was to attract development assistance to the region and improve the effectiveness of aid by coordinating the actions of major development partners.

Alongside these new initiatives, Macron made it clear that, in the face of continuing anti-French demonstrations, he expected the leaders of the G5 Sahel states to reaffirm their support for French operations in the region. However, the way in which they were summoned to Pau by President Macron, demanding that they 'clarify' formally their support for France's intervention, was experienced by G5 leaders as a summons and seen as disrespectful (Carayol, 2023; pp. 195–196; Melly, 2021). This contributed to the souring of France's relations with Mali and Burkina Faso, which would later lead to the expulsion of French troops from these countries.

Indeed, after the Pau summit, Macron's military policy in the Sahel began to unravel rapidly. In August, a military coup removed the Malian President, Ibrahim Boubacar Keïta, who was arrested and replaced by a military-backed transitional government. This not only complicated the political landscape but also raised questions about previous claims of political progress within the country. Moreover, eight years after President Hollande launched Operation Serval in January 2013, with French troop losses above 50, the cost of its military operations in the Sahel rising and facing a potentially difficult election in 2022, Macron was under pressure to bring forward an exit strategy. He drew back from announcing an expected reduction in French troop numbers at the G5 Sahel summit in Chad on 15–16 February 2021, although the delay proved to be only temporary as, a few months later, Macron announced the end of Operation Barkhane (Larcher, 2021). Events on the ground then moved quickly, obliging Macron to further rethink France's Sahel strategy. Mali suffered a second military coup in May 2021, as the army sought to reassert control over the political transition. This was followed in January 2022 by a military coup in Burkina Faso – which removed President Roch Marc Christian Kaboré from power – and the Malian government's expulsion of the French ambassador. At the same time, Danish troops, who had arrived in Mali to join the Takuba task force, were told to leave, while troops belonging to the Russian private security company, Wagner, arrived in the country in December 2021 and started undertaking military operations alongside Mali's armed forces. In May 2022, the Malian government announced the country's withdrawal from the G5 Sahel, accusing it of being under 'foreign' (in other words French) influence (Soyez, 2022). Subsequently, shortly after Macron's re-election in May, the Takuba task force was closed down and all French troops left the country by the end of August 2022. In January 2023, the Burkinabè government made the same demand – that France withdraw its troops from the country. Following a further military coup in Niger in July 2023, the new government expelled the French ambassador and announced that it would evict French (and US) troops from the country.[3]

France as the *'gendarme* of Africa': a long history of interventionism

In seeking to break with the past in the field of military policy, the problem for Macron was that, when elected in 2017, he found himself trapped in a 'logic of intervention'. First, France, as the former colonial power, has a well-established interventionist reputation as the *'gendarme* of Africa' in its post-colonial sphere of influence (Vallin, 2015). Even as it denied that its intervention had any ulterior motive and asserted that its intervention was humanitarian, it could not escape this history. To be sure, following criticism of its role in Rwanda before and after the 1994 genocide, France made efforts to 'multilateralise' its military interventions in Africa (Chafer, Cumming and van der Velde, 2020). However, even when not acting alone but at the head of an international assemblage of external actors,[4] as with Operation Serval and subsequently Operation Barkhane in the western Sahel, France has not avoided accusations of neo-colonial interventionism

(Carayol, 2023 p. 280). This perception was reinforced when, in 2019, troops from Operation Barkhane intervened unilaterally in support of Chad's autocratic leader Idriss Déby's efforts to crush an insurgency against his regime by bombing rebel convoys that were converging on the country's capital, N'Djamena. Barkhane's brief was to carry out counterterrorist operations against jihadist forces that are seen as everybody's enemy, but, in this case, French forces intervened to save Déby, a close ally of France, from rebels opposed to his regime. Chad continues to represent, for France's military establishment as it has for successive French presidents, 'the centrepiece of [France's] regional security architecture' in Africa (Bensimon, Ricard, Vincent and Châtelot, 2023). As a result, the importance attached to the France–Chad security partnership overrode any concerns about the Déby regime's well-documented human rights abuses and use of violence against opponents. France was further criticised for double standards when, following the death of President Déby in 2021, the new regime in N'Djamena simply overrode the constitution and announced his replacement by his son, General Mahamat Idriss Déby Itno, as the new leader of the country. Macron's decision to attend the late President Déby's funeral gave the impression to many that France supported this abuse of Chad's constitution and that his commitment to democratisation on the continent was both selective and less than wholehearted. This perception was reinforced when, in contrast to its reaction to the Chadian regime's actions, the French government criticised the Malian junta when it seized power in two military coups in 2020 and 2021. In this case, France insisted that new elections should take place by February 2022. The impression thus created, that France applies double standards in its deployment of military force and indeed more generally in its dealings with Sahelian governments, fuelled renewed criticism of France's military presence and role in the region, as the increasingly frequent demonstrations against the French presence, notably in Mali and Burkina Faso, showed (Debos, 2019; International Crisis Group, 2019). As time went on, the failure of France and its partners to either deliver improvements in security and governance or promote development, played into the narrative that France was in the Sahel to defend its own interests, not to improve the lot of the people of the region (Haidara, 2020).

Second, France had convinced its allies that the jihadist groups operating in the Sahel were not just a local problem but also a European one – due to the threat of uncontrolled migration from the region if it imploded – and a global one, due to the threat of terrorism; yet, there was no evidence that the groups operating there represented a threat beyond the region itself. Nevertheless, France having convinced its allies to support its intervention in 2013–2014, it was now difficult for Macron to change course, even as the security situation was worsening, because that would be to admit that the strategy had been mistaken[5] (Bertrand, Chafer and Stoddard, 2023). He therefore chose to continue France's military intervention in the Sahel and renew the commitment to the 'war on terror' launched by his predecessor.

Macron thus struggled to bring about the break with the past that he had promised. To be sure, he faced a difficult situation because, by 2017, the security situation in the western Sahel was worse than when Operation Barkhane was launched in 2014, and no exit strategy was in place, hence, the decision to promote the idea of the G5SJF to take over responsibility for counterterrorism operations from French troops. However, for the armies of five of the poorest countries on the planet, lacking military capacity, with no experience of fighting an asymmetric war against non-state, armed groups, nor indeed of joint operations, this was never a realistic prospect. In the end, French military policy in the western Sahel was overtaken by events. Demonstrations against the French military presence increased, and the growing hostility was dramatically illustrated when, in November 2021, protesters held up a French military convoy for several days on its journey through Burkina Faso and Niger (Bensimon and Vincent, 2021). Following the two coups in Mali, the government's decision to invite the Russian private military contractor, Wagner, into the country and the subsequent coup in Burkina Faso in 2022, Macron announced a reconfiguration of the French military presence in the region, with a lighter footprint and French forces only intervening at the express request of the host government (Roger, 2021). However, the reality was that the French intervention had failed to improve human security in Mali and the region and, following the expulsion of French troops from both Mali and Niger, Macron was forced to launch a wide-ranging review of France's military policy. At a press conference at the Elysée Palace on 27 February 2023 (Macron, 2023), he once again sought to reset the relationship, recognising implicitly in so doing the failure of his earlier attempts at a reset (Abboud and Schipani, 2023). He acknowledged an urgent need to rethink France's military presence in Africa and gave an undertaking that there would no longer be any purely French military bases in Africa (apart from Djibouti, which is presented as an Indo-Pacific, rather than an African, base). If implemented, this would signal a major change of policy. He also promised that, in the future, any military bases would be 'co-managed' with host countries, although it is not clear exactly what this might mean in practice nor what the timetable is for achieving this, partly because implementing it will require a thorough revision of the defence and military assistance agreements that France has with African governments. *Affaire à suivre.*

Economic and business policy

As an economic liberal (and former banker), a key priority for President Macron has been to increase economic ties with Africa's largest economies in Africa, such as South Africa, Nigeria and Ethiopia, which is why, in the 15 months after his election, he became the first president to visit the two major anglophone countries in West Africa, Ghana (November 2017) and Nigeria (July 2018). Apart from economic opportunities for French business, he hoped that this would compensate French companies for their declining share of trade with Francophone Africa and help them to free themselves from the networks of *la Françafrique*. Another new initiative was the role envisaged for the African diaspora (not only Francophone) in France. At the 2021 Montpellier Africa–France summit, Macron restated a favourite theme of his – that diasporas are a 'factor of development for Africa' (Destimed, 2021) – and promised changes to the ways in which the *Agence Française de Développement* (AFD) works to promote African enterprise (Caslin, 2021). However, the main issue that dominated the economic and financial relationship with Francophone Africa during Macron's first term was not France's declining share of trade with the region but the continuing argument about the CFA franc and its future.

Concerning economic policy, a report on how 'to relaunch a French economic presence in Africa', jointly commissioned by the Ministry of Foreign Affairs and the Ministry of the Economy and Finance and chaired by former Agriculture Minister Hervé Gaymard, was delivered in April 2019. The context for the report was a steep fall in French businesses' market share in Francophone countries from 25 per cent in 2001 to 15 per cent in 2017 (Gaymard, 2019, p. 17). In a more positive vein, the report suggested that French exports to the continent had doubled (from US $13 billion to $28 billion) to an 'African market whose size had multiplied by four from around $100 to $400 billion' (2019, p. 8). It also noted an upward trend in French foreign direct investment (FDI) in the energy sector in West, Central and Southern Africa, including Anglophone (Nigeria) and Lusophone (Angola) countries (2019, pp. 21–22). With a view to strengthening the position of French business on the continent, the report made 47 proposals, including a recommendation that French overseas development aid (ODA) should support national businesses on the continent more directly (2019, p. 9). To this end, it recommended that the government should 'consider a progressive broadening of the notion of development assistance towards a renewed one of development investments from which each side will benefit' (2019, p. 8). This idea is reminiscent of the notion of *mise en valeur* put forward by Colonial Minister Albert Sarraut 100 years ago, when he advocated investment in the colonies that would be beneficial both to the colonial power and to colonised populations (Sarraut, 1923). This did not happen in 1923 and it remains unclear to what extent it will be implemented, as the impact of this two-fold 'new' French strategy has still to be seen in terms of FDI and trade. This is especially true in French-speaking countries since, significantly, the focus in Paris is continent-wide and not confined to the Franc zone, with Anglophone Africa being specifically targeted. In any case, France does not have sufficient resources alone to make infrastructure investments on the scale needed to make a significant impact and compete with China. This no doubt explains the report's recommendations to jointly identify 'points of common economic interest in Africa between Germany and France' and to persuade the EU to prioritise infrastructure investment, a key priority for the AFD (Gaymard, 2019, p. 9). Thus, as with military policy, Macron's policy on financial assistance to Africa favours a multilateral approach.

Macron has shown an increasing interest in the African diaspora in France, especially in dual nationals who he sees as having the potential to make a significant contribution to Africa's development. Africa receives 70 billion euros per year in remittances from its diasporas, of which 10 billion euros come from France, one of the world's top ten exporters of funds (Baumard, 2019). The idea would be to encourage dual nationals to use these funds – or at least a proportion of them – differently, so that they would not only go to families but would promote development through investment in start-ups and small- and medium-sized companies in Africa. For Macron, these funds could complement French ODA but would also provide a new type of economic link between France and Africa that bypasses the financial channels associated with *Françafrique*.

Finally, under Macron, there has been a significant change of approach to the CFA franc. In December 2019, at a joint press conference in Abidjan, Macron and his Ivoirian counterpart, President Ouattara, announced reforms to the West African CFA franc zone. The CFA has been criticised over many years as a neo-colonial construct – a relic of *Françafrique* whose origins lie in the colonial period – and these criticisms have become stronger and more widespread in recent years (Taylor, 2019). The reforms announced in Abidjan claimed to address three of the most widely made criticisms of the zone. First, the name of the currency would change to the 'Eco' from the CFA franc, considered too redolent of the currency's colonial origins. Second, the requirement for member states of the *Union Economique et Monétaire Ouest-Africaine* (West African Economic and Monetary Union: UEMOA) to deposit 50 per cent of their foreign reserves with the *Banque de France* would be ended. Third, French officials would be withdrawn from the central bank's board ('*L'Obs avec AFP*, 2019). Critics have questioned the significance of these changes. The 'Eco' was the name that ECOWAS had chosen in June 2019 for its planned single currency, and Anglophone members, Nigeria in particular, were affronted that a group of Francophone countries had, from its perspective, hijacked the plan for a West African single currency (Assoko, 2020). As a result, the proposal to rename the currency has, it seems, been dropped, at least for now. Finally, although the requirement to deposit part of their foreign reserves in Paris was removed, as were

French representatives on the central bank's board, they were replaced by a reporting mechanism that enables France's Finance Ministry to maintain its oversight of the zone's finances (Pauron, 2022). Moreover, other features of the zone have remained unchanged: the fixed parity with the euro is maintained, Paris retains its role as guarantor of the currency, and finally, these reforms apply only to the eight UEMOA countries of the West African franc zone and not to the six in the Central African zone.

Macron set out to 'reset' the economic and business relationship between France and Africa. However, as the Gaymard (2019, p. 3) report acknowledges, this requires long-term planning: 'The Franco-African economic relations of 2050 are constructed today'. It is therefore probably too early to judge the impact of his initiatives in this area. One thing Macron has clearly not been able to change is the continuing decline in the importance of trade with Africa, from 30 per cent of France's external trade in 1960 to 6 per cent today (Gaymard, 2019, pp. 16–17). Trade with sub-Saharan Africa has declined and, by 2021, it represented only 2 per cent of France's total external trade (Châtelot and Bensimon, 2023). The effort to increase trade with countries outside Francophone Africa has also had limited success (Glaser and Airault, 2021, pp. 75–80). On the other hand, one notable change is that Macron is the first president to have no minister for 'cooperation' or development in his government (Gaulme, 2021).

Concerning the CFA franc, Macron also wanted to 'reset' the relationship. However, as with military policy, he found himself constrained by a past that he could not change and by the failure to reach an agreement between Franczone member states on the way forward. There are also strong vested interests, particularly among the French-speaking elites and middle classes in Francophone Africa, for the zone to be retained: it facilitates international travel, provides relative price stability for imported goods and ensures that money can be converted freely into a stable international currency. Consequently, the rhetoric of change has overridden, indeed obscured, the lack of substantive change in this area of policy.

Politics

In the political sphere, here again Macron wanted to break with the past by freeing himself from the 'institutional straitjackets' of *la Françafrique* and seeking out new interlocutors (Kessous, 2021). We see this in his pattern of official visits to Africa and in the relationships he has sought to cultivate with civil society, both in Africa and among the African diaspora in France, for example, through the creation in 2017 of the CPA, composed of 11 people, mainly dual nationals and people from civil society chosen by the president to provide him with an 'alternative view' of the continent; this was consistent with Macron's wider approach to Africa policy, in that it bypassed officials and diplomats. Innovation was also discernible in the new format Africa–France summit in Montpellier in 2021, to which no African heads of state were invited. We also see this attempted *'rupture'* at the symbolic level in his efforts at reconciliation with Algeria and in his Ouagadougou speech of 2017, when he praised Thomas Sankara, promised to open the French archives relating to his assassination and vowed to return to Africa cultural artefacts that were taken during the period of colonisation. He also reiterated France's commitment to the promotion of democracy in Africa, a pledge originally made by President Mitterrand at the 1990 La Baule Franco-African summit (Borrel, Boukari-Yabara, Collombat and Deltombe, 2021, pp. 482–485), and to the promotion of *Francophonie*, an organisation of multilateral cooperation between countries using the French language.

As discussed earlier, Macron's first visit to Africa in 2017 was to Mali. However, in attempting to underline his commitment to a change of approach to the continent, he became the first French president to visit the two major Anglophone countries in West Africa – Ghana and Nigeria. Beyond the economic logic to this visit, there was also a political logic. France has had difficult relations with Nigeria dating back to de Gaulle's support for Biafran secession during the Nigerian civil war (1967–1970). By choosing to visit Ghana and Nigeria, Macron wanted to send a message to African political leaders and civil society that France had changed, that it wanted to engage with new interlocutors and establish new partnerships beyond its traditional African *pré carré* (sphere of influence) through culture, sport and economic development. Significantly, therefore, after visiting Nigeria's capital – Abuja – and meeting President Muhammadu Buhari, he travelled to Lagos, where he visited the New Afrika Shrine nightclub, formerly run by the legendary Afrobeat musician Fela Kuti who was frequently put in prison during the 1970s and 1980s for his outspoken criticism of Nigerian military rule. As in Ouagadougou, Macron sought to appeal directly to African youth, to encourage them to get involved in politics: 'Fela was not just a musician. He was a politician who wanted to change society', Macron told the young audience from the stage. 'So if I have one message for young people, it's this: yes, politics is important; yes, be involved' (Mumbere, 2018). During his first term, he also visited Kenya and Ethiopia (March 2019), again both outside France's traditional *pré carré*.

Macron broke with protocol in another way when, on a visit to Algeria during the 2017 presidential election campaign, he described colonisation as a 'crime against humanity', although this was not an unqualified condemnation of colonisation, as he continued: 'While recognising this crime, I do not want us to fall into a culture of guilt (*'culpabilisation'*), which is not at all constructive'. His choice of words nonetheless provoked a reaction from the mainstream and extreme right; François Fillon, for example, condemned his declarations as 'unworthy of a candidate for the presidency of the Republic'

(Berdah, 2017). Once elected, he visited Morocco and then returned to Algeria on an official visit in December 2017, when he repeated that he wanted to 'turn the page' on the past and look towards the future (Sulzer, 2017). Reiterating that he was the first president born after the Algerian War, he sought to engage, as in Ouagadougou, with young people, a point reinforced by the fact that he was accompanied by young entrepreneurs ('*startupeurs*') and figures from the world of culture. He also, in a break with presidential tradition, went for a walkabout in Algiers, talking with people in the street and, in a gesture of reconciliation, laid a wreath at the memorial to the martyrs of the Algerian War. However, the symbolism of his visit and the determination to look to the future could not prevent the resurgence of conflicted memories of a shared past, or contentious issues between the two countries – such as the decision by the French government to further restrict visas for Algerians wishing to visit France (see Chapter 14).

Franco-Rwandan relations have been difficult since the 1994 genocide, when France supported the Habyarimana government held responsible for it. Here again, Macron sought to turn the page on the past and normalise relations. He met President Kagame during the UN General Assembly in September 2017 and again at the International Solar Alliance launch meeting in March 2018 – and then supported Rwanda's Foreign Minister, Louise Mushikiwabo, for the post of Secretary-General of the Organisation Internationale de la Francophonie (OIF). The desire to regularise relations with a country that has made notable economic and social progress since the genocide was clear, and diplomatic relations were restored in 2021 when Macron nominated an ambassador to Kigali for the first time since 1994. Support for Mushikiwabo also reflected Macron's desire for a change of approach in promoting the French language through the OIF. In March 2018, he announced an 'overall plan … to write a new page [in the history] of *Francophonie*' and to 'restore the French language to its rightful place in the world', while also recognising that France is no longer 'the sole owner of its language' (Macron, 2018). Supporting an African to lead the OIF is also consistent with Macron's conviction that the future of *Francophonie* lies in Africa and that its centre of gravity is located 'somewhere around the Congo basin' (Kpoda, 2018).

Franco-African summits have been a leitmotif of French presidencies since Georges Pompidou – and Macron's presidency has been no exception. Having hosted a Paris summit on the financing of African economies, to which over 30 heads of state – not only Francophone – were invited, Macron hosted a new format Africa–France summit in Montpellier on 8 October 2021. This was perhaps the most striking attempt to break out of the 'institutional straitjackets' of the Franco-African relationship. No heads of state were invited; instead, a few carefully selected representatives of civil society, especially young people and people whom Macron considers can deliver change – *les acteurs du changement* (entrepreneurs, intellectuals, researchers, artists, sportspeople and influencers) who could help to redefine the France–Africa relationship – were invited. At the summit, Macron took part in a wide-ranging debate with 15 young Africans, not only from Francophone Africa, in which France found itself criticised for its attitudes – 'its arrogance, its paternalism' – and its practices on the continent. For example, a young Kenyan woman demanded that France put an end to *la Françafrique* and its opaque practices and pointed to the contradictions of French policy, on the one hand promoting democracy, but on the other mired in issues of racism in France itself. The summit concluded with a speech in which Macron sought to focus on the future rather than the past, a future in which France would 'take ownership of its 'Africanity' (*'assume sa part d'africanité'*) thanks to the seven million French people who are 'closely linked, often through family, to Africa' (Bourdillon, 2021). He also promised changes in the traditional political and economic 'cooperation', renaming development aid 'solidarity investment', and that the AFD would be retitled. Finally, he announced the creation of two funds of 30 million euros each, one to promote democracy and the other to develop the continent's digital infrastructure, as well as the restitution to Benin of 26 cultural artefacts taken from the palace in Abomey during colonisation (*Le Monde avec AFP*, 2021; see Chapter 14 for a detailed discussion of this issue).

Thus, Macron's ambition to break with the past and reset Franco-African relations for the future is not in doubt. Yet, his achievements have fallen short of his ambitions. The desire to open up Franco-African relations to countries beyond its traditional *pré carré* dates back to Giscard's presidency, but what is new is the amount of effort that Macron has put into pursuing this objective, notably through his official visits to the continent. However, as Antoine Glaser and Pascal Airault point out, these overtures to non-Francophone Africa have not, thus far, yielded the hoped-for results (Glaser and Airault, 2021, pp. 78–82).

His ambition to change *Francophonie* came up against a similar problem. In 2018, Macron wanted to enlist Alain Mabanckou, an African intellectual and winner of the Renaudot Prize for literature, to contribute to a 'work of reflection' around the French language and *Francophonie*. However, in a very public rebuff, Mabanckou (2018) wrote an open letter to Macron criticising this plan. *Francophonie*, he wrote, 'is unfortunately still seen as the continuation of France's foreign policy in its former colonies'. He went on to criticise 'institutional *Francophonie*', which has never raised its voice against autocratic regimes or rigged elections and continues to tolerate the lack of free speech in Africa, 'orchestrated by monarchs (*sic*) who speak French and subjugate their people *in French*' (emphasis in the original). In short, Macron's plan to promote the French language and reinvigorate *Francophonie* was seen by critics as a renewed expression of French neo-colonialism. His plan to return cultural artefacts to Africa was similarly ambitious, but he subsequently had to scale it back because of the complexity of the issues raised and the resistance it provoked, resulting in what Glaser and Airault (2021, p. 153) have described as a 'minimal restitution of Africa heritage'.

Finally, to what extent did the 2021 Africa–France summit in Montpellier represent a genuine break with the past? The French president certainly wanted it to be radically different. He presented it as part of his effort to 'reshape the Africa–France relationship' and 'entrepreneurship, civil society, diaspora, youth, new technologies, [...] opportunities for economic cooperation were all key words at the heart of the discussions shaping this summit' (Domingues Dos Santos and Schlimmer, 2021). However, despite Macron's stated commitment to the promotion of democracy, there was little time allocated for the discussion of overtly political issues. The format was certainly new, with the focus on invited interlocutors from civil society, not heads of state or diplomats, none of whom were present. Nevertheless, beyond the format, the summit can still be seen as falling within a long tradition of Franco-African summitry. In this respect, at least, it seems that old habits – and practices – die hard.

Presidential style and policy errors

President Macron's Ouagadougou speech, in front of 800 students, was billed as marking an important moment in the development of a new partnership with Africa, when he would set out the main points of his new Africa policy. He did, indeed, announce some important changes. Yet the speech is remembered by many across the region for his joke made at the expense of the Burkinabè President, Roch Marc Christian Kaboré, which was seen as patronising and disrespectful because of Macron's use of the familiar *tu* form when speaking to him (Bensimon *et al.*, 2023). Likewise, Macron's decision to summon the leaders of the G5 Sahel to Pau to 'clarify their position concerning French military operations in the region', as discussed earlier, went down equally badly (Kpatindé, 2020). The form and tone of the summons came across to African leaders – both in the region and beyond – as condescending and paternalistic (Châtelot and Bensimon, 2023). His decision not to invite any African heads of state or government to the Africa–France summit in Montpellier was also experienced as disrespectful and was not well received.

The perceived arrogance of Macron's tone and style has thus been at odds with his ambition to establish a new Franco-African partnership. His presidency has also been marked by a series of policy errors and missteps that have led many Africans to question his commitment to change. The inconsistency in his responses to military coups – no sanctions against the coup-makers in Guinea (2021), Chad (2021) and Gabon (2023) but vociferous condemnation of those responsible for the coups in Mali (2021), Burkina Faso (2022) and Niger (2023) – has led many Africans to question both France's commitment to democracy on the continent and the real motives for the French presence in the region. Similarly, the decision to attend the late Chadian dictator Idriss Déby's funeral – the only Western leader to do so – added to anti-French sentiment in the country and the region, as discussed earlier.

His handling of the military governments of Mali, Burkina Faso and Niger after the military coups has been marked by a series of missteps that have further undermined France's position in the region, strengthening the position of the military juntas and hardening anti-French sentiment in public opinion. His public support for the Economic Community of West African States' (ECOWAS) threat of military action against the coup-makers in Niger, which was later dropped, was a godsend, as it solidified the (false) portrayal by the juntas of ECOWAS as a French stooge doing France's bidding. The subsequent decisions – the cancelling of aid, the closure of French consulates and the refusal to issue visas (making it impossible for students, artists, musicians and business people to go to France) and the subsequent closure of the French *lycée* in Niamey – were seen as punishing the local population, further playing into the hands of the juntas by stoking anti-French feeling in the region (Olivier de Sardan, 2024). Finally, the quiet abolition in March 2022 of the Presidential Council for Africa (CPA), which Macron had created in 2017, suggests that he did not attach sufficient value to the alternative views of the continent with which he had been provided by its members (Assemblée Nationale, 2022, p. 55).

Conclusion

Prior to the election in 2017, Macron made clear his ambition to set Franco-African relations on a new footing. Once elected, he quickly set out his stall, making a series of pronouncements about the changes he wanted to bring about. As a (neo)liberal, he wanted to break down the 'closed shops' of *la Françafrique*, put an end to its often-occult networks and 'normalise' France's relationship with the continent. He wanted to leave the past behind; his gaze was determinedly turned towards the future and how to support the building of a (neo)liberal Africa. Hence, for example, his courting of African entrepreneurs and start-ups, his efforts to get French businesses more involved in Africa beyond the traditional French *pré carré* and to promote Western-style democracy. Thus, at Ouagadougou, he stated that he was no longer willing to rely on the eternal rule of autocrats, and he has repeatedly sought to promote African civil society, emphasising his support for the democratic youth in Africa. He has sought to mobilise the African diaspora in France to back his ambition for a new relationship with Africa and is the first president to name a French citizen of African origin as an ambassador on the continent (Jules-Armand Aniambossou was appointed ambassador to Uganda in 2019 and subsequently to Ghana in 2022). The plan to return cultural objects to Africa, albeit hitherto in limited numbers, should also be noted.

To further these ambitions, there has, on the face of it, been a significant change in terms of presidential discourse and method. Yet France has a long history of involvement with Africa, especially North-West, West and Central Africa, which in many ways intensified after political independence. For all his focus on the future, he could not escape this past. The result is that style has often triumphed over substance; despite the emphasis on change, there have been many continuities with the past in Macron's Africa policy. Indeed, as Macron himself admitted in an interview in 2020: 'You're not going to change a 70-year-old system in a matter of three years, that would only be aiming for a quick fix' (Institut Montaigne, 2020). Moreover, because of Africa's continuing geopolitical significance for France and the importance it has traditionally attached to Francophone African votes at the UN as a multiplier of French power on the global stage, Macron could not simply overturn the 'special relationship' with Africa, particularly in a context in which France's presence and leverage on the continent are being challenged not only by China and Russia but also by new external actors such as India, Turkey and the Gulf states. Furthermore, France is often considered by its allies as an 'African power', and there is therefore an expectation, among its allies at the UN but also among some African leaders, that France will take the lead in dealing with security issues in its 'backyard'. These factors – and the fact that France's presence and activism on the African continent remain central to its global power status – are the structural givens which are at the root of the path dependencies that shape Macron's Africa policy.

These structural constraints on change have been compounded by what is perceived on the continent as the president's arrogance and by a series of policy errors and missteps, which have led to a growing rejection of what many Africans see as French interference on the continent. Its military presence, the maintenance of the CFA franc, its incoherent policy on the promotion of democracy and the continuing demonstrations of paternalistic attitudes towards Africa among its governing elites have been particular bones of contention for Francophone African intellectuals and many of the younger generation of Africans. The frequency of anti-French street demonstrations and campaigns in the press and on social media during his presidency suggests that Macron has not only failed to set the country's relationship with the continent on a new footing but may actually have made it more difficult, at least in the short term, to achieve this aim.

Notes

1 The CFA (*Colonies françaises d'Afrique*) franc was created in 1945 as the currency of France's colonial empire in sub-Saharan Africa. Today it refers to two currencies, the West African CFA franc, used in eight West African countries, where CFA stands for *Communauté financière en Afrique* and the Central African CFA *franc*, used in six Central African countries, where CFA now stands for *Coopération financière en Afrique*.
2 See Antil (2020) for the background to the establishment of the G5 Sahel.
3 A further military coup took place in France's African '*pré carré*' – in Gabon – in August 2023. This is discussed in the final section.
4 These include the UN MINUSMA peacekeeping mission (France was the penholder for the UN Security Council resolution establishing the mission in Mali in 2013), the EU's Training Mission in Mali (EUTM-Mali), its Capacity Building Missions in the Sahel (EUCAP Sahel Niger and Mali) and the International Coalition for the Sahel. France was also the driving force behind the establishment of the G5SJF (Desgrais 2018; Dieng et al., 2020).
5 Interview with a policy officer, European External Action Service, Brussels, April 2022.

References

Abboud, L. and Schipani, A. (2023) 'Emmanuel Macron embarks on African tour as France seeks to redefine its role', *Financial Times*, 27 February.
Antil, A. (2020) 'Le G5 Sahel et le concept de "sécurité-développement"', *Recherches Internationales*, 117, pp. 59–74.
Assemblée Nationale (2022) *Projet de rapport d'information sur les relations entre la France et l'Afrique*. Paris: Commission des Affaires Etrangères.
Assoko, J. (2020) 'Réforme du franc CFA: comment la fracture sur l'eco a éclaté au grand jour au sein de la Cedeao', *Jeune Afrique*, 21 January.
Barma, A.Y. (2017) 'G5 Sahel: Macron en VRP, l'Arabie Saoudite promet 100 millions de dollars', *La Tribune Afrique*, 5 December.
Baumard, M. (2019) 'La diaspora africaine de France envoie-t-elle ses 10 milliards annuels à la bonne adresse?', *Le Monde Afrique*, 24 January.
Bensimon, C. and Vincent, E. (2021). 'Au Sahel, un convoi de l'armée française face à la colère populaire'. *Le Monde*, 30 November.
Bensimon, C., Ricard, P., Vincent, E. and Châtelot, C. (2023) 'La politique africaine d'Emmanuel Macron: histoire d'une rupture', *Le Monde*, 4 November.
Ben Yahmed, M. (2017). 'Emmanuel Macron: "J'agirai en Afrique en toute transparence, loin des réseaux de connivence"', *JeuneAfrique*, 14 April.
Berdah, A. (2017) 'En Algérie, Macron dénonce la colonisation: "C'est un crime contre l'humanité"', *Le Figaro*, 15 February.
Bertrand, E., Chafer, T. and Stoddard, E. (2024) '(Dis)utilities of force in a postcolonial context: Explaining the strategic failure of the French-led intervention in Mali', *Journal of Intervention and State-Building*, 18(3), pp. 286–305.
Borrel, T., Boukari-Yabara, A., Collombat, B. and Deltombe, T. (2021) *L'empire qui ne veut pas mourir. Une histoire de la Françafrique*. Paris: Seuil.
Bourdillon, Y. (2021) 'Emmanuel Macron veut que la France assume "sa part d'africanité"', *Les Echos*, 9 October.
Carayol, R. (2023) *Le mirage sahélien*. Paris: La Decouverte.
Caslin, O. (2021) 'Afrique-France: à Montpellier, Emmanuel Macron prend une série d'engagements', *Jeune Afrique*, 8 October.

Chafer, T., Cumming, G.D. and van der Velde, R. (2020) 'France's interventions in Mali and the Sahel: A historical institutionalist perspective', *Journal of Strategic Studies*, 43(4), pp. 482–507.

Châtelot, C. and Bensimon, C. (2023) 'France-Afrique, la cassure', *Le Monde*, 2 November.

D'Alançon, F. (2019) 'Opération Barkhane: Emmanuel Macron réclame un appui clair des pays du Sahel', *La Croix*, 5 December.

Debos, M. (2019) 'Que fait l'armée française au Tchad?', *Libération*, 8 February.

Desgrais, N. (2018) 'La force conjointe du G5 Sahel, nouveau mythe de Sisyphe?' *The Conversation*, 17 July. https://theconversation.com/la-force-conjointe-du-g5-sahel-nouveau-mythe-de-sisyphe-99803.

Destimed (2021) 'Nouveau sommet à Montpellier: Jour 1 de nouvelles relations Afrique-France?', 14 October, available at: https://destimed.fr/Nouveau-Sommet-a-Montpellier-Jour-1-de-nouvelles-relations-Afrique-France.

Dieng, M., Onguny, P. and Ghouenzen Mfondi, A. (2020) 'Leadership without membership: France and the G5 Sahel Joint Force', *African Journal of Terrorism and Insurgency Research*, 1(2), pp. 21-41.

Domingues Dos Santos, E. and Schlimmer, S. (2021) 'New Africa France Summit: the concealed continuation of Emmanuel Macron's Africa policy', *Editoriaux de l'IFRI*, 27 October, available at: https://www.ifri.org/en/publications/editoriaux-de-lifri/lafrique-questions/new-africa-france-summit-concealed-continuation.

Dossier Emmanuel Macron et l'Afrique (2017) *Jeune Afrique*, 30 April.

Faivre, A. (2017) 'Face au discours de Macron à Ouagadougou, l'Afrique attend de voir', *Le Point*, 29 November.

Gaulme, F. (2021) 'La politique africaine de la France: l'heure du renouvellement?', *Etudes*, 4(April), pp. 7–17.

Gaymard, H. (2019) *Relancer la présence économique française en Afrique: urgence d'une ambition collective à long terme*. Paris: Ministère de l'Europe et des Affaires Étrangères/Ministère de l'Économie et des Finances.

Glaser, A. and Airault, P. (2021) *Le piège africain de Macron: du continent à l'Hexagone*. Paris: Fayard.

Haidara, B. (2020) 'Pourquoi l'opinion publique malienne a une vision négative de l'opération Barkhane', *The Conversation*, 10 February. https://theconversation.com/pourquoi-lopinion-publique-malienne-a-une-vision-negative-de-loperation-barkhane-130640.

Hewlett, N. and Kuhn, R. (2022) 'Reflections on the 2022 elections in France', *Modern and Contemporary France*, 30(4), pp. 393–409.

Institut Montaigne (2020) 'Macron in Africa: letting go, not going anywhere', 20 May.

International Crisis Group (2019) 'Rebel incursion exposes Chad's weaknesses', 13 February.

Kessous, M. (2021) 'Les diasporas, l'autre ambition de la politique africaine d'Emmanuel Macron', *Le Monde*, 29 October.

Kpatindé, F. (2020) 'A Pau, pour parler du Sahel, des "doyens ouest-africains" agacés par le "petit frère" Macron', *Le Monde*, 13 January.

Kpoda, Z. (2018) 'Secrétariat général de l'OIF: les Africains feront-ils barrage à la réélection de Michaelle Jean?', *L'Observateur Paalga*, 10 May.

Larcher, L. (2021) 'Sahel: Emmanuel Macron annonce la fin de l'opération Barkhane', *La Croix*, 10 June.

Le Monde avec AFP (2021) 'A Montpellier, Emmanuel Macron annonce la création d'un fonds pour le développement de la démocratie en Afrique', *Le Monde*, 8 October.

L'Obs avec AFP (2019) 'Ce que va changer la fin du franc CFA annoncée par Macron et Ouattara', 23 December.

Mabanckou, A. (2018) 'Francophonie, langue française: lettre ouverte à Emmanuel Macron', *L'Obs*, 20 March.

Macron, E. (2017) 'Discours d'Emmanuel Macron à l'université de Ouagadougou', 28 November, available at: https://www.elysee.fr/emmanuel-macron/2017/11/28/discours-demmanuel-macron-a-luniversite-de-ouagadougou

Macron, E. (2018) 'Une ambition pour la langue française et le plurilinguisme', 20 March, available at: https://www.diplomatie.gouv.fr/en/french-foreign-policy/francophony-and-the-french-language/france-s-commitment-to-the-french-language/

Macron, E. (2020) 'Conférence de presse conjointe à l'issue du Sommet de Pau', 13 January, available at: https://www.elysee.fr/emmanuel-macron/2020/01/13/sommet-de-pau-declaration-conjointe-des-chefs-detat

Macron, E. (2023) 'Discours du président: le partenariat Afrique–France', 27 February, available at: https://www.elysee.fr/emmanuel-macron/2023/02/27/discours-du-president-de-la-republique-dans-la-perspective-de-son-prochain-deplacement-en-afrique-centrale

Melly, P. (2021) 'Relations Afrique–France: pourquoi la France fait face à tant de colère en Afrique de l'Ouest', *BBC News Afrique*, 7 December.

Mumbere, D. (2018) '"Join politics": Macron tells Nigerian youth to emulate music legend Fela Kuti', *AfricaNews*, 4 July.

Olivier de Sardan, J.-P. (2024) 'Macron ou la catastrophe africaine', *AOC*, 8 February, available at: https://aoc.media/opinion/2024/02/07/macron-ou-la-catastrophe-africaine/

Pauron, M. (2022) 'Franc CFA: "Une réforme administrative, pas monétaire"', *AfriqueXXI*, 7 April.

Pigeaud, F. and Sylla, N.S. (2021) *Africa's last colonial currency. The CFA Franc story*. London: Pluto Press.

Roger, B. (2021) 'Sahel: Macron annonce la fin de l'opération Barkhane sous sa forme actuelle', *Jeune Afrique*, 10 June.

Sarraut, A. (1923) *La mise en valeur des colonies françaises*. Paris: Payot.

Soyez, N. (2022) 'Le Mali quitte le G5 Sahel: quel avenir pour une organisation régionale déjà fragile?', *TV5 Monde*, 16 May.

Sulzer, A. (2017) 'En Algérie, le jeune Emmanuel Macron au défi des vieux dossiers', *L'Express*, 4 December.

Taylor, I. (2019) 'France à fric: the CFA zone in Africa and neocolonialism', *Third World Quarterly*, 40(6), pp. 1064–1088.

Vallin, V. (2015) 'France as the gendarme of Africa, 1960–2014', *Political Science Quarterly*, 130(1), pp. 79–101.

Verschave, F.-X. (1998) *La Françafrique: le plus long scandale de la République*. Paris: Stock.

14
MACRON'S NEW BEGINNING: COMING TO TERMS WITH THE COLONIAL PAST THROUGH RESTITUTION, RECOGNITION AND EMPATHY

Martin Evans

Abstract

Under his tenure, Emmanuel Macron has invested a huge effort into addressing the painful legacies of French colonialism in general and the Algerian War in particular, so that coming to terms with the colonial past has become a defining dimension of his presidency. This chapter analyses the political calculations behind this very high-profile process. It assesses why Macron saw himself as the first Head of State to properly be able to do this, principally because he is the first president born after the end of the French Empire in 1960 and after the end of the Algerian War in 1962. The chapter focuses on two key processes enacted by President Macron: the first, over the restitution of African objects acquired during colonialism and the second, over truth and reconciliation in respect to the Algerian War. It focuses on how Macron used cultural diplomacy, through restitution, to try to turn the page of the French Empire and open up a new era of postcolonial relations with sub-Saharan Africa and Algeria. In conclusion, the chapter considers Macron's initiatives, in particular the specific emotional language he has used, within a broader global history of confronting difficult pasts.

> Memorial issues are at the heart of the life of nations. Whether they are used, repressed or assumed, they say something about what you want to do with your country and your geopolitics.
> (Emmanuel Macron speaking to journalists from *Le Monde*, *Le Figaro* and Radio J on the return night flight from an official visit to Israel, 24 January 2020 –Smolar, 2020)

DOI: 10.4324/9781003323259-14

Introduction

Coming to terms with colonialism in general and the Algerian War in particular has been a defining aspect of Emmanuel Macron's presidency. Specifically, he has presented his age and his lack of connection to this past as the opportunity to re-set the historical dial in respect to France's Africa policy and, especially, Franco-Algerian relations. Then, in turn, he has connected this generational re-set over Africa to reconciliation within France, not just in terms of the societal groups the most affected by the consequences of the Algerian War but also in respect to what Macron has claimed is the ongoing link between the alienation of French citizens of Algerian heritage and the growth of homegrown Islamist 'separatism' – and, by extension, terrorism.

As such, Macron's determination to confront colonialism is part of a wider shift in the past–present dynamics within French society. Throughout the 19th century and the first half of the 20th century, one dominant dynamic was driven by conflicting narratives about the meaning of the 1789 Revolution, which, after 1918, was joined by the past–present dynamic over the memory of World War One. Then, in 1945, these dynamics shifted to World War Two, in particular in the wake of the student revolt of the late 1960s that challenged the dominant Gaullist and Communist resistance narratives, both of which played down collaboration in order to project an image of themselves as the leaders of the mass French Resistance movement. Now, however, since the beginning of the 21st century, these dynamics have shifted again to focus on the French Empire and, in particular, the Algerian War – one which Macron has inscribed into the nation's memorial culture during his first presidential term.

At the most basic level, Macron saw this processing of France's problematic colonial past as a response to the denial, since the end of the Algerian War, of successive presidents who, through official amnesia, had sought to forget the divisions of the whole decolonisation process. In Macron's view, this denial has ultimately been damaging since it has stopped France from facing up to a necessary truth: this past is a massive history – after all, the French Empire was only second in scale to the British, which is still present and continues to shape society – as well as the on-going relationship with the former African colonies, as discussed in this volume by Tony Chafer (Chapter 13).

Furthermore, for Macron, this unfolding past–present colonial dynamic is particularly acute when it comes to Algeria, due to the longevity of colonial rule (132 years), the fact that Algeria was administered as an integral part of France, the presence of 1 million settlers out of a population of 10 million in 1954 and the violent nature of French Algeria's final *dénouement*. This had more far-reaching consequences than the other moments of

French decolonisation, be they the end of the Fourth Republic, the engagement of conscripts, the 'return' of the settlers or the massacres of pro-French Algerians (Evans, 2012). Then, each of these specific groups became involved in fashioning their own memory narratives of the Algerian War, to which must be added Algerians (numbering 436,000 in July 1962) whose descendants – born in France over the ensuing decades – had the right to French citizenship.

For Macron, therefore, a crucial dimension of his policy has been addressing each of these narratives to consider what they say about France now and how they can be brought together through a process of reconciliation. In this way, Macron is reconnecting with the presidency, between 1995 and 2007, of Jacques Chirac, who he sees as a model in terms of the politics of memory. After all, it was Chirac who, having officially recognised the Vichy Regime's role in the Holocaust, went on to recognise that what took place in Algeria between 1954 and 1962 had the status of war – a word withheld at the time in favour of 'law and order' problem. Chirac then inaugurated national *Harki Day* on 25 September 2001 in order to commemorate the suffering of pro-French Algerians – *les harkis* (derived from the Arab word for movement), the term used to designate Algerian units recruited by the French army. This process of reconciliation slowed down under President Sarkozy before being revived under President Hollande and then really reignited under Macron.

Given this importance, this chapter assesses the political calculations behind Macron's coming to terms with the colonial past. It examines the purpose of the process, his method, the reactions and the concrete outcomes. The conclusion evaluates how his intervention sits within a wider global history of countries coming to terms with problematic pasts.

Election 2017: from candidate to president

The fact that Algeria became a central part of Macron's political vision can be traced back to his visit to Algiers in mid-February 2017 as a presidential candidate. Interviewed on the Algerian television channel *Echorouk News* on 15 February, Macron condemned past French actions in Algeria. By 21st-century standards of human rights, these actions, he stated, would be termed as 'crimes against humanity' that, he underlined, France had to confront. Apologising, he stated:

> Colonisation is part of French history. It's a crime, it's a crime against humanity, it's real barbarism. And it's part of that past that we have to face up to, apologising to those towards whom we have committed these acts.
>
> *(Le Monde/AFP, 2017)*

By any stretch of the imagination, these words were unambiguous; when posted online, there was uproar from his main rival, Marine Le Pen, leader of the far-right National Front. For her, this was an anti-patriotic act of self-flagellation designed to ingratiate himself with French voters of immigrant origin and made even more shameful because he uttered these words in Algeria.

This attack prompted Macron to clarify his remarks. Confronted a few days later with angry protestors in Toulon, in the south of France, home to a large number of *pieds-noirs* (former settlers who left Algeria after independence and their descendants), he defended himself on the grounds that he had not meant to say that those who were living in Algeria and who served in the French army were guilty of 'crimes against humanity'. Instead, he contended, it was about recognising the responsibility of the French state.

In defending his comments thus, Macron did not concede any substantive ground to his opponents on the right and far right. Rather, he opened up a clear dividing line over the Algerian War between himself and Le Pen, which meant that the Algerian question became a defining issue in Macron's campaign.

In 2017, Macron won an emphatic mandate, which he immediately seized upon to honour his promise to confront colonialism and the Algerian War. In specific terms, this policy was based upon a three-pronged approach, where the first stage was a presidential pronouncement, the second, a detailed report and the third, a concrete action.

Museums and memory: the Sarr–Savoy report

This three-stage approach was first laid out over the restitution of sub-Saharan African objects in French museums, a long-standing issue that Macron sought to resolve through his speech at the University of Ouagadougou in Burkina Faso in November 2017 (Macron, 2017). With the Head of State, Roch Marc Christian Kaboré, at Macron's side, this intervention was a carefully staged piece of political theatre. By addressing an audience of 800 students, it underlined his desire to engage directly with the future generation through a far-reaching speech that lasted over one and a half hours, followed by 40 minutes of questions.

On one level, his address represented diplomatic continuity: traditionally the first presidential official visit outside of Europe is always to sub-Saharan Francophone Africa, which is then used as a platform to strengthen Franco-African ties. However, on another level, it was a dramatic break. Deploying all his oratorical skills, his words articulated a new vision of Franco-African relations. From now on, he claimed, this relationship would be more open and equal. It would dispense with the networks of corruption that had marred post-independence Franco-African relations since 1960. Significantly, too, he promised, this would be a relationship based upon historical honesty; one that recognised the need for truth both in terms of specific episodes – such as the controversial French role in the Rwandan genocide of the mid-1990s – and the wider recognition of colonialism as a crime. Here, Macron presented his condemnation of colonialism as a generational shift:

> I am, like you, from a generation which never knew Africa as a colonised continent. I am from a generation for which one of the most beautiful memories was the victory of Nelson Mandela and his fight against apartheid. I am from a generation of French people for whom the crimes of European colonisation cannot be disputed and are part of our history.
> *(2017, para. 9/10)*

On this basis, the most dramatic aspect of the speech was his recognition of the need to restitute African objects in French possession: 'I want, within five years, the conditions to be met for the temporary or permanent restitution of African heritage in Africa' (Macron, 2017, para. 136). It was a historic moment. Now Macron became the first president to support the return of African artefacts. None of his predecessors had taken such a stance. Even Chirac, who established the Quai Branly Museum as a museum of indigenous objects committed to an equal dialogue across different global cultures, was adamant that these objects, no matter how they had been acquired, must remain the property of the French state.

These forceful words were then backed up by the commissioning of a report in March 2018 to be compiled by two experts in the field: Felwine Sarr and Bénédicte Savoy (2018). Sarr is a Senegalese writer and economist, while Savoy is a historian of French art. There then followed months of collaborative work between France and the former sub-Saharan colonies in the form of meetings, workshops and online conversations that culminated in a report presented to the president in November entitled *The Restitution of African Cultural Heritage. Toward a New Relational Ethics.*

In considering the restitution of African objects, the report is clear that the focus here is on sub-Saharan Africa. Stating that Algeria needs a separate, stand-alone study, the report underlines the singularity of sub-Saharan Africa, given the intensity of the cultural violence at stake. Since according to the report, approximately 90 per cent of all cultural heritage from sub-Saharan Africa is held in Western collections, with no other continent suffering from this scale of dispossession, the result is an imbalance where African museums have few African objects to display, while European museums have so many, including huge amounts in storage. This imbalance, the report argues, explains why the question of cultural redress is so pressing; Sarr and Savoy see the solution as twofold – the timely restitution of artefacts must go hand-in-hand with the development of a new methodology that is based upon collaboration guided by 'dialogue, polyphony and exchange' (2018, p. 18).

The report is divided into three chapters: *To Restitute*, *Restitutions and Collections* and *Accompanying the Returns*, each of which addresses the complex legal, historical and cultural questions at stake. At the core of the report is a new framework for restitution based upon a cooperative methodology. Here, the authors suggest both the criteria for restitution as well as a concrete timetable for the French and African authorities to follow. Significantly, this timetable is not immediate but gradual. Nor does it recommend a sweeping return of all African cultural heritage from France. Rather, Sarr and Savoy state that the case for permanent restitution depends upon the specific context of acquisition: if the objects were illegally acquired, there must be permanent restitution. For them, this means those objects that arrived in France because of three specific contexts: war booty from colonial military campaigns, 'scientific' expeditions and donations to museums from colonial soldiers and administrators. The report contains an inventory of these specific contexts and recommends, in the form of bold lettering, that the French government is open to restitution. This, they propose, must be done through bilateral diplomatic arrangements to be made with African governments, based on proposals by African experts.

The report also contains a comprehensive appendix that outlines the methodological process followed by Sarr and Savoy, supported by documents, charts and figures on the collections in France as well as information on museums in Africa. A key part of this appendix is a detailed inventory of the 88,000 objects from sub-Saharan Africa, of which approximately 70,000 are held in the Quai Branly Museum in Paris, which explains why this institution occupies such a central position in the report.

Responses and outcomes

Through the report, Macron sought to place France at the vanguard of restitution amongst European countries. With the use of 'culture', he wished to position France at the cutting edge of diplomatic relations with Africa and, on this basis, the Ministry of Culture and the Ministry of Europe and Foreign Affairs jointly organised a forum – 'African heritages: succeeding together our new cultural cooperation' – in July 2019, which brought together French and European professionals. Using the report as a starting point, the forum discussed what a new approach to European cultural relations with the African continent should look like, one where African heritage must continue to be showcased in Africa *and* Europe.

With this new approach, the forum underlined that museum practice is not simply about returning objects. Restitution is seen as one issue amongst many that also include the development of exchanges between French museums and African institutions, the circulation of objects, the strengthening of partnerships in terms of training, the need to better document the exact nature of the African collections in Europe and the challenge of transmitting to the French public the history of African works preserved in French museums. As a measure of its ambition, the French government underlined that all the key cultural institutions – the Louvre Museum, the National Heritage Institute, the RMN-Grand Palais and the Quai Branly Museum – would play a leading role in building this cultural cooperation: a new common imaginary that would be a model to the rest of the world. In the wake of this forum, a process was put in place, where policy leads to action properly recognised by the law. On this basis, it was decided that each request would be examined on a case-by-case basis by the competent French authorities in consultation with the requesting state and the relevant cultural and scientific actors concerned.

Following this schema, the first concrete act of restitution was the return from the Quai Branly Museum to Benin of 26 works taken by the French Army in 1892 from King Béhanzin's palace during the conflict with the Fon Kingdom of Dahomey in West Africa. The second was then a long-term loan to Senegal of the sword of El Hadj Omar Tall – a 19th-century Islamic scholar and military commander – and its scabbard, preserved by the Army Museum. According to Sarr and Savoy's criteria, these were two unambiguous examples of objects acquired as spoils of war through colonial conquest and, in both cases, restitution was facilitated by a new law passed in December 2020. In September 2021, this process was further enhanced by a publicly accessible digital research webpage published by the *Institut National d'Histoire de l'Art* (INHA), which provides access to an annotated map of objects from Africa and Oceania in more than 240 French public collections, a digital catalogue that opens the way to further requests from African countries.

Algeria

Over Algeria, Macron's actions did not begin with a report but, rather, with a symbolic act in September 2018: a personal apology to Josette Audin, the 87-year-old widow of Maurice Audin, the anti-colonialist militant who disappeared at the height of the Algerian War in Algiers in 1957. Sitting with her and their two children, Michèle and Pierre, in her fifth-floor flat in the Paris suburbs, surrounded by a small entourage of journalists, politicians and historians, Macron recognised the French Republic's responsibility for Audin's death in custody and asked for forgiveness. It was a historic gesture. Although his predecessor, François Hollande, had admitted that Audin died in detention, Macron's apology went much further. Deploying the full weight of presidential protocol, his (2018) letter to Mme Audin recognised that Audin's disappearance was the result of the special powers accorded to the French Army by a parliamentary vote in March 1956: the first time a French president had officially acknowledged that the French Army carried out systematic torture, sanctioned and backed up by the French legal system. He also announced that archives would be fully opened to historians, families and organisations seeking the truth about the Algerian War.

In initiating this reconciliation process, Macron looked to the guidance of France's most well-known historian of Algeria: Benjamin Stora. On one level, this choice was very different to that of Sarr and Savoy. He was much older – 66 in 2017 – and his profile was more established, in terms of publications, numerous televised documentaries as well as regular media appearances commenting on this history. He had also worked at the Ministry of Education and was appointed by the Socialist President François Hollande to be Chair of the Research Committee of the French National Museum of the History of Immigration between 2014 and 2019. However, given his Algerian Jewish heritage – born in Constantine in 1951 – and as a former stalwart of the Trotskyist Movement, who joined the Socialist Party in the mid-1970s, this choice was condemned in National Front circles, for whom he was a historian with a left-wing agenda.

Yet, the reason why Macron chose Stora rather than one of the younger historians of the Algerian War – such as Sylvie Thénault or Raphaëlle Branche – is in part due to his approach. For Stora, the Algerian War is a symptom of a colonial syndrome that mirrors the country's problems in acknowledging the Vichy Regime's collaboration with the Nazi occupation (1991). In his view, France is a society in denial over the Algerian War and, through his work, he has long sought to overcome this amnesia – an approach that has framed much of Macron's understanding of the Algerian question. Drawing upon Stora, Macron wanted to achieve a healing process between, on an international stage, France and Algeria and then, within France, all the different communities directly affected by Algeria.

Alongside Audin, the other high-profile gesture of reconciliation was the restitution of 24 Algerian skulls dating from initial French colonisation, whose existence had come to light in the early 2010s when Ali Farid Belkadi, an Algerian historian, discovered them in a shoebox in the archives of the Museum of Mankind in Paris. His campaign for repatriation culminated in the Algerian government making a request to Macron for their return shortly after his 2017 victory, a demand to which Macron immediately agreed, seeing this as a first step in his policy of Franco-Algerian *rapprochement*. On this basis, a French-Algerian committee was set up in late 2018 to catalogue the remains that could be returned and, by June 2020, it had identified 24 to be sent back out of a total of 45.

However, the research was cut short by Macron's office, principally because he wanted the skulls returned by 5 July 2020, Algeria's Independence Day, in a bid to curry favour with his Algerian counterpart, President Abdelmadjid Tebboune. Macron's hope was that this gesture would persuade the Algerian president to collaborate in his more ambitious efforts at Franco-Algerian reconciliation. Consequently, the bones were returned under a hastily drawn-up agreement signed by both governments in June 2020, which stated that the remains had been loaned to Algeria 'for a period of five years', pending a proper restitution enshrined in law.

Macron's intervention meant that the way was open for a full Algerian state ceremony bringing the skulls back, which began when they were flown into Algiers from France. At Algiers airport, the remains were given a heroes' welcome by a military guard of honour and by President Tebboune, who bowed in front of each coffin while a Muslim cleric recited a prayer for the dead. The coffins were then put on public display at the Palace of Culture before being buried in a special funeral on the 58th anniversary of independence.

The Stora Report

Macron declared that the return of the remains was a gesture of 'friendship', which was part of his wider efforts to 'reconcile the memories of the French and Algerian people' (Macron, 2020). In this sense, the return of the skulls was part of a careful choreography by Macron. Through this gesture, he hoped that Tebboune would cooperate on the centrepiece of his Algeria strategy: the commissioning of Benjamin Stora, just three weeks later, to compile a special report on Algeria.

Stora immediately began working on the report, which he presented personally to Macron on the steps of the Elysée in January 2021 in front of the assembled media. The report was a weighty document of some 160 pages that was quickly published on the Elysée website and then as a book (Stora, 2021). In style, this report is very different to that of Sarr and Savoy. Jointly authored, their report was the product of a collective process of reflection, whereas Stora worked alone. There was no collaborative framework, whereby other people, either historians or people directly affected by the war, could have input into the process of reflection. Instead, he worked alone, a method that was reflected in the fact that the report bore his name. The result, therefore, was very much about his own knowledge, experience and approach, which has come to see the impact of Algeria upon French society in terms of a painful psychological history that needs to be addressed.

Written in measured prose, the report's tone is balanced, as seen in the choice of the first two quotes: one by Albert Camus – the French settler who rose to become a world-famous writer and was killed in a car crash in January 1960 – and the other by Mouloud Feraoun, the Algerian intellectual assassinated by an extremist settler organisation in March 1962. Both are unconventional figures. In January 1956, Camus sought to stop the cycle of violence with a Civil Truce, while Feraoun – although a supporter of independence – felt ill at ease with some of the violence of the FLN (National Liberation Front). By citing the two together, Stora is, therefore, self-consciously foregrounding voices from the Algerian War itself, which he sees as humane and open to dialogue, thereby framing his own perspective.

The first section explores the memorial landscape in the two countries, shaped by both the exceptional violence of the Algerian War and its longevity. Noting that, unlike France and Germany, there is neither a common school textbook nor a friendship treaty, Stora examines the two different official memorial narratives in France and Algeria. In France, the official narrative has been defined by forgetting. During the conflict, French governments withheld the word 'war'. Indeed, it was not until 1999 that the French state recognised that what took place in Algeria *was* a war. The consequence of this official amnesia, Stora argues, has been a proliferation of separate community narratives from below, from settlers, veterans or French citizens of Algerian heritage, each of which eschews mutual understanding in favour of an assertion of their group identity. Invariably, he argues, each narrative invokes some sense of victimhood coupled with a quest for justice and recognition. In contrast, in Algeria, the memory of the Algerian War is one of hyper-memory. It is the foundation stone of the post-independence state. Memorials to the 'one and a half million martyrs' are everywhere, while the state calendar is defined by a constant cycle of commemorative events relating to 'the Algerian Revolution'. For Stora, the challenge is how to achieve reconciliation in this charged climate, especially since many of these memorial narratives are so unwilling to listen to other narratives or engage with the complexities of history.

The second section focuses on inter-state relations and, here, Stora charts the different interventions by successive French presidents and civil society groups in the two countries. Thus, de Gaulle's ideological position of casting himself as the great decoloniser in Algeria gave way to muted pragmatism under Pompidou, Giscard and Mitterrand, who avoided any ideas of a grandiose reconciliation in favour of practical issues of the economy and migration. It was not until the arrival of Jacques Chirac as president in 1995 that the Elysée Palace engaged with the question of memory at a state level, which resulted in a number of high-profile gestures already outlined, as well as Chirac's state visit to Algeria in 2003. This visit, in particular, seemed to put Franco-Algerian relations on a new footing, opening up the possibility, Stora claims, of a friendship treaty. However, this high point was sabotaged by the row over the 2005 law passed by the French National Assembly, which recognised the 'positive role of France in North Africa', even if it was later rescinded by Chirac. Thereafter, Chirac's two immediate successors, Sarkozy and Hollande, continued to give importance to the

Algerian question. Sarkozy condemned colonialism in a speech in Algeria in 2007, while Hollande publicly recognised the 17 October 1961 massacre of Algerians in Paris. However, neither talked of an apology, let alone a friendship treaty. As such, Stora argues, Macron went much further and has been more ambitious in trying to produce truth and reconciliation between the two countries and within French society.

The third section examines the challenges faced. Stora comments on the absence of French films on the Algerian War when compared to US cinema. He also refers to other countries confronting problematic pasts, from South Africa through to Chile, Spain, Russia and Japan. By situating Algeria within this much wider global context of memory cultures, Stora is underlining that the Franco-Algerian relationship is not unique. Furthermore, he is looking at the lessons that can be learnt from these examples and, with this in mind, the final part of this section outlines a set of feasible steps that could be taken. For Stora, it is crucial to push the process to another level, and he pinpoints three issues: complete disclosure of all the details of French nuclear testing in the Algerian Sahara between 1960 and 1966, the restoration and upkeep of French cemeteries in Algeria and the re-edition and translation of key books on the Algerian War. Alongside these, he also discusses the need to focus on 'the disappeared', a common feature of all the different Algerian memory narratives, to open all the archives and to educate French society on the history of French anti-colonialists. These measures, he feels, have the potential to bring both Algeria and France together and to produce a healing process within French society amongst those groups most affected by the aftermath of the conflict.

The report concludes with a series of concrete proposals: calling for the constitution of a 'Memory and Truth Commission' bringing together French and Algerians from academia, civil society and politics, Stora outlines a 27-point programme for this Commission to consider. First and foremost, these proposals include the creation of a commemorative culture that, by addressing certain key dates – such as the Evian Agreements of 19 March 1962 that brought the conflict officially to an end or the 17 October 1961 massacre in Paris – will bring together all the groups concerned in a bid to arrive at a less-divisive and more-inclusive narrative based upon reconciliation. Equally, Stora underlines the importance of addressing the question of 'the disappeared' on all sides of the conflict, of restoring French and Jewish cemeteries in Algeria, of working together on the aftermath of French nuclear testing and the precise mapping of French mines laid during the conflict and of declassifying – and giving open access to – all the archives.

Importantly, too, Stora stresses the need for cooperation between Algerian and French researchers that can be facilitated through academic exchanges and a visa system that allows Algerian students to come to France for a prolonged period and *vice versa*. Studiously avoiding any talk of any official apology on the part of the French state, the report prefers to talk of realisable goals, where the aim is to establish bridges between the different community memory narratives as well as between Algeria and France. In this respect, Stora talks of an honest and more inclusive memory narrative that, by reaching out to French citizens of Algerian heritage and Franco-Algerian citizens, could be a powerful counter to alienation from French society and the pull of Islamist extremism.

Responses and outcomes

Inevitably the report produced an immediate reaction, in part because its publication was accompanied by a high-profile media campaign by Stora, who carefully positioned himself as a historian and not a politician. From the Algerian government, the response was a blanket condemnation. According to government spokesman Ammar Belhimer, the report 'lacked objectivity' and, he continued, by putting Algerian victims and French perpetrators on the same footing, it failed to acknowledge 'war crimes and crimes against humanity' committed by the French colonial system (Le Troquier, 2021). Likewise, Mohand Ouamar Benelhadj, the secretary general of Algeria's main war-veterans group, denounced the report on the organisation's Youtube channel as a cover up 'concealing colonial crimes' (*Le Monde/AFP*, 2021a).

Yet, amongst Algerian commentators across the media and social media, there was a wide range of responses. Some echoed the Algerian government, while others were more welcoming with many shades of grey in between. The Algerian writer, Kamel Daoud, turned the focus away from France to Algeria in an unsparing manner (Daoud, 2021). In his opinion, for all the talk of an apology, the Algerian regime does not want one because to close the colonial chapter in a definitive way would mean that the regime would have to finally face up to the future. For this reason, Daoud maintained, much of the official Algerian reception, to Stora, was disingenuous because, preferring to replay the narrative of the colonial victim, it did not engage with his findings. Thus, Stora was accused of refusing the idea of an apology, even though he himself said that, personally, he 'had no problem' with such an apology. Equally, the Algerian government and Algerian commentators largely ignored the fact that President Tebboune had appointed an Algerian counterpoint to Stora, the historian Abdelmadjid Chikhi, to produce an equivalent Algerian report; yet, his own report had not been forthcoming. Even so, blaming the lack of an Algerian report on the impact of Covid-19, Chikhi criticised the Stora Report as a 'Franco-French' affair (*Le Monde/AFP*, 2021b).

In terms of gauging Algerian reactions, one distinction that emerged was the difference between Algerians in Algeria and Algerians in France: Algerian nationals living in France, Algerian–French dual nationals and

French citizens of Algerian heritage. For the former – Algerians in Algeria – the most pressing questions are those of an apology and state-to-state relations, while for the latter – Algerians in France – there is an additional question about what this report means about their place in French society. Thus, the prominent French-Algerian journalist Nabila Ramdani, writing in *Foreign Policy*, condemned Stora's overall approach: 'Rather than an apology, reparations and the possibility of prosecutions, tokenism and a desire to downplay unspeakable crimes that are in living memory appear to have guided Stora's work' (Ramdani, 2021). She was particularly condemnatory about the way in which Stora claims that educating young French Muslims about the Algerian War is a 'necessary safeguard' against 'Islamist terrorism'. For her, such a link is unproven. Moreover, she continues, it leads to a manipulation of history, whereby the report focuses, in the introduction, on the brutal attacks carried out in France by Islamist terrorists in 2021 when, in fact, it should be addressing the 132-year catalogue of French colonial violence in Algeria.

In a similar vein, according to the Algerian journalist Benamar (2021), the historian Malika Rahal, director of the *Institut d'Histoire du Temps Présent,* found the report confusing because it conflated two different issues:

> It is a complicated object that emanates from the current French context. From a political point of view, it responds to the request of the French president and it is confused on several levels, in the sense that it brings together questions that should be separate. It seems wrong to me to want, in the same movement, to repair French society, to enable it to find a consensus on the colonial past and, on the other hand, to improve diplomatic relations with Algeria. These are two separate issues that cannot be addressed in the same report.

Rahal's comments underline just how far historians were at the forefront of the discussion, in both Algeria and France, where reactions were also very varied. In the Algerian daily *El Watan*, Ruscio (2021) was broadly positive, as was Blanchard (2021) in *Libération*, while, in *Le Monde*, Thénault (2021) was highly critical in her evaluation, feeling that Stora's psychological model was misguided. The most vociferous criticism, however, came from Olivier Le Cour Grandmaison, who accused Stora of allowing himself to be used for political purposes by Macron. In the context of the right-wing shift of the presidential candidate for re-election, Le Cour Grandmaison (2021) argued, Stora had produced a report that ignored any apology, underplayed the violence of the original 1830 invasion and set up the violence of the coloniser and colonised as being in some way equivalent when, in reality, they were very different. On the right and far right, the conclusion was the exact opposite: Stora had gone too far. Perpignan's mayor, Louis Aliot, of the far-right

National Rally party (formerly National Front) tweeted 'shameful' in reaction to Stora's recommendations, which he said denigrated the memories of French war victims. Meanwhile, Dalila Kerchouche, the writer and *harki* activist, could not contain her anger in *Le Monde* (2021). Like so many activists, she had been expecting much from the Stora Report yet, in practice, for her, Stora barely addressed the *harki* issue – a lacune which left her cynical about any reconciliation process. Perhaps unsurprisingly, the report satisfied no one and this, in turn, led to some re-evaluation on the part of Stora. He acknowledged that he might have skirted too quickly over the Algerian side of the equation and that, since this report was commissioned by Macron, the result was inevitably a largely French perspective.

The official presidential response was published online on the presidential website later on the day that Stora presented the report to Macron. Praising the quality of Stora's work, Macron now highlighted three specific memorial days that he wanted to use to build reconciliation within French society: the commemorations of 25 September (National Day of Tribute to the *Harkis* and to the members of the auxiliary forces of the French army in Algeria), of 17 October 1961 and of 19 March 1962.

By identifying three specific memorial days, each encapsulating different memory narratives, Macron wished to embody the recognition of suffering on all sides; a desire that explains why, in the end, 19 March 1962 – the date of the cease-fire – was replaced by 26 March 1962, the moment when settlers protesting at imminent Algerian independence were shot down by French soldiers, an event that precipitated the mass exodus of settlers. In this way, Macron wished to establish a specific pattern of remembering: one that flattened the Algerian War into one story of violence where everyone was a victim, thus putting all violence side-by-side whether it be that suffered by the *harkis*, the Algerians or the settlers.

As such, in the run-up to the 2022 presidential election, which coincided with the cycle of 60th anniversaries marking the denouement of the Algerian War, Macron sought to be scrupulously even-handed. So, on the one hand in September 2021, the 20th anniversary of the establishing of *Harki* Day, he asked for forgiveness for the abandonment of the *harkis* who were left to be massacred in Algeria by the FLN as pro-French collaborators (Crapanzano, 2011), while, on the other, on 17 October 2021, he laid flowers at the bridge over the Seine, the first president to attend such a commemoration. Likewise, he paid tribute to the nine anti-colonial French protestors killed at Charonne metro station in February 1962, while admitting that the March 1962 shooting of dozens of European supporters of French Algeria on the rue d'Isly in the heart of Algiers was 'unforgivable' and a 'massacre'. In each case, however, although admitting the scale of the violence, he always stopped short of an apology. Nor did he return to the language of 'crime against humanity' from five years earlier.

Such balance, in keeping with his repeated use of the phrase 'at the same time', came from a clear calculation. In the run-up to the election, he did not want to be accused by his main rival, Marine Le Pen, of promoting post-colonial guilt, especially given the 'manifesto' from former French Army chiefs, published provocatively on the 60th anniversary of the 1961 putsch by army generals in Algeria, which characterised France as a society under threat from Islamist extremism. However, nor did he wish to be attacked by the left as a president who had caved in to the French–Algeria lobby. Instead, he underlined that addressing the Algerian War was now a vital way to combat Islamist extremism, and here, Macron's principal target was 'community separatism', referred to as *communautarisme* in French, a word that is invoked as a threat to republican unity because it encapsulates the fracturing of society into separate ethnic, cultural and religious groups. By reconciling the different communities affected by the Algerian War, Macron wanted to reinforce basic republican values in a show of patriotic unity. In this context, the specific keywords were 'shared', 'common' and 'recognition' (Bobin and Faye, 2022). This focus upon French society, originally just one part of Macron's grand reconciliation project, reflected not just the forthcoming election but his frustration with the Algerian regime's refusal to engage with the process in any meaningful way. In part, this refusal stemmed from the fact that Tebboune could not see any immediate advantage in supporting an initiative that, ultimately, had come from the former colonial power and was driven by a French agenda. He did not want to lay himself open to the attack of being pro-French. Faced with this impasse, Macron invited 18 young French people marked by the Algerian War to the Elysée Palace on 30 September 2021, and here, Macron did not hold back. Describing the Algerian regime in place as a 'political-military system' whose backbone was an ongoing exploitation of memory (*rente mémorielle*) and 'hatred of France', he posed questions about the existence of 'the Algerian nation before colonisation' (Kessous, 2021). The speech produced fury in Algiers, with Tebboune telling *Der Spiegel* in an interview on 9 November 2021:

> You can't question a people's history and you can't insult the Algerians ... With this comment, Macron placed himself on the same side with those who justify colonisation.
>
> *(Sandberg and Bolliger, 2021, para. 8)*

At this point, reconciliation with Algeria seemed further away than ever, which, in turn, explained Macron's renewed emphasis on healing French society. In the meantime, Stora also responded to Macron's critics. Ever present as a figure in each of the memory events between September 2021 and March 2022, Stora was adamant that he was not Macron's lackey and also that Macron had made real progress, achieving more, in one year, than in the previous 60 (Stora, 2022).

Change or continuity?

In so many ways, Macron's coming to terms with the colonial past must be understood less as a break and more as a reconnection with the Chirac presidency between 1995 and 2007. Indeed, in an aeroplane taking him to Jerusalem in January 2020, Macron confided to journalists that, during his tenure, he wanted to face up to France's Algeria past in the same way that Jacques Chirac had done over the role of the French state in the Holocaust (Smolar, 2020). Moreover, during his second term, Chirac established the National Museum of the History of Immigration because, by telling the story of the contribution made by migration to French society, he wanted to combat ethnic exclusion. So, in a similar vein, Macron sees a link between facing up to the Algerian War – and colonialism more generally – and to the fight against Islamist extremism *and* racism. For Macron, France must not be trapped by a colonial past, as he made clear in a speech on 2 October 2020:

> Added to all this is the fact that we're a country with a colonial past and traumas it still has not resolved, with facts that underpin our collective psyche, our project, the way we see ourselves. The Algerian War is part of this and, basically, this whole period of our history is being replayed, as it were, because we have never unpacked things ourselves. And so we see children of the Republic, sometimes from elsewhere, children or grandchildren of today's citizens of immigrant origin from the Maghreb and sub-Saharan Africa, revisiting their identity through a post-colonial or anti-colonial discourse.
>
> *(Macron, 2020, para. 17)*

At the same time, this strategy of inclusion went hand-in-hand with a very tough stance on border controls because, in the run-up to the 2022 presidential election, Macron did not want to be open to any attack from Le Pen on the subject of border security. This is why he substantially cut visas to Algerians, Moroccans and Tunisians in autumn 2021, a move that produced a diplomatic furore in both Algiers and Rabat, when Macron was accused of courting Le Pen's electoral base.

However, once re-elected, Macron renewed his effort to reach out to Algeria. In August 2022, he made an official three-day visit to Algeria, during which the subjects ranged from the Ukraine War through to security in the Sahel region, energy, visas, the management of illegal immigration across the Mediterranean and reconciliation over the Algerian War. Then, six weeks later, the Prime Minister, Elisabeth Borne, returned with 15 ministers – and further talks reinforced a new mood of cooperation and rapprochement. Now, more than ever, Macron had made Tebboune's Algeria into France's privileged partner in the Maghreb, a stance that simultaneously harmed international relations with Morocco, which, as Algeria's main regional rival, felt shunned by this policy.

Conclusion: empathy but no apology

However, while huge question marks remain over the possibility of Franco-Algerian reconciliation, what remains of Macron's Algeria policy is his attempt to arrive at a reconciliation within French society itself, as an internal problem. Here, it is important to underline that Macron has stopped well short of Chirac's unprecedented official apology for the French state's role in the Holocaust. Nor has Macron ever reiterated, as president, what he said as a candidate in 2017, calling colonialism a 'crime against humanity'. Instead, Macron has crucially eschewed the language of *apology* in favour of the language of *recognition* on the part of the state. Thus, during each of the 60th anniversaries, his words and body language were consoling emotional gestures, which recognised the violence suffered by each community, thereby putting everyone's experience side by side. Specifically, he wanted to bring together the different memory narratives under one more singular republican narrative, wherein the unifying thread was not an apology but a common understanding of one another's pain.

In this sense, Macron's carefully crafted actions must be put into a much broader global history of countries confronting difficult pasts, such as post-apartheid South Africa or Northern Ireland in 1998. Macron's initiatives have been about healing French society and arriving at a new relationship with Algeria, where he has developed a very specific emotional register that is psycho-historical. It draws upon Stora's interpretation of France as a society in denial over the Algerian War, which Macron is trying to remedy through truth. However, above all, this register is empathetic. Rejecting the language of apology, it draws upon the language of empathy to bring all the different 'victims' together, a process that, Macron hopes, will ultimately help France to transcend the Algerian War and produce a more inclusive and more cohesive society.

Acknowledgement

I would like to thank Nadja Makhlouf for her invaluable comments on the first draft of this chapter.

References

Benamar, K. (2021) 'Malika Rahal, historienne: "Le rapport Stora est un objet compliqué"', *Liberté*, 30 January. (liberte-algerie.com) (accessed 05 January 2024).
Blanchard, P. (2021) 'Dense et riche, le rapport Stora peut permettre d'aller au delà du conflit franco-algérien', *Libération*, 20 January.
Bobin, F. and Faye, O. (2022) 'Emmanuel Macron et l'Algérie, une longue histoire contrariée', *Le Monde*, 25 August.
Crapanzano, V. (2011) *The Harkis: The wound that never heals*. Chicago: University of Chicago Press.
Daoud, K. (2021) 'The west is too obsessed with its colonial guilt', *Financial Times*, 24 February.
Evans, M. (2012) *Algeria: France's undeclared war*. Oxford: Oxford University Press.
Kerchouche, D. (2021) 'France-Algérie: "Les harkis méritent mieux qu'un rapport mémoriel lacunaire et cynique à leur égard"', *Le Monde*, 28 January.
Kessous, M. (2021) 'Le dialogue inédit entre Emmanuel Macron et les "petits-enfants de la guerre d'Algérie"', *Le Monde*, 2 October.
Le Cour Grandmaison, O. (2021) 'Sur le rapport de Benjamin Stora: le conseiller contre l'historien', *Le Club de Mediapart*, 28 January.
Le Monde/AFP (2017) 'En Algérie, Macron qualifie la colonisation de «crime contre l'humanité», tollé à droite', 15 February.
Le Monde/AFP (2021a) 'En Algérie, les anciens combattants rejettent le rapport Stora sur la réconciliation des mémoires', 1 February.
Le Monde/AFP (2021b) 'Pour Alger, c'est comme si le rapport Stora sur la réconciliation des mémoires entre la France et l'Algérie "n'existait pas"', 24 March.
Le Troquier, P. (2021) 'Rapport Stora. Le gouvernement algérien déplore la non-reconnaissance des "crimes coloniaux" de l'État français', *Courrier international*, 10 February.
Macron, E. (2017) 'Discours d'Emmanuel Macron à l'université de Ouagadougou'. https://www.elysee.fr/emmanuel-macron/2017/11/28/discours-demmanuel-macron-a-luniversite-de-ouagadougou (accessed 5 January 2024).
Macron, E. (2018) 'Déclaration du Président de la République sur la mort de Maurice Audin'. https://www.elysee.fr/emmanuel-macron/2018/09/13/declaration-du-president-de-la-republique-sur-la-mort-de-maurice-audin (accessed 5 January 2024).
Macron, E. (2020) 'La République en actes: discours du Président de la République sur le thème de la lutte contre les séparatismes'. https://www.elysee.fr/emmanuel-macron/2020/10/02/la-republique-en-actes-discours-du-president-de-la-republique-sur-le-theme-de-la-lutte-contre-les-separatismes (accessed 5 January 2024).
Ramdani, N. (2021) 'Macron's Algeria report isn't progress, it's a whitewash', *Foreign Policy*, 1 February.
Ruscio, A. (2021) 'Histoire France-Algérie: Il faut s'engouffrer dans la brèche ouverte par Benjamin Stora', *El Watan*, 2 February.
Sandberg, B. and Bolliger, M. (2021) 'You can't question a people's history and you can't insult the Algerians', *Der Speigel*, 9 November.
Sarr, F. and Savoy, B. (2018) *La restitution du patrimoine culturel africain: vers une nouvelle éthique relationnelle*. Paris: Seuil.
Smolar, P. (2020) 'Emmanuel Macron fait de la guerre d'Algérie le défi mémoriel de son quinquennat', *Le Monde*, 25 January.

Stora, B. (1991) *La gangrène et l'oubli: la mémoire de la guerre d'Algérie*. Paris: La Découverte.
Stora, B. (2021), *France-Algérie: les passions douloureuses*. Paris: Albin Michel.
Stora, B. (2022) 'Guerre d'Algérie: Emmanuel Macron a plus fait qu'en soixante ans de présidence française', *Libération,* 15 April.
Thénault, S. (2021) 'Sur la guerre d'Algérie, parler de "réconciliation" n'a pas de sens', *Le Monde,* 5 February.

15
RECOGNITION AND SURVEILLANCE: EMMANUEL MACRON'S RELIGIOUS POLICY

Philippe Portier

Abstract

This chapter analyses the religious policy pursued by Emmanuel Macron since his election in 2017. It takes place in a context marked, in the eyes of the Head of State, by a destabilisation of solidarities in French society under the effects of globalisation and individualisation. The author argues that at the root of this risk of anomie, Macron sees a growing tendency for a part of the Muslim population to turn inwards upon itself – a phenomenon which he calls 'separatism' – to the point of leading to violent radicalisation. This analysis led the president to develop a policy of secularism to restore cohesion to French society, marked by two characteristics. The first is the principle of recognition: breaking with the initial model of privatisation of religion, the aim is to integrate religious authorities into the mechanisms of symbolic and material management of society. The principle of recognition is coupled with that of surveillance. Macron's concern over the development of a radicalised Islam is reflected in what the author sees as an unprecedented policy of control over religious denominations, culminating in the law of 24 August 2021 on 'reinforcing respect for the principles of the Republic'.

Introduction

French secularism was established at the turn of the 19th and 20th centuries. When the Republicans came to power in 1879, they undertook to put an end to the system of recognised churches known as the *Concordat regime*, agreed between Napoleon Bonaparte and the Pope, which had regulated relations between the state and religious authorities since 1801–1802. A partial separation, essentially excluding religious teaching and ecclesiastical staff from the public school system took place in the 1880s. This movement culminated in 1904 when religious congregations were banned from providing school education. The 'great separation' between Church and State, which was very liberal in its approach, was marked by the law of 9 December 1905, whose first two articles set the general framework for the new regime. Article 1 affirmed the principle of freedom of conscience, to which was added that of freedom of worship, seen as the right to express one's religious opinions, beyond the confines of places of worship, in the social space itself. To preserve the principle of equality without which, according to the Republicans, freedom of conscience would be impossible, Article 2 then laid down the rule of the religious neutrality of the state, stating that 'the Republic does not recognise, subsidise or pay the salaries of any religion'. At its inception, French secularism therefore clearly dissociated the state order from the religious order, which the Catholic Church did not initially accept and, for some time, it remained attached to the idea of an institutional alliance between the two powers.

Secularism only entered the common consciousness after the Second World War (Portier and Willaime, 2022). The 'war of the two Frances' seemed to be over. Of course, controversy resurfaced from time to time. However, as in 1959, when the Debré law was passed (supported by the right, it introduced the financing of private schools) or in 1984, when the Savary project was discussed (presented by the left, it aimed to nationalise private education), it was only partially focused on the issue of schooling, seen as being of secondary importance. Politicians were keener to discuss economic issues and European integration. This appeasement was driven by two closely related factors. On the one hand, there was the evolution of the Catholic magisterium: the Church, against which the republican order had been partly established, renounced its overtones of protest and approved the secular regime. On the other hand, the secularist movement faded away: public opinion, even the most secularised sections, could no longer identify with the anticlerical rhetoric of teachers' unions, associations of freethinkers, Masonic denominations and popular education movements. Furthermore, the secular front lost the school battles of 1959 and 1984: the Debré law was passed, and the Savary law was withdrawn.

But the secular quarrel resurfaced in the 1980s – albeit on a different basis – and has continued ever since. At its root lies an observation: after asserting, as they did during the 1983 'March for Equality', the same rights as their fellow citizens – in other words, a 'right to indifference' – in order to enter mainstream society, Muslims, especially younger generations, have cultivated a singularity, expressing itself in the demand for special rights. In September 1989, a movement launched by high-school students in Creil, near Paris, called for Muslims to be granted leave of absence on religious grounds, special menus in public authority canteens and the wearing of religious symbols such as headscarves in administrative areas. Some political players, more on the left than the right, initially accepted this differentiation. This was the case, for example, for the Socialist Minister for Education in December 1989, when he accepted, subject to certain conditions, the wearing of headscarves in public schools, considering that their display was not contrary to secularism. This position was reversed in the 2000s, in the wake of the shock produced by terrorist attacks, the rise of extreme-right-wing ideas among the electorate and the impact of controversial books such as *Les territoires perdus de la République* (The Lost Territories of the French Republic), published under the pseudonym of Brenner (2004), which painted an alarming picture of the anti-semitism, racism and sexism, particularly amongst pupils of North African descent, observed by schoolteachers. The idea developed that secularism had to be used not to support this movement but to control it.

Laws such as that of 15 March 2004 – which outlawed the wearing of conspicuous signs of religious affiliation in public schools – and new regulations, numerous charters and vade-mecums, were all designed to achieve this goal. Secularism underwent what has been called a 'substantialist turn' (Portier, 2016).[1] In the past, secularism was seen as a system for preserving freedom of conscience, based on the separation of political and religious institutions. But against a backdrop of cooperation between the state and religious authorities, secularism has been increasingly asserting itself as a regime for imposing the moral law defined by government. There are no real differences in this respect between presidents – Jacques Chirac, Nicolas Sarkozy, François Hollande – from 1995 to 2017. All of them, using their own rhetoric, have contributed to this new type of edifice: the rights of the individual, yes, but within the confines of the famous 'values of the Republic'. Some analysts, attentive to certain liberal overtones of his speeches during his first election campaign in 2016–2017, may have believed that Emmanuel Macron, elected on 14 May 2017, would initiate a return to the *status quo ante*. By underlining his complicity with 'globalised neo-Protestantism' (Debray, 2019a), these analysts sometimes evoke his adherence to the American model. However, an examination of the first seven years of his presidency positions him differently: in reality, he has in no way broken with the 'securitarian' line of his predecessors. Indeed, arguably, he has consolidated, even 'radicalised' some of the measures they had introduced into law, to use the pejorative expression he used in 2016 to denounce the hard secularist line of his rival, Manuel Valls, François Hollande's prime minister.

Driven by a fear of anomie, his religious policy, which has changed little since 2017, articulates, in contrast to the attachment to separation held dear by the founders of the Third Republic, two elements – recognition and security – which, far from opposing each other, are, on the contrary, united around a common objective of 'disciplining' the social conscience.

The obsessive fear of disconnection

President Macron's positions on secularism cannot be approached without taking into account his reading of the changes in the society he intends to lead. His manifesto book, *Révolution* (Macron, 2016), introduces an analysis of the historical dynamics that mark our era from this perspective and which have been maintained since. Despite the Covid pandemic and the war in Ukraine, his analysis of the world is marked by the principle of trust: we must believe in progress, not only in its technical and scientific dimension but also in its ethical and political dimension.

Following in the general vein of the journal *Esprit*, of which he was a long-standing member of the editorial board, Macron first and foremost highlights the recent recompositions of our democratic society. For a long time, he explained, France had been marked by a kind of ontological certainty: the common idea was that history was necessarily leading us towards an improvement in our social being, in a world now free from want. This harmonious conception of historical development was all the more easily expressed in that everything then, by virtue of the very configuration of social structures, seemed controllable, carried along by the slow march of time. The state exercised its sovereignty over a culturally unified population within the framework of a territorial space protected from external intrusions by strong borders. However, these social universes no longer have this security of enclosure. On 29 August 2017, when he opened the Ambassadors' Conference at the Elysée Palace in Paris, he said: 'We still need this [old] world – it was the triumphant world of the *"Trente Glorieuses"*, then the pitiful *"Trente Piteuses"* – but we have entered a new world'.[2] This emerging image of modernity brings with it two changes. The first concerns spatiality. Like other Western countries, France has found itself caught up in the movement of globalisation. Multiple movements have disrupted its national mode of management: economic and financial flows, information flows with the digital revolution, legal flows with the integration of national laws into supranational organisations, viral flows as we saw with the pandemic and demographic flows under the effects of immigration. This last point brings us back to the question of religion. In the past, France was united around the 'Judeo-Christian' frame of reference,[3] but over the last four decades, it has opened up to new influences, such as Islam, which is in many ways out of step with the majority ethos. The second change concerns temporality. Here, this refers to the principle of acceleration. The equilibrium of our times is constantly upset by the obsession with surpassing oneself: 'The globalisation of flows continues to accelerate (…), leading to the advent of a more rapid and changing economy, made up of brutal technological ruptures' (Macron, 2016, p. 56). The same applies to biology. In this respect, Macron insists on the demand of a growing part of the population to extend individual rights to issues such as surrogate motherhood and assisted dying, which, in the past, were governed by the canons of religious morality.

The transition to this image of modernity must not be rejected, the movement must be embraced, as he notes: 'For many of our fellow citizens, the civilisation we are entering is synonymous with regression, loss of control, anxiety and insecurity. But can we replace the world as it is? I don't think so' (Macron, 2016, p. 53). This acceptance of time is due to the fact that, for Macron, at its core, today's open society brings a degree of prosperity and inventiveness not found in the previous world. It ushers in a Renaissance-like change. 'In this context of crisis, the best can be born' (Macron, 2016, p. 64). This optimistic approach to history does not, however, mean that Macron wants to take the new world as it comes: he refers to the 'risks' that accompany it. The first of the two main risks is alienation. In today's society, individuals are often dissociated from their essence. Their future, Macron explains, is to be autonomous. In his speech to the French Parliamentary Congress on 3 July 2007, he said: 'I believe in the spirit of the Enlightenment, which means that our objective is the autonomy of free, conscious and critical beings'. However, the lives of many of our contemporaries, subjected to the cold rationality of the contemporary state, do not reflect this image. This observation holds in the economic sphere: whilst valuing individual success, Macron is concerned about the poverty and exclusion of those who have not been able to adapt to the demands of the economy. The same applies in the bioethical sphere: the desire for unlimited procreation can lead, as has been seen with surrogate motherhood, to commodification of the body. In other words, the risk of alienation and the risk of separation. It has been said that Macron fails to think about the social bond (Debray, 2019b): for him, nothing is a body, everything is an ephemeral association of isolated 'monads'. This is an interpretative exaggeration. Macron has constantly expressed his fear of seeing the national community lose its cohesion by allowing individuals to withdraw, at a distance from the common order, into partial circles of ethnic, religious or regional identification. Islam, which has grown considerably in France, presents us with this challenge: Macron notes that some of its followers are tending to cut themselves off from the mainstream French community. In his July 2017 address to the *Conseil Français du Culte Musulman* (the French Council for Muslim Worship) and as he pointed out even more forcefully in his press conference at Mulhouse on 18 February 2020[4] and in his speech at Les Mureaux on 2 October of the same year,[5] this withdrawal into the Muslim enclosure is all the more worrying as it can spread codes of existence, which are dissociated from the values of freedom and equality upon which French society is founded. This risk analysis has given rise to a programme of action. For the president, the state is not simply the producer of an external order within which calculating rationalities can flourish, without concern for the common good. While it must adapt to the demands of the economic market, which, according to a 'neo-liberal logic', presupposes a policy of 'modernising' social systems and public action (Dolez et al, 2019, 2022; Revault d'Allonnes, 2019), and to changes in ethical awareness, it is also responsible for setting limits on the utilitarian inclinations of its constituents: against alienation, by reviving a policy of solidarity; against separation, by producing a politics of unity.

Macron therefore believes that political power, while committed to modernising the system, must oppose these individualistic drifts. However, it is essential that the state's actions take place within a space grounded in tradition. As he put it in his speech at the Pantheon on 4 September 2020:[6] 'The Republic is both will and transmission'. The influence of Paul Ricoeur can be seen here. Macron was his editorial assistant in the late 1990s when the philosopher wrote *La mémoire, l'histoire et l'oubli* (2000) and, like Ricoeur, Macron also believes that history, if it is not to lapse into *hubris*, must be weighed down by a memory, which is often carried by religions (Dosse, 2017). He assigns a dual function to this religious memory, which sits alongside secular memory (notably that represented by the great figures of the Pantheon). On the one hand, he explains, religion is a factor of identity, helping to shape the national essence. Much like Nicolas Sarkozy, on many occasions, Macron has referred to France's 'Christian roots' as a 'self-evident historical fact'.[7] Everything about France reminds us of this: its monuments, first and foremost the Notre-Dame-de-Paris cathedral, which he declared, when fire broke out in April 2019, to be 'the cathedral of an entire people and its thousand-year-old history';[8] its heroes, such as Joan of Arc; its writers, from Bernanos to Mounier (whose open-minded Catholicism he appreciates) and its very concepts, such as the 'common good' which are central to his texts.[9] In this memorial landscape, Catholicism is often central. Protestantism and Judaism have also contributed to shaping the nation's character, transmitting, in their own harmonious ways, a sense of its ultimate values, such as dignity, freedom, hospitality and a taste for the universal.[10] Religion is also a source of inspiration. At this historic moment when so many questions are being asked, Macron explains that politics needs an ethical recharge and practical assistance. Religions can play this supporting role. The transcendence they convey introduces, at the very heart of the exercise of the state, a space between the ruler and their role. It prevents them from escaping reflection on the moral significance of their actions (Ricoeur, 2019). The title of 'Vigil of the Republic' bestowed by the president on the Protestant denomination[11] is an extension of this affirmation.

Religion thus stabilises society. It helps to bind society to a historical origin and an ethical substance. However, as Macron points out, it would be wrong to reduce it to its collective function alone. Although the right to the social expression of religion must be guaranteed, it is because religion also responds to a subjective need. Perhaps the experience of his conversion at the age of 12 at the Jesuit College of La Providence in Amiens, followed by a Catholic baptism, has left its mark. Macron considers that faith, even if it does not necessarily express itself in the form of a historical religion, is consubstantial with human existence. As he has said on several occasions: 'Metaphysics is a place that we know is there, a place outside places (…). I believe we have an ontological need for it (…). Humans have a need for the absolute. This relationship with transcendence is what characterises us'.[12]

Turning to religion

The secularism of the Third Republic, which succeeded Napoleon Bonaparte's Concordat regime, was based on a radical separation of institutions: religion was relegated to a space outside the state and henceforth found a home solely in civil society – comprising both private and social spheres. Article 2 of the law of 9 December 1905, cited earlier, is a clear indication of this break with the previous order. Recent decades have, to some extent, put this on hold. The state, subject to the demands of identity and driven by managerial imperatives, opened up, under the presidency of General de Gaulle, to a form of partnership with religious institutions – and President Macron has not strayed from the path traced by his predecessors. His analysis of contemporary challenges also leads him to position his religious policy within the framework of a model of recognition.

This model is based, first and foremost, on a safeguarding programme. Throughout French history, there have been attempts to eradicate historic religions in favour of the 'republican faith', as was the case for some years under the Revolution in 1792–1794. Macron rejects this tradition. Strongly asserting his conviction during the 2017 campaign (Macron, 2016, p. 171), he has consistently repeated this position since his election. For example, on 18 March 2019, during a debate at the Elysée Palace with a group of intellectuals, he stated:

> Secularism is a principle of the Republic that ensures and protects everyone's freedom. It allows everyone to believe or not to believe, and to do so freely. And to avoid interfering in the life of any religion, it implies the neutrality of public services and is therefore a framework (…). Secularism has no adjective, nor have I ever made it a form of religion of the Republic.[13]

In this light, the freedom to believe (or not to believe) has found itself, under his presidency, even more protected than in the past. The penalties for interference, provided for in Article 31 of the law of 9 December 1905, were greatly increased by the law of 24 August 2021: the number of chaplains working in prisons and the armed forces, either paid or employed by the state, increased during the Macron presidency,[14] following the line of development outlined earlier. In addition, the president has blocked proposed legislation from the right (*Les Républicains*) and the far right (*Rassemblement National*) to give legal force to the contents of a 2012 ruling depriving mothers accompanying schoolchildren on outings of the right to wear headscarves. He similarly opposed plans to ban manifestations of religious affiliation at university. The president undoubtedly has a preference for 'reasonable' faith, which he says brings him closer to liberal Protestantism.[15] This is the source of his criticism of contemporary literalism, which, as can be seen in certain evangelical and Muslim spheres, locks believers into a fideistic enclosure that exposes them to the temptation of breaking away from the surrounding world. Macron acknowledges, however, that this is no more than a personal preference, which has no business interfering with the order of law: 'I will never ask anyone in the Republic to believe moderately or not, I'm not interested in that. I want everyone to be able to believe freely, to be as absolute in their faith as they need to be'.[16]

Yet, Macron's policy goes beyond this negative protection, adding, in a positive way, a support mechanism. This raises the question of whether freedom of religion has become a 'positive right' as much as a 'negative right'. Material assistance to religious denominations began to develop in France in the 1960s. Several pieces of legislation were passed, some of which concerned the school system. Under the Debré Law of December 1959, private schools – which today are still predominantly Catholic, despite a few dozen Jewish and Muslim schools – were granted public subsidies, after signing a contract with the state, to cover a large part of their staff and operating costs without affecting their 'specific character'. Public grants were reinforced by the Guermeur Act of 1977 (aimed at giving private school teachers the same social benefits as public school teachers), the Rocard Act of 1984 (allowing the contractualisation of agricultural teaching establishments), the Carle Act of 2009 (establishing parity in local funding for private and public elementary schools) and the regulations resulting from the Lang/Cloupet[17] agreements of 1992–1993, notably concerning funding for private school teacher training. There are a few political groups in France, such as Jean-Luc Mélenchon's *La France Insoumise*, who advocate the nationalisation of all private schools. Of course, Macron has done nothing of the sort, perpetuating the private system with a larger budget than in previous periods.

Other measures affect the churches themselves. Since the 1960s, in contradiction to Article 2 of the 1905 law, which forbids the Republic from 'subsidising religious denominations', the number of indirect subsidies has increased. Examples include the 1961 law allowing public authorities to guarantee loans to associations involved in building places of worship, the

1987 law on sponsorship, which allows taxpayers to deduct 66 per cent of sums allocated to religious associations from their taxes and the 2006 laws legalising the use of long leases granted by local authorities to build religious buildings. These liberties, which Macron renewed, have recently been supplemented by other texts. The law of 29 July 2019 bases the reconstruction of Notre-Dame-de-Paris on special regulations that differ from town planning law but also offer tax rebates of up to 75 per cent on donations. In an unprecedented move, the law of 24 August 2021, discussed below, enabled religious associations to own and manage buildings that they have acquired free of charge and to keep the rents paid on them. It should be added that, under Macron, the special status of Alsace-Moselle has so far been modified only marginally.[18]

Finally, Macron's programme is based on a system of association. Despite the 1905 law, Republican governments have always maintained relations with religious authorities, and the leaders of the Fifth Republic gradually strengthened and institutionalised these relationships. This is also the case – and even more so – with Emmanuel Macron. In the words of Murray Edelman, some of his meetings represent a symbolic policy (Edelman, 1985), with the aim of recalling the contribution that religions have made to the social constitution of the nation. The president's attendance at dinners organised by the *Conseil Représentatif des Institutions Juives de France* (the Representative Council of Jewish Institutions in France, CRIF) and the Charles Gide Protestant Association, are examples of this, as is the participation of his ministers, notably the Minister of the Interior, in ceremonies organised in their ministries by religious institutions. Visits to places held in high regard in religious memory are also extremely significant, and in this respect, Catholicism certainly dominates: Macron's visits have included the Basilica of Saint-Denis, where the kings of France are buried, Mont-Saint-Michel, the collegiate church of Semur-en-Auxois and Strasbourg Cathedral. He also visited Rome in 2021, where he received the insignia of canon of the Lateran Basilica, in accordance with a tradition dating back to the 17th century (although not all presidents of the Fifth Republic have observed this tradition). Attendance at the mass celebrated by Pope Francis in Marseilles in September 2023, criticised by some on the left, also testifies to a special link with Catholicism[19] that France, he said at the College of Bernardins on 19 April 2018, has unfortunately allowed to become distended.[20] But other faiths have not been overlooked: Macron also visited the Grande Mosquée de Paris, the Martin Luther King space in Créteil and the capital's Grande Synagogue. In December 2023, Macron's relationship with Judaism was the subject of a particularly visible display when, during an official ceremony, he allowed Chief Rabbi Khorsia to light the Hanukkah candles in the salons of the Elysée Palace, provoking a protest from secularist groups and from political opponents on the left and right.

In addition to this symbolic aspect, there is also a managerial one. Macron attaches particular importance to discussions with religious authorities – not only with Pope François, with whom he has met four times, but also with French religious authorities, who he even invites to dinner. Following a formula inaugurated by the socialist Prime Minister Lionel Jospin in 2002, every year, the prime minister, together with the Minister of the Interior, receives a delegation from the Catholic Church at Matignon, led by the Nuncio and the president of the Bishops' Conference, to review issues of interest to both parties. He also sometimes organises more targeted meetings, involving all communities when the situation so requires, as was seen, for example, during the pandemic. Other ministers have set up similar meetings. These discussions are not limited to sectoral issues relating to the preservation of religious freedom; they also involve exchanges of views on social policy (e.g. on the question of migration), bioethics and, with the Pope, international politics. This dialogue sometimes takes on a practical dimension. Political and religious authorities also get together – in a context, let us not forget, where the state, as Macron himself says (Macron, 2016, p. 75), is not capable of solving everything – to jointly implement concrete policies, such as those concerning the reception of refugees, support for immigrants, relief for the needy and mediation in difficult neighbourhoods.

This path of recognition bears witness to a certain 'corporatisation' of French politics. Religious and political institutions find themselves interacting on the basis of an exchange of services. Politics, in response to the challenges of the times, recognises the usefulness and freedom of religion. In return, religion, happy to regain the publicity of which it was deprived by the secularist movement, provides its resources of connection and meaning. However, the relationship between the two is asymmetrical, and the government has the final decision. This was demonstrated in 2020 at the time of the pandemic: despite requests from the episcopate, the governments of Edouard Philippe and Jean Castex decreed a ban on masses, refusing to include them as part of the nation's 'essential' activities. Macron has shown himself no more open to the Catholic Church's requests on the issue of abortion: in February 2024, he pushed through the constitutionalisation of women's right to abortion. The same assertion of sovereignty was made in 2024 during the debate on the end of life: although religious authorities were received by Macron, they were unable to prevent the introduction of a bill in favour of assisted dying.

The power of the state

On several occasions, Macron has explained that, given the current sense of disconnection, social life needs to regroup around a pole of incarnation. It is up to the state – and more specifically the Head of State – to occupy this role, not the religious authorities. Although they are invited to the dinner table of the Republic, they can only act, like other actors in civil society, by accepting their inclusion in the legal order that political power defines. This has always been Macron's doctrine. He set out the principle in his 2017 campaign, notably in his manifesto publication *Revolution*:

> If freedom of conscience is total, intransigence with regards to respect for the laws of the Republic is absolute. In France, some things are non-negotiable. Basic principles of civility are not negotiable.
> *(Macron, 2016, p. 172)*

This assertion, found in all his subsequent speeches, certainly meets the key criterion of legal modernity, based on the principle of sovereignty. However, it is supplemented by new content: the rule to which religions are called upon to refer is no longer, as in the past, the procedural law of classical liberalism but a substantive law,[21] based on the social ethos that the state believes can be found in the deep-rooted structures of national culture.

This policy of sovereignty is based, first and foremost, on an analytical moment. Macron finds himself confronted with a denominational landscape that has undergone a profound transformation over the past 40 years. Sociological research readily considers that it has been affected by two contradictory movements. The first is the deepening of secularisation: in France, declarations of religious affiliation have declined considerably: compared to just 5 per cent in the 1950s, 58 per cent of the population now say they have no religion (Portier and Willaime, 2021). The second trend is the reconfirmation of religiousness. Among those who state a religious affiliation, a strong tendency to cultivate a normative faith can be seen. This is true of all religious 'families'. But it is Islam, in particular, which today represents around 10 per cent of the total population in France compared to 1 per cent in 1981, which attracts attention, particularly from Macron (2016, p. 172).[22] Surveys show that, particularly among the younger generations, ritual obligations and moral disciplines are being observed to a far greater degree than in the past. It has been pointed out that this orthodoxy is often accompanied by a distancing from political law: for 65 per cent of young Muslims at secondary school aged 15 and over 'The laws of religion count for more than the laws of the Republic'.[23] A whole debate has sprung up around what has been referred to as this 'revenge of Allah'. For some analysts, this religious affirmation is not necessarily in contradiction with the republican concept of 'living together': provided it is accompanied by respect for the rights of others, it can form part of an overall process of civic integration. This is the approach taken by intellectuals associated with the *Vigie de la Laïcité*, created in 2020 around Jean-Louis Bianco, former president of the

Observatoire de la Laïcité, historian Jean Baubérot, advocate of liberal secularism and sociologist Michel Wieviorka. But for others such as the members of *Printemps Républicain*, founded by Laurent Bouvet in 2016 after the Charlie Hebdo and Bataclan attacks, with the support of Marcel Gauchet and Elisabeth Badinter, Catherine Kintzler and Dominique Schnapper, this is a worrying development and is the source of both the 'communitarianism' and terrorism that have haunted French society since the 1990s.

Before his election, it was said that Macron was aligned with the first interpretation. Yet, nothing could be further from the truth. His criticism of the 'radicalisation of secularism' – which he has expressed throughout his time in office – has in no way prevented him from defending a strict position on the matter, as early as 2016 in *Révolution,* where he stated that 'A certain number of Salafist associations are waging a cultural battle with young people everywhere (…). Let us not be afraid to wage a relentless battle against them. The state's duty is to be inflexible' (Macron, 2016, p. 174). Advised by sociologist Gilles Kepel, he repeated this speech in his address to the *Conseil Français du Culte Musulman* in July 2017[24] and even more vividly in his speeches in Mulhouse and Les Mureaux in 2020, cited earlier. From his texts, as from those of his Interior Ministers, an interpretation similar to that formalised by Gilles Kepel and his school of thought emerges, whereby, as a result of the penetration into the Muslim world of movements close to Islamism, religious radicalism, which puts the law of God before the law of people, can lead to a move towards 'separatism', a word used by Elisabeth Badinter, which the president substituted for the word 'communitarianism' in October 2019 (Portier, 2022)[25] where terrorist temptation can take root. As he put it in the speech at Les Mureaux:

> Within this radical Islamism – and this is the crux of the matter, so let's address it and call it what it is – there is a declared, open determination, a methodical organisation to contravene the laws of the Republic and create a parallel order, to establish other values, to develop a different organisation of society, which may be separatist at first, but whose ultimate aim is to take control, complete control. Insidiously, this leads to radicalisation. Nearly 170 people, to give just one example, are being monitored for violent radicalisation here in the Yvelines department.[26]

In his bid to reassert the power of the state, Macron is also constructing a normative discourse with the aim of determining the frame of reference for the new policy of secularism. The phrase 'values of the Republic' is essential here. It was hardly ever used before 1990. Associated with the idea of secularism, it was crystallised in the early 2000s. François Baroin's report *Pour une nouvelle laïcité* (For a New Secularism), submitted to Prime Minister Jean-Pierre Raffarin in July 2003, uses the term several times, stating:

Today, we need to reaffirm the values of the Republic and therefore secularism. Freedom of expression must also be reconciled with personal emancipation and freedom of conscience. At some point, we have to have the courage to say that human rights and secularism can be contradictory.
(Baroin, 2003)

President Jacques Chirac used the same expression 17 times in December 2003 at the ceremony to present the report of the Stasi Commission 'on the application of the principle of secularism in the Republic', during which he announced his decision to introduce a bill banning conspicuous religious symbols in public schools. In any case, the idea caught on: it was taken up by subsequent governments, both right-wing – under Nicolas Sarkozy between 2007 and 2012 – and left-wing, during the presidency of François Hollande, under the impetus of Manuel Valls, who became Prime Minister after a spell as Interior Minister.[27] This discourse of values aims to give secularism a new purpose: its authors call on it to place social existence under the canopy of a moral consensus. The same terminology is used in Macron's speeches. The word appeared 16 times in his address to Congress on 3 July 2017, 6 times in his address to the *Conseil Français du Culte Musulman* a few days later and 9 times in his *La République en actes* speech at Les Mureaux on 2 October 2020, cited earlier. An inheritance of words and of ideas: it is all about rectifying the public mind by imposing, in a way that modifies the original meaning of the secular regime, a response to the demands of 'civility', itself identified with compliance with the 'minimum requirements of life in society'.[28]

A re-reading of the explanatory memorandum to the law of 24 August 2021, 'reinforcing respect for the principles of the Republic',[29] reveals Macron's intentions. He articulated two key ideas, which had already been set out in the speech at Les Mureaux. On a descriptive level, the memorandum recalls, in line with the motif mentioned earlier, that society is grappling with a separatist dynamic that is threatening social cohesion:

An insidious but powerful communitarian infiltration is slowly corroding the foundations of our society in certain territories. This infiltration is essentially of Islamist inspiration. It is the manifestation of a conscious, theorised, political-religious political project (…) that misunderstands the Republic and flouts the minimal requirements of life in society.

On a prescriptive level, he called upon the nation to reconstitute its cohesion around the unifying project of the Republic:

Our Republic is our common good. It has imposed itself through the vicissitudes and upheavals of national history, because it represents much more than a simple way of organising power: it is a project. But this project is a demanding one and requires the support of all the citizens who make up the body of the Republic.

This call for a united front is an organic model, in stark contrast to the original structure of secularism. In the wake of the Enlightenment, secularism required citizens to respect the procedural rules of the democratic order, based on the simple horizontal limitation of individual freedoms. Macron's proposal is of a different nature – far more vertical and less pluralist. By referring to the 'values of the Republic', it aims to unite individuals around a shared morality that they are required to approve through a positive act of will. The content of this socio-ethical construct is becoming increasingly clear: it incorporates the equality of sexual orientations, the freedom of sexual behaviour, the equality of women and men, the primacy of positive law over religious law and the sacred nature of the flag and the motto of the Republic. Within the president's entourage, this may also be extended to a certain way of dressing and eating.[30] Again, is this a 'civic' conception of the nation? Probably not: by transforming these principles of life into obligations of being and linking them to the code bequeathed by France's Judeo-Christian and rationalist history, Emmanuel Macron is, in fact, constructing a 'culturalist' scheme for living together. He constantly proclaims this, as in his New Year's greetings to the French people for 2024: 'France is a culture, a history, a language, universal values that are learned from the earliest age'.[31]

This system of discipline is complemented by a third, transformative, aspect. The former 'recognised churches' are the object of occasional admonitions from the State. In October 2021, before the National Assembly, Macron's Interior Minister, Gérald Darmanin, took issue – albeit very mildly – with the attitude of the President of the French Bishops' Conference, Mgr de Moulins-Beaufort, who, in a radio broadcast, had asserted, with regard to a possible challenge to the secrecy of confession, that the law of the Republic could not prevail over the law of God. However, reproaches are rare, all the more so as the Head of State often voices his 'admiration'[32] for these religious families who have accepted modern times.[33] Islam is not treated with the same tact: Macron, who wishes to demonstrate his distance from the extreme right, explains that it is not 'compatible' with the Republic and must be reformed. To adapt it to the demands of French culture, the Macron government has embarked on a vast reform of the secular laws of the Third Republic. The project was revealed by the newspaper *L'Opinion* in October 2018[34] but had been in preparation since at least the beginning of that year. It was the subject of an official announcement, accompanied by a catalogue of practical measures proposed to parliament and in his speeches in Mulhouse and, particularly, Les Mureaux. Opposition from religious forces, at least from Catholics, Protestants and Muslims,[35] did not lead the government to shelve it, nor did the petition from certain intellectuals close to the *Printemps Républicain* movement, who considered that, if police measures could be implemented against 'Islamic separatism', this should be done without touching the law of 1905. After a wide-ranging debate involving not only parliament but also public institutions like the National Consultative Committee on Human Rights and the Defender of Rights – which opposed the project – and private groups such as the *Grand Orient de France* and the *Printemps Républicain*, which ultimately supported it, the final text was promulgated on 24 August 2021.

Supported by groups supporting Macron and the right, this text touches upon an extensive number of sectors (the law of worship, the law of associations, health law, sports law, criminal law, family law, inheritance law, etc.). The provisions it introduces into French law have the effect, with a few exceptions, of reducing the scope for religious freedom. Let us cite just two examples: freedom of association and freedom of education. With regard to freedom of association, the 1905 law minimally regulated the management of religious associations, all the more so as it stated in Article 4 that they may 'conform to the rules of general organisation of the church whose exercise they propose to ensure'. The 2021 law considerably tightens up their operating principles, particularly those concerning membership of religious associations, the conditions under which meetings are held, controls on funding (particularly from abroad) and accounting. If associations governed by ordinary law – organised under the 1901 Act, which, under French law, can perform a religious function – wish to receive a public subsidy, they must now sign a 'contract of republican commitment' in which they undertake to respect the principles of liberty, equality and fraternity, not to call into question the secular character or symbols of the Republic and to refrain from any action prejudicial to public order and human dignity. With regard to freedom of education, the law of 28 March 1882 established that instruction could be given in public schools, private schools or, after a simple declaration to the public authorities, within the family. However, this freedom has now been restricted: homeschooling is now subject to a system of authorisation. As for education in private schools, this is now subject, along the lines already announced in the 2018 Gatel law, to tighter controls by the state. Furthermore, in September 2023, the then Minister of Education, Gabriel Attal, now prime minister, issued an internal ruling extending the scope of the 2004 law by including *qamis* and *abayas* in the category of conspicuous religious symbols – and therefore prohibited in public schools. In December 2023, this set of rules was supplemented by provisions prohibiting the recruitment of foreign imams seconded to France. The Immigration and Integration Act of 26 January 2024 added further provisions to the *corpus juris*, requiring immigrants to pass on the values of the Republic to their children, while facilitating the expulsion of those who transgress them.

This pattern of intervention,[36] which owes much to the need to respond to the demands of a public opinion increasingly marked by the words of the *Rassemblement National* (previously *Front National*), concerns Islam first and foremost. Moreover, the state is striving to place it under the control of bodies that it defines. In place of the Sarkozy-style *Conseil Français du Culte Musulman*, set up on the basis of elections that left plenty of room for intervention by foreign states and following an approach already at work in 2016 under the presidency of François Hollande, it has substituted a more open partnership structure bringing together, in the words of the President of the Republic, 'the living forces of the Muslim faith [with a view to] building an Islam of the Enlightenment'.[37] In this model, these voices are chosen by the political powers themselves. Moreover, the general population is not excluded from this 'republicanisation' of conscience. From schools to government departments and civil associations, all French citizens are now subject to multiple training courses on secularism,[38] culminating in the 'official day of secularism' on 9 December. This 'civic rearmament', as Macron calls it, is being carried out under the aegis of new institutions: the *Conseil des Sages* (Council of Elders) within the Ministry of National Education – made up mainly of people who support 'strict secularism' – and the *Comité Interministériel de la Laïcité* (Interministerial Committee for Secularism) – made up of government officials – which has replaced the *Observatoire de Laïcité* (Secularism Observatory), which the authorities deemed too flexible regarding identity-based manifestations.

Conclusion

The past seven years have seen a continuation in France of the model for the public management of religious affairs that has been gradually established since the early 2000s. Emmanuel Macron has even accentuated some of its features. The system of regulating belief that he defends is based on two principles. First, the principle of openness. His world is that of liberalism. Society, he says, can only serve the good of individuals and the prosperity of society by letting private initiatives play a role in all areas. Internally, this vision feeds the 'trickle-down' economic theory, according to which the wealth of the 'lead climber' ends up benefiting everyone. It also leads him, as he said after the pandemic, to welcome scientific and technical conquests and to promote, as indicated by his interventions on questions of procreation, euthanasia, abortion and the extension of rights affecting intimacy. Externally, Macron distrusts the economic and legal programmes of today's populist movements to build borders: his European policy bears witness to this, as do his stances in favour of free trade. The second principle is that of stabilisation. Macron's vision includes a Ricoeurian aspect: the expansion of subjective sovereignty, when unchecked, can lead to social dislocation if it is not countered by elements of meaning external to itself. This is where the politics of secularism come in. Here, we return to the hypothesis put forward in the introduction: in the world of the Third Republic, secularism was a system for *preserving freedoms*. In short, it was conceived as a procedural, abstract and general framework, allowing everyone to cultivate their beliefs or non-beliefs as they wished, without the state – which was 'separate from the Churches' – being able to directly influence the organisation and activity of religious institutions. The 1905 law followed in the wake of others that had extended freedom of expression, recognised freedom of funerals and instituted freedom of association. Under Emmanuel Macron and in a continuation of a policy inaugurated by Jacques Chirac and accentuated by Nicolas Sarkozy, the secular regime has taken a different turn. Within the framework of asymmetrical cooperation between the state and religious authorities, it is now seen as a means of disseminating values, with the aim of placing citizens, in the exercise of their subjective freedom, within the orbit of the good as defined by political power. This evolution, which can be seen in other European countries, undoubtedly reflects the (trend towards the) installation of our political systems in the space of what political theory sometimes calls 'authoritarian liberalism' (Portier, 2024; Spitz, 2022). In the past, the public mind was independent of the state. It has now been rediscovered, through the effect of a policy of uniquely material and cultural securitisation, subject to the state's sovereign power.

Notes

1 Substantialist secularism describes a regime for regulating belief in which the state is not content to preserve freedom for all, but in which, on the contrary, it attempts to guide its implementation on the basis of the morality (the substance) it defines.
2 Unless otherwise noted, other speeches by Macron can be accessed at the Elysée website: https://www.elysee.fr/recherche?prod_all_fr%5Bquery%5D=discours&prod_all_fr%5Bpage%5D=3https://www.elysee.fr/.
3 Speech at the European Jewish Center, 29 October 2019.
4 https://www.elysee.fr/emmanuel-macron/2020/02/18/proteger-les-libertes-en-luttant-contre-le-separatisme-islamiste-conference-de-presse-du-president-emmanuel-macron-a-mulhouse
5 Speech at Les Mureaux in English at https://www.elysee.fr/en/emmanuel-macron/2020/10/02/fight-against-separatism-the-republic-in-action-speech-by-emmanuel-macron-president-of-the-republic-on-the-fight-against-separatism
6 https://www.elysee.fr/emmanuel-macron/2020/09/04/150-ans-en-republique
7 Speech at the Collège des Bernardins, 19 April 2018. https://www.elysee.fr/emmanuel-macron/2018/04/09/discours-du-president-de-la-republique-emmanuel-macron-a-la-conference-des-eveques-de-france-au-college-des-bernardins

Recognition and surveillance **319**

8 https://www.vie-publique.fr/discours/268513-emmanuel-macron-16042019-notre-dame-de-paris-incendie#:~:text=L
9 Speech at the *Forum économique mondial à Davos*, 24 January 2018.
10 Speech by French President Emmanuel Macron on the 500th anniversary of the Protestant Reformation, Hôtel de Ville, Paris, 25 September 2017. Speech at the European Jewish Centre, 29 October 2019.
11 As previous note: speech 25 September 2017.
12 On this point, Interview with *Famille Chrétienne*, 21 December 2017.
13 Debate with intellectuals, 18 March 2019. 'Grand débat des idées, le direct: Emmanuel Macron échange avec des intellectuels', France Culture. Vidéo et podcast: le débat d'Emmanuel Macron avec des intellectuels en intégrale (radiofrance.fr)
14 There were 280 military chaplains, both active and reserve, in 2017; the target was 360 by 2022. It should be noted, however, that the crisis in the hospital sector has led to a reduction in the number of paid positions in this sector, albeit with an increase in the number of volunteers.
15 Interview with *Famille chrétienne*, 21 December 2017.
16 Debate with intellectuals, 18 March 2019.
17 Jack Lang was Minister of National Education; Max Cloupet, General Secretary of Catholic Education.
18 Alsace-Moselle has a specific status based on local law and the 19th century system of recognised religious denominations since it was under German control when the 1905 law was passed, following the Franco-Prussian war. In addition to the possibility of intervening in schools, the government continues to provide churches with salaries for some of their staff and the possibility of obtaining subsidies for their public events and property operations. Clerics are appointed with the agreement of the political authorities.
19 President Macron claims to be one of its devotees, at least culturally.
20 From time to time, he can also be seen attending mass with Brigitte Macron, his wife, a former Catholic school teacher who seems to have retained a close link with the faith.
21 See note 1.
22 He states 'We have to be honest. While fundamentalism is at work in all religions, the heart of the debate occupying our society today concerns Islam'.
23 Ifop study for DDV (Le Droit de Vivre) and the LICRA carried out by self-administered online questionnaire from 15 to 20 January 2021 among a sample of 1,006 people, representative of the secondary school population aged 15 and over.
24 'It's essential that we win this battle against the preachers of hate who, in the name of Islam, today in a clandestine manner, still proceed with preaching contrary to the values of the Republic, to what is at the heart of Islam'.
25 He gave a half-hearted explanation of this evolution in Mulhouse in February 2020: communities are tolerable in a Republic. From this point of view, his model is one of integration rather than assimilation.
26 He declared in Mulhouse on 18 February 2020 (see link note 4): 'The problem we have is when, in the name of a religion or affiliation, you want to separate yourself from the Republic, and therefore no longer respect its laws, and therefore you threaten the possibility of living together in the Republic, in this respect, that you yourself get out, but you threaten the possibility for others to do so'.
27 Despite resistance from a number of other ministers, such as Najat Vallaud-Belkacem, Minister of Education.
28 By linking secularism to its mission of ensuring 'civility' and promoting the 'minimum requirements of living together in French society (in the words borrowed

from the explanatory memorandum to the 11 October 2010 law on covering the face in public spaces), President Macron has considerably extended the scope of state intervention in behaviour management.
29 https://www.vie-publique.fr/loi/277621-loi-separatisme-respect-des-principes-de-la-republique-24-aout-2021. Given the warning contained in the Conseil d'Etat's opinion on the government's proposal, the word 'principles' is undoubtedly used more often than the word 'values'.
30 Comments made notably Jean-Michel Blanquer, Minister of Education, and Gérald Darmanin, Minister of the Interior.
31 https://www.elysee.fr/emmanuel-macron/2023/12/31/voeux-aux-francais-pour-2024
32 See the president's various interventions with regard to the Catholic Church after the attack on Father Hamel in Saint-Etienne du Rouvray in August 2016.
33 Speeches about Catholicism, Protestantism and Judaism are always laudatory. These three religious families have built the nation and, at different paces, supported the Republic.
34 While stating that there was no need to create new laws, Macron had already proposed a whole series of measures in *Révolution* in 2016, which are to be found in the 2021 law on separatism.
35 The Jews were in his favour.
36 Macron has declared that he wants to accompany this work of security integration with a heavyweight social intervention scheme. See in particular his speech in Mulhouse, 18 February 2020.
37 Speech for the Forum de l'Islam de France à l'Élysée,16 February 2023.
38 See the significance attached to Moral and Civic Education in school curricula under the action of Jean Michel Blanquer as Minister of Education. The decree of 3 May 2017 made it compulsory for paid chaplains to obtain a state-issued diploma in civil and civic training. Also, noteworthy is the creation of the French Institute of Islamology.

References

Baroin, F. (2003) *Pour une nouvelle laïcité. Report to Prime Minister Raffarin*. Rapport de François Baroin « Pour une nouvelle laïcité » (Club Dialogue & Initiative) [Réseau Voltaire] (voltairenet.org).
Brenner, E. (2004) *Les territoires perdus de la République*. Paris: Fayard.
Debray, R. (2019a) *Le nouveau pouvoir*. Paris: Editions du Cerf.
Debray, R. (2019b) *Du génie français*. Paris: Gallimard.
Dolez, B., Fretel, J. and Lefebvre, R. (eds) (2019) *L'entreprise Macron*. Grenoble: PUG.
Dolez, B., Douillet, A.C., Fretel, J. and Lefebvre, R. (eds) (2022) *L'entreprise Macron à l'épreuve du pouvoir*. Grenoble: PUG.
Dosse, F. (2017) *Le philosophe et le président*. Paris: Stock.
Edelman, M. (1985) *The symbolic uses of politics*. Chicago: University of Illinois Press.
Macron, E. (2016) *Révolution*. Paris: XO.
Portier, P. (2016) *L'État et les religions en France. Une sociologie historique de la laïcité*. Rennes: Presses Universitaires de Rennes.
Portier, P. (2022) 'Laïcité dans les programmes présidentiels de l'élection 2022', *Le Grand Continent*, April. https://legrandcontinent.eu/fr/2022/04/06/la-place-de-laicite-dans-les-douze-programmes-presidentiels/
Portier, P. (2024) 'La crise de la laïcité française', *Critique*, 924, pp. 59–70.

Portier, P. and Willaime J.-P. (2021) *La religion dans la France contemporaine. Entre sécularisation et recomposition.* Paris: Colin.
Portier, P. and Willaime, J.-P. (eds.) (2022). *Religion and secularism in contemporary France.* London: Routledge.
Revault d'Allonnes, M. (2019) *L'esprit du macronisme.* Paris: Seuil.
Ricoeur, P. (2000) *La mémoire, l'histoire et l'oubli.* Paris: Seuil.
Ricoeur, P. (2019) 'Le pouvoir. Fin du théologico-politique', *Esprit*, 457, pp. 112–129.
Spitz, J.-F. (2022) *La République? Quelles valeurs? Essai sur un nouvel intégrisme politique.* Paris: Gallimard.

EPILOGUE: 6 JANUARY 2025

Susan Collard

Given the tumultuous nature of the events that have characterised French politics since the submission of this manuscript in late July 2024, the editors have kindly allowed me to add an epilogue to bring the analysis of Macron's presidency as up to date as possible prior to publication.

The Olympic truce

Following the snap legislative election held in June and July, in which the NFP left alliance won the greatest number of seats, it proposed (after much consultation) a candidate, Lucie Castets, to form a new government. However, the president (who has sole power to nominate the prime minister) rejected this proposal on the grounds that her government would be immediately censured by the other opposition groups, though he was no doubt also motivated by his determination not to allow the repeal of the pension reform, demanded by the NFP. He preferred instead to buy himself time to consider his choice of prime minister by announcing an 'Olympic truce': despite Attal's formal resignation on 16 July, his government would remain in place as a 'caretaker government,' only dispatching urgent business, until its replacement after the summer. This was controversial, not only because it left a potential political vacuum in the event of a major crisis or terrorist attack during the Olympics, but also because important preparations should have been underway for the annual budget to be presented to parliament in the autumn.

Moreover, since 17 ministers had won seats in the recent election, the rule of separation of powers set out in Article 23 of the Constitution should have meant their giving up one of those roles. But instead, outgoing ministers were allowed to participate in the internal elections in the National Assembly (NA) in July for the key posts which deliver influence over how parliamentary business is conducted (presidency and vice-presidency of the Assembly, and the eight permanent committees and membership of the *bureau*). These internal elections proved to be intensely political, with complex wheeling and dealing between and within the various parliamentary groups. Much of this activity aimed to minimise the potential influence of the National Rally (RN), despite its being the single party with the greatest number of seats. As a result, the outgoing 'macronist' president of the NA, Yaël Braun-Pivet, managed to retain her position, while the RN ended up with no representation on the *bureau*, which is now dominated by the NFP. This intense infighting was a strong indicator of how politics would play out amongst the newly elected deputies when the new parliamentary session started in early October.

The Barnier government

On 5th September, Macron finally announced that he was appointing Michel Barnier as prime minister. UK readers will remember Barnier as the Chief Negotiator for the Brexit agreement with the EU, but he also had extensive experience as French EU Commissioner, as a minister, deputy, MEP and in various levels of local government. Politically, Barnier came from the centre-right, as did Macron's first two prime ministers. He had stood in the internal primary held by *Les Républicains* in 2022 to select their presidential candidate, in which he came third out of five contenders, having run a campaign which was unexpectedly hard-line, especially on immigration.

Forming a government was no easy task, given the aim, agreed with the president, of including only parties considered as being within what was called the 'republican arc', excluding the two extremes (RN and LFI). Solidarity within the NFP meant that Barnier was only able to persuade one representative of the left to join him: Didier Migaud, president of the HATVP (discussed in Chapter 4) who became Minister of Justice, ranked second in formal order of importance. The government, announced on 21 September (with a couple of additions a week later), was composed of 39 ministers and secretaries of state: about half of them came from the former presidential majority, 8 of them represented other small right-wing or independent parties, and 10 were from the most conservative wing of *Les Républicains* (which had only won 38 seats), notably hard-liner Bruno Retailleau in the key post of Minister of the Interior. The party's new leader, Laurent Wauquiez, who had previously refused to join a coalition with the president's supporters, had changed his position since the new prime minister was from his own party. But this was no ordinary coalition, and debate followed as to how this new set up could be defined: was it cohabitation?

Coalitation? Cohabilitation? Or even collaboration, as suggested by the leader of the communists? In the end, the term '*socle commun*' was agreed upon: a term used in the education system to define a 'common core'. This enabled the participating parties to feel that they were 'responsibly' supporting the overall aims of the government, whilst retaining enough independence to play a constructively critical role.

The fact that this new government was such a poor reflection of the election results inevitably provoked an outcry of 'denial of democracy' from opposition groups, especially within the NFP. It had already instigated an unprecedented attempt to bring about the 'destitution' (impeachment) of the president by invoking Article 68 of the Constitution, whereby the incumbent can be removed from office "in the event of a breach of duty manifestly incompatible with the exercise of their mandate". Although there was little support for this proposal, it was a reminder that the autocratic style of the 'hyperpresident' remained at the heart of the political crisis.

For Macron, the marked turn to the right of Barnier's government - compared to the broader support he had rallied behind him in previous governments - was mitigated by the assumption that his economic programme, especially the pension reform, would not be upended by the new prime minister, especially since key positions, especially in the Finance Ministry, were still held by '*macronistes*'. When the prime minister delivered the ritual 'declaration of policy' to the NA on 1 October, he emphasised the need for dialogue, respect, and a general 'change of method' in governing. In terms of policy, although short on detail (understandably given the time he had to prepare), he outlined five priorities: to improve quality of life, give better access to public services; reinforce security; take a pragmatic approach to problems relating to immigration; and encourage more 'fraternity' across a range of policy areas. For the economy, he pledged to reduce the public deficit to 5 per cent by the end of 2025 (and to 3 per cent by 2029), by imposing higher taxes on large profit-making companies and the wealthy (effectively suspending Macron's business-friendly reforms) and by making a range of spending cuts. He also said he wanted to make improvements to certain problematic aspects of the 2023 pension reform. On institutional reform, he agreed to consider proposals for a change in the electoral system to include some form of proportional representation, once again seen as a potential key to unlocking the stalemate in the NA.

Barnier's initial task was to try to pass the budget for 2025, an annual ritual that dominates the autumn session of parliament, and which had to be passed before 21 December for it to be implemented. Elisabeth Borne had reluctantly resorted to using the controversial Article 49.3 to force her budgets through in 2022 and 2023 without a vote, and it was pretty much a foregone conclusion that Barnier would have to do the same, exposing his government to an inevitable vote of no-confidence by the opposition. Whilst

Borne was able (with difficulty) to survive these pressures, the numerical composition of the new NA made Barnier's government much more vulnerable - providing of course that the opposition groups on both left and right were prepared to support the same censure motion (discussed in Chapter 3). This possibility hung over the new prime minister like the sword of Damocles throughout the parliamentary debates over the budget.

These debates became even more intense as figures were published showing an apparently sudden and sharp decline in the state of the economy: the public deficit was now forecast to hit 6.1 per cent of GDP by the end of the year instead of the 4.4 per cent anticipated (already far higher than the 3 per cent officially required by EU fiscal rules), and public debt had risen to 110.6 per cent of GDP. This triggered an immediate blame game, as explanations were sought for the causes of this unexpected and catastrophic state of affairs. A Senate inquiry which reported on 19 November held the previous governments under Borne and Attal responsible, for not having taken action when economic forecasts first gave indications of problems in late 2023. In response, Borne argued that she was preoccupied at that time with passing the 2024 budget and the immigration bill. For his part, Attal listed various actions he had taken after taking office, and accused Barnier of not acting immediately after his appointment to implement by decree some of Attal's plans, which had been suspended by the dissolution of the NA. The bitter recriminations within the '*socle commun*' did not bode well for the future of this fragile construct. In attempting to implement a 'responsible' strategy to tackle the disastrous economic situation, by delivering 60 billion euros of savings, Barnier found himself stuck between a rock and a hard place: attacked from both sides of the opposition, as well as from within his own camp, including *macronistes* defending the legacy of 'macronomics'.

At the same time, a rise in unemployment and a wave of job losses in big companies like Michelin and Valeo revealed other problems which cast a shadow over the legacy of Macron's attempted 'reindustrialisation' plan based on business-friendly supply side economics (*politique de l'offre*). The government also faced demonstrations by farmers, angry not only at the prospect of the signing of the MERCOSUR agreement by the EU, which they argue represents unfair competition for French agriculture, but also over unkept promises made to them by Attal's new government earlier in the year regarding the problem of agricultural over-regulation.

The critical moment for Barnier's government was expected at some point in December: the LFI leader Jean-Luc Mélenchon - keen to precipitate a presidential election in which he assumed he would be the candidate of the left, rather than push for the appointment of the NFP candidate as prime minister - announced that the NFP would table a censure motion if Article 49.3 was used to force the budget through. Le Pen's RN, having initially adopted a more conciliatory line, in keeping with its projected image as a party committed to responsible government, later hardened its position, threatening to support the NFP's motion if Barnier failed to meet their budgetary 'red lines'. This change of tack was no doubt at least partly influenced by a court recommendation made in late November (at the end of a trial of party members, including herself, accused of embezzling funds from the European Parliament) which could result in her being denied eligibility to stand in the next presidential election. Since that decision would be announced on 31 March 2025, it was in Le Pen's interest to push for the early resignation of the president, leading to a new election before that date. By bringing down the government, she, like Mélenchon, hoped to force Macron's hand.

Despite making several concessions, Barnier refused to meet all her demands, and on 4 December, the RN deputies voted in support of the NFP's motion of no confidence. This had been tabled two days earlier after the prime minister had decided to invoke Article 49.3 to push through the part of the budget relating to social security financing (the PLFSS). The combined vote of 331 deputies from both alliances brought down the government after only 91 days in office, making it the shortest-lived government in the Fifth Republic.

For the reasons explained in Chapter 3, this was only the second time in the history of the Fifth Republic that a government had been voted out in this way. The only precedent was in 1962, when parliament strongly rejected de Gaulle's attempt to encroach on its sovereignty by introducing universal suffrage for the presidential election (instead of by an electoral college). The president had responded by dissolving the NA and holding a controversial referendum (ignoring the procedures set out in the constitution) in which 62.25 per cent of the electorate gave him the answer he wanted. In that case, the vote of no confidence in the government led to the strengthening of de Gaulle's position. Here, by contrast, with the collapse of Barnier's government Macron was further weakened, especially since the budget had not been approved. This unprecedented scenario tipped the situation into an even deeper crisis with no obvious solution, but which prompted much speculation about possible outcomes.

From Barnier to Bayrou

The following day, Macron spoke on television for about 10 minutes, thanking the outgoing prime minister and promising to announce his replacement very soon. He insisted he would remain in office until the end of his five-year mandate and criticised the extremes of right and left for uniting against the government in what he called 'an anti-republican front', designed to create chaos in pursuit of their own interests rather than the national interest. There was no expression of remorse over his decision to dissolve the NA; rather, he regretted that it had not been well understood. He called for a new era of compromise, putting an end to divisions to prevent a return to 'immobilism', and hoped that in the 30 remaining months of his mandate, progress could be made in tackling France's many problems. However, there was no indication that Macron himself had any intention of compromising on his own political programme.

Intense consultations followed, and it was well over a week before the Elysée announced on 13 December the nomination of François Bayrou, leader of the centrist party the MoDEM, as the new prime minister. This was clearly not a straightforward choice: although Bayrou had supported Macron since 2017, and in many ways represented many of the core values of 'macronism', there was strong resistance to him from some quarters, and the president had initially told him that he would not be choosing him to lead the next government. But Bayrou had retaliated by threatening to withdraw the MoDEM's support, and Macron gave in. By all accounts, this is the first time that a prime minister has imposed himself on a reluctant president. Former President Sarkozy, who has a history of acrimonious relations with Bayrou, wasted no time in criticising this appointment in the press, saying: "I am sorry for France faced with this distressing spectacle, and sorry for the president of the Republic who has submitted to *combinaisons* that no-one understands".[1]

Once in office, Bayrou faced the same challenges as Barnier in trying to constitute a government which would incorporate representatives from across the 'republican arc', excluding the extremes of left and right, but ideally including the socialists. He started badly by making several beginner's errors, such as forgetting to thank the president for appointing him in his first speech as prime minister, a ritual prerequisite. His consultations were then suddenly disrupted by the catastrophic impact of a cyclone in the overseas department of Mayotte (off Madagascar in the Indian Ocean), following which the president and prime minister both (separately) flew out to assess the situation and show support for the victims. For Macron, this turned out to be a disastrous exercise in political communication when he responded to angry residents, who were complaining that they still had no water or electricity, by saying that he wasn't responsible for the cyclone and that 'if Mayotte was not part of France, they would be 10,000 times deeper in the shit'.[2] Once again, the president's apparent lack of empathy and his habit of 'plain speaking' (*parler cash*), did him a great disservice in terms of his public image. For Bayrou, his decision to prioritise attending a meeting of the municipal council in Pau where he is (and intends to remain) mayor, before going to Mayotte, was also seen as a political blunder, especially as the new prime minister used the occasion to raise the issue of a return to allowing multiple office holding, which was seen as out of step with the more urgent demands of the immediate crisis.

The composition of Bayrou's government was finally announced on 23 December, despite this being allocated a day of mourning for the victims in Mayotte, and extraordinarily, the 35 new ministers took up their positions, in front of TV cameras, on Christmas Eve. Interestingly, the new government included two former prime ministers, significantly placed in second and third positions in the formal ranking of ministers. These were Elisabeth Borne and Manuel Valls, occupying key posts as ministers of state: Borne heads up a Ministry for National Education, Higher Education and Research, while Valls has responsibility for all of France's overseas territories in an unprecedented full-blown ministry dedicated to the '*outre-mer*'. The two other ministers of state are Gerald Darmanin (ranked 4th), previously Interior Minister but who was not in the Barnier government, who now became Minister of Justice, and Bruno Retailleau (ranked 5th), who retained his position as Minister of the Interior. The idea is that these two will work in tandem to take a firm stand on law and order and on dealing with migration, issues identified in polls as high priority by a significant part of the population.

Politically, it remained a government representing the centre and centre-right allegiances of the former presidential alliance: over half of them had been in the Barnier government, with 14 of them retaining their same posts, but there were fewer representatives of *Les Républicains* (7 instead of 13). Bayrou, like Barnier, was unable to persuade any significant socialists to join him: having failed to retain the previous Minister of Justice, Didier Migaud, the only representatives with (past) associations with the left were: Manuel Valls, former prime minister to President Hollande (considered a 'social-traitor' by most of his former party members); the mayor of Dijon, François Rebsamen, as Minister for Territorial Planning (*Aménagement du territoire*), who had left the Socialist Party in 2022 to endorse Macron; and Juliette Méadel, who was excluded from the party in 2018 for having supported Macron in 2017, and who now became a junior minister under Rebsamen with responsibility for urban cohesion policies (*politique de la ville*).

With the new government in place, politics then took a break until the president's annual TV intervention on 31 December to convey his New Year wishes to the nation.[3] The broadcast innovated by starting with video footage, commented by Macron, of France's great achievements in 2024, including the constitutionalisation of the right to abortion, the D-Day commemorations, the Olympic Games and the spectacular restoration of Notre Dame Cathedral. Reverting then to the traditional speech from the Elysée Palace, he unexpectedly acknowledged that the dissolution of the NA had not brought the clarity he had anticipated, nor had it prevented a regrettable decline into political 'immobilism'; instead, it had simply created more divisions. In a rare demonstration of humility, he even accepted his full share of responsibility for this. He then urged the population to pull together in a collective effort (*un resaisissement collectif*) to build compromises and greater stability. He alluded to the possibility of giving the nation a say on certain important but undefined issues, without clarifying whether this might mean another election, a referendum, or some other form of consultation. In fact the whole speech was generally weak on specifics, but in terms of overall direction, it was clear that the 'project' he claimed to be outlining was in reality just more of the same.

On 3 January, the new government met for the first time as the weekly Council of Ministers, but the meeting was short and discussion of Mayotte was deferred to a separate crisis meeting. Bayrou's watchwords for the new government were reconciliation and stability, whereas Macron invited the new ministers to show unity and audacity, to make good use of their powers to issue decrees (*la voie règlementaire*) and to take full advantage of the administrations under their control (see Chapter 9). Ministers were asked to consult as widely as possible in order to feed into the prime minister's inaugural 'declaration of policy' to be delivered in parliament on 14 January, which will outline his proposals for legislation, including the budget. From then on, the fate of the new government looks uncertain.

What next?

Bayrou described the challenges facing his government as being of 'Himalayan' proportions, with his first and most urgent task being to prepare and win approval for a new budget, without succumbing to a censure motion as Barnier did. In a long TV interview broadcast just after announcing his government, the new prime minister expressed his confidence that he could succeed in this. Parliament had unanimously voted a special law on 16 December enabling the 2024 budget to be carried over, avoiding the situation of shutdown experienced in the USA. But Bayrou, who has historically shown great concern for France's problem of growing debt and deficit, must still find ways of addressing the same economic difficulties as Barnier: cutting expenditure and increasing revenue. A key player in managing these choices will be Eric Lombard as new Finance Minister, alongside former 'macronist' minister Amélie de Montchalin, now responsible for the Budget and Public Accounts. Lombard has not previously held any elected or ministerial office, and despite a successful background in banking, he identifies as being on the left, with whom he maintains good relations. However, his views are those of a Rocardian social-liberal and are highly compatible with the general direction of Macron's economic reforms, which therefore probably remain in safe hands.

The key stumbling block in budget negotiations will be the fate of the 2023 pension reform, which the left wants to repeal, or at the very least suspend, pending a revised agreement. Maintaining this emblematic reform has been a constant red line for Macron, as for Barnier and Bayrou, even if certain adjustments might be considered. This explains why both Barnier and Bayrou failed to persuade any socialists to join them in their efforts to build a majority from within the 'republican arc'. There is in fact division within the Socialist Party over the line it should take on this, but since its electoral fortunes are currently tied to its membership of the NFP alliance, and since another election in 2025 is quite possible, their hands are somewhat tied. In due course, this might change if the Bayrou government is willing and able to introduce some form of proportional representation, freeing the socialists from their rather unnatural electoral alliance with LFI. But more immediately, Bayrou must win their approval for a revised budget, or at least a commitment not to back a vote of no confidence, without alienating his support from the right, which is committed to the pension reform. This will involve some hard bargaining: the socialists will need to secure sufficient recompense for what would effectively mean the break-up of the NFP. Thus, whereas with Barnier, it was the RN that held the greatest bargaining power, for Bayrou, it is more likely to be the socialists.

If he is successful, he could possibly remain in place till the next presidential election, normally due in 2027. But if he fails, Macron will be under more pressure to resign early and allow a reboot of the whole political system. This is however unlikely, if only because it would probably result in a run-off between the leaders of the two extremes, Mélenchon and Le Pen, that Macron is determined to prevent. Since the socialists are not in favour of an early presidential election (because they do not currently have an agreed candidate and would not want to support Mélenchon), they could perhaps be persuaded to help Bayrou remain in office. If his government does not survive, and if Macron chooses not to resign, the president will have to search again for another prime minister and the cycle of immobilism will continue, with increasingly negative implications for France's international standing. This would no longer be a political crisis, but an institutional one, raising the question of the need for significant constitutional reform, or even regime change.

Macron could also use his constitutional power to dissolve the NA again and hope for a better outcome, but since legislative elections cannot be held until at least a year after the last ones, the earliest possible date would be July 2025. Given the disastrous impact of the 2024 dissolution, which he has now acknowledged, it is highly unlikely he would repeat this move. In any case, most observers doubt that a new election would produce a significantly different outcome. The stalemate would therefore not be resolved, unless perhaps if parliament could agree on a modification of the electoral system (see Chapter 3) to introduce proportional representation, which has wide support across the parties and amongst the population. Yet even this might not bring sufficient clarity to the situation: in a recently published study by the *Fondation Jean Jaurès*,[4] the former deputy and academic Emeric Bréhier calculated what the results of the 2024 election would have looked like if proportional representation had been used, modelled on two possible different systems. If they had used the method adopted for senatorial elections, which is a complex mix of proportional and majoritarian systems based on the population size at departmental level, 80 per cent of the deputies would have been elected using proportional representation. The main beneficiaries would have been the RN and its allies, who would have won an additional 39 seats, bringing their total to 180, but still far off an absolute majority of 289. The *Républicains* (who want to keep the current system) would have gained six seats. The NFP would have lost 17 seats, leaving it with only 161 deputies, and the presidential alliance would have lost 28 seats, retaining only 134.

If they had used the model adopted for the European elections (national party lists), the RN and allies would have made gains of 20 seats, but the small parties like the Communist Party would have failed to even reach the 5 per cent minimum threshold without alliances. The ecologists would have lost 13 seats and LFI would have lost 12. By contrast, the socialists would have gained 21 seats. These calculations show that reaching a cross-party consensus on what model to adopt would be highly problematic and would not provide a return to absolute majorities. So although many other models could be investigated, electoral reform seems unlikely to offer a way out of the current crisis, even if it might address the problem of democratic representation (see Chapter 3). If tripartism is to remain the norm, as seems likely, the only way of preventing immobilism is political: parties and politicians will have to accept the need to work better together. Yet that prospect still seems a long way off.

Macron's legacy?

However the current domestic crisis unfolds, it is now abundantly clear that Emmanuel Macron's deliberate disruption of French politics has not delivered the transformation he hoped for, but rather, a return to the immobilism of the past. Not since 1934 have there been four prime ministers in the same year. Once again, the country is locked in a struggle between the pursuit of change and resistance to it. Nor have the president's attempts to reset France's relations with certain priority areas abroad yielded any positive results. Its relationship with Algeria (see Chapter 14) is now at an all-time low, symbolised by Algerias's imprisonment in November of the Franco-Algerian writer Boualem Sansal on spurious political grounds. The recent announcements of the expulsion of French troops by the governments of Chad, Senegal and Ivory Coast were another reminder of Macron's failure to establish a new partnership with *la Françafrique* (see Chapter 13). Even in the all-important European arena (see Chapter 7), Macron's ambitions have been thwarted, and his inability to prevent the signing by the EU President of the Commission in December 2024 of the MERCOSUR agreement (with four South American countries), which he considers to be unacceptable, is an indicator of his weakened position, marking a decline in French influence in the EU.

With over two years till the end of the Macron's mandate in 2027, it seems premature to invoke his future legacy. But it is hard to envisage at this stage how he could recover sufficient authority and legitimacy to maintain the pursuit of his long-term political 'project'. At the same time, any prospect that the weakening of the president might herald a rebalancing of power towards parliament is counteracted by the fragmentation of political representation in the NA and by the intensity of ideological opposition between the main alliances. Ironically, the only policy proposal that could command a majority is the repeal of the pension reform, to which executive power (and the Senate) is strongly committed.

How could things have gone so wrong? For the reasons explained throughout this volume, and notwithstanding any positive achievements that for now have been totally eclipsed from public consciousness, Emmanuel Macron personally carries much of the blame for the increasing strength of animosity that has developed towards him over time, and which has prevented him from completing the deep transformation of France he had envisaged. In short, he has been his own worst enemy. As we have seen, he willingly became the most extreme incarnation of what the renowned political scientist, Maurice Duverger, famously described in 1974 as the 'republican monarch' (Duverger, 1974), arguing that this was what the French people wanted. But when Macron was drawing on Roman mythology to theorise his desire to be a 'Jupiterian' president, he might also have looked to Greek mythology, in which the crime of 'hubris' is punished by the gods. In this context, his arrogance and overconfidence invite a parallel with Icarus, who flew too close to the sun, ignoring all warnings until his wings melted and he fell into the sea and drowned. Perhaps Macron's fundamental mistake was to think that he could revisit the aspirations of the Revolution whilst 'at the same time' playing the role of monarch. This proved to be a paradox too far for the French people, who have not forgotten that it was the Revolution that led the King to the guillotine.

Notes

1. https://www.latribune.fr/la-tribune-dimanche/politique/francois-bayrou-a-matignon-c-est-affligeant-l-hiver-amer-de-nicolas-sarkozy-1013981.html
2. https://www.theguardian.com/world/2024/dec/20/emmanuel-macron-swears-amid-furious-exchange-with-cyclone-hit-mayotte-islanders
3. https://www.elysee.fr/emmanuel-macron/2024/12/31/voeux-aux-francais
4. https://www.jean-jaures.org/publication/ce-que-la-proportionnelle-peut-apporter-ou-non-a-la-democratie/

References

Duverger, M. (1974) *La Monarchie républicaine, ou comment les démocraties se donnent des rois*. Paris: Robert Laffont.

INDEX

5G 230
100-day period of appeasement 58

abortion 311
abstentions 77
accreditation 72; Anticor 81
addiction salée 33
ADEME *see* Agency for Ecological Transition
adequationist obsession 209–210
administrative deconcentration 181
adult education 209
advisors, corruption 79–80
AFA *see* Anti-Corruption Agency
AFD *see* Agence Française de Développment
affairs 67
AFM *see Avance sur frais de mandat*
Africa policy 16–18, 278–279; apologies to Josette Audin 289–290; economic and business policy 270–273; interventionism 268–270; museums and memory 286–288; policy errors 277–278; politics 273–277; promises of change 264–265; restitution of African heritage 288–289; Stora report 291–294; *see also Françafrique*
Africa-France summit (2021) 274
Agence Française de Développment (AFD) 271

Agency for Ecological Transition (ADEME) 223
Algeria 18–19, 284–285, 289–291, 298; crimes against humanity 285–286; Stora report 291–298
Algerian liberation movements 243
Algerian War 68, 243–244, 275, 285, 290, 298
Algerian-French dual nationals 294
alienation 306
Aliot, Louis 295
allowances, National Assembly 82
Alsace-Moselle 310, 319n18
alternance 190; presidential elections 2
alternance training 171
ambitions of Macron 3–4
amendments 46–47
America First 142
Amish model 230
Anglophone 271–272
Anglophone countries 274
ANPE *see* National Employment Agency
Anticor 78, 81
anti-corruption 71
Anti-Corruption Agency (AFA) 72
apprentices 210
apprenticeship training centres 170
arresting troublemakers 249–251
Article 49.3 56, 58, 106, 109n5, 325–326

Assédic (Association for Employment in Industry and Commerce) 172
assisted dying 311
Association for Employment in Industry and Commerce (*Assédic*) 172
Association of Mayors 51
Attal, Gabriel 6, 37, 59, 106, 175, 185, 207, 316, 323, 326
Attali, Jacques 187
Attali Commission 21–22
Attali, Jacques 187
Audin, Josette 289–290
Audin, Maurice 289
authoritarian liberalism 254–255
automobiles, environmental and climate policy (ECP) 232
autonomy 306
Avance sur frais de mandat (AFM) 81
Avec Vous 55
average annual growth rate 156

BAC *see Brigades Anti-Criminalité*
Bac Pro diploma 169
BAC *see Brigades Anti-Criminalité*
baccalauréat exam (*bac*) 211
Bad Godesberg conference (1959) 5
Balladur, Edouard 71
banlieues 16, 245, 248, 253, 255–256
bans: on headscarves 309; on hiring family members 74; on wearing of Muslim abaya 59; *see also* Penelopegate
banlieues 16, 245, 248, 253, 255–256
Bardella, Jordan 59, 107
Barnier, Michel 324–325
Barre, Raymond 31
Bataclan concert hall, terrorist attack 245, 313
Bayrou, François 34–35, 52, 54, 73
Béchu, Christophe 234–235
Belkadi, Ali Farid 290
Benalla, Alexandre 74–75
Benalla Affair 47, 75, 123
Benalla, Alexandre 74–75
Benelhadj, Mohand Ouamar 294
Benelux countries 137, 139
Bérégovoy, Pierre 31, 70
Berger, Laurent 32
Besoin d'Europe 3
BFM TV 120–121, 128
Big Walk (*Le Grande Marche*) 90
Birds Protection League (LPO) 232
Black Lives Matter 257

Blanquer, Jean-Michel 32, 191, 202, 211, 216
blocked vote 57, 59
BNF *see* National Library
Bollore, Vincént 10–11, 120–121, 126
Bordella, Jordan 151
border security 298
Borne, Elisabeth 31–32, 57, 59, 124, 185, 299, 325–326
'both left and right' paradox 34–37
Bourdin, Jean-Jaques 128
Braun-Pivet, Yaël 324
Brexit 134–135
Brigades Anti-Criminalité (BAC) 252
budget for 2025 325
Bundesbank 166
Burkina Faso 265–270, 278, 286
business conditions 159, 169
business policy in Africa 270–273

cabinets, downsizing of 188–189
cahiers de doleance 49
Cahuzac, Jérôme 71–72
Camus, Albert 291
Canal+ 121
Cap Collectif 49
Cap emploi 173
capitalism, state-centred capitalism 181
carbon border adjustment mechanism (CBAM) 147
carbon tax 136
Carle Act of 2009 309
Carrefour du Developpement 69–70
Castaner, Christophe 233
Castets, Lucie 3, 323
Castex, Jean 31, 124, 189, 193, 231, 311
Catholicism 19, 307, 310
CBAM *see* carbon border adjustment mechanism
CCC *see* Citizens Convention on the Climate
CDD *see* contract of limited duration
CDI *see* contract of unlimited duration
Central Service for the Prevention of Corruption (SCPC) 70
centre 99–100
Centres de formation d'apprentis (CFA) 170
CESE *see* Economic, Social and Environmental Council
CFA *see Centres de formation d'apprentis*

CFA *franc see* Colonies françaises d'Afrique
CFA *see* Centres de formation d'apprentis
CFPs *see* Individual Professional Training Accounts
CFSP *see* Common Foreign and Security Policy
Chad 269
Chamber of Civil Society 46
Charles Gide Protestant Association 310
Charlie Hebdo 245, 313
charter schools 211
CHESP *see* Cycle des hautes études du service public
Chikhi, Abdelmadjid 294
Chirac, Jacques 2, 5, 18, 25, 71, 116, 244, 285, 287, 292, 298, 314
Chouviat, Cédric 256
Christian roots 307
Ciotti, Eric 10–11, 60, 101
Circular Memorandum 195
Citizens Convention on the Climate (CCC) 7, 52–53, 232; socioecological justice 228–229
Citizens' Initiative Referendums (RIC) 48, 52
Citizens Vests (*Gilets citoyens*) 49, 52–53
civic rearmament 317
civil servants 13, 43, 67, 180, 182–183, 188; functional politicisation 197–198; pressure on 188–192
civil service 182; refounding of the system 192–197
CJR *see* Court of Justice of the Republic
class sizes, education system 211
Climate Bank 234
climate change 220; Citizens Convention on the Climate (CCC) 52–53; sovereignty agenda 233–236; *see also* environmental and climate policy
CNCCFP *see* National Commission on Campaign Accounts and Political Finance
CNDP *see* National Commission for Public Debate
CNDS *see* Commission nationale de déontologie de la sécurité
CNews 10, 120, 126

Coalition for the Sahel 267
coalition-building 137–139
codes of conduct 75–77, 84n22
cohabitation 2
collective contractual termination 169
collective debt management 11
collective redundancy procedures 169
collèges 207; *see also* higher education
Collomb, Gérard 102
colonialism 17, 265, 283–285, 298–299; condemnation of 286–288, 292–293; empathy for 299
Colonies françaises d'Afrique (CFA franc) 264–265, 271–273, 280n1
Comité de déontologie 82
Comité Interministériel de la Laïcité (Interministerial Committee for Secularism) 317
commemorative culture 293
Commission Mixte Paritaire (CMP) 59
Commission nationale de déontologie de la sécurité (CNDS) 244
Common Foreign and Security Policy (CFSP) 143
communautarisme (community separatism) 297
communication style of Macron 125–129
communitarianism 313
community policing 16, 244
community separatism 297
Compagnies Républicaines de Sécurité (CRS) 247–248
companies, lack of career development and internal promotions 165
competitiveness: high tax wedge 162–163; labour market 159–163; reforms to 166–167
Concordat regime 302
concours (competitive exams) 182, 186, 193, 205, 207, 208, 212
Conference on the Future of Europe 148
conflict of interest 66, 71–73, 78–79
Conseil des Sages (Council of Elders) 317
Conseil Français du Culte Musulman 317
Conseil National de la Refondation (CNR) 57
Conseil Présidentiel pour l'Afrique (Presidential Council for Africa CPA) 265

Index   337

Conseil Représentatif des Institutions Juives de France 310
Constitution of the Fifth Republic 24–25
Constitutional law 46
constitutional reform 45–47, 56
constructive opposition 10
consultancy firms 33, 69, 80, 184
contaminated blood scandal 78
continuity, education system 209–210
contract of limited duration (CDD) 164
contract of unlimited duration (CDI) 164
convaincre 22
Convention on the future of Europe 148
corporatisation 20, 311
corps intermédiares 54, 57
corruption 8, 66–68; parliamentarians 76–77
Council for Economic, Social and Environmental Council (CESE) 52
Council of Citizen Participation 54
Council of State 55, 194, 196
Court of Accounts 74, 196
Court of Appeal 196
Court of Justice of the Republic (CJR) 78
Couve de Murville, Maurice 31
Covid recovery package 15
Covid-19 crisis 30, 32, 55, 121, 124, 138–141; policing 257; recovery agenda 231; Resilience and Recovery Facility (RRF) 146; whatever it costs approach 147
Covid-19 Scientific Council 33
Covid-19 vaccines 140
CPA *see* Presidential Council for Africa
CRIF *see* Representative Council of Jewish Institutions in France
crime 244
crimes against humanity, Algeria 285–286
crisis of authority 188
crowd management 249–251; low-cost crowd control 251–253
CRS *see Compagnies Républicaines de Sécurité*
CRTE *see* Recovery and ecological Transition Contracts
CSE *see* Social and Economic Committee
curriculum 206–207

Cycle des hautes études du service public (CHESP) 194

DACs *see Directeurs d'Administration Centrale*
Daoud, Kamel 294
Darmanin, Gerald 59, 103, 107, 257, 315
Dati, Rachida 11
de Gaulle, Charles 24–25, 31, 42, 68, 264
de Montchalin, Amélie 193, 197–198
debates 116; 2022 campaign 118
Debré law 303, 309
debt 11, 135, 138–139, 146–147, 325
debt mutualisation 138
decentralisation *see* environmental and climate policy
declaration of interests 77
declarations of assets 76
Defender of Human Rights 316
Défenseur des droits 243
dégagisme 2
de-industrialisation 160
Delevoye, Jean-Paul 77
Delfraissy, Jean-François 33
délocalisation 161
Demeter Unit 233
democracy 27, 43, 50–51; European democracy 149; representative democracy 53, 55
Democratic Renewal 57
Democratie Ouverte (DO) 49
development assistance 271
DIESE *see* direct authority, of an interministerial delegation
digital terrestrial television (DTT) 119
direct authority, of an interministerial delegation (DIESE) 195, 198
Directeurs d'Administration Centrale (DACs) 189–191
disintermediation 30, 33
disposable income 156
DiTP *see* Ministry and Interministerial Delegation
DO *see Democratie Ouverte*
dogmatism, versus pragmatism 230–233
domestic intelligence service 248
downsizing of ministerial 189
drivers of environmental and climate policy 222–224

dualisation of labour market *see* contract of unlimited duration
Dupond-Moretti, Eric 78–79
Dussopt, Olivier 192
Dussopt Law (2019) 168, 193
Dussopt, Olivier 192

E12 *see* European Intervention Initiative
EC agenda 235–236
EC concerns *see* environmental and climate (EC) concerns
EC rhetoric *see* environmental and climate (EC) rhetoric
École de guerre (war college which trains military officers) 194
École Polytechnique 183
ecological planning 233–236
ecological transition 230–233
ecology 226–227
Economic, Social and Environmental Council (CESE) 45–46, 54–55, 229
Economic and Monetary Union (EMU) 160–162, 166–167
Economic Community of West African States (ECOWAS) 278
economic policy, in Africa 270–273
Economic, Social and Environmental Council (CESE) 45–46, 54–55, 229
economic uncertainty 159
ecotax 225
ECOWAS *see* Economic Community of West African States
ECP *see* environmental and climate policy
EDF *see* European Defence Fund
education 201–204, 215–216; apprentices 210; class sizes 211; *concours* (competitive exams) 205, 207–208; curriculum 206–207; educational justice 204–205; enhancing labour supply 169–170; failure of 165; *formation continue* (adult education) 209; higher education 207–208, 212; home-schooling 210; junior high schooling 207; marketisation of 214–215; meritocracy 14, 206–207, 210–214; *Parcoursup* 212–213; social justice 208–209; teacher recruitment 205
Education Act 1866 204
educational failure 208
educational justice 204–205
educational reforms 165
EELV electorate, pragmatism 227
EE-LV *see Europe Ecologie-Les Verts*
EELV electorate, pragmatism 227
EGM *see Escadrons de Gendarmeries Mobiles*
El Khomri Law of 2016 12, 36, 168
election of Emmanuel Macron 2–3, 5–6, 27, 35, 43
Élysée, as definer of news media 122
EM *see En Marche!*
emotional neutrality, policing 247
emplois croisés 75
employment rate 157–158
EMU *see* Economic and Monetary Union
En Marche! (EM) 26, 90, 92–94, 106, 114; *see also La République en Marche*
en même temps 34, 59
ENA *see* National School of Administration
enarques 183–185, 187
energy transition 224, 232–233
Ensemble! (Together!) 3, 56, 60, 106
environmental and climate (EC) concerns 221, 224–226, 230; overview of Macron's pledges since 2016 226–227; Yellow Vests movement 228–229
environmental and climate (EC) rhetoric 220–222
environmental and climate policy (ECP) 14, 221, 236–237; drivers of 223–224; ecological planning 233–236; ecological transition 230–233; failure of 227–228; in the Fifth Republic 222–223; pragmatism and ecological reality 226–227; socioecological justice 228–229; water 236; Zero Net Artificialisation 235
EP *see* European Parliament
EP Quatar corruption scandal 151
EP *see* European Parliament
EPC *see* European policy
EPF *see* European Peace Facility
equality, educational meritocracy 210–214
Escadrons de Gendarmeries Mobiles (EGM) 247
esprit de corps 183–184, 188, 196
ethical awareness 307

ethical standards 75–76
Ethiopia 271
EU accession 141
EU Birds Directive 232
EU Directive on adequate minimum wages 139
EU Rapid Deployment Capacity 145
EU solidarity 140
EU treaty reform 151
Eurobarometer 150–151
Europa City commercial hyperplace 228
Europe 134–137
Europe Ecologie-Les Verts (EE-LV) 97
European army 142–143
European coalition-building 137–139
European Commission 138; Next Generation EU (NGEU) 15, 138–139, 146
European conventions 148
European Council 137–138
European Defence Fund (EDF) 136, 144
European democracy 149
European Green Deal 15, 230–231, 233–234
European Intervention Initiative (EI2) 144–145
European Parliament (EP) 97; results of 2014 and 2019 elections 98
European Peace Facility (EPF) 145
European policy 133–134, 150–151; coalition-building 137–139; Covid-19 crisis 139–141; sovereign Europe *see* sovereign Europe
European Political Community (EPC) 141
European security 142–144
European sovereignty: and French national interests 145–147; security 142–145; *see also* sovereign Europe
European Union: accession of countries 141; Common Foreign and Security Policy (CFSP) 143; defence fund 144–145; directives 81, 137, 139, 164, 232; enlargement 141–142; European Green Deal 230–231, 233–234; own-resources revenue 147; sanctions 141
euros, competitiveness 161
Eurozone 5, 11, 134
Eurozone budget 136
exchange rates 160

exchange-type communication 129
exit ranking 194
external competitiveness 159–163

Face a l'info 120
failure of: education system 165; environmental and climate policy 227–228
fatigue informationelle 121
Faure, Olivier 102
fear of disconnection 305–308
Feraoun, Mouloud 291–292
Fessenheim nuclear plant 225
FGF-Force Ouvrière union 197
Fifth Republic (1958–1988) 2–3, 25, 42, 59–61, 182; environmental and climate policy 222–223; political corruption 68–70
Fillon, François 8, 31, 34, 65–66, 73, 79, 95–96, 274
Fillon affair 34
financial balance of unemployment insurance 172
financial transparency 69–70
firing processes 169
First Republic 42
flat tax on capital gains 36
flexibility, job market and reforms 90, 168, 254
FN *see* National Front
food, environmental and climate policy 232
forcing through laws 56, 58–59
formation continue (adult education) 209
Fourth Republic (1946–1958) 2, 42
Fraisse, Rémi 225
Françafrique 263–264, 272, 276, 278; military cooperation 266–268
France24 11
France Médias 11
France Télévisions 11, 120
France travail 172–173
France–Chad security partnership 269
Franceinfo 120
Franco-German tandem 137–139
Francophone Africa 271
Francophonie 274, 276
Franco–Rwandan relations 275
free candidacy 83n2
free markets 5
freedom of association 316

French national interests: and European sovereignty 145–147; security 142–145
French Review of Public Administration (RFAP) 194
French secularism 302–303
French situation 27
Front National (National Front, FN) 89, 91, 93; *see also Rassemblement National*
fuel tax 48
functional politicisation 185, 197–198

G5 Sahel 265, 268, 277
G5 Sahel Joint Force (G5SJF) 17, 266
Gabriel, Sigmar 136
Gatel law (2018) 316
Gaullian approach to campaigns 118
Gaullian leadership 122
Gaullist party 89
Gaza crisis 124
GDP per capita 156
gendarme of Africa, France as 268–270
Gendarmerie Nationale 243, 247
gendarmes (police) 244, 252; reduced reliance on specialised units 247–249; *see also* policing
gender-parity laws 44
general culture dissertation, elimination of 194
general delegates 93–94
General review of Public Policies (RGPP) 181
General Secretariat for Ecological Planning (SGPE) 235
General Vision of Public Policies (GPPR) 80
Georgia, EU accession 141
German-Russian North Stream II pipeline project 138
Germany: competitiveness 161, 166–167; Franco-German tandem 137–139; labour costs **162**; payroll tax 162–163
Ghana 271, 274
Gilets citoyens (Citizens Vests) 49, 52–53
Giscard d'Estaing, Valéry 24, 31, 35, 115, 119, 150
globalisation 5, 159–160, 305
Glucksmann, Raphaël 102
glue-traps hunting 232
GND *see* Great National Debate

good governance 71
governing through crime 249
GPPR *see* General Revision of Public Policies
Grand Orient de France 316
grandes écoles 203, 207–208
Grands Corps 13, 183, 186, 191, 196; ending of 192–193
Great National Debate (GND) 7, 29–30, 43, 47–51
Greece, labour costs **162**
green economy 220, 226
Greens 102–103, 108
Grenelle de l'environnement (national debate held in 2007) 229
grievance registers 50–51
growth, inclusive growth 5
Guermeur Act of 1977 309
Guillaume, Marc 191
Gumbel, Peter 165

Habermas, Jürgen 136
Hamon, Benoît 36, 95
Hanouna, Cyril 121
Harki Day 285
Harkis 296
HATVP *see* High Authority for Transparency in Public Life
hauts fonctionnaires 13, 183; *see also* state nobility
headscarves, banning of 309
High Authority for Transparency in Public Life (HATVP) 8, 72, 74–76; advisors 79–80; consultancy firms 80; declaration of interests 77; declarations of assets 76–77
High Court of Justice 78
high tax wedge 162–163
Higher Civil Service 12–13
higher education 13, 207–208; access to 212
high-school protests 249
hiring of family members 74–75
historical development 305
Hollande, François 5, 25, 34, 71, 95, 114, 122, 126, 156, 181, 224–226, 245, 266, 268, 285, 317
home-schooling 210
Horizons 56
Hulot, Nicolas 15, 227–228
Humboldt University speech (January 2017) 135, 147
hunting 232

hybrid media system 118–121
hyper-presidential intervention 6–7
hyper-presidentialisation 42

IIAP *see* International Institute of Public Administration
illegal taking of interest 79
ILO *see* International Labour Organization
Immigration and Integration Act (2024) 316
Immigration Bill 58–59
immobilism 4
immobilisme 2
inclusive growth 5
income 156
incumbency, importance of 99
Indemnité representatative de frais de mandat (IRFM) 81
Index of Professional Gender Equality 173
Individual Professional Training Accounts (CFPs) 170
industrial relations 155–156
infotainment 115
INSP *see* National Institute for Public Service
instability after 2022 election 106–108
Institut National de l'Audiovisuel (INA) 11
Institute of Public Service (ISP) 193
institutional continuity, education system 209–210
institutional reformism 181
intermediary bodies (corps intermédiares) 4
intermediary elections, 2017–2022 97–99
Interministerial Committee for Secularism 317
International Institute of Public Administration (IIAP) 194
International Labour Organization (ILO) 160
interventionism 268–270
invasion of Ukraine 140–142
IRFM *see* Indemnité representatative de frais de mandat
Islam 306, 312
ISP *see* Institute of Public Service
Italy: competitiveness 161; labour costs **162**
iTélé 120–121

Jacob, Christian 101
JAM *see Les Jeunes avec Macron*
job families 195
joint defence budget 144
joint defence doctrine 143
joint doctrine of action 145
joint intervention force 143
Joly, Eva 35
Jospin, Lionel 35, 181, 244, 311
journalism, corruption 68
journalists, communication style of Macron 126
Judaism 19, 307
judicial repression 251
judicialisation 16, 249–250
junior high schooling 207
Jupiterian-participatory paradox 6, 30–34
Juppé, Alain 71, 95–96, 181
jurisprudence Balladur 79

Kaboré, Roch Marc Christian 277, 286
Kepel, Gilles 313
Kerchouche, Dalila 296
Kohler, Alexis 79

La Droite Républicaine 10
La Françafrique 16–17; *see also* Africa policy
La France Insoumise (LFI) 9, 57, 95, 102, 108, 309
La Grande Marche (the Big Walk) 90
La République en Marche (LaREM) 8–9, 88, 92–94, 97, 99–101, 104, 106, 108–109
La Stratégie du météore 115
Labour Code 168
labour costs **162**
labour market, dysfunctions 159
labour market: Economic and Monetary Union (EMU) 160–162; enhancing quality of labour supply 169–173; high tax wedge 162–163; Macron's reforms to 166–176; poor external competitiveness 159–163; regulation 164; skills mismatch 165–166
labour market, dysfunctions 159
labour reforms 12
labour supply, enhancing quality of 169–173
labour unions *see* unions
labour-participation rate 157–158

Lagarde, Christine 149
lame duck incumbent 124
Lang/Cloupet agreements 309
LaREM *see La République en Marche*
Law for the Freedom to Choose One's Professional Future 192
Law of Civil Service Transformation 192
Law on Energy Transition for Green Growth (LTECV) (2015) 225
LCAP law *see Loi pour la liberté de choisir son avenir professionnel*
LCI 120
Le Bodo, Agnès Firmin 77
Le Canard Enchaîné 68
Le Cour Grandmaison, Olivier 295
Le Défenseur des droits 244
Le Maire, Bruno 107
Le Monde 123, 126
Le Pen, Marine 9, 34–35, 55, 91, 96, 101, 103–106, 116, 134, 244, 286, 326–327
Le Point 115
lead-climber theory 4
leadership projection 118
l'échec scolaire (educational failure) 208
L'École Superiuere des Sciences Economiques et Sociales (ESSEC) 212
the Left 102–103, 190
legal modernity 312
legislative election, 2022 election 104–106
legislative pacts 10
Lejeune, Geoffroy 121
Les Guignols de l'Info 121
les harkis 285
Les Jeunes avec Macron (JAM) 90
Les Républicains (LR) 34–35, 44, 60, 93–98, 101, 106, 216, 324
'Letter to the French People' 49
LFI *see La France Insoumise*
liberal socialism 5
limits on multiple office-holding 44
linguistic registers, of Macron 29
lobbies 81
lobbyists, registering 72
L'Obs 115
Loi Debré 204
Loi organique sur les lois de finances (LOLF) 181
Loi pour la liberté de choisir son avenir professionnel (LCAP) 169–173

LOLF *see Loi organique sur les lois de finances*
looters, prosecuting 250
low-cost crowd control 251–253
LR *see Les Républicains*
LREM *see La République en Marche*
LTECV *see Law on Energy Transition for Green growth*
Luchaire Affair 69–70
Luhaka, Théo 242
Lusophone 271
lycée 207, 211, 213

Macron, Brigitte 115
Macron Ordinances 159, 168
Macronism 35, 37
macronistes 324–326
Mali 278; Operation Barkhane 266–269
managerial disintermediation 6
March for Equality 303
Marchand, Mimi 115
marcheurs 90, 93–94, 184
Maréchal, Marion 108
marketisation of education 214–215
marketisation of society 5
Marseillaise 241–242
masks for Covid-19 140
material assistance to religious denominations 309
May Day (2018) 47
McKinsey 33, 80
Méaux, Florence 195
media 10–11, 118–121; 2017 campaign 114–117; 2022 campaign 117–118; corruption 67–68; Elysee as definer of 122; over-exposure 26; ownership of 120; privatisation 119; trust of public 121
Mediapart 128
Mélenchon, Jean-Luc 9, 35, 95, 97, 102–103, 106, 108, 118, 309, 326
memorial culture 284
memorials for Algeria 292, 296
memory 286–288; religion 307
Memory and Truth Commission 293
MERCOSUR agreement 326–327
meritocracy 14, 205–208, 210–214
Merkel, Angela 137
Meseberg Declaration 137
Messmer, Pierre 31
Michel, Charles 138
Migaud, Didier 85n46, 324

military cooperation, *Françafrique* 266–268
military policy 17
ministers, corruption 77
Ministry and Interministerial Delegation (DiTP) 181
Mission Cadres Dirigeants 195
Mitterrand, François 2, 25, 31, 34–35, 119
MoDem *see Mouvement Démocrate*
Modernisationof Public Action (2012–2017) 181
modernity, transition to 305–306
monarchical presidency 42
monarchist-populist 6
monarchist-populist paradox 27–30, 42
monetary union 166–167
Montagne d'Or gold mining project 228
Montebourg, Arnaud 95
monuments, religion and 307
moralisation of public life 73–75
morality 8
motion de rejét prealable 59
Mouvement Démocrate (MoDem) 56, 73, 93, 106
municipal racketeering 69
Museum of Mankind 290
museums 286–288; restitution of African heritage 288–289
Mushikiwabo, Louise 275
Muslim Islamists 19
Muslims 19; special rights 303–304

Nadal, Jean-Louis 81
National Assembly 3, 43; abstentions 77; allowances 82; composition in 2017 92; composition in 2022 107; constitutional reform 45–47
National Commission for Public Debate (CNDP) 49
National Commission on Campaign Accounts and Political Finance (CNCCFP) 70
National Consultative Committee on Human Rights 316
national curriculum 206–207
National Debate on Energy Transition 224–225
National Employment Agency (ANPE) 172
National Front (FN) 89

National Institute for Public Service (INSP) 13, 193–194, 196
National Library (BNF) 49
National Low-Carbon Strategy (SNBC) 225, 231
National Museum of the History of Immigration 298
National Rally (RN) 3, 9, 11, 60, 323, 326
National Refoundation Council 148–149
National School of Administration (ENA) 13, 182–183
NATO 138, 143
Ndiaye, Pap 216
N'Djamena 269
neoliberal reforms 5
neoliberal turn 255
neoliberalism 5
networks of connivance 67
New Hanseatic League 139
New Popular Front (NFP) 3, 9, 60
New Popular Green and Social Union (Nupes) 106
New Public Management 182
news management 118, 122, 124
Next Generation EU (NGEU) 15, 138–139, 146
NFP *see* New Popular Front (NFP) 324
NGEU *see* Next Generation EU
Niel, Xavier 126
Niger 268, 278
Nigeria 271–272, 274
Non-Governmental Organisations (NGOs) 71, 81
Notre Dame des Landes airport 228
Notre-Dame-de-Paris 310
nuclear power 232–233
nuclear testing, in Algeria 293
nuclear waste landfill 225
NUPES alliance 9, 60
Nupes *see* New Popular Green and Social Union
NUPES alliance 9, 60

Observatoire de Laïcité (Secularism Observatory) 317
Observatory of Debates 49
Ode to Joy (Beethoven) 133, 241
OECD *see* Organisation for Economic Co-operation and Development
Office de Radio-Télévision Française (ORTF) 119

OIF *see* Organisation Internationale de la Francophonie
Olympic truce 323–324
one-hundred-days milestone 189
Operation Barkhane 266–269
Operation Serval 266, 268
ordinances 193
Ordinary law 46
Organic Law 46
Organisation for Economic Co-operation and Development (OECD) 156; tax wedge 163
Organisation Internationale de la Francophonie (OIF) 275
ORTF *see Office de Radio-Télévision Française*
outsourcing 33
own-resources revenue 147

P3S *see* Partnership for Security and Stability in the Sahel
Palais d'Iena 54
pantouflage (revolving doors) 183, 186
parachuting 165
Parcoursup 14, 212–213
Paris Administrative Tribunal 81, 230
Paris Agreement on Climate Change 15, 220–221, 227
Paris Match 115
parliamentarians 74, 76–77
parliamentary expenses 81–82
parliamentary government 25
parliamentary majorities, National Assembly 2017 92–93
parliamentary reserve 74
participation rate 157–158
participative governability 55
Partnership for Security and Stability in the Sahel (P3S) 267
party finance, regulation of (1988–1995) 69–71
path dependency, education system 210
pauperisation 214
payroll tax 162–163, 167
Pech, Thierry 52–53
Pécresse, Valérie 36, 101, 105
Penelopegate 34, 65–66, 73, 96
pension reform 32–33, 57–58, 124, 325; protests 258–259
People's Primary movement 103
Permanent Structured Cooperation (PESCO) 143
Perrineau, Pascal 49

personal ambitions of Macron 89–91
personal parties 26
personalisation 6; of political competition 26
PESCO *see* Permanent Structured Cooperation
Philippe Circular Memorandum (2017) 198
Philippe, Edouard 31, 92, 106–107, 124, 188, 254, 311
Philippe Circular Memorandum (2017) 198
Philippon, Thomas 157, 165
pieds-noirs (former settlers who left Algeria after independence and their descendants) 286
Piette, Emilie 195
Place Publique 108
Plénel, Edwy 71, 128
Pôle emploi 172
police 15–16; *see also* policing
Police Nationale 242–243, 259
Police Prefect 16
police problem 243
police scandals 256
police trade unions 256–258
police violence 246–247, 256
policing 242–246, 258–259; authoritarian liberalism 254–255; community policing 244; Covid-19 crisis 257; crowd management 249–251; low-cost crowd control 251–253; protest policing 249–251; reduced reliance on specialised units 247–249; repression of Yellow Vests movement (2018–2020) 246–247
policing trap 256–258
policy errors, Africa policy 277–278
policy venues 222
political corruption 66–68, 82–83; advisors 79–80; anti-corruption 71; codes of conduct 75–76; conflict of interest 71–73, 78–79; consultancy firms 80; *En Marche!* 90; *Les Républicains* 98; lobbies 81; ministers 77; moralisation of public life 73–75; parliamentary expenses 81–82; regulation of party finance (1988–1995) 69–71; transparency 71–73; unchecked corruption (1958–1988) 68–69
political decentralisation 181
political elites 78; *see also* state nobility

Index **345**

political finance, regulation of party finance (1988–1995) 69–70
political opportunity structure 222
political parties: 2017–2022 97; *Ensemble!* (Together!) 3, 56, 60, 106; *Front National* (National Front, FN) 89, 91, 93; Gaullist party 89; LaREM 8–9, 88, 92–94, 97, 99–101, 104, 106, 108–109; *Les Républicains* 94–97; *Mouvement Démocrate* (MoDem) 56, 73, 93, 106; National Front (FN) 89; New Popular Front (NFP) 3, 9, 60; New Popular Green and Social Union (Nupes) 106; *Rassemblement National* (RN) 88, 97, 103–106, 138, 230, 317; Socialist Party 5, 34–35, 44, 89, 102–103, 108; Union for a Popular Movement (UMP) 94–95
political polarisation 121
political work 203
politics, Africa policy 273–277
Pompidou, Georges 31, 275
Portugal, labour costs **162**
power elite 183–184; *see also* state nobility
power of the state 311–317
pragmatism 34; *vs* dogmatism 230–233; and ecological reality 226–227
presidential candidacy 113–118; 2017 campaign 114–117; 2022 campaign 117–118
Presidential Council for Africa (CPA) 265
presidential elections 2, 25–26; 2017 election 8, 66, 88, 91, 93, 96, 285–286; 2022 election 9, 11, 54, 88–89, 104–106, 108, 120
Presidential Ordinance (2 June 2021) 185
presidential photographs, Macron, Emmanuel 28–29
presidential style, Africa policy 277–278
presidentialisation of politics 6, 26
presidentialism 42
press conferences, 2nd Act 51–52
pressure on top civil servants 188–192
primary schools 211
prime minister, role of 31
primo-deputies 44
principle of recognition 302
print media 119

Printemps Republicain movement 316
private life, sharing of 115
private sector, education 214–215
privatisation 4; of media 119
productivity levels 161
Property Wealth Tax (IFI) 36
protection of whistle-blowers 81
protective Europe 136, 139–140
protest policing 249–251, 255, 257–258
Protestantism 19, 307, 309
protests: arresting troublemakers 249–251; crowd management 249–251; pension reform 258–259; *see also* Yellow Vest movement
Proto, Sébastien 186
proximity policing 244
PS *see* Socialist Party
public communicative style 126
public debt 325
public expenditure 33
public problem 65–66, 71, 82, 203, 205, 208, 215, 217n4, 242, 258
Public Transformation 181

Quai Branly Museum 18, 287; restitution of African objects 289
quality of labour supply, enhancing 169–173

radicalised Islam 302, 313
Radio France 11, 120
Radio France Internationale (RFI) 11
Radio France 11, 120
Radio-Télévision Française 68
Raffarin, Jean-Pierre 313
Rahal, Malika 295
Ramdani, Nabila 295
Rassemblement National (RN) 88, 97, 103–106, 138, 230, 317
Reagan, Ronald 4
The Real Debate 49
recognition 310–311; religion 308–311
reconciliation, with Algeria 289–291
reconfirmation of religiousness 312
Reconquête 108
Recovery and Ecological Transition Contracts (CRTE) 231
Recovery and Resilience Plans (RRPs) 146
Recovery Plan 231
Red Caps movement 225
Redouane, Zineb 242, 246

refounding of civil service system 192–197
regional elections, results of 2021 election 99
register of abstentions 77
registers for expressing grievances 49–51
regulated markets 5
regulation of labour 164; Macron's reforms to 167–169
regulation of party finance (1988–1995) 69–71
religion 19, 307–308; turning to 308–311
religious authorities 311
religious denominations, material assistance to 309
religious memory 307
religious morality 306
religious policy 302–306, 317–318; fear of disconnection 305–308; power of the state 311–317; taxes 310; turning to religion 308–311
religiousness 312
Renaissance 56, 59, 108–109
Rencontres de Saint Denis 58
Rendez les doléances! 51
Renseignements généraux 248
rent-seekers 4
rent-seeking 4
REPower EU legislative proposal 235
Representative Council of Jewish Institutions in France (CRIF) 310
representative democracy 53, 55
representativity of LREM 44–45
repression of Yellow Vests movement (2018–2020) 246–247
republic arc 324
resignation of Macron, possibility of 327
Resilience and Recovery Facility (RRF) 146
restitution of African objects 287–289
restitution of Algerian skulls 290–291
Retailleau, Bruno 324
'revenge of Allah' 312
review of directors 190–191
revolving-doors practices 183, 186
RFAP *see* French Review of Public Administration
RGPP *see* General Review of Public Policies

RIC *see* Citizens' Initiative Referendums
Ricoeur, Paul 307
The Right 101–102, 190
RIP *see* Shared Initiative Referendum
rise of Macron 186–188
RN *see* National Rally
; *Rassemblement National*
Roblot-Troizier, Agnès 82
Rocard, Michel 56
Rocard Act of 1984 309
Rocard Government (1988–1991) 181
Rocard, Michel 56
RRF *see* Resilience and Recovery Facility
RRPs *see* Recovery and Resilience Plans
Russian invasion of Ukraine 140–142
Rwanda 265, 268, 275

Sahel Alliance *see* Partnership for Security and Stability in the Sahel
'at the same time' (*en même temps*) doctrine 26
Sankara, Thomas 265
Sapin I 72
Sapin II 72, 81
Sapin law 70
Sarkozy, Nicolas 8, 25, 31, 46, 59, 71, 78, 96, 115, 181, 244, 249, 293, 314
Sarr, Felwine 287
Sarr-Savoy report 18, 286–289
Savary law 303
Savoy, Bénédicte 287
Scandinavian flexicurity model 166–167
Scandinavian model 166
Schnapper, Dominique 53
Scholz, Olaf 137, 142
schooling of Macron 186
Sciences Po Paris 194, 212
SCPC *see* Central Service for the Prevention of Corruption
second presidency of Macron 55–61
secularisation of France 312
secularisation of teaching 204
secularism 19, 302–305, 308–311, 313–315, 317; substantialist secularism 318n1
Secularism Observatory 317
security, sovereign Europe 142–145
separatism 302, 313
sexual behavior 315
sexual orientation 315

SGPE *see* General Secretariat for Ecological Planning
Shared Initiative Referendum (RIP) 52
shooting of teenager in Paris 128
Sixth Republic 42
skill shortages 159
skills mismatch 165–166
small- and medium-sized enterprises (SMEs) 167
SNBC *see* National Low-Carbon Strategy
Social and Economic Committee (CSE) 168
social cohesion 314
social conscience 305
social inequalities, between public and private school 214
social justice 4, 203–204, 208–209
social media 120
social relations, within firms 165
Socialist Experiment 4–5
Socialist Party 5, 34–35, 44, 89, 102–103, 108
Socialist Party–Les Républicains duopoly 94–97
Socialist-Green agreement 224
socioecological justice 228–229
socle commun 324, 326
Sorbonne speech (September 2017) 11, 136–137, 142–148
South Africa 271
sovereign Europe 135–137, 141–142, 147–150; security 142–145
sovereignty 312
sovereignty agenda, ecological planning 233–236
Spain 138, 169, 293, 327
spatiality 305
specialized police units 247–249
Spitzenkandidaten process 149
spoils system 190
Stability and Growth Pact (SGP) 147
state, power of 311–317
state administrators 196
state nobility 13, 180, 185; Macron's rise in 186–188
state reform memorandum 181
state-building 180–181
state-centred capitalism 181
State-in-majesty 181
Stora, Benjamin 290–294
Stora report 291–294; responses to 294–298

'Strategic Compass' 145
strict secularism 317
substantialist secularism 318n1
suburban youth, Yellow Vests protests 16
surrogate motherhood 306
surveillance 302

Takuba 267
talent pool 195
Talents concours 193
tax wedge 167
taxation 159
taxes 36; breaks for religious donations 310; ecotax 225; fuel tax 48; high tax wedge 162–163; payroll tax 162–163, 167
teacher recruitment 205
teaching unions 207
Tebboune, President 291, 297
technocracy 186
technocratisation 13
television 119–120
temporary employment 164
territorial reforms 181
terrorism 249, 269, 313
terrorist attacks 245
Thatcher, Margaret 4, 22
Third Republic (1870–1940) 2, 42, 66–67; education 204
Thiriez, Frédéric 192–193
Thiriez Report 195
TI *see* Transparency International
top-down presidential communication 128
Touché pas a mon poste 121
trade-openness ratio 160
trading favours 66
Transitions Pro 171
transparency 71–73
Transparency in Public Life 72
Transparency International (TI) 71
transpartisan commission 55
Traoré, Adama 245, 257
Treaty of Maastricht 166
trickle-down economics 4
truck tax 225
Trump, Donald 15, 142, 220–221, 227
trust of media 121

UEMOA *see* West African Economic and Monetary Union

Ukraine 11, 15, 235; invasion of 140–142
UMP *see* Union for a Popular Movement
unchecked corruption (1958–1988) 68–69
Union nationale interprofessionnelle pour l'emploi dans l'industrie et le commerce) 171, 173
unemployment 156–157, 161, 170, 174, 326; monthly unemployment rate (1983–2021) 157; *see also* labour market
unemployment-insurance system 171–173
Union Économique et Monetaire Ouest-Africaine (West African Economic and Monetary Union) 272–273
Union for a Popular Movement (UMP) 94–95
Union nationale interprofessionnelle pour l'emploi dans l'industrie et le commerce (Unédic) 171
Union of Civil Administrators (USAC) 194
unions 12; police trade unions 256–258; teaching unions 207
United Nations, MINUSMA peacekeeping mission 280n4

Valeurs actuelles 128
Valls, Manuel 95, 102, 114, 304, 314
values of the Republic 304, 313–315
Van Beneden, Elise 75
Van Ruymbeke, Renaud 67, 71
VAT 162
Véran, Olivier 57
Versailles Declaration 144
verticalisation of presidential power 30–34
verticality 31, 55
Vidal, Frédérique 202
Vigie de la Laïcité 312
visits to religious places 310
vocational education, reform of 170–171
voluntary violence 75
von der Leyen, Ursula 138, 140, 149
voter trust 121
VSD 115

Wagner 268
water 236
Water Plan 32
Wauquiez, Laurent 10, 101, 324
weak political leadership 223–224
Wealth Tax (ISF) 36
Weber, Manfred 149
West Africa 271–272, 274
West African Economic and Monetary Union (UEMOA) 272–273
Western Balkans 141
whistle-blowers 81
World Bank 71

Yellow Vests movement 7, 13, 15–16, 20–21, 32, 43, 100, 121, 123, 127–128, 185, 189, 241–242; protests 29, 47–51, 248, 252–255; repression of 246–247; socioecological justice 228–229
Yellow Vests protests 16
Youth for Climate 230

Zecler, Michel 258
Zemmour, Eric 105–106, 108, 120
Zero Net Artificialisation (ZNA) 235

For Product Safety Concerns and Information please contact our
EU representative GPSR@taylorandfrancis.com Taylor & Francis
Verlag GmbH, Kaufingerstraße 24, 80331 München, Germany